WHAT PEOPLE ARE SAYING ABOUT

CHAOS ETHICS

An elegant yet passionate defense of ethics, the book carefully considers various conflicting accounts of what it means to live a good life before settling on imagination and narrative as chaotic and transient foundations of ethical thinking. Ethics for Bateman is both necessary and necessarily tumultuous; it is also a story which we should try and tell as best we can. Thought-provoking, engaging even if at times controversial, Chaos Ethics is a pleasure to read – and to agree and disagree with.

Joanna Zylinska, Professor of New Media and Communications, Goldsmiths, University of London, and author of *Bioethics in the Age of New Media* and *The Ethics of Cultural Studies*

"A revelatory reading of both my own and other's work – a genuine philosophy for the 21st century."

Michael Moorcock, award-winning fantasy and literary author

Chaos Ethics

Chaos Ethics

Chris Bateman

zero books

Winchester, UK
Washington, USA

First published by Zero Books, 2014
Zero Books is an imprint of John Hunt Publishing Ltd., Laurel House, Station Approach,
Alresford, Hants, SO24 9JH, UK
office1@jhpbooks.net
www.johnhuntpublishing.com
www.zero-books.net

For distributor details and how to order please visit the 'Ordering' section on our website.

ISBN: 978 1 84694 605 9

A CIP catalogue record for this book is available from the British Library.

Design: Stuart Davies

Printed and bound by CPI Group (UK) Ltd, Croydon, CR0 4YY

CONTENTS

Biographical Notes

Chris Bateman is an outsider philosopher, game designer, and author. Graduating with a Masters degree in Artificial Intelligence/Cognitive Science, he has since pursued highly-acclaimed independent research into how and why people play games, and written extensively on the neurobiology of play. In 2009, he was invited to sit on the IEEE's Player Satisfaction Modeling task force, in recognition for his role in establishing this research domain, and in 2013 he became the first person to be awarded a doctorate in play aesthetics.

He has a lifelong interest in mythology and religion, and has travelled the world studying religious practices and beliefs. He has taken part in everything from Native American sweat lodges to Pagan solstice celebrations, as well as visiting Buddhist and Shinto shrines in Japan, and witnessing traditional tribal religions in Africa whilst briefly living in the Sahel Reserve near the Sahara desert.

Chris works in the digital entertainment industry as an expert in game design, narrative and player satisfaction modeling, and has worked on more than forty published games. As a game designer and writer, he is best known for the games *Discworld Noir* and *Ghost Master*, as well as the books *Game Writing: Narrative Skills for Videogames, 21st Century Game Design* and *Beyond Game Design*. He also conducts research and teaches at the University of Bolton.

His work in philosophy includes *Imaginary Games*, which explores the relationship between art and play, and *The Mythology of Evolution*, which examines the role of imagination in the evolutionary sciences. His blog *Only a Game* (http://onlyagame.typepad.com) deals with both philosophy and game design, and contains a prolific array of articles, many of which have been featured elsewhere.

Preface

In 1874, the Yorkshire-born philosopher Henry Sidgwick published the book that is viewed as the culmination of the classical utilitarian tradition, *The Methods of Ethics*. In his original conclusion, Sidgwick worried that there might be an irreconcilable conflict between self-interest and moral duty, one that threatened to undermine any belief that the imperfect moral order we encounter in the world could be reconciled with the perfection of "Universal Reason". This conclusion depressed him, and he ended the first edition by lamenting that:

> ...the Cosmos of Duty is thus really reduced to a Chaos: and the prolonged effort of the human intellect to frame a perfect ideal of rational conduct is seen to have been foredoomed to inevitable failure. (Sidgwick, 1874).

In a way, my stepping point for this book of moral philosophy is to challenge Sidgwick's pessimism by asking: would moral chaos really be such a disaster? To put this same question the other way around: is a perfect ideal of rational conduct necessarily a good thing? It seems to me, viewing our world from a very different vantage point to Sidgwick, that the exactitude of moral order that this and many other brilliant academics have craved would risk a disaster far worse than mere chaos – which, we ought to bear in mind, is *precisely what we find ourselves in, and always have.*

We have always lived in chaos and tried to condition it with order. However, we used to believe that behind that chaos was a perfect order that we merely failed to live up to, something I find increasingly difficult to accept. Instead, I want to suggest that behind our flawed attempts at law might also hide a perfect chaos, and the challenge facing us now is not to become masters of order, nor indeed to become masters of chaos, but to become masters at *balancing* order and chaos. To attain this, we must first understand both the moral law *and* moral chaos – and this means exploring not only ethical traditions built on order, but also those ethics that thrive in its absence.

However, Sidgwick is not really the beginning of my story, and were it not for Derek Parfit's love of Sidgwick's "great, drab book" (Parfit, 2011) I might never have encountered the above quote, which so wickedly incited my mischievous nature. No, like so much of my life, this story begins for me with a game – and not just any game, either, but *Dungeons & Dragons* (Gygax and Arneson, 1974), the most influential game in the history of game design. As a game designer by profession (whilst also a philosopher by vocation), I've spent a considerable amount of time explicating the numerous connections between *Dungeons & Dragons* – or D&D for short – and the design of contemporary games, and indeed dedicate a section of my first book of philosophy, *Imaginary Games* (2011), to discussing this strange and wonderful history. But I never thought that this game would also provide the circumstances that would lead to my first book in moral philosophy.

Zero Books had already accepted two proposals from me, but I was keen to get them to take a book of ethics as well, since it was a topic I'd been enjoying writing about for some time. The trouble was, the way I'd presented my proposal was either too esoteric for any prospective audience or not radical enough for the tastes of Zero's editor-in-chief. I had the basis for the book worked out, but what I was missing was a title – something less enigmatic than my draft title *Enemy: A Morality Tale*, but more exciting than my suggested alternative *Universal Ethics* – a title that now sounds bland even to me!

It was at this juncture that Jon Cogburn, who had been very generous with his support for my first philosophy book, *Imaginary Games*, invited me to submit a chapter to a volume of popular culture philosophy he was working on. I've always found these kinds of books a little shoddy, I admit, and it wasn't something I'd wanted to pursue previously. However, Jon and his co-editor Mark Silcox were working on a book connecting philosophy to *Dungeons & Dragons*, and had already recruited a number of people whose work I respected. He gave me one of his draft chapters to read, a piece that discussed recent changes in the rules of the game that abandoned one of the oldest aspects of its design. Jon argued that the changes TSR (now owned by Wizards of the Coast, now owned by the transnational toy corporation Hasbro) had made to the rules were justifiable on philosophical grounds. I was shocked at his claims, and wrote a lengthy email to him defending the original rules – text that eventually made it into the final book as my essay "Chaotic Good in the Balance" (Cogburn and Silcox, 2012).

The rules in question are what are known as the alignment system: in the original versions of D&D, this was based on two tripartite divisions – into Good, Neutral and Evil, and into Lawful, Neutral and Chaotic. This produced nine different alignments – Lawful Good, Neutral Good, Chaotic Good, Lawful Neutral, 'True' Neutral, Chaotic Neutral, Lawful Evil, Neutral Evil and Chaotic Evil. For over thirty years, these nine different positions caused players of this game to think about the relationship between order and chaos on the one hand, and good and evil on the other. Then, in the recent fourth edition of the game, the alignment system was downsized to just Good, Lawful Good, Evil, Chaotic Evil and Unaligned. Jon argued that this was consistent with prevailing views in moral philosophy – I countered that his view was based on a very narrow examination of the state of contemporary ethics.

The new alignment system says, in effect (and Jon's arguments in his essay "Beyond Chaotic Good and Lawful Evil?" support this claim) that law and order are *always* good, while chaos is *always* evil. This is something that as a Discordian I simply could not accept, since the essence of that grand and ridiculous religion is precisely that both order *and* chaos can be beneficial. More importantly, as a lifelong admirer of the novels of Michael Moorcock, I found in the dismemberment of the original alignment system an immeasurable slight against one of the authors whose work significantly influenced both D&D in general, and the alignment system specifically, since the Law and Chaos dimension of the classic alignment system is based entirely on metaphors Moorcock had tirelessly developed over decades of writing. These metaphors still have a great deal to teach us, and part of my motive in writing this book is to do what should have been done years ago – to link Moorcock's work back into the philosophical traditions that helped inspire it.

As soon as I had written to Jon about the connection between the ethics of the radical French philosopher Alain Badiou and the D&D alignment of Chaotic Good – not to mention my suggesting to Jon that from a Christian perspective Jesus was precisely an embodiment of Chaotic Good – I knew that the book proposal I was trying to get accepted at Zero wasn't about Universal Ethics. It was about Chaos Ethics. Thus it was that I came by my title, my theme and my purpose in writing this book: to rehabilitate disorder in the eyes of a culture that associates chaos solely with anarchy and disaster, and that refuses to recognize what the *Principia Discordia* calls the Law of Eristic Escalation: "Imposition of Order = Escalation of Chaos" (Hill and Thornley, 1970). Anybody who has had to work within the strictures of an overly officious bureaucracy is well aware of this principle! Indeed, what I espouse here is not a formula for anarchy – as Greg Hill quipped, anarchy has too many rules, like hating the government – but rather a potential antidote to that mindless bureaucracy Hanna Arendt called "the rule of no-one" (Arendt, 1958), perhaps the cruelest and most tyrannical form of government we have discovered thus far.

Having mentioned two of my religions at this point, I suppose that I ought to come clean and confess to being a deeply religious individual – after all, I have no fewer than five religions, which is considerably more than most devout people can claim! These religions have greatly affected my own personal morality, perhaps more so than studying moral philosophy has, but of the five it is Christianity and Discordianism that have had the most impact on my ethics. Ironically, despite the Discordian religion being set up as a counter-point to the conservative lawfulness of the Christian-suffused United States of the 1960s, the two religions are surprisingly complimentary – although their practitioners, I might add, tend not to be complimentary to one another! The reason for this is that much of what we call Christianity today is rather what Søren Kierkegaard condemns as merely *Christendom* (Kierkegaard, 1859) - the attempt to wed state law to Christianity will always struggle to be authentically Christian. If I could contribute one thing back to Christianity to thank this tradition for what, via my parents, it has given me, it would be to show how moral chaos is precisely the duty of anyone who claims to follow the teachings of Jesus.

That I have been heavily influenced by religious traditions does not mean, of course, that I expect my readers to have a religion, or even a *non-religion* of the kind I compare and contrast with the older traditions in the final chapter of *The Mythology of Evolution* (Bateman, 2012). I would like this book to have something to offer anybody, from any background, although I suspect it is unrealistic to think that it can be read by just anyone. This book expects the reader to be intelligent and capable of critical thought, just skeptical enough to avoid believing too quickly, but not so skeptical as to be incapable of believing anything beyond the orthodoxy of disbelief. This book expects the reader to bring their own morality to the table where it can be carefully examined, not to measure if it is right or wrong against universal standards, but to see if the reader can endorse their own ethics without resorting to the tub-thumping politics that would make an enemy of everyone whose moral viewpoint differs from our own. Indeed, this book asks that we all set political conflict aside while we unravel the deeper problems in ethics, instead of deciding what is right and trying to enforce it upon everyone else. Only when we understand moral chaos can we hope to establish laws worth upholding.

All philosophical writing risks alienating some readers as a result of a complex technical vocabulary, but I have tried to keep this problem somewhat under control here. Where possible, I have used everyday language to express concepts, sometimes briefly mentioning the normal terms in philosophical circles for context. My inspiration in this is the incomparable Mary Midgley, who has a far greater faculty for presenting philosophy stripped of jargon than I will ever manage. To help with accessibility I have also tried to minimize unnecessary distinctions, and for instance assign little importance to differences between the terms 'morals' and 'ethics'. In general I have preferred 'ethics' when it refers to a moral system or a particular approach to morality, and have used 'moral' as a more general adjective, constraining 'ethical' to meaning 'aligning with a given moral system'. Additionally, there is a glossary of the terms used in the book at the back, and key terms are italicized as they are introduced. I hope that this will help compensate for my inability to present this monograph without magniloquent terms such as 'monograph' and 'magniloquent'.

Once again, I have an endless list of people whom I must thank for their assistance in the development of this manuscript and its investigations. First and foremost, Allen Wood, whose magnificent edition of Kant's *Groundwork* was the first step on the journey into moral philosophy that brought me here, and who has been so incredibly helpful with sourcing various materials – and so wonderfully horrified when I first began to hint at what I was attempting to write about! I can only hope that what I have written meets with some tiny part of his approval, since I am certain much of it will meet with his justifiable disdain. The inadequacies of this venture are, of course, entirely my own responsibility and I can indemnify my spectral mentor in Kantian ethics of any blame for my own, doubtless considerable, errors.

I also must thank a great many other academics for their time and insight, including Ben Abraham, Lee Braver, Molly Scott Cato, Tamar Szabó Gendler, Graham Harman, Christine Korsgaard, Mary Midgley, Kendall L. Walton, Joanna Zylinska, not to mention the aforementioned Jon Cogburn, without whom I might never have found a title, much less wrote the book that you now hold in your hands. Also, to those who are not academics – both those whose materials I have referenced, including Roger Barry of the *Manaraefan Herred* Viking re-enactment society, and those who have helped me otherwise. Particular gratitude is due the tireless support staff at the University of Bolton, and especially the librarians Sheila Coakley and Denise Mercer who have endured my endless requests for inter-library loans and the sourcing of obscure papers.

Then there are the hordes of people who have helped me on either the manuscript itself or the long process leading up to it (many of them unwitting accomplices in my crimes!), including Neil Bundy, Peter Crowther, Ben Cowley, Nick Elliott, Jack Monahan, Jon Rouse, Wayne Thompson, translucy, Kelly Waldrop-Briggs, everyone at Chorlton Unitarian Church (true agents of chaos!), and a host of other people who, via my blog *Only a Game*, helped shape my views on all manner of ethical issues over the past decade. Especial thanks are due to everyone at my blog who discussed the trolley problem with me, including Bezman, Tom Camfield, Duoae, Corvus Elrod, Darius Kazemi, Marc Majcher, Duncan Monro, John Peacock, and Foster Nichols. I also owe a debt of gratitude to Cathy Bryant for getting me interested in philosophy in the first place, many moons ago in a very different life to the one I am living now. If it were not for her, the course of my life would have been very different indeed!

Lastly, but certainly not least, there are those who provided invaluable feedback on the draft manuscript including Vitor Bosshard, Gary Jones, Theo Malekin, Matt Mower, Michael Pereira, Sushma Sahajpal, and Oscar Strik, many of whom have been great friends of this project – some from as far back as the germinal 'Ethics Campaign' on my blog! The final version of this book is greatly improved by virtue of their contributions, although it goes without saying that any remaining mistakes are mine and mine alone. Michael and Oscar in particular went above and beyond the call of duty in providing assistance, and for this I am forever in their debt.

I must offer some apologies as well. Firstly, to every Kantian scholar who will gnash their teeth when they read what I have done to Kant's ethics in this book. I certainly do not claim to be the best source for an accurate portrayal of what Kant actually thought – I heartily recommend Wood's *Kant's Ethical Thought* or *Kantian Ethics* for this. However, I would like to think that what I have done here is still very much in the spirit of Kant's project – and welcome feedback either way in this regard. Apologies are also due to any moral realist who feels I have besmirched their position in some way – realisms hold little appeal for me, but I have adored the work of many realists, including Parfit, Wood and of course Kant himself. I certainly do not intend to imply any superior moral stance to anti-realists, non-cognitivists or any of the ragtag fleet of positions that flail wildly against the consistently clearer arguments of realists, for all that I cannot actually commit to any kind of realism personally.

I may also have to apologize to every rigorous teacher of moral philosophy and meta-ethics for riding roughshod over the fine and nice distinctions that these fields have accumulated internally over the years – but I hope we can all recognize that the complexity of the resulting maze is such that it has become a barrier to getting people interested in a truly fascinating field. Although I spent a long time learning the terminology in use, in my ongoing project to bridge the gap between academic philosophy and the world at large I have to be prudent about the choice of terms. Much of this book simplifies to a point that professors of philosophy could only respond by tearing out what little hair they have remaining after enduring the frustrations of university bureaucracy. To all such people, my sincere apologies: I wanted to write for a wider audience, and I needed to cast off a lot of baggage to make that journey possible.

Additionally, I must express regret for my omissions, particularly to those people whose work I have not been able to incorporate into the research for this book. Explicit apologies are offered to the object-oriented ontologists in this regard – but I believe they may forgive me if I reveal that it was catching up with Latour that robbed me of the time necessary to absorb their many intriguing books. However, I *do not* thank Ian Bogost and Graham Harman for teaching me the phrase 'Latour litany', which Ian coined to describe long lists of objects used for rhetorical effect (Harman, 2009) - it has made me second guess every list I have put into the manuscript! Ian also made me doubt whether I should be using the well-worn phrase 'always already'. There have been so many times that I have edited the phrase in and out of the manuscript that I cannot begin to guess whether it will appear in the final version!

Beyond those mentioned above, I would also like to echo my gratitude to the list of people I have already thanked for the first two books in this 'trilogy' - *Imaginary Games* and *The Mythology of Evolution* – and I must single out Mark Vernon once again for setting me off on the path to becoming a published philosopher (admittedly by turning me down!) and Tariq Goddard for giving me a home for my ramblings at Zero Books. As far as trilogies go, this one is entirely insane – a book on the relationship between art and games, a book on the utter nonsense that the alleged war between Science and Religion has unleashed around the sciences, and now a book on how chaos can be as moral (or more moral!) than order. But all three books are about the role of imagination in life – in art and in play, in science and religion, and in morality and ethics. Although any of these books can be enjoyed in isolation, I offer particular appreciation to anyone who manages to read and enjoy all three books as a trilogy, and hope you have enjoyed this journey as much as I have, but with hopefully a fraction of the toil it has required of me.

Finally, I must offer even greater gratitude than usual to my wife, Adria Smiley, for her assistance in making this book possible. Although she has always supported my writing, on this project I found myself in need of even more direct aid and if it were not for her assistance in compiling quotes from a mountain of papers literally the size of my head it is highly doubtful I would have been able to complete the manuscript in time. Marriage to Adria has been a splendid chaos indeed, and becoming a parent has only intensified our descent into disorder. This has not been an abandonment of freedom and order, but a relinquishing of the vain desire to be the master of one's own fate, a wish that is never as desirable as it first seems. Better to live happily in chaos than to be forever cursed to seek an order beyond possibility – an adage that applies to marriage just as it does to life.

1

Moral Discord

A Paper Time Machine

Fear seizes me the moment I imagine using it once more. So many times I've considered destroying it, setting it ablaze and watching it burn down to nothing but grey ash. For this is no device made of glittering metal, ivory and crystal, like the titular machine in H.G. Wells' novel, it is a shelf full of books, pages and pages of my own words written down day after meticulous day over three decades. To anyone else, a mere collection of diaries – in my hands alone it becomes something far more terrifying: a paper time machine that allows me to enter my own past and confront the strange and disparate people I have been.

Why should my diaries frighten me? After all, we can all imagine ourselves in the past, recalling memories of things long gone. But with memory, there is little possibility of discovering something unexpected – what we remember is almost always consistent with the story we tell about who we are. When I use my paper time machine, however, there is an ever-present risk that I will learn something new, or discover something disturbing. I used to read an old diary every year for fun – until I started finding things I didn't want to know, events in my history that conflicted with who I thought I was or am. Exploring my past became an upsetting ordeal, and I came to be afraid of the things I had once written down in innocent earnest, anxious about confronting the people I used to be. Now, I rarely open any volume unless there is a pressing need to check some fact of my earlier lives, and I strive to avoid needing to go back to these ghosts of myself.

Part of the issue is simply the greater perspective I have gained with age – reading my younger selves occasionally reveals another side to a situation I had originally understood differently. It's distressing to realize that the girl you obsessed over for a decade was, for a while at least, actually interested in you – but you did nothing because your ridiculous pining prevented you from recognizing an opportunity. It's disturbing to discover anger and hatred pouring out of your pen from times you remember fondly, and saddening to read your hope and optimism about something that was ultimately doomed to failure. Experience allows for insights that are impossible in its absence, and time, the medium within which our lives occur, conflicts with memory, the medium in which our identities coalesce. As the nineteenth century philosopher Søren Kierkegaard remarks in his own diaries, life must be understood backwards, yet it must be lived forwards – and this makes it impossible to fully comprehend your own life temporally, since there is no point of rest from which to interpret your past (Kierkegaard, 1996). This restlessness is part of what makes my own time travel so utterly unbearable.

Contemporary philosopher Derek Parfit offers a way I might preserve my sanity in the face of my own historical diversity – but at the price of the coherent narrative I relate about my life that gives it unity. He suggests rather than thinking of ourselves as persons whose stories begin at birth and end at death, we can split our lives into different chapters – making us into what Thomas Nagel calls *series-persons* (Parfit, 1984). As well as suggesting certain ancient approaches to identity, this idea resembles the concept of regeneration in the British time travel adventure *Doctor Who*. Originally added as a MacGuffin to allow for a change of actor, over the decades it has become a cornerstone of the show's mythology: instead of dying, the Doctor regenerates into a new body with the same memories but a different personality. Like the fictional Time Lord we all become different people over time – although we do not, of course, experience dramatic transformations of body with accompanying special effects. No, our lives feel continuous as they are lived – it takes something like my paper time machine to reveal the discontinuity of these regenerations, these series-persons we once were. Nagel rejects his idea as unwise, but Parfit embraces it, suggesting that by accepting it a person's constituent series-persons "can start to speak through the mouth that both share."

Some caution is required with this series-person concept since how we conceive of ourselves has a significant effect on how we relate to morality, as the philosopher Tamar Szabó Gendler (2002) has cogently argued against Parfit. She notes that questions of how our past and future selves relate to us are intimately tied up with concepts such as fairness, responsibility, and justice – not to mention rationality – and that we should be cautious about disrupting these kinds of associations. However, while Parfit effectively wants us to consider replacing our concept of person with the concept of series-person, I don't want to go anywhere near this far. Our sense of who we are *as a person* is something that relates to who we have been *as series-persons*, and the idea we have been different at different times of our lives is much less disruptive than Parfit's efforts to reform our understanding of personal identity. All I want to do here with the concept of a series-person is to split my history into different identities, to divide my time machine into sets of volumes, each representing a different series-person, a different regeneration of me, without denying that these are still essential parts of who I am now.

My diaries begin when I am twelve, back when I was a Christian teenager. This religious-me is the first series-person I can reach in my time machine, although these early diaries are not very articulate, and my own memories have to fill in a great many gaps. This is always the nature of my time travel, however – written word and remembered events combine into an experience of the past, which is why it is disconcerting when the two conflict. Religious-me at twelve has recovered from a period of extended depression, but is still discovering who he is and what he might be. This me talks to God in his bedroom at night, and is bullied for his faith by his peers – I can literally count the Christians who are 'out' at my middle school on one hand. Everything he does is measured not by how he might gain from it, but by what it would mean to everyone around him, both friends and enemies (although for him the two are impossibly hard to tell apart). He may be young and foolish, but he's also smart, erudite, and absurdly well-read on numerous topics – he can describe the basics of atomic structure, chemical bonds and optical physics to a degree of detail that confounds his teachers, let alone his fellow students. He is a young geek in training, and finds no conflict between his love of God and his love of the sciences.

Compare this to the series-person I was in London over a decade later, for five volumes of my time machine. Let's call him wild-me. Although he cannot admit it to himself, he is angry at religious-me and does not like to think of those days. The death of his mother led to a string of 'regenerations' before eventually taking him to the big city for a job as a professional game designer and writer. Wild-me drinks gargantuan quantities of beer and vodka, he smokes unearthly quantities of marijuana with his housemates, and he occasionally experiments with amphetamines and other illegal drugs, although he always thoroughly researches what he is taking first. Despite his rather shocking immoderation, there is nothing he wouldn't do for his friends or his work colleagues, except perhaps commit some blatant injustice. He didn't hesitate to let a friend stay with him indefinitely when circumstances would have otherwise rendered him homeless, even though doing so meant violating his contractual agreements. Frankly, the law is not something he respects, and the only thing he shares in common with religious-me is a yearning to find a soul mate – something he doubts will happen or is even a meaningful phrase, even though unbeknownst to him this life-changing event lies on the imminent horizon. He is a geek in the big city, still finding himself as he simultaneously loses himself, and he finds no conflict between his drug taking and his strong commitment to doing whatever might be good or right.

Then there is the series-person I am now – a dedicated husband and a loving father, a university professor-in-the-making, an occasional lay minister at a local Unitarian church, and a regular invited speaker at academic events, even sometimes on the radio. There are many regenerations between current-me and wild-me, changes wrought by my international relationship with my wife, years of running my own company, and the gradual transformation from lover to family man, first by dog and then by child. The questions and issues I deal with now are so very different from the concerns of my youth, which seem alien indeed. And here's the odd thing: while wild-me would condemn religious-me for his naïve commitments to religious traditions he deems archaic and immoral, and religious-me would be utterly horrified by the limitless excesses and brazen lawlessness of wild-me, this me, the series-person I am now, respects both of these former selves. Indeed, whatever their individual flaws he would defend both these earlier identities as good series-persons, as moral beings.

How can this be? It's not simply because they are me (or parts of the story of me, at least) since I would not similarly defend the brief episode of vandal-me in my late teens, nor the reckless-me who took to the wheel of a rusty and overpowered Ford Cortina with gleeful abandon. Similarly I would be quite unwilling to call business-me unequivocally moral while I was seeking investment for a start-up company, if only because I am deeply conflicted about the way capital investment functions and what this means for the world at large. It is clear that I do not judge all my regenerations in a positive ethical light – but these particular two I still commend for their morality, even though either would castigate the other without hesitation. So many different stories that were and are me – but not all of them have a sense of morality at the heart of their narrative. There is something about both these specific episodes in my life that I find worthwhile – even though the virtuous Christianity of religious-me and the individualist drug circle community of wild-me are so far apart as to barely feel like the same planet, let alone the same person.

This seems to present something of a paradox – for if, as a long-established tradition in moral philosophy has it, what is right can be specified as a universally binding *moral law*, it would seem odd that two so very different persons (series or otherwise) could both be paragons of some kind of virtue. But if there is no such thing as the moral law, if the comparatively young tradition that conceives of morality as mutable and different for everyone were valid, then I could have no basis for either praising or disparaging any of the people I have been – every stop in my time machine would be immune to any kind of overarching criticism because there could be no absolute vantage point from which universal ethical judgments could be made. Kierkegaard's problem would run even deeper than it first seemed, not only denying us any way to understand our lives as a temporal sequence but preventing us from making any kind of moral assessment whatsoever.

In so much as this is a genuine problem, it speaks to the heart of a question that moral philosophy must answer if it is to have any continuing relevance. It may seem as if these issues could be satisfactorily resolved simply by rejecting my premise that both my former selves can be morally defended. For this, all you would need is a basis for criticizing one or both of these younger versions of me – a moral law of some kind that aligned with either the perspective of religious-me, or wild-me, or with neither. Yet however you might do this, it cannot solve *my* problem, since any such approach must necessarily throw me to the wolves. What I need to escape the conflict my paper time machine forces me to confront is some way of dealing with the fact that I am now quite unlike either of these earlier people who helped make me who I am today, even though I still wish to defend them as ethical beings. A moral law cannot unite these disparate identities into a single ethical perspective without being so thin as to risk meaninglessness. What I need has to allow that not only are many different things good, but many different things can be right, and it has to do this without reducing ethics to nothing more than an illusion or a façade. What I need isn't a moral law at all, or at least it cannot be anything like what this phrase usually means. What I need is something akin to a moral chaos.

When I defend religious-me and wild-me as good people, I'm not trying to claim that they were good in the same way, and neither am I claiming that what is good about them is the way they helped me become who I am now (although this is *also* a way in which they were good). Rather, I am claiming that there is something good about who I was at these different points of my life that is also good in *other people* who are similar to whom I was at these times. This runs radically contrary to any concept of 'good' that supposes a unitary account of what is ultimately good or right. But of course, we live at a time when singular ideals of this kind are no longer taken for granted, and indeed the prevailing trend outside of religious or non-religious orthodoxy is to adopt an entirely contrary perspective – the idea that there are an infinite number of kinds of good, that each person establishes their own good, or that there is nothing right except what we judge right for ourselves as individuals. This is a view attributed to the French existentialists such as Jean-Paul Sartre who claimed that "Man is nothing other than he makes himself to be" (Wild, 1965).

In ethics, the former ideology is broadly that of moral law, which operates on the basis of a single set of moral standards that we can be obligated to follow because they alone are right or good. Conversely, the latter ideology denies the meaningfulness of moral law, offering instead a deflation of the truth of morality to the point that 'it's all relative'. According to philosophers like Parfit, if this perspective were true it would be tantamount to *nihilism* – it would mean that *there are no moral truths at all,* nothing at all matters, and life itself is ultimately meaningless (Parfit, 2011). Parfit resists this conclusion, and instead tries to rescue the moral law by reformulating it, but it is far from clear that he succeeds. His assumption is that if there is no moral law, there can be no morality at all, and he is not alone in thinking this.

In what follows, I shall argue against *both these assumptions.* Instead of claiming there are no moral truths, I shall defend the idea that ethics are meaningful, and that things do indeed matter. But rather than opposing nihilism with moral law, I shall be arguing for *moral chaos* – or more specifically, I will argue that there are positive aspects to chaos that we all too often overlook. I certainly do not intend the phrase 'moral chaos' to have a pejorative edge – indeed, precisely by the adjective 'moral' I seek to pick out from the anarchy of disorder whatever may yet be good, whatever might yet be *moral.* Moral chaos, therefore, is something I intend to show as desirable, but I have an uphill battle since the tradition of moral philosophy and ethics in general has almost exclusively dealt with moral *order,* and especially with the aforementioned moral law. Chaos, it is assumed, is inherently bad, wicked, evil, whereas law is inherently good, blameless, righteous. It is precisely this assumption that I seek to overturn.

Laws – actual laws, that is – are not necessarily good, they are never beyond blame. Following the law is certainly not guaranteed to be righteous. Few if anyone doubts this, because we all come across bad laws, stupid laws, and laws that are so antiquated they are impossible to take seriously, like the requirement under English law that all men attend archery practice. The moral law, however, shields itself from such criticisms because moral law is an ideal, what I shall call a *moral fiction*, which is not the same as claiming it is false. The use of 'law' in the phrase 'moral law' was always a metaphor – it appeals to a parallel between laws (the rules of a nation) and moral law (the rules of good conduct). Presupposed in that metaphor is the idea that law is positive, and therefore that chaos (being antithetical to law) is negative. Thus the entire mythology of the moral law attempts to paint disorder as something terrible, the monstrous absence of law. It is this myth that needs overturning, not so that a myth of moral chaos can replace it, but so that we can understand how *both* moral law and moral chaos are necessary if we are to attain anything that we might hope to call good.

Intolerant Tolerance

It may seem that by 'moral chaos' I simply mean the acceptance of different ethical points of view, what can be called pluralism or *multiculturalism*. Yet the ideology of tolerance that goes by this name is far from moral, for all that it may indeed be chaotic. If nihilism suggests that nothing has meaning, multiculturalism achieves the same stalemate by declaring that *everything* is meaningful to *someone*. Multiculturalism claims to level the playing field between different cultures by admitting that the moral perspectives of a New Yorker, an Argentine farmer, a Yoruban 'witch doctor', a Ukrainian merchant, and an Australian aborigine are impossible to compare, and that therefore we must treat all these ethical worlds as entirely separate, with no possibility of evaluation or communication between them. Everyone is locked away in their own little world, and all we can do is accept it – to *tolerate* it.

Supposedly, this tolerance is an acceptance of difference, but scratch the surface of pluralism and it quickly becomes apparent that it conceals a depth of prejudice far worse than the bigotry that is its putative enemy. As the French philosopher Alain Badiou (2001) has argued, liberal ideals of tolerance and the acceptance of difference simply don't stack up in practice. Many of those liberally-minded individuals who espouse multiculturalism have a general inability to even *accept* difference:

> ...the self-declared apostles of ethics and of the 'right to difference' are clearly *horrified by any vigorously sustained difference*. For them, African customs are barbaric, Muslims are dreadful, the Chinese are totalitarian, and so on. As a matter of fact, this celebrated 'other' is acceptable only if he is a *good* other – which is to say what, exactly, if not *the same as us*? Respect for differences, of course! But on condition that the different be parliamentary-democratic, pro free market economics, in favor of freedom of opinion, feminism, the environment... That is to say: I respect differences, but only, of course, in so far as that which differs also respects, just as I do, the said differences (Badiou, 2001).

Badiou offers a stunning indictment of those political ideals that preach tolerance, while practicing intolerance! This bigotry-against-bigots has crept into liberal thought in a way that has become poisonous to any hope of living together since it is torn apart (as Badiou attests) by the tensions it manifests between praising tolerance and condemning fanaticism, between demanding acceptance of difference but vilifying racism, and between insisting upon our recognition of others while declaring fixed boxes within which our identities must fall. These problems are felt every day in the politics of the United States and elsewhere when advocates of liberal doctrines refuse to accept the needs of their conservative rivals, yet claim to be espousing a politics of inclusion – a strange kind of inclusiveness that purports to shelter the minority while leaving the majority out in the cold!

Intolerant tolerance operates perniciously to seal off discussions and privilege one ideal over all others. Primarily, there is the problem identified by Badiou: respecting differences presents itself as an openness to diversity but manifests as a closed-minded hatred of anyone who does not accept the definitions of what is acceptable that are being tacitly enforced. It is thus mandatory to accept gay people, but acceptable to exclude and denigrate Christians – precisely on the assumption that they do not accept gay people. I say 'assumption', because in point of fact there are plenty of gay Christians, not to mention Christians in support of diverse sexual and gender identities. Those most vocal in speaking out against certain kinds of bigotry risk becoming bigots themselves as they imagine the worst kind of generalizations and apply them to anyone even remotely close to disagreeing with their views.

Similarly, it is mandatory to accept feminism in some form or another, and acceptable to exclude and denigrate Muslims on the presumption that they do not accept women as equals. Sunera Thobani (2007) stresses that this undermines the very feminist ideals being praised, since it portrays Muslim women as victims who need to be rescued from their religion and culture. There is no discussion with the women themselves to establish what problems they actually face – there is apparently no need, since it is clear in the eyes of the intolerantly tolerant that "the 'good' Muslim woman is the one who will readily propagate western gender and sexual norms" as well as condemning other Muslims "for refusing to laud the magnanimity of the west towards Muslim women." Once again, acceptance of diversity means nothing more or less than acceptance of one specific image of diversity – it certainly does not entail the kind of dialogue that would be required to establish *what* living with diversity might entail in practice.

It is not just religious practitioners who are the targets of this intolerant tolerance, however, since it manifests wherever any of the fault lines in contemporary identity politics are felt. Consider Slovenian philosopher Slavoj Žižek's observation that certain proponents of multicultural tolerance are all-too-quick to accuse Balkan state citizens such as him of allowing ethnic cleansing to happen (Žižek and Daly, 2004). Race, gender, sexuality, culture, economic class... wherever there is difference there is tolerance, and wherever there is tolerance there is intolerant tolerance. Moderate voices are lost in the clamor of righteous bigotry. If someone should speak aloud their concerns about immigration, they can be denounced as a racist and thus scorned, ridiculed – even persecuted. Perhaps whoever speaks this way is indeed a racist – but to idolize racial categories and thus scorn anyone who refuses to toe the pre-established lines of tolerance is not a morally superior attitude, it is merely an attitude of moralistic superiority.

This problem is even deeper than it first appears. Moral philosopher Allen Wood (2008) wisely suggests that "being tolerant might require us to permit someone to preach intolerance", but regrettably there seems to be a sense that 'being tolerant risks preaching intolerance'. The community that advocates inclusion and tolerance – what we might call the liberal traditions as against the conservative traditions – prescribes what is acceptable and what isn't acceptable, often on the basis of appeals to specific liberal ideals such as inclusion, equality, diversity and so forth. But in all cases, there is a preconceived image of who will be included, what equality must entail, and which identities will constitute desirable kinds of diversity. Dissent, no matter how temperate, must be punished and those who do not include the same elements in their catalogue of approved identities become the enemy and must be denounced – ensuring the circularity of making prejudice the central problem. As the dogma becomes 'Only those who tolerate what we tolerate can be tolerated', toleration itself becomes a kind of blinkered bigotry, a way to exclude any other perspectives from consideration. This is the essence of intolerant tolerance: to prevent persecution, we must persecute! The liberal notion of tolerance, as Žižek (2008) suggests, is sustained by violence.

It is not, when considered carefully, enormously surprising that everyone has their own peculiar prejudices, nor that being opposed to these kinds of bigotries inevitably fosters a different kind of bigotry. As Hannah Arendt (2005) remarked, it is entirely impractical to live a life free of prejudice since this would "demand a superhuman alertness", an impossible capacity to constantly confront the totality of the world at every moment. We all come to the world from a specific set of circumstances, and the liberal extolling of difference does not transcend this, it is just another one of these backgrounds. When we denigrate the fervent nationalist for their love of a mythic nation on the grounds that this turns them against people from other nations we effectively perpetuate the very same mistake – we wield our own ideal as a weapon and use it to prevent other people from having theirs. If we seek the moral high ground by observing that our ideal is more inclusive, this escalation falls prey of the same problem: why must they accept our ideal of inclusiveness when we cannot accept their ideal of national identity?

Beyond the serpent eating its own tail inherent to this hatred of haters, intolerant tolerance represents a far bigger threat to our hopes of living together because it eliminates any possibility of treating others as genuine equals. This problem, which Isabelle Stengers (2003) calls 'the curse of tolerance', stems from the idea that we can easily divide knowledge from belief. It is a curse "upon anyone who thinks they are free to redefine, in their own terms" the way other people inhabit the world. When we think that we *know* but that others merely *believe*, we automatically elevate ourselves to a position of supremacy. This division goes hand in hand with the activities of the contemporary sciences, which are embedded within this distinction between knowledge and belief. As Wittgenstein (1980) observed, evaluating beliefs as an inferior form of knowledge misses the point that "although it's *belief*, it is really a way of living, or of assessing one's life." Tolerance is a curse because it marks an *inability* to understand others, and this in turn conceals an even greater inability to understand *ourselves*.

Consider the case of the photograph, which certain tribes 'believe' will steal their soul – for the Kayapo of the Amazon, for instance, the phrase 'to take a picture' literally means 'to steal a soul' (Moraes, 2011). Ah, how we mock such 'primitive belief' - especially since many people today do not even believe in a soul, much less that a photograph could capture it. Yet how is this caution concerning the capture of images in photography significantly different from the intuitive idea that pornographic photographs can demean women? Anyone who does not believe that a photograph can command power over people is invited to pay closer attention to the contents of tabloid newspapers. The curse of tolerance asks that we humor the naivety of those who 'believe' that photographs can steal souls, but ignore the naivety of those who 'know' that photography is an entirely harmless capturing of photons. Tolerance destroys the otherwise palpable possibility that each could learn from the other's way of being in the world.

Am I really saying we must give up on being tolerant? It may be difficult to appreciate just what I am arguing for at this point, since abandoning the forbearance of multiculturalism for some kind of monoculture is clearly to accept *greater* not lesser intolerance, and it may be tempting to call our current clumsy attempts at pluralism the lesser of two evils. Yet the terrible consequences of a split between intolerance (monoculture) and intolerant tolerance (multiculturalism) is the capacity of those nations that are balanced between this false choice to pursue abominable foreign policies of invasion, internment, torture, and worse, precisely because whichever fork is taken results in the same inability to truly acknowledge other ways of being in the world. That multiculturalism is a form of imperial monoculture in disguise is precisely Badiou's accusation, and this allegation should be taken very seriously indeed. Finding a better way of living together is an urgent concern – and multiculturalism *cannot* offer this while it secretly masks its own horrific prejudices.

Arendt suggests that if we want to dispel prejudices, we need to uncover the prior judgments that brought them about: without establishing the truth within prejudice "whole battalions of enlightened orators and entire libraries of brochures will achieve nothing" (Arendt, 2005). But perhaps the most significant truth to be uncovered within our intolerance is that *all bigotry is fundamentally the same*, it is, as Emmanuel Lévinas (1978) suggested, "the same anti-semitism" that has created so many victims of hatred of so many kinds over so many centuries. If intolerant tolerance seems innocent compared to the genocides of the past, it is perhaps because we valorize our tolerance *as if* it were moral – and fail to see how in actuality it destroys any possibility of equality, permits extermination by asking that we do not interfere, and sanctions massacre by defining enemies who must be stopped at any cost. Intolerant tolerance is not the ethical achievement of our civilization, but the barbaric heart of our own immorality.

Wasted Wastrels

It would scarcely be possible to detail all the prejudices that people deploy to partition themselves from others, but one such distinction deserves particular attention since it masks deeper issues that ought to be dug up and examined in the light. Whoever uses drugs, the official story states, can justifiably be denigrated – even though this accusation is leveled primarily against *illegal* drugs. There is, it is assumed, no such thing as a virtuous drug user, essentially by definition, since drugs are presumed to enslave people against their will and ruin lives.

These are far more delicate affairs than the established dialogue has allowed for! In the United States, to be branded as an abuser of drugs is to risk your job, your reputation, and your livelihood. Indeed, a great many employers in that nation routinely conduct laboratory analysis of their staff's urine in order to verify their purported virtue, and feel entirely justified in doing so.

In order to comply with the official story about drugs, it would be necessary for me to play the game of wringing my hands, decrying my behavior during my wild years, declaring my repentance, and warning everyone of the terrible dangers of drugs. As it happens, I do indeed want to warn of a danger with drugs – but it is not the one that is usually offered in this regard. Crucially, I am not willing to turn my back on my former self and declare him wicked or evil – but neither would I want to hide behind some vague libertarian concept of freedom that would endorse absolutely anything done with consent. It is far from clear how an adequate concept of consent can be brought to bear in contexts such as drugs that threaten to distort our basic assumptions concerning free will.

I am quite unable to denounce my experimentation with drugs of so many different kinds during my time in London because to do so would be to turn my back on everyone I have met who uses these illegal chemicals and plants, thus condemning them as immoral. This I cannot honestly do. Yet at the same time, I dread to think that my son might grow up thinking that the kind of hedonistic, experimental carnage I indulged in when I was younger was sensible, desirable, virtuous, or worthy of imitation. So I face what appears to be a dilemma: betray friends and acquaintances who either did or still do take illegal drugs, or risk encouraging my son to emulate the chapters of my life I would least want him to copy. The only way I might resolve this is to provide a moral defense of drug-taking that was not at the same time an endorsement of its practices – and this may seem impossible.

It would be wrong to think of this as a uniquely contemporary problem, however, since two of the greatest philosophers from the eighteenth century both passed comment upon the odd moral question of getting wasted. The Scottish philosopher, David Hume, whose work I greatly admire but rarely agree with, speaks strongly in *favor* of the merits of intoxication. Hume, admittedly, is only talking about alcohol, but he not only praises the merits of a good night's drinking, he provides a morality for its undertaking:

I hate a drinking Companion, says the Greek Proverb, who never forgets. The Follies of the last Debauch should be buried in eternal Oblivion, in order to give full Scope to the Follies of the next (Hume, 1751).

You can't always tell with Hume whether he is entirely sincere, or just trying to get a rise out the Christian orthodoxy of his time, who clearly irritate him on all manner of topics. Still, the drinking ethic espoused here is close to the drug ethic that I followed in London – and indeed, it is worth noting that of all the damage caused by this excess, it was certainly my rapacious appetite for beer that caused the most problems. I woke up one morning after one of Hume's fine debauches to discover I had the shakes, and quickly totted up my weekly consumption in my head. At fifty pints a week, sometimes having as many as five pints of Guinness in a single lunch break, I knew it had got out of hand, and thus reined in my drinking dramatically from that point onwards.

Compared to Hume, the Prussian philosopher Immanuel Kant is willing to countenance much less leeway when it comes to intoxication. "A human being who is drunk", he objects, "is like a mere animal, not to be treated as a human being". According to his argument, putting yourself into a state of incompetence violates a duty you have towards yourself, what we might now call a duty of care. Kant notes that although such "debasements" are usually caused by "fermented drinks" they can also result from "other narcotics, such as opium and other vegetable products". He warns that these are particularly seductive because under their influence people "dream for a while that they are happy and free from care", but cautions not only about the debilitating weakness that follow afterwards but also the need to increase dosage to get the same effect (Kant, 1785). This is a surprisingly familiar complaint to be echoing across a gap of two centuries!

Yet even a stuffy goody-two-shoes like Kant isn't calling for total abstinence, since he immediately counters that it is possible to justify "a use of wine bordering on intoxication" on the grounds that it "enlivens the company's conservation" and helps people talk more freely. Both Hume and Kant are thus willing to allow that a little libation can serve the social good of a group of friends, but the latter shares his concerns about how to address the problem that once intoxicated there is momentum already pushing towards greater and greater excess. Who among the young bar-hoppers has never been out for 'a quick drink' that ended in a mighty bender, with only a catastrophic hangover as a memorial for whatever it was that took place the night before? More poetically, Kant asks: "who can determine the measure for someone who is quite ready to pass into a state in which he no longer has clear eyes for measuring?"

However, Kant utterly condemns both opium and strong spirits on the basis that those who take them become reticent, and withdraw into silent euphoria. In a more contemporary turn of phrase, they drop out, or become shut-ins. I should like to call those people Kant censures for debilitating themselves with drink or drugs by the old Victorian word *wastrel*, which originally meant an idler or a spendthrift, in order to make clearer what exactly is the moral problem in this regard. It is not that getting wasted is the issue so much as it is becoming a wastrel – and it is this distinction that is all too often ignored in discussions of drugs. The assumption is that certain drugs must be illegal because addiction is a disease they *cause*, which is another way of suggesting that such substances *cause* wastrels. But this is an implausible understanding of the topic that is in desperate need of revision.

I should like to contrast two very different examples from my own experience. Firstly, a student whom I lived with during my first year at university, who like me was starting out on an astrophysics degree. Let's call him Norton. He was, as far as I can tell, a bright fellow with excellent prospects, but he had discovered during his late teenage years a predilection for smoking marijuana. It seemed to those of us living with him that he was perpetually stoned, and never seemed to be thinking clearly. He believed, insanely, that because he was studying astrophysics he only needed to attend those few courses that directly related to this topic, thus missing most of the foundational work in physics that was a requirement for the degree. He consequently failed his first year and dropped out, going to live with a band of squatters who panhandled for a living. The last time I saw him, he was begging for money outside of a cinema I was waiting to enter. He couldn't seem to understand why I didn't want to give him my spare change.

Compare Norton to someone I knew in London. Let's call him Tommy. He lived in a dilapidated high rise building near Clapham Junction, the kind of wretched housing where the elevators seldom work, and even when they do they stink of urine. Tommy not only smoked pot, he was also a small time dealer in that particular drug, as well as a light heroin user. In fact, he once absent mindedly offered me a smoke that had been laced with smack before remembering that I avoided the stuff, and praising me for doing so. He was full of stories about why heroin was nasty, and savaged Danny Boyle's adaptation of *Trainspotting* on the grounds that it made junkies seem glamorous and fun. He knew it was neither. But Tommy was not a wastrel – in fact, he worked very hard fitting bathroom tiles whenever he could get work doing so. While Tommy was not, of course, a paragon of virtue neither was he someone worthy of contempt. Between the two, I have far more reason to disparage Norton the wastrel than Tommy the dealer and reluctant addict.

It is worth comparing these contrasting examples to the official story that illegal drugs cause addiction and thus cause wastrels. Norton smoked pot and did become a wastrel – but Tommy took not only this drug but also the far more potent heroin and *didn't* become a wastrel. Furthermore, although he recognized the destructive consequences of heroin abuse, I can't say that he was anything like an archetypal junkie. The story that 'drugs cause wastrels' is problematic because the same drugs in different hands have different effects. We could retreat to a softer position, one that recognized the involvement of the individual in the outcomes, but then we'd have to give up this concept that drugs *cause* addiction and wastrels.

Even the association between destructive addiction and illegal drugs requires closer scrutiny. Alcohol, nicotine and caffeine are all legal, but can be at least as addictive as the illegal drugs – including heroin (Stolerman and Jarvis, 1995). We routinely *overestimate* the power of illegal drugs and *underestimate* that of legal drugs. On the basis of my own experiences I can report that some of the locally-grown tobacco on sale in smoke shops in Tennessee is unbelievably potent compared to what is typically sold to smokers, and far stronger than the amphetamines I took in London on a few rare occasions. The same is true of the wonderful green tea known as *matcha* used in the Japanese tea ceremony, which had me buzzing in Kyoto far more than anything I took in my wild years. Yet I have never been addicted to nicotine, despite wild-me smoking tobacco on-and-off for a short while, and although I am a habitual tea drinker like my father before me, this addiction has not obviously caused me any problems. Treating drugs as causes of addiction, and drug addiction as the cause of wastrels, is to indulge in a misleading simplification.

Compare what may seem to be a very different circumstance: the use and abuse of firearms. As the French intellectual Bruno Latour remarks, those who wish to limit the unrestricted sale of guns use the slogan "Guns kill people", while their opponents offer the reverse claim that "People kill people, not guns" (Latour, 1994). The first slogan is parallel to the claim that drugs cause wastrels – it places responsibility for a state of affairs entirely into things. The second slogan places responsibility entirely upon the shoulders of individuals and denies any relevance for the gun in unlawful shootings. Yet oddly, the people who blame things in the case of firearms tend to accuse *people* in the case of drugs, and those who blame people in respect of gun violence tend to point the finger at drugs in the context of addiction and wastrels. While it may at first seem reasonable to treat guns and drugs in this radically different way, if we stare down this odd disconnect it begins to appear quite absurd that we could draw a line between beings and things and assign responsibility only ever to one camp or the other.

Latour (1991) traces responsibility for this division to none other than Kant, for it is Kant's critical philosophy – responding to sceptical concerns that had been raised by Hume – that institutes a division between subject and object, between beings and things. To be fair, the distinction had been around earlier, in the invention of the laboratory by Boyle and the concept of politics devised by Hobbes, not to mention the philosophy of René Descartes, but it was Kant's nerdy brilliance to make it central to how the world would be understood by everything 'modern' - and the sciences in particular. The entire philosophical tradition that descends from Kant's pioneering work has, Latour suggests, only sharpened the divide between subject and object, nature and society, to the extent that we have become quite unable to recognize the incredible interplay *between* beings and things – an issue that both wastrels and gun control help bring into focus.

Kant's moral philosophy builds upon his critical philosophy and gave us the tradition of secular humanism from which human rights and other such fixtures of contemporary ethics have developed. Part of this tradition is the concept of *autonomy*, or self-governance, which as Jerome Schneewind has demonstrated is established as a core moral concept by Kant as the culmination of philosophical discussions over the preceding centuries (Marshall, 1999). Without this, we would not have the culture of individualism that we have today – and so much the better say critics such as Alasdair MacIntyre (1984). Most of us, however, value the ideals of individual freedom that have prospered from these intellectual seeds, and it has become central to a kind of ethic of authenticity underlying the idea that people can and should make themselves what they will (Taylor, 1992).

The problem with Kant's conception of autonomy is that it grants too much power to the individual – it locks up all moral concerns in the mind of the individual moral *agent*, that is, anything that can take an action of moral relevance. It risks suggesting that people kill people or become addicts with absolutely no involvement from guns and drugs. Against this, Latour and others such as Peter-Paul Verbeek (e.g. 2009a) offer what I shall call a *secular animist* approach that views agency not as the sole province of an autonomous agent but as distributed among networks of beings and things. As Latour (1994) puts the matter: "It is neither people nor guns that kill." Rather, responsibility for action must be shared among *everything* that is involved.

Although there is much about an ethics of secular animism I would praise – particularly in understanding contentious questions such as wastrels and guns – there are some problems with the approach. For a start, it is not something everyone is willing to accept. There are critics who do not find the arguments of Latour or Verbeek compelling and who insist on maintaining the conventional understanding of our tools – that they are neutral, or "at most bearers of instrumental value" (Peterson and

Spahn, 2011). I am unconvinced that we are on the fringe of an animist moral revolution that will convince everyone, for all that I *am* convinced that the secular animist perspective is a vital voice that we lost at some point over the preceding millennium.

Part of the problem, as Kant and Hume recognized, is that morality *requires* us to have the freedom to act as individuals since if we lack this any concept of responsibility falls by the wayside. Kant's solution, which builds upon Hume's recognition that free will becomes incoherent unless causality acts consistently, is to suggest that we approach the world from two different stances. On the one hand, we have the *theoretical* view that dominates the empirical sciences – that of causal relations. On the other hand, we have the *practical* view that dominates ethical thought – that of individual freedom and autonomy. Kant, quite brilliantly, recognized that there was no contradiction inherent in holding these disparate views (Buss, 2008) - that nothing can remove our responsibility to decide what to do, even if our decisions could ultimately be understood as resulting from purely mechanical causal processes (Wood, 1999).

My own small contribution to this matter is to suggest that both the theoretical and the practical perspective depend intimately upon *mythologies*, collections of imaginative patterns using fiction and metaphor to establish particular ways of looking at the world. In my previous book of philosophy, *The Mythology of Evolution*, I was able to demonstrate how the theoretical perspective of the sciences is – and must be – intimately tied up with their mythologies (Bateman, 2012). Now, I must complete this argument by showing that the practical perspective of ethics is also saturated by mythologies – and we can no more eliminate them from our morality than we can from the sciences. We are beings with intimate connections to our stories and we can no longer afford to think that moral importance resides purely in beings, for it also entails both our things and the mythologies that conjoin them. Morality is thus not merely about reason and rationality – it is also about *imagination*, and it is only within our mythologies that reason and rationality have meaning.

The question of what causes wastrels is a terrific demonstration of the salience of this argument, since when the topic of free will is investigated experimentally it transpires that *belief in free will is conducive to its exercise.* In an extremely revealing study, Kathleen Vohs and Roy Baumeister (2009) demonstrate that by exposing people to scientific literature that seems to suggest that we *don't* have free will – that we are dominated by unconscious processes, or genetic determinism, or neurochemical domination – people become more willing to cheat, steal, or act aggressively and less willing to help others. Conversely, artificially bolstering belief in free will had no significant effect – suggesting that we ordinarily believe in our autonomy as moral agents (the mythological legacy of Kant's philosophy that we have all inherited). As Kant had intimated centuries earlier, a belief in free will is a requirement for its exercise!

This work was conducted specifically to address the question of individual freedom in the context of drug addiction, and Vohs and Baumeister conclude that the medical conception of addiction that emerged around the turn of the twentieth century is deeply flawed. Medical addiction treats drug abuse as if it were a disease, and treats the drugs themselves as a contagion like a virus or a germ (the wastrel equivalent of 'guns kill people'). In this perspective, addiction acquires the implication of a loss of autonomy. This mythology (and Vohs and Baumeister expressly use this term, albeit within 'scare quotes') actively increases the chances that people who use drugs will become wastrels, since those who have made bad choices tend to like the idea that they were not really responsible for their actions. Catering to this perspective "excuses their behavior and sometimes contributes to enabling them to continue making similar choices." It is neither drugs nor people that cause wastrels – it is drugs, people, *and their mythologies*, all of which are intimately entangled. Insisting on the story that it is illegal drugs that cause addiction creates a self-fulfilling prophecy.

Understanding wastrels in this way also allows us to get away from one of the most damaging aspects of the way this issue is framed – the idea that it is solely *illegal* drugs that contribute to people becoming wastrels. On the contrary, whether it is painkillers, antidepressants or treatments for attention 'deficits', our medical bureaucracy offers a mythology of drug use that produces its own vast swath of addicts, wastrels, and disempowered individuals. It is far from clear, for instance, that someone who is depressed is actually helped by a doctor absolving them of any responsibility and whacking them out on pills. A doctor's medical training should have no bearing on the moral dimensions of wastrels, and cannot make the routine daily obliteration of personality acceptable, whether we're talking about anti-depressants or merely mood-savaging ADHT 'medication'. Next to what is thoughtlessly done to people with mind-wrecking pharmaceuticals under the guise of medicine, a great deal of illegal drug use begins to seem radically less serious.

As Bertha Alvarez Manninen (2006) has argued in her application of Kant's ethics to the question of medical drugs, whether or not a particular pharmaceutical is *effective* against a particular situation should not obscure the question of whether it is *desirable* to use it in this way. Drugs are now being deployed not just to alleviate severe cases of mental dysfunction, but to 'treat' just about any situation where people are unhappy. Circumstances that were once seen as opportunities to grow through personal struggle and self-insight are being replaced with medical 'treatments' that offer to 'fix' emotional distress chemically. Manninen even notes that the quintessential experience of growing up and discovering yourself has been "relabelled as a medical affliction that can only be 'cured' by using psychoactive medication."

The system of metaphors that underlies this medicalized fixation with treating human beings as broken machines is intimately connected with the theoretical perspective Kant contrasted to the practical perspective of morality. It is part of a vast and complex imaginative system that animates, and all too frequently distorts, the work of the sciences. I have called this mythology *orthodox science fiction,* which in literature is synonymous with what is called 'hard' science fiction (Bateman, 2012). Just as Charles Segal (1986) suggested that the myths of the ancient Greeks only made sense when they were thought of as an interrelated system he termed a megatext, there is an equivalent collective mythological framework connected to the sciences. The assortment of scientific theories, experimental apparatus, methodologies, textbooks, and research papers that are currently endorsed by the academic community form what I call the *science megatext* – an invaluable guide to research endeavors from a theoretical perspective, but far from morally innocent from a practical perspective. The mythology of orthodox science fiction that is rooted in the science megatext has serious effects throughout the contemporary world, and intersects with the questions of secular animism concerning our relationship with our supposedly neutral technology.

Cyberfetish

From before the term itself had been coined, science fiction set itself apart from other kinds of literature through its relationship to the empirical sciences. Whereas prior to the eighteenth century the term 'science' had referred to all kinds of knowledge (including philosophy), the meaning of the word in English transformed in the wake of the Enlightenment to refer specifically to the kind of laboratory-driven, experimental methods that had been established by Robert Boyle in the seventeenth century. Changes in the understanding of facts were coupled with changes in the content of fiction. Although there were certainly earlier examples, particularly the novels of Mary Shelley, the form of the science fiction genre was set in place by the 'scientific romances' of the nineteenth century (a term alluding to the medieval chivalric romances, not to 'romances' in the sense of romantic love).

H.G. Wells and Jules Verne compete for the title 'Father of Science Fiction' and also represent something of a schism in how the genre could be pursued – whether the "Verneian category of 'hard', unspeculative fiction or the more imaginative, socially committed mode of Wells" (Barthelmess, 1987). Verne was apparently influenced by the non-religion of *positivism* founded by Auguste Comte (1830, 1858) whereas Wells confessed "a real personal dislike" of Comte, while still grudgingly acknowledging "a sort of priority he had in sketching the modern outlook" (Wells, 1934). In much the same way that myth cycles form the literary foundation of conventional religions (as with the Ramayana or Mahabharata in the Hindu traditions), science fiction was to constitute the mythological foundations for the non-religion of positivism, which can be seen as collecting together such disparate identities as scientific materialists, atheists, Marxists and scientific humanists under one roof much as 'theist' collects Christians, Muslims, Zoroastrians and members of the Bahá'í Faith under one tent (which is to say, only in the most generic of senses).

In the contest between Verne's and Wells' approaches, it was to be the orthodox science fiction that would largely win out. This was particularly the case in the United States where pulp magazines were to give voice to authors now synonymous with the genre such as Isaac Asimov in the 1940s and 50s, and Robert A. Heinlein in the 60s. The most famous publications associated with the rise of popular science fiction were the magazines *Astounding Science Fiction*, which tellingly changed its name from the more general title *Astounding Stories* in 1938, and *Amazing*

Stories, which in 1926 became the first periodical specifically devoted to science fiction. Like all the pulp magazines, these titles were gaudy and lurid in their presentation and printed on cheap paper, often with ragged edges that resulted from their low-cost production techniques (and to which the term 'pulp' refers).

In the pages of these early science fiction magazines, scientists comprised the majority of both the heroes *and* the villains, although businessmen tended to be portrayed as substantially more villainous than scientists, as Walter Hirsch noted in his examination of three decades of pulp science fiction. Orthodox science fiction seized moral law away from religious traditions and reimagined its meaning, making those with scientific skills into prophetic figures. The scientist was generally seen as quite removed from the society they lived in, with their major activity in the pulp stories being saving humanity. After World War II, however, this emotional investment in the scientists as messianic figures begins to give way to the idea that humanity perhaps might not be able to save itself, and technologically advanced aliens start arriving to do it for us (Hirsch, 1958). Of course, this loss of faith in the human scientist did not denote a loss of faith in mythological Science – it was precisely their technological superiority that qualified the extra-terrestrials to act as saviors, a theme that can still be found today in the deeply positivistic reimagining of *Doctor Who* currently airing on the BBC.

In the 1980s, a radically new direction in science fiction was to appear that eventually came to be known as the cyberpunk movement. Five authors stand out as the center of what was at first simply called 'the Movement', and later 'the Mirrorshades Group': William Gibson, Rudy Rucker, Lewis Shiner, John Shirley, and Bruce Sterling. Although they did not coin the term 'cyberpunk' - like most artists their label was foisted upon them by critics – it stuck firmly. The name had an irresistible appeal, and it seemed to link this movement with its predecessor, the

New Wave science fiction of the sixties and seventies – John Brunner, Michael Moorcock and (perhaps more than anyone) J.G. Ballard were icons of this time who went on to influence the nascent cyberpunks far more than the traditional science fiction writers. Whereas the pulp magazines had been invested in orthodox science fiction, New Wave had been unconcerned with the scientific accuracy of their content and far more interested in experimentation with a more literary style, one that focused on the existential crises of their characters rather than the nuts and bolts of their settings.

Although William Gibson is the cyberpunk author most associated with the movement, Bruce Sterling did the most to try and rescue it from being perceived as mere dystopianism. His edited collection, *Mirrorshades: the Cyberpunk Anthology* (1988), remains the definitive tribute to the first wave of cyberpunk authors, and its preface is the most illuminating presentation of what the movement was about. Sterling notes the importance of the rapid acceleration of technology to its ethos. Gone is the comfortable distance between an imaginary Science and a somewhat distant society that populated the pages of *Amazing Stories*, rather there is almost a trace of the monstrous products of technology foreshadowed by Mary Shelley's *Frankenstein* (1818) - but no longer set aside in isolated laboratories. Technology has collided with life and can no longer be pried apart. As Sterling puts the matter in the preface to *Mirrorshades*:

> ... the gap is crumbling in unexpected fashion. Technical culture has gotten out of hand. The advances of the sciences are so deeply radical, so disturbing, upsetting, and revolutionary, that they can no longer be contained. They are surging into culture at large; they are invasive; they are everywhere. The traditional power structure, the traditional institutions, have lost control of the pace of change.

Thus the origin of the movement's name – high tech (cyber) fusing with counter-culture (punk). Sterling comments that for he and the other original cyberpunks "technology is visceral... it is pervasive, utterly intimate. Not outside us, but next to us. Under our skin; often, inside our minds." The prevailing themes of those original cyberpunk stories revealed a horror and a fascination in this collision, epitomized in George Alec Effinger's *When Gravity Fails* (1988), whose protagonist has great anxiety about the vast array of 'add-ons' and 'moddies' that everyone else is using to get wired. The ethical stance of cyberpunk was not in unequivocal support of this blind fusion between humanity and machine. Gibson laments on occasion his fans inability to spot the irony that animated *Neuromancer* (1986) and its sequels – their fervent desire to be part of the fallen future he depicted was distinctly distasteful to him.

That the cyberpunk movement was more of a warning than an exaltation of technology can be seen most clearly through the book that came out of an unorthodox collaboration between pivotal members of 'the Movement', William Gibson and Bruce Sterling. *The Difference Engine* (1991) is considered to be one of the first-wave of 'steampunk' novels, a genre that crossed cyberpunk themes with Victorian settings. This particular book operates overtly as an alternate history for the 1850s in which Charles Babbage successfully constructs a mechanical computer, but covertly as a commentary on the 1990s. Sterling confirms precisely this in an interview from shortly after its release, remarking that it's "about the 1990s, let's face it". He makes the point that "the present is somebody else's past" and that for all the criticisms we may have of the Victorians, we can still see their achievements all around us. Conversely, our legacy is less impressive: "What the hell are we leaving? Mounds of disposable diapers, basically, a ruined atmosphere..." (Fischlin, Hollinger and Taylor, 1992).

As it transpired, the original cyberpunk vision of resistance to institutional power against a backdrop of technological future shock quickly gave way in the fanbase to a fetishist fantasy about body modification, a desire for cybernetic limbs and mental union with the computer, epitomized by the non-religion of The Singularity, whose future visions are so hilariously reminiscent of the eschatology of traditional religious mythology that their signature event was quickly dubbed 'the Rapture of the Nerds'. Cyberpunk thus eroded down to mere *cyberfetish*. Gone was the grassroots rebellion, now substituted by fanciful dreams of trading flesh for tech – a reverie intimately connected with the vacuous hope of techno-immortality. There is no ethical side to these phantasmagorical distortions of cyberpunk – it is simply a reflection of the base self-centered egoism that Gibson and Michael Swanwick exposed in their short story "Dogfight" (1987).

When I say 'cyberfetish', do I mean cyberfetish*ism*? The latter would stress a parallel to Karl Marx's commodity fetishism, which compares the strange importance we place on goods and money to the attitudes that tribal animists display towards their totems or fetishes (Marx, 1867). There has been a revival of interest in this idea in recent years, particularly in viewing capitalism as a form of animism (Holert, 2012). As with the formative influences on science fiction, it was Comte who had helped put fetishism onto the intellectual map when he proposed it as the first stage of human religion, his final stage being positivism, in which Science replaces religion (Comte, 1830). From this interest in tribal fetish-making came both Marx's commodity fetishism and also to the use of the term 'fetish' to mean an erotic fixation, as discussed by Freud and others.

The way I use 'cyberfetish' implies both the exaltation of technology (cyberfetishism) *and* technology as equivalent to an animist fetish (the cyberfetish), since the two go hand-in-hand. Just as a traditional maker of fetishes credits their creation with powers that would be dismissed as 'mere belief' with intolerant tolerance, so *we* credit our technology as a whole with spectacularly grandiose powers. Technology has become our preferred fetish, since many believe it will grant immortality, create perfect slaves, and allow us to 'conquer' the universe. Indeed, orthodox science fiction repeatedly assures us of the inevitability of these awesome achievements. Cyberfetish also carries a sense of irresistible attraction, thanks to the sexual implications the term 'fetish' has gained, and this allusion is also something I explicitly intend to allude to with the term.

In its most extreme manifestations, cyberfetish is brazenly absurd in its longings, and a profound betrayal of cyberpunk's roots. It is also deeply ridiculous in its iconic manifestations: why desire cybereyes when your smartphone is forever at hand to snapshot your life and distribute it online to your friends? We are all trivially cybernetic now but more than this, as Donna Haraway shrewdly observed in 1985 at the height of the cyberpunk movement, *we were always cyborgs* (Haraway, 1991). The distinctions we make between our bodies and our machines are contrived; our prostheses are as much a part of our lives now as they ever were, although their nature has changed and their diversity has skyrocketed. Of course you are a cyborg when you get behind the wheel of your car, or browse the internet, or even read this book – and I am a cyborg every time I dare to use my paper time machine. But the ancient Greeks were also cyborgs when they began using notebooks, and early humans were cyborgs when they made flint tools and painted images onto cave walls. Yet even this doesn't go back anywhere near far enough. The surgical implantation of an artificial hip doesn't make your granny more cyborg than you – the bird was a cyborg the moment it built its first nest, the beaver's dam profoundly reconfigured the world millennia before we began to fear our capacity to do so.

The cybernetic moment is not union with the machine, but its usage. Cyborg existence began with tools, long before humanity.

The more intense advocates of cyberfetish seek to narrow the gap between human and machine, flesh and metal, but this change is all but meaningless when measured against those original cybernetic moments, when animals began to explore the boundless realms of tools and technology. We have, without a doubt, accelerated the process immeasurably within the last century – and it was this that the cyberpunks alternately warned us about, or hoped we could use to change the world before it could change us. Cyberfetish abandons this dream, preferring instead to surrender. I had always hoped cyberpunk might serve as a timely warning, instead it has devolved into a fatalistic fixation with nothing to offer but escapism. Alas, cyberpunk is dead – and with it the hope that technology might be our deliverance. Now it becomes ever-clearer that 'Science as salvation', as philosopher Mary Midgley (1992) has dubbed it, is a mythology as problematic as any other messianic prophecy, whether from religion or non-religion, and trusting the sciences to save moral law is a fool's errand.

If it is all too easy to laugh at the more extreme manifestations of cyberfetish, it is sobering to recognize that we all seem to fall prey to its milder forms. Illustrations of our barely-noticed dependency upon technology can be found everywhere around us: in the medical mythology that authorizes the kinds of horrendous drug interventions discussed previously, the radical monopoly of the car and its asphalt infrastructure (Illich, 1974), or the ubiquity of the smartphone – a pocket robot that is advertised precisely by the claim of technical omnipotence implied by the phrase 'we have an app for that'. Indeed, 'dependency' is the perfect word for cyberfetish since it is little more than technological addiction, two centuries of exalted engineering bringing endless proliferations of devices designed to do everything on our behalf. Computers were only the culmination of this sequence – from Victorian steam engines to the automated jukeboxes of the 1940s and 50s, we were so busy expecting human-shaped androids we failed to notice that we had already surrounded ourselves with robots. Machines, as the orthodox science fiction authors predicted, will do everything for us – even help destroy us if we're not careful.

To be clear, responsibility for this encroachment of cyberfetish upon every aspect of human existence cannot be constrained to just the positivists alone, since the majority of Christians and members of other religious traditions have been equally content to incorporate orthodox science fiction into their mythologies, and equally complicit in the mythic vision of progress that cleared the path for cyberfetish like a bulldozer leveling a rainforest. Even the oft-murmured phrase 'technological advances' is inescapably infused with cyberfetish! If we wanted to fairly judge our relationships with our machines, we could not possibly view everything that has occurred in the previous century as an 'advance', as a manifestation of inevitable and desirable progress. On the contrary, the honest way to talk about such things would be 'technological changes', since we all recognize that not all change is positive. Thinking that every development, refinement, and obsolescence of our tools has been as 'an advance' could be the very definition of cyberfetish.

How did we get ourselves into this horrific mess where we are unable to even contemplate the moral and practical dimensions of our technology because we are fooled into thinking that every change is necessarily a positive accumulation? Part of the problem is that the story of 'progress' has become the unrecognized backdrop of our thinking. As Hannah Arendt remarked, it is difficult to address many of our contemporary problems because we lost any viable concept of authority when we switched to a mythology of the ever-improving future:

> ....with the beginning of the modern age, the old belief in the sacredness of foundation in a far-distant past gave way to the new belief in progress and in the future as an unending

> progress whose unlimited possibilities could not only never be bound to any past foundation, but which also could only be arrested and frustrated in their limitless potentiality by any new foundation (Arendt, 2005).

What alternatives to cyberfetish might we have? Enter the secular animists, with their radical new conception of agency and their attempts to foreground what has for too long been concealed in the background. Their position is parallel to that of the cyberpunks, equivalent to Sterling's recognition of a pervasive technology that is not on the outside, but "under our skin" and "inside our minds". They are the late-breaking philosophers of cyberpunk, not looking to smash the machines like the Luddites of the industrial revolution (who were perhaps the first victims of cyberfetish, humans made obsolete by mechanized textile mills), but instead desperately trying to understand the hidden dimensions of technology and "morally assess technologies with respect to the role they play" (Verbeek, 2006) instead of pretending that the ethical dimensions of human existence have been utterly unaffected by the unleashing of machines that have entirely reconfigured every aspect of our lived experience.

As Peter-Paul Verbeek warns, if we do not have frank and open discussions about the effects of technology, only the designers of devices will be in a position to dictate the moral effects of our manufactured things. Against this implicit technocracy, he and the other secular animists propose finding a "democratic way to 'moralize technology'" (Verbeek, 2006). This ethical and political discussion cannot simply be couched in the extreme poles of individual autonomy and technological oppression, because technology now shapes not only who we are but also how we can live (Verbeek, 2009b). The battle cry of secular animism is not 'down with machines' but Verbeek's plaintive call 'let's make things better'. But this 'better' is not the "unending progress" that Arendt recognizes as having become our new mythology, but rather a long-overdue call for us to look our robots in the 'eye' and think about what they are, what they do, what they make us do, and how we should like our relationship with them to continue.

We can no longer afford to accept an ethics that is incapable of imagining the effects of technology upon agency, but we equally cannot risk losing sight of the central importance of beings in what happens. Latour proposes we imagine our tools as having 'scripts' that are inscribed in them by design (Verbeek, 2006), while Thomas Powers and Deborah Johnson (2004) suggest we might think of our artifacts as having a kind of intentionality without mentality. Powers and Johnson suggest:

> We see no reason to confine 'agent' or 'agency' to the class of humans, or even to the class of living organisms... The central issue is whether it is essential for something to be an agent—a moral agent—that it causes an action through intentional states that are also mental states. We have argued that artifacts have intentional states that cause behavior and change in the world, but we have not claimed that these intentional states are mental states. Does the concept of agency require that the cause of moral action be confined to the realm of the mental?

This returns us to the questions raised by drugs and guns, and the contradictory presuppositions deployed to either demand or deny their causal roles in the ethics of addiction or murder. Oddly, there is a strange sense that we are now facing the reverse of the problem that Kant faced when he had to rationalize the necessity of causation with the freedom required for morality. As Powers and Johnson put it "Kant abandons the causality of the mental in order to get to moral evaluation, we abandon the mentality of the causal in order to get to the same place." Thus they suggest that beings such as humans have mental states that are intentional, but technology can have a kind of intentionality without being mental – the intentionality that was put there by design. When it comes to our tools, they suggest, the two influences come together such that there is effectively "a complex of agency consisting of user, artifact, and designer."

But there is no need to accept such an unusual construal of agency to get to the heart of the moral problem of cyberfetish. Responding to the work of Verbeek and Latour, Auke Pols (2012) offers a different way to understand the distribution of agency between beings and things, one that is far closer to the conventional wisdom in moral philosophy. He suggests that the effect of technology upon human morality can be understood simply by recognizing that the facts about things "alter our reasons for action". Latour's design-inscribed 'scripts' describe the possibilities inherent in any given tool, and this can be expressed in purely factual terms: no-one was ever shot dead with a bullet that was not fired from a gun, and every gun that has been shot has been fired by a human – at least so far. It is, after all, horribly ironic that for all Asimov's (1942) meticulous specification of the necessary limits of robot morality in the pages of *Astounding Science Fiction*, the most fervently pursued research into autonomous robots today aims to make them into killers. Perhaps we should hope that whoever designs such an abomination might not be able to hide behind the increasingly implausible claim that the design of technology is immune from ethical consideration.

On the Roads

While living in the US, I had an opportunity to partake in a traditional Lakota sweat lodge that had been arranged by the pagan community in Tennessee and Georgia. This was an incredible experience in itself, but it was not just the purification ceremony that stuck in my memory. Our host for the ritual, a robustly built Native American with a refreshingly pragmatic view on life, arrived in a quite substantial pickup truck and remarked (with a wry grin) that if his ancestors had been able to drive off-road vehicles, they would have done so. I understood the point he was making, which went to the practicalities of making use of what is available, but it also helped dissipate the naïve image of tribal cultures 'living in harmony with nature'. It is not that the tribes of the Great Plains were not mindful of their relationship with other beings and things, but it could not be claimed that their tradition would therefore be resistant to cyberfetish. On the contrary, they were just as likely to be caught up in the mythology of technology as any other human.

In this case, it has to be noted that there was no conceivable way that a nomadic people like the Lakota could possibly have used cars since despite the way we tend to think about our technology, it never operates in isolation. Setting aside the incredible collection of enterprises involved in designing and building an automobile, there is no way to operate a motorized vehicle without an infrastructure that not only mines and processes oil, it constantly delivers it to a distribution of depots for its eventual use. The idea of Native Americans roaming the plains in jeeps hunting herds of buffalo is entirely absurd – they could not have maintained their lifestyle if they changed to these kinds of tools. The illusion that this would have been possible illustrates the subtle ways in which cyberfetish fools us into thinking of each tool as an isolated capability, instead of something that gains its effectiveness only by drawing against an immense network of industrial productivity. Even this book that you are reading now could not have reached you without power stations, internet relays, software developers, and either forests and paper mills (for a paper copy) or mining, refining, and manufacturing (for an electronic copy).

Technology is not what we think it is, particularly when we imagine it as a source of entirely neutral tools with no effect on the world except when wielded by human hands. Consider the strange juxtaposition of automobiles and firearms in the debate over technological death in the United States. In defending their beloved guns from the attempts to legally limit their acquisition, opponents of gun control sometimes invoke the argument that cars kill more people than guns, yet nobody is campaigning to ban cars. In response, advocates of gun control generally ignore the most morally salient part of this ad hoc rhetoric and instead point out all the licensing and restrictions that apply to cars, using this to support their claim for equivalent legislation restricting access to guns. On either side of the gun debate, cyberfetish operates to blind people to the rather modest thought that *the fact that people driving cars kill people is a morally relevant aspect of car-ownership*.

For me, the ethical problems of automotive technology are considerably more serious than those of domestic firearms, and not just because cars and their drivers do indeed kill more people than guns and their firers. In 2010, the United States lost about 38,000 people to car accidents and 32,000 people to gun related deaths, about two thirds of which were suicides (Kennedy, 2013). Anyone who thinks *either* of these statistics can simply be ignored is blinded by cyberfetish, and anyone who thinks the only conceivable way to address these losses of life is to battle over the legislature hasn't really appreciated the moral importance of these 70,000 tragedies. If you think the cyborg made of gun-and-human is addicted to a specific technology, how much more is this true of the cyborg made of car-and-human! It is as unthinkable that people would give up their cars as it is that a wild animal would be permitted to roam the United States killing the equivalent tens of thousands of people each year – and both sides of this equation hint at some strange gaps in our ethical thought.

The renegade Catholic priest Ivan Illich is one of a very small number of people who recognized the radical injustice of an infrastructure that not only kills thousands but is also deeply counterproductive, since the more roads are built, the more cars flow into them, and the more traffic grinds to a standstill. Illich saw that cars were a radical monopoly that no-one was contesting – a mandatory requirement of living in technologically-obsessed societies unable to distinguish between a useful application of tools and the necessary futility of scaling up beyond the point of effectiveness (Illich, 1974). Because we all accept that cars are now a staple of 'modern' living, we are all complicit in the deaths that result from their use, the pollution and environmental damage produced by their use and manufacture, and the frustration that is inherent to a system that forces vast numbers of people to travel at the same time and through the same routes. Whatever your political stance, at least one of these concerns should matter to you.

However, as passionately as I share Illich's recognition that limiting the speed of urban transportation to that of a bicycle would be a better solution to the problem of local transport in most cities, I do not want to engage in politics until we can successfully talk about ethics. My particular interest here is not in the politics of infrastructure but in the morality of cars and their drivers – and in particular the difference between the laws that govern the roads and the chaos that is lived upon them. In this context, the question of how many people are killed by a technology that is presumed necessary takes on an additional meaning beyond the problem that cyberfetish consistently blocks our ability to think about what a good life could be if stopped believing in an infinite cycle of slightly better things. A short anecdote will help illustrate the point I want to draw out of our roads.

A few years back, I was invited to speak at a conference in Hyderabad and was delighted to get a chance to travel to India. While I was there, my hosts discovered my love for the Indian sport of kabaddi, and thus arranged for me to attend a show match in my honor on the other side of town. It was a particularly memorable part of the trip for me, in part because I had a chance to watch the fog gently lifting from Hussain Sagar, the lake near the center of the city that was built in the sixteenth century, and to see, albeit from a distance, many of the Hindu temples and Islamic mosques that are scattered around the region. However, what was particularly eye opening about this journey across town was the unadulterated carnage on the roads of Hyderabad. The streets were packed with cars, motorcycles, trucks, vans, auto-rickshaws, bicycles, and bullock carts, all weaving around each other in an anarchy of motion. I desperately tried to perceive some pattern within it all – were they overtaking each other in some orderly fashion, or just jostling for position as they made their way towards their disparate destinations? In the UK, road usage is governed by what is called 'the highway code', which describes the laws and best practices for transportation. I couldn't see any sign of logic to the traffic on the Indian roads, so I eventually asked my driver if he could explain the local rules of the road to me. He replied: "don't hit the other vehicles!"

If the Indian roads are governed by a formal highway code of any kind, I was unable to ascertain what it might be beyond the directive my driver mentioned. The situation was only marginally better in Mumbai, where I had first arrived, because there were more vehicles and so the gridlock kept the average speed to just a slow crawl! It is probably no surprise, therefore, that Indian road traffic deaths are rather numerous – constituting more than a third of the accidental deaths in that nation, some 160,000 fatalities each year (National Crime Records Bureau, 2011). This is considerably higher than the roughly 32,000 people who died in road traffic accidents in the United States last year – proclaimed as a 'record low' (Reuters, 2012). But then India has four times as many people living within its borders. Compared by population, both nations' motorized transport manages to kill over a hundred and twenty people each year for every million inhabitants.

Do not think, however, that I mean to suggest that the anarchy on the Indian roads is equivalent to the purportedly lawful driving in the United States in terms of safety. On the contrary, if the comparison is made on the number of motorized vehicles, rather than on the total population, a very different picture is revealed. In the US, most people are all but required to own a car, and the fatalities per million motor vehicles are around one hundred and fifty. In India, only the richest members of the population can afford a car or a motorcycle, and the traffic fatalities per million vehicles are more than *three thousand*! This means that for every car on the US roads that is involved in killing someone, twenty cars in India are responsible for the death of an innocent. Having seen the way they drive in Hyderabad, I scarcely doubt this horrific figure!

One big difference between the two nations is the existence of a legally-enforced highway code, although just how well it is enforced is somewhat questionable. While living in Knoxville, Tennessee, I studied the local rules of the road in order to earn my driving license, and was shocked by how dreadful the drivers of Tennessee were at keeping to their stated rules – even the police officers rarely used their indicators before performing any maneuver, no matter how unexpected. Still, guidelines badly followed are apparently still considerably safer than a complete absence of guidelines, which is perhaps what we would expect. We are led to believe, after all, that our laws are there for our mutual benefit – that we would all be worse off without them. The comparison between India and the US in terms of traffic fatalities seems to bear out this assumption.

Our experiences on the road offer a convenient analogue for a key aspect of our moral lives. For instance, most of us will have had the experience of driving on a highway and being cut off by another driver who careens past us, apparently oblivious to both our presence and our safety. Often, this is one of those instances that evokes rage in us - "what does that maniac think they're doing?" But our judgment on the roads is not to be trusted too easily, since we only see what little we can perceive with our forward vision and mirrors. An observer from a better vantage point may be able to tell that the driver who cut us off was swerving to avoid another driver who changed lane unexpectedly, perhaps responding to an obstacle that came into their path. We feel morally justified in our anger at the driver that cuts us off, but we really have *no idea* why they did what they did, and it is only an assumption – one that may be entirely false – that the other driver was reckless.

An example from my wife's driving experiences may help bring this point into focus. While driving through Manchester during heavy traffic, her car started to emit a sputtering sound and the engine revs began to drop. Eventually it stalled and wouldn't restart, and although she was able to pull over to the edge of the road she wasn't able to get completely clear of the junction, making things unavoidably awkward for the other drivers. Because of the breakdown, she immediately called our mechanic to discuss what could be done on her cell phone. Another driver, seeing my wife at the side of the road talking on her phone, pulled alongside, rolled down her window, and disparagingly announced: "I can't believe you pulled over just to answer your phone!" My wife, understandably, was rather less than happy at this complete misreading of the situation, and offered a few choice words of her own. This emphasizes my general point that the anger we experience when we make moral judgments about other drivers is always based on incomplete information, and is rarely if ever entirely trustworthy.

Along the same lines, most of us have become angry in situations whereby other drivers seem to be completely ignoring the rules of the road. The impression that our judgments of their driving are correct can be incredibly strong – even in cases when it turns out, on closer inspection of the highway code, that the other driver was doing precisely what was expected of them and what you were demanding them to do was actually *against* the stated rules. Other examples fall between the cracks of what is specified, as when my wife becomes livid that a 'Johnny Special' has ignored the lines of cars waiting to merge after road works and pushed their way ahead of everyone else. She's angry because what the driver has done isn't fair, but it isn't strictly against the rules of the road, which in most regions has nothing to offer on this kind of situation.

I want to treat our experience of the roads as an allegory for our experience of contemporary ethics. It is all too easy to become angry at other people's transgressions of the moral law we carry around in our heads, whereas we remain incredibly forgiving of our own trespasses. After all, we always know our own situation, and mitigating circumstances abound. Other people, on the other hand, do not get the benefit of the doubt so easily – especially when we suffer inconvenience or danger as a result of their actions. This bias is so intimately bound up with our humanity that psychologists never tire of naming new phenomena that riffs off this theme – confirmation bias, selective perception, hyperbolic discounting, bandwagon effect (Baron, 2007), the list grows longer almost every year.

The great achievement of psychologists over the last century has been to confirm what ethicists have long claimed, that we humans are biased towards ourselves and our own prior beliefs, to the extent that we judge others by standards for which we almost always manage to exclude ourselves. As Gendler (2007) states: "It is no exaggeration to say that the tendency towards first-person exceptionalism is among the most widespread and pervasive of our tendencies toward bias." Yet this ability to hold others to standards that we are willing to exclude ourselves from is not just a problem for individuals, since entire nations permit themselves the moral latitude to ignore their ethics when they become inconvenient. Isn't this the reason that the 'predatory' effects of cars are not treated as tragedies deserving action, but as unfortunate side effects to be regretted but ignored?

The whole purpose of the appeal to a moral law – one perfect moral law – was that irrespective of our personal biases, we might have a code of conduct we could *all* abide by since it was the perfect rational ideal for our behavior. But when we look at our moral behavior in a narrowed circumstance – say, upon the road – we find that this idea is highly problematic. Accepting that no actual highway code is perfect, are we even tempted to say that there is an ideal set of rules for motorized transportation? Is there, in short, a moral law for drivers that goes above and beyond the local strictures of various highway codes? Could there be such a thing? If we cannot apply the ideal of moral law in this one limited case, how could we possibly hope to establish a perfect moral ideal that would cover *all* our behavior? Yet give up on the moral law for drivers, and what are we left with: Indian traffic, with its concomitant reckless killing of innocents. We seem to face a genuine dilemma – between insisting on an absolute moral law we cannot demonstrate even in limited circumstances, and abandoning all notions of moral law completely. Neither option is desirable!

But if we go back to the roads and watch what happens upon them, we may be surprised at how often drivers act for the benefit of strangers. Every day, I see drivers who give way to other drivers even though the highway code frowns upon them doing so in that particular circumstance. I see drivers stopping to help other drivers who have broken down, even though the rules have nothing to say about this. I see drivers who stop to pick up hitchhikers, even though conventional wisdom warns against the risks of doing so. In short, I find moral chaos on the roads as much as – perhaps more than – I find moral law.

A Truce for Politics

This book is an exploration of moral chaos, but it is not an unequivocal attack on moral law. On the contrary, neither moral law nor moral chaos is going to be capable of bearing the burden that ethics will place upon their shoulders once the scale of our problems has been entirely understood. We need to find a balance between the two, but this is not easy – especially when discussion of moral philosophy is obsessed with the moral law and deathly afraid of chaos. Overcoming intolerant tolerance requires embracing chaos in a way that goes far beyond the limitations of multiculturalism, but if our only moral option lay in disorder there might be no way of freeing ourselves from cyberfetish – we might learn to live together just in time to drive ourselves to extinction. The challenges we face go far beyond questions of what laws we shall enact, we have to establish how we can willingly accept limitations we do not even want to acknowledge as necessary, and this is a problem that might be insurmountable in the contemporary political climate.

According to a popular view, eloquently expressed by Isaiah Berlin, politics is nothing more or less than "ethics applied to society" (Berlin, 1988). Our laws, therefore, which are the product of political action, are purported to be merely our ethics elevated to the level of the nation. I find in this idea a disturbing distortion of the relationship between politics and ethics, since – to invert the famous quote by Carl von Clausewitz – politics is now the continuation of war by other means. The reason our political situation is in perpetual stalemate (especially in the United States) is precisely because we have given up on the difficult challenges of ethics in favor of continuing a long and entrenched battle to politically defeat our opponents *who are definitely wrong*. Just consider the stalemate over gun control I alluded to earlier as but one example of this problem. In place of this, I offer a ceasefire on the political stage – a chance to parlay with our political foes, and perhaps transform them into something less than enemies.

This call for political disarmament goes hand-in-hand with Chantal Mouffe's (2005) passionate recognition that conflict and disagreement are quintessential to any genuine attempt at political life. As she suggests, chaos and instability cannot be eliminated from democratic politics except by voiding the whole concept of democracy. Mouffe condemns any attempt to shortcut disagreements by enforcing a conception of rational consensus, since any attempt to do so must exclude all the currently unheard voices from future participation in politics. Instead, she proposes that we change from seeing our political opponents "as an enemy to be destroyed" and begin to see them as adversaries who ideas we may combat, but whose "right to defend those ideas we do not put into question."

This truce is not an abandonment of political life, but an attempt to restart it. If politics concerns the public determination of *how* we shall live together, then the *politics as war* we are currently practicing is fundamentally self-defeating. It denies any possibility of living together and instead demands that we fight amongst ourselves with the sole aim of enforcing our views upon others against their consent. But to get beyond this, to try and create something like an ethically-grounded political life, requires that we understand morality – and this is certainly a more difficult task than simply deciding who is right and then striving against those who are wrong on the battleground of our legislative institutions! It is this challenge we must overcome first, because until we appreciate that moral discord is the indispensible starting point for moral politics we are doomed to face unending struggle.

If I may resort to a gaming metaphor, the stakes of this game are worth the risks – since if I can convince you to set aside your prior political commitments, even briefly, so that we can have a discussion about the moral ideals that support those beliefs, it may be possible to see all the major political disputes as the frontlines of a clash of ideals, a conflict that moral philosophy is already well equipped to tackle if only we would give it a chance. I can place on the table, as prizes potentially to be won, the resolution of otherwise insoluble political issues such as abortion, gay marriage, the status of animals, the destruction of the environment, and the perpetual state of war. None of these issues will ever be resolved politically as long as the warring parties cannot appreciate the moral ideals of their opponents.

This opening chapter traces the topics that the book as a whole aims to address: the relationship between morality and imagination, the contrast between moral law and moral chaos, the unrecognized dangers of intolerant tolerance, and the growing crisis of cyberfetish as our technological obsessions reconfigure not just human life but the face of our planet. My paper time machine brought to light the ambiguity concerning the different kinds of good that we can experience and raised the question of how they might somehow be brought together. The way we currently deal with our multiplicity of ideals is to seal them off from one another in multiculturalism, but this blocks communication precisely when we should be trying to talk to one another about what has gone awry. To escape this particular problem requires a means of escaping both nihilism and relativism, and it is these issues that the next chapter investigates by asking "Who Killed Morality?"

Once the problems of relativism are resolved, we can begin to examine the diversity within morality, which is conceptualized in this book both in terms of both moral law *and* moral chaos. "Law and Chaos" explores these ideas through the novels of Michael Moorcock and an examination of all the different kinds of ethics that humanity has expounded. This chapter also demonstrates how morality can be understood not as something dependent upon rationality, but as something emerging from imagination. "Wild Ethics" takes these concepts further by considering how both imagination and morality have developed over the last four billion years, as well as pondering how hesitation could be as moral (or more moral) than certainty. These opening four chapters collectively lay down an understanding of the relationship between morality and imagination by exposing the many different mythologies that lie beneath ethics – both those that depend upon ideals of law, and those that draw against ideals of chaos.

Having provided some understanding of morality as imagination, the troubles inherent to collisions of radically different ideals are diagnosed in "Moral Horror", which suggests that political stalemates occur because the conditions for our outrage are not in alignment. This begins a series of discussions concerning issues in politics that might be better resolved if we considered them as ethical problems. "The Tragedy of Bureaucracy" asks about the petty evils of institutions and exposes the impossibility of merely calculating what is good. "Rights and Wrongs" shows how this distortion of moral imagination among the corporations leads to dishonor and catastrophe when it occurs in our national institutions. This chapter also presents the merits of moral law by drawing against the most influential philosopher to rigorously pursue such ideals, Immanuel Kant, and the dangers of moral law by contrasting this with the philosophy of Alain Badiou.

The theme of cyberfetish introduced in this chapter recurs throughout the book as one of the most pressing issues facing us, even though it manifests in many different ways. It confuses our moral understanding of death (a point discussed in "Moral Horror"), corrupts bureaucracy by replacing human interrelation with robotic automation ("The Tragedy of Bureaucracy"), and deprives soldiers of their honor by turning warfare into extermination ("Rights and Wrongs"). In the penultimate chapter, "Ethical Things", the question of how we can deal with both other beings *and other things* is positioned as a challenge for how we represent ourselves politically. This is brought into focus through Isabelle Stengers and Bruno Latour's attempts to conceive new ways of interrelating that might actually allow us to live together, instead of just fighting amongst ourselves.

Finally, in "Balance" all these topics are concluded by considering them not just as political issues but as problems concerning how we are morally represented. Here, both Moorcock's and William James' concept of a *multiverse* is related to our moral diversity to provide different answers to the questions raised by multiculturalism, and a possible solution to intolerant tolerance. This in turn gives us a way to approach and perhaps resolve cyberfetish, or at least to begin to discuss it seriously. Throughout, a practical acceptance of the moral value of chaos is offered as an alternative to the endless warfare of a politics divorced from ethics, a conflict that allows us to ignore our own moral lives because we are too busy trying to force our ethics onto other people. If political issues are only ever a choice between competing visions of the moral law, we can expect this battle to be eternal. But perhaps it was never just a choice between different moral laws – perhaps it was always also a choice between different kinds of moral chaos.

2

Who Killed Morality?

The Authority of Science

On the twelfth of December 2011, I saw a British tabloid newspaper headline in my local chip shop that genuinely surprised me. The *Daily Mirror*, a popularist paper more likely to have celebrity gossip on the cover than anything I might be interested in, ran with a story (admittedly below one on the latest TV talent contest winners) attacking the integrity of that venerable British institution, the BBC. The front page headline read: "Beeb Faked Frozen Planet" (Stretch, 2011), referring to the recently-aired nature documentary *Frozen Planet*, narrated by the venerable broadcaster Sir David Attenborough. The purported scandal focused on the portrayal of a pregnant polar bear giving birth – presented in the episode in question as if this event had happened deep beneath the arctic snows, but in fact shot in a zoo. The BBC had not concealed the origin of the footage – their website showed how it was constructed – but the voiceover that accompanied the sequence created the impression that viewers were watching the births 'in the wild'.

Why was this 'revelation' so shocking as to justify a front page news story? Although other tabloids also reported the story in one form or another, the allegedly more respectable British broadsheet newspapers largely mocked the 'fake' scandal, being far more upset by the news that the final episode of *Frozen Planet*, focusing on climate change, wasn't going to be aired in every country because of differing degrees of skepticism towards the concept. Although the outrage channeled by the tabloids in this matter was focused upon the integrity of the BBC, I want to suggest that this incident offers a fascinating window on the question of authority in contemporary life. For on the one hand we have the claimed authority of newspapers to present the truth – which many of us now seriously doubt – and on the other we have the claimed authority of the sciences to present the truth – which is only now beginning to be seriously questioned.

Hannah Arendt, writing in the mid-twentieth century, lamented that "authority has vanished from the modern world", claiming that authority – the capacity to demand obedience – had been primarily inherited from Rome, and after the fall of that city by its successor, institutional Christianity (Arendt, 1961). While the Romans certainly used a great deal of violence to maintain their empire, authority in Arendt's sense is incompatible with coercion or force since when such methods are applied authority has already failed. Similarly, it is incompatible with persuasion, since whenever arguments are applied there is clearly a lack of authority. The Romans, and after them the Roman-influenced Church, had been able to draw from a foundation in the past as a cornerstone for authority, but today this appeal no longer has the influence it had just a few centuries ago. Revolutions, Arendt notes, do not manage to re-establish authority, and contemporary politics are thus left without any clear way to determine permissible actions, since there is nothing self-evident that could be trusted to make this judgment.

Among the few survivors of this collapse of authority are news institutions and the sciences, which are both notable because their appeals to authoritative assertions are also subject to an infinite regress of future revisions and justifications. The *Daily Mirror* article claimed that the polar bears were filmed in a German zoo, but this was later corrected to one in Scotland. The sciences declared asbestos a wonder material in the 1950s – then corrected this to a toxic hazard a few decades later. Both the news and the sciences have a claim to pronounce truth – but this authority is quite unlike the Roman authority that sprang from the peculiar mythology of the City of Rome, with its legendary foundation. Traditional authority may have gradually revised its institutions, but the claim to authority was not something in itself that anyone expected to be subject to constant revision.

Notice that in the case of the *Frozen Planet* furor, the supposedly more insightful newspapers were unfazed by the recognition that the nature documentary had involved a little showmanship. Intellectuals today know that the alleged neutrality of documentaries cannot be plausibly sustained – especially since music can be used almost invisibly as a means of subtle influence. A later BBC nature documentary, *Africa,* plays sinister overtones while talking about naked mole rats, leaving us in no doubt that we are supposed to be slightly disturbed by the queen's dominance of her colony (*Africa,* 2013a). The presentation of the sciences on television is *never* neutral, any more than newspaper reporting could ever be entirely neutral. But still, a great many people believe that Science itself has privileged access to truth – albeit a slightly neutered concept of truth, subject to perpetual revision – and indeed when reacting in anger to the presentation of scientific findings in one way or another there is at heart a faith in the authority of Science to proclaim truth, as if it were the last remnant of the Roman empire.

In some respects, this analogy is not entirely without merit, since our sciences have descended directly from Christianity, and have an institutional character imbued with this echo of Roman mythology that was acquired via the Church. However, the sciences have inherited much more from that other great predecessor to institutional Christianity: Greek philosophy, in particular the work of Plato, or rather the legacy of Plato since there is a vast gap between Plato's actual philosophical views and what has been made of it over the intervening millennia. Nonetheless, it was Plato who first imagined that some people would be able to step outside of the manifest deceptions of social life and see into a true world beyond, as depicted in his famous Allegory of the Cave (Plato, 380 BC). For Plato it was the philosopher who held this power over the authority of truth, but via Rome, via the Church, that authority has now been inherited by Science. The scientist is widely believed to have the incredible power to step outside of their social circumstances, uncover the truth, and then return to the social world to report it.

As a researcher myself, I know how farcical this claim must be, and many other scientists would judge this as an utterly credulous perspective on the work of the sciences. Yet this view of Science as either the arbiter or provider of truth is incredibly widespread today – and the authority of Science is the last bastion of an alleged capacity to end disputes. Which makes it all the more ironic that the sciences are now rocked on a regular basis with purported scandals over the *failure* of scientific claims to cash in on this authority, something abundantly clear in the case of climate change that also intersects with the polar bear story via the broadsheets. According to proponents of climate change (the new name for 'global warming') it is a proven fact, beyond dispute, and thus those who do not accept the authority of Science in this matter are deluded. Of course, the hilarious flipside of this is that so-called 'climate deniers' (a phrase wonderfully far from neutrality!) *still* appeal to the authority of Science in their attempts to reveal the widely-reported scientific consensus as having distorted the evidence. Something has gone terribly wrong when the last remaining source of unshakable authority is being evoked by *both sides* of a dispute in the sciences!

Bruno Latour, described variously as a sociologist of science, an anthropologist, and a philosopher, has been an astute observer of this final and inevitable breakdown of the authority of Science. He views contemporary disputes over the authority of the sciences as rooted in part in a strange division of cultures, between the scientists on one side and the humanities on the other. The former camp declares scientific findings as accurate only when they have been "purged of any contamination by subjectivity, politics or passion" while the latter views contact with science, technology and objectivity as a corruption of humanity or morality. Latour views *both* these attempts at 'purification' as misguided, and offers alternative ways of thinking about the meaning of research that help connect the sciences to the communities they are always imbedded within (Latour, 1999).

Borrowing heavily from Isabelle Stengers (1997), Latour suggests that when researchers succeed in their job, we can understand them as *speaking for* other entities – after all, the suffixes '-logy' and '-logist' used to provide specific titles to sciences and scientists descends from the Greek term 'logos', meaning 'speech' or 'story'. The key to understanding the sciences in Latour and Stenger's view is to recognize the *reliable witnesses*. When a researcher in animal behavior, known as an ethologist, speaks about how animals act and react in a manner faithful to the creatures in question, the *animals* are a reliable witness, and the researcher can be said to be a *spokesperson* for the animals in question. Similarly, when a physicist uses an accelerator to create microscopic collisions and reports the discovery of a new particle, the *particle* is a reliable witness, for which the physicist is a spokesperson. This is not how we usually think about the sciences, but it helps clarify the relationship between research and instrumentation – not to mention assist in putting politics and the sciences on an even footing, which is precisely Latour's objective in *The Politics of Nature* (2004), a book that I will have cause to refer to often.

This concept of spokespeople and reliable witnesses contrasts with the usual assumption that researchers 'read Nature'; that the facts are in the world and can simply be lifted off it, like looking up an answer in an encyclopedia. This metaphor emphasizes how strange our view of the sciences has become: we all too easily ignore the methods, devices and theories researchers deploy in order to make entities 'speak'. When someone claims that 'facts speak for themselves' they have usually been swept away with enthusiasm for Science, and may in the process lose their status of spokesperson by no longer reporting on behalf of reliable witnesses. According to Latour, it is not the facts that 'speak for themselves' but the investigated entities that speak via various forms of mediation – laboratory instruments, experiments, protocols and so forth. The trustworthiness of a scientist does not lie in an ability to obtain a magical state of objectivity, but in their capacity to develop methods that produce reliable witnesses (Holifield, 2007).

In adopting this novel approach of discussing research in the context of recognizing spokespeople for reliable witnesses, I share some of Latour's goals in terms of improving both our understanding of the sciences and of truth. Both Latour and I have always been critical of Plato's Allegory of the Cave, which implies that it is somehow possible for certain special people (philosophers for Plato, scientists in a contemporary context) to mysteriously travel between the world of appearances and the alleged 'true' world beyond. Latour's complaint is that this obfuscates the actual practices of researchers and sets up a strangely mystical view of what they do (Latour, 2004). My related complaint is that this view of 'Science as truth' is a mythology that distorts our perceptions of both the sciences and of truth (Bateman, 2012). The political philosophy that Latour advocates in this regard involves a tricky contradiction that will eventually need to be addressed, but for now we can at least clarify the claims of researchers by talking of reliable witnesses and spokespeople.

If these terms read rather strangely, I hope the merits of this wording will become clearer the more it is used within this book. It is worth bearing in mind that when I talk of 'those who speak for the microbes' or 'the spokespeople for the rocks', I am talking about more than just individuals, but the entirety of the people and things involved in making microbiological or geological assertions, which includes numerous organizations, researchers, devices, theories, texts and so forth. Such scientific spokespeople may be mistaken – they may lack reliable witnesses, or they may have found reliable witnesses but misrepresent them, but this risk goes with any kind of representation.

Furthermore, although I will mostly use this terminology to talk about the claims of researchers, these are not the only people who have claims to being spokespeople in this sense: the Maasai Lion Guardians are not scientists, but they may have a better claim to speak for the lions of the East African savannah than anyone else (*Africa*, 2013b). Similarly, the sandstone formation in Australia's Northern Territory known as Uluru or Ayers Rock says one thing through the mouths of geologists, but quite another through the voices of Australian aborigines. When a political advocate speaks on behalf of the latter, they too are a spokesperson – and they too can be accused of lacking a reliable witness, although in this political context the process by which this can be ascertained is quite different. When an experimenter becomes a spokesperson they let things speak "in a way that all other scientists recognize as reliable" (Stengers, 1997), but when a politician becomes a spokesperson their reliability is something that can only be assessed by those they claim to represent.

The question of the authority of Science is of direct relevance to any attempt to discuss ethics, in particular because if the sciences are the only source of facts and truth then the only valid kind of morality would have to be scientifically derived. Indeed, in the blind acceptance of the authority of *medical* sciences that is rampant today it sometimes seems as if the only form of ethics that is construed as meaningful is medical ethics. I have grave concerns about this narrow understanding of morality whenever it manifests – both because it distorts our attempts to discover what might be a good life (the vocation of moral philosophy since the Greeks), and because 'medical ethics' conceals some of the most terrible and invisible aspects of the contemporary technological world. As Ivan Illich (1973) repeatedly stressed, medicine has ceased to be about assisting people with their healing and dying and become instead a global bureaucracy that disempowers people, interfering with their ability to take care of themselves. This medical cyberfetish is so widespread that we have become unable to separate those therapeutic tools that can improve health and save lives from an institutional quagmire that all too frequently becomes a terrible threat to health (Illich, 1975). If ethics is about living a good life, it may have to part company with a 'medical ethics' that uses the authority of Science to *prevent* individuals from thinking about the moral problems of living and dying.

Before we can begin to talk about ethics, however, we must exhume what remains of traditional morality from the grave it has been buried in for a century or so, and before we can begin any kind of salvage operation it may be necessary to establish some ground rules. Firstly, ethics is a topic for *everyone*: moral philosophers may study the complexities of the subject, but ethicists are to morality what cartographers are to navigation – experts seeking to assist everyone with their own individual problems, whatever they might be. Secondly, no-one can be permitted to short-circuit the challenges inherent to moral enquiry – neither those who believe in a God who has specified all the rules in advance, nor those who believe in a nebulous Science that can uncover what is morally necessary have any business dictating to everyone else what must be so in ethics. Thirdly, which is the inverse of the previous point, everyone is free to interpret what traditional religion or the sciences appear to say on various topics: we can certainly help influence people when their interpretations appear to run awry, as they so often do on both accounts, but the freedom of belief at the heart of our cosmopolitan societies means *no-one can dictate what you think.* Neither priest nor scientist can do any more than offer testimony on their area of expertise, and neither – despite popular misconceptions – has a miraculous hotline to truth, nor the authority to force us to accept their conclusions.

Perhaps, having read that paragraph, you feel confident that I am about to assert that value judgments are subjective, that we each get the freedom to determine right from wrong. However, freedom of belief should not be confused with what is derided in the phrase 'moral relativism', and freedom of belief does not mean freedom from criticism. We are free to believe irrational things – such as my belief in the inherent goodness of humanity, something that I also believe is false. You may criticize either part of that previous clause (and with good reasons!) but doing so doesn't in any way undermine my freedom, since our capacity to raise such criticisms is a necessary part of how freedom must operate in practice. Yet if value judgments were entirely subjective, such criticisms would be entirely pointless on moral subjects since *nothing in morality would matter*, an argument forcibly pursued by Derek Parfit (2011) in defense of the idea that actually some things *do* matter, and morality is not just a mirage.

Parfit's extended arguments in defense of morality are indicative of just how bizarre discussion of ethics has become – was it really necessary for a moral philosopher to produce nearly *fifteen hundred pages* to defend the idea that morality is meaningful? Part of the problem is the extensiveness of the presumption that values are entirely subjective, a belief that has suffused contemporary society in those nations wealthy enough to afford such luxurious doubts. The authority of morality, it seems, lies dead and buried, and we are left solely with these valueless values that are a matter for private concern only. Ethics is left toothless and unimportant, a mere matter of taste. This sad state of affairs is inexorably coupled to the strange idea that facts are the exclusive domain of the sciences, that empirical investigation is the only way to establish objective truth. Yet trying to keep facts and values so far apart from one another is asking for trouble!

Who killed moral authority, and why? This is the question I hope to answer in this chapter. I will endeavor to explain how morality went from something that had both civil and religious authority to our strange state of affairs where there is a vast gulf between those things we call 'facts' that are entirely objective and those things we consider 'values' that are entirely subjective. It's a mystery that is intimately connected with the question of the authority of Science, and this topic has a significant history, one that will have to be briefly traced if the problems are to be untangled. It's the history of the *fact-value distinction*, the first piece of evidence we have to examine in order to work out whodunit...

The Vienna Wall

This detective story begins in the eighteenth century with David Hume's publication of *A Treatise of Human Nature* (Hume, 1739). Hume had little patience for sloppy thinking and remarks in this book that he is shocked at how often discussions of morality switch suddenly from considering of the way things are – described by "is" and "is not" - to discussions of the way things should be – described by "ought" and "ought not". Hume cautioned against such inferences if they cannot be explained, and raised the problem of exactly *how* an 'ought' might be derived from an 'is'. This is sometimes called the *is-ought problem*, and it is frequently taken to be the genesis of the fact-value distinction.

Actually, blaming Hume for this problem is extremely unkind as it makes it sound as if he was an enemy of the study of ethics, as those that later instituted the fact-value distinction surely were. But as Hilary Putnam points out, Hume's observation was not meant to stop moral philosophy but merely to clarify some of the lazy habits that were common in the ethical thinking of his day (Putnam, 2002). What's more, it seems that Hume recognized the problems that his caustic observations about sloppy moral thought might cause since in his *Enquiries*, which are revisions of his *Treatise* that he claimed more accurately represented his position, he excised the discussion of the is-ought problem entirely, preferring to focus on other points (Hume, 1748 and 1751). For both these reasons, I shall offer a posthumous pardon to Hume and point the finger of blame to considerably more recent philosophers.

The prime suspects in this investigation are identified by Putnam: the logical positivists of the Vienna Circle in the 1920s. We have already met the non-religion of positivism as founded by Auguste Comte, but more generally a *positivist* can be understood as someone who aims to minimize belief in untestable things, that is, to minimize *metaphysics* – a perfectly reasonable goal for all that I do not personally ascribe to it or believe that it is attainable. Positivism is usually pursued by placing especial trust in the capacity of the sciences to attain to truth, an ideal that, after Latour (2004), I shall mark with the capitalized term *Science* to distinguish it from *the sciences*, which refers to those varied traditions that pursue empirical research. Although positivists are an important part of our contemporary societies, they can become rather militant on some issues, as can theists, Marxists, environmentalists and, well, almost any group you'd care to mention – but no-one, no matter what their commitments, should be allowed to circumvent the discussions required to make moral and political life possible.

The logical positivists were especially fervent in their opposition to metaphysics, and in *The Mythology of Evolution* (Bateman, 2012) I already painted these philosophers in a slightly villainous light because their desperate attempts to clarify the truth of Science led to such a disastrous misunderstanding of the sciences. The fact-value distinction is the other crime that can be laid upon the doorstep of these meticulous hoodlums, but the root of the problem is precisely the same: the logical positivists sought to dismiss everything that could not be verified as meaningless. This attack on metaphysics was also extended to ethics, as can be seen in a famous statement from Rudolph Carnap's *The Unity of Science* (1934):

> All statements belonging to Metaphysics, regulative Ethics, and (metaphysical) Epistemology... are in fact unverifiable and, therefore, unscientific. In the Viennese Circle, we are accustomed to describe such statements as nonsense...

Thus for the Vienna Circle, ethics was nonsense and – worse yet! - *unscientific*. This goes far further than Hume, whose is-ought problem was at most just the expression of a *doubt*, as Alasdair MacIntyre (1984) notes. Carnap and the Vienna Circle, on the other hand, believed they could savage morality from a position of certainty, and were thus empowered to neatly divide the world into those testable matters that the sciences could process into truth – facts – and some vestigial matters of moral judgment that could never attain such purification – values. Thus the logical positivists built what I shall call *the Vienna Wall*, the dichotomous distinction between facts and values that has caused nothing but trouble ever since. Everything true, objective and factual is on one side of this wall, while the barbaric vagueness of meaninglessness, subjectivity and values is safely excluded on the other side.

Oh the trouble this distinction has caused – and all the more so because it seems so innocent! There is, after all, some kind of useful distinction to be drawn between ethical judgments and other kinds of judgment, although as Putnam notes just because there's a distinction between (say) chemical judgments and judgments outside the field of chemistry doesn't mean this difference is of any particular importance to the world at large. As Mary Midgley (1978) points out, however, it is just not that simple to draw a line between facts and values. Although it is a fact that something is "food or poison, that it is dangerous, dirty, unique, or legal", there is always some kind of evaluation involved in reaching the conclusion that these are indeed facts, and this involves "standards quite alien to physics". It is actually rather strange to think that facts and values could simply be segregated – yet this is precisely what the Vienna Wall was supposed to achieve!

The pragmatist philosopher William James, in a lecture given in 1891, shows the direction the wind was blowing with respects to the all-too-easily drawn demarcation between facts and values. He notes that moral words like duty, good, and bad can have no possible relevance in a world without sentient life – the only habitat for moral relations is a mind since "no world composed of merely physical facts can possibly be a world to which ethical propositions apply" (James, 1891). James sought to clarify and protect ethics from the problems it was facing at the time – but by constraining morality to the mental world, he made it easier to dismiss ethics as 'merely subjective', as the logical positivists attempted to do shortly afterwards.

The Vienna Wall is built upon a valid but trivial foundation, the claim that ethical judgments are different in kind to other kinds of decision making, but once all its bricks were in place it no longer served to distinguish ethics from other fields, but to deny moral philosophy and morality any access to the facts. Indeed, the fact-value distinction demands that values be excluded from facts, and that facts be excluded from values – such that any poor value who attempts to infiltrate the wall to make it into the realm of facts will be mercilessly shot on sight, as will any fact that dares to fraternize with lowly values. Unfortunately for the Vienna Circle, the "most influential marketers of the fact/value dichotomy" as Putnam remarks, their barricade is as utterly insane as the Berlin Wall from which my metaphor is drawn. Nonetheless, it certainly proved popular with many twentieth century moral philosophers, who eagerly pounced on the possibility of reimagining morality as something utterly divorced from fact!

There seems to have been an appetite for this kind of thinking in the early twentieth century, and MacIntyre notes that G.E. Moore's *Principia Ethica* had also been snapped up by a generation of intellectuals eager to find a new approach to moral thought and make a break with the moral philosophy of the nineteenth century. Here's another suspect worthy of investigation in the mystery of the murdered moral authority! Moore's book denies that the term 'good' can be defined in any factual manner, and furthermore claims that there is no way to reach moral conclusions from purely factual premises – a reinforcement of Hume's is-ought problem (Moore, 1903). Oddly, Moore's arguments were incredibly weak, yet as MacIntyre observes a great many intelligent people leapt upon this book as a resolution to all the problems of ethics despite the "great silliness" entailed in its approach, which essentially rested on reducing moral claims to opinions that could never acquire the dignity of facts.

For both Moore and the logical positivists, a growing hostility towards traditional religion (long viewed as the guardian of morality) contributed to this hastily pursued divorce between facts and values. The Christian Church in the Victorian era had steadfastly held onto its moral authority, even while the British and other empires were enthusiastically betraying everything Christianity was supposed to entail. With the Vienna Wall erected, religion could be deemed safely removed from importance – it could be thrown over the wall to languish among the subjectivity of values, while the facts would finally be free from the distorting influence of ecclesiastical power. If every murder investigation needs to find means, motive and opportunity, the Vienna Wall is the means and toppling the moral monopoly of the Churches is a plausible motive!

Alas, the consequences of the fact-value distinction for moral philosophy have been nothing less than disastrous, as so many since have recognized. Latour has been particular lucid in this regard – and especially vocal about our need to knock-down the Vienna Wall:

> The tempting aspect of the distinction between facts and values lies in its seeming modesty, its innocence, even: scientists define facts, only facts; they leave to politicians and moralists the even more daunting task of defining values. Who would not feel the comfort in such a formulation? The bed is still warm; all one has to do is slip in and settle at once into the sleep of the just. It is from this long dogmatic sleep, however, that we have to awaken. For what reason would it be more difficult to declare what things are worth than to declare that they are? (Latour, 2004)

Latour identifies problems with both sides of the fact-value divide. In the case of 'facts', and especially in terms of the relationship between the sciences and matters of fact that the Vienna Circle was counting upon, it is a definite weakness of the 'fact' concept that it obfuscates rather than clarifies the relationship between experiments, theories and conclusions. Scientific facts never appear from nowhere as a fully formed statement – they emerge from a complicated process of refinement and investigation as an end product, and it is one of the strengths of the sciences that affirming something as a final result involves a great deal of uncertainty in the interim. The fact-value distinction has the illusion of virtue within the sciences where it seems to serve as a defense against the influence of ideology on research – but as I demonstrate in *The Mythology of Evolution* in the case of evolutionary science, the metaphors that the sciences depend upon to do their work can *never* be entirely neutral. As Latour observes:

> If we were to show, for example, that immunology is entirely

> polluted by war metaphors, that neurobiology consumes principles of business organization in enormous quantities, that genetics conceives of planning in a determinist fashion that no architect would use to speak of his plans, we would be denouncing a number of frauds used by smugglers to conceal debatable values under the umbrella of matters of fact.

These smugglers, deftly bringing their values across the borderline defended by the Vienna Wall, are presumed not to live up to the objective standards of the sciences – but as Putnam points out, *these standards entail values*. Terms like 'coherence', 'simplicity', 'elegance' and 'rigor', often used to express judgments within the physical sciences, *are values* – and we would struggle to conceive of any way of carrying out scientific work that did not entail values. Not moral values, in this case, but what are termed epistemic values i.e. values concerning knowledge, but the fact-value distinction is supposed to block such bastardization and keep the sciences pure - "just the facts, ma'am". Unfortunately for anyone who desires such an outcome, it is entirely impossible.

The problem is no better the other way around, and Latour notes that the biggest challenge which the term 'value' faces in the shadow of the Vienna Wall is that the territory it is supposed to denote is entirely dependent upon having *already* defined facts. Values are merely second rate, as the distinction between objective fact and subjective value makes abundantly clear. Accepting the fact-value distinction is entirely disastrous for moral philosophers, as they are forced to live in the gulag with the other subjectivities on the value side of the wall – they can appeal to universality, seek foundations, but denied facts they are rendered utterly powerless and without reasonable influence. As Latour laments, the more we distinguish between facts and values, the worse our predicament gets since it becomes impossible to disentangle what is from what ought to be. Hume's doubt has returned as a veritable quagmire of uncertainty!

But what would happen if we were to tear down the Vienna Wall? No-one is going to be satisfied at giving ideological smugglers a free ride between either side of town if this means an inability to distinguish between legitimate scientific research and its distortion by prior beliefs! Yet as it happens, we *already* face this problem: as I have argued elsewhere, the sciences have been ideologically distorted for quite some time – not least of all by Science! - and the fact-value distinction has done nothing to prevent it. If anything, it has made the situation worse by concealing those values that were necessary for constructing accurate facts, and denying those facts that were essential for applying values. We have to recognize, as Latour states, that "people deliberate and decide *just as much* about facts as about values," for all that this admission may at first seem scandalous.

Facts and values, as Putnam eloquently observes, are intimately *entangled*, and this entanglement is something we have to learn to live with, not something we can simply block out with an artificial barrier. Midgley makes the same point: as she remarked to me in respect of this topic, a great many words are both factual *and* evaluative – and this shows up "something dubious about the whole contrast". We could not assign importance to anything without taking into account both factors, since importance, as she suggests, is "not a blank abstract 'simple' quality" but something that requires us to "weigh the facts" about ourselves (Midgley, 1978). Recognizing this problem is vital to making a better world, since as Mariam Fraser (2006) observes "it is difficult, if not impossible, to consider what ought to be done in a world in which what is truly important cannot be definition be known." The logical positivists conception of fact was horribly impoverished, and their concept of value deeply confused. Rather than clarifying our thinking – on matters of fact or on ethical concerns – the Vienna Wall has prevented us from understanding either, blocking both discussion and thought.

The mystery begins to be unraveled. We have our suspects – Moore and the logical positivists – and we know how they did it. They severed facts from values with the Vienna Wall, and left the power of authority solely with the former, savaging morality and leaving it for dead. We also have a possible motive, namely the attempt to shatter the monopoly on morality claimed by ecclesiastical authority. Did these conspirators decide it would be easier to do away with traditional morality rather than trying to wrest authority away from the Church? This doesn't seem to quite capture the spirit of early twentieth century philosophy, which was more concerned with elevating the sciences than slaying religions. Something is wrong with our putative motive, and we are still missing one vital piece of the puzzle – the opportunity. How did such an extreme measure as the fact-value distinction come to be viewed as reasonable and desirable by so many intellectuals? Like so many detective stories, the answer is to be found deeper into the backstory...

Nietzsche's Abyss

It is part of the nature of philosophy as a field that its influence tends to be felt gradually, and the thoughts of any given philosopher usually do not attain maximum potency until after their death. So it is that the philosophical direction of the twentieth century can be traced to thinkers in the previous century, and in particular to three people whom Hannah Arendt dubs "the nineteenth century rebels against tradition": Marx, Kierkegaard and Nietzsche (Arendt, 1961). This is not to lay the blame for the terrible direction of history in the previous century upon the shoulders of these individuals – Arendt avows that this would be "even more dangerous than it is unjust". Rather, the "rebellion of the philosopher against philosophy" was a desperate act intended to save us all from the growing realization that not only could we not find meaningful answers, it was not even clear we could ask meaningful *questions.*

I will say little about Marx, in part because I have asked that we set aside politics as warfare, but Kierkegaard and Nietzsche are absolutely central to our detective story since it is these founders of what is termed *existentialism* that pry open the cover from the great pit within which morality now languishes. Are they suspects in our murder investigation? Perhaps... Certainly both Nietzsche and Kierkegaard argued forcibly against the prevailing moral attitude in Europe, which was grounded in Christianity. Kierkegaard did so in the hope that what was authentically Christian could be recovered, whereas Nietzsche had a pathological hatred of all things Christian and sought to bring this religion to an end – a situation he naively expected to come about within his lifetime (Nietzsche, 1888). The motive I suggested above might not be correctly attributed to Moore and the logical positivists, but it *does* apply to Nietzsche and Kierkegaard.

Nietzsche's writings are forever mischievous – he seems to have taken an impish glee in undermining the nonsense of his time, and it is perhaps because of this spirited defiance that he has so many admirers today. However, he is frequently misunderstood – and in no small part because he is often self-contradictory, allowing individuals to take from his writings whatever they wish as long as they don't try and square those thoughts against the entirety of Nietzsche's writings. There are essentially two general views of Nietzsche's overall position, both of which are defensible (Wilkerson, 2009). On the one hand it can be claimed that he embraced nihilism – the view that life or morality is essentially meaningless – and promoted an exploration of the human condition in an essentially literary fashion. Alternatively, it can be suggested that he merely *predicted* the threat of nihilism that would come from puncturing religious orthodoxy (his famous "death of God") and strived to produce a new approach to affirming life, knowledge and morality. On either approach, Nietzsche felt that exemplary human beings had to craft their own identities through a self-realization that could not rely on anything transcendent (such as God).

However, I believe that the reason Nietzsche appears to embrace nihilism (the first interpretation) is precisely because he was trying to resist it (the second interpretation), a position which is supported by Parfit's discussions of the troubled German philosopher. In assessing Nietzsche's perspective, Parfit suggests that Nietzsche was deeply concerned by his loss of belief in God (as were many thinkers in the nineteenth century) in part because knowing humanity had been created by God would allow life to be given meaning via the goal that God had set. Losing that belief meant giving up any hope of securing meaning, and it is this crisis that Nietzsche attempted to address. But alas, like so many philosophers, Nietzsche is far better at diagnosing the problem than he is at offering a solution. He seems to suggest that there is a solution to be found by simply affirming the way things are – to transform every "It was" into an "I wanted it thus" (Nietzsche, 1883-85). Parfit dismisses this as an "incoherent fantasy". Throughout his later work, Nietzsche strives to find a way to "revalue all values" - to invent a new kind of morality – but mostly, he just ends up attacking Christian values instead. In his last published attempt at this problem, Nietzsche finds himself hoping for some kind of novel new nobility whose "formula for happiness" would be "a Yes, a No, a straight line, a goal" (Nietzsche, 1888). Parfit rather humorously responds: "That is not a helpful formula".

In seeking to tear down Christianity while acknowledging that it is precisely religion that was forming the moral foundation of European society at the time, Nietzsche reveals the abyss of nihilism – like a great black hole in the heart of morality that could not be seen because it emits no light. This was not a welcome discovery for anyone, and having revealed the chasm Nietzsche desperately tries to cover it over or transform it into something positive – and indeed goes mad trying to find a way out of the disaster he has foreshadowed. In one of his many pithy remarks he warns that "if thou gaze long into an abyss, the abyss will also gaze into thee" (Nietzsche, 1886). Despite failing to dig himself out of this infinite hole, and thanks in large part to a growing discontent with Christianity, Nietzsche's philosophy found an eager audience. Indeed, the late Victorian era was crying out for alternatives to Christianity, and as I noted in *The Mythology of Evolution*, 'Darwin's bulldog', T.H. Huxley, was able to offer evolution as a religion long before it was a truly viable science. Michael Ruse even suggests that having a "secular religion" to oppose the forces of the Anglican Church aided the process of social reform considerably (Ruse, 2003).

There have been few writers who have offered as coherent a critique of Christianity as Nietzsche, and there is perhaps only one philosopher who can claim to have surpassed him in this regard: Søren Kierkegaard. Kierkegaard's advantage over Nietzsche, in many respects, is that whereas Nietzsche sought to destroy Christianity having abandoned his faith, Kierkegaard's purpose was to attempt its recovery. The core of Kierkegaard's argument is that the Europe of his time (slightly earlier in the nineteenth century than Nietzsche) is dominated by something that purports to be Christian, but which can only be a corruption of it. On this point, Nietzsche and Kierkegaard broadly agree. But Kierkegaard, as a Christian who retained his faith in God, wishes to restore Christianity to its original teachings rather than abandon it entirely. Almost his entire philosophical career is dedicated to exposing the utter failure of the people of his day who called themselves 'Christian' to live up to the ideals of that religion.

Kierkegaard used the term 'Christendom' to disparage the Danish church, and by extension all of organized Christianity in the Europe of his day. It was his view that rather than authentically following the teachings of Jesus, those who called themselves 'Christians' had simply reduced Christianity to a set of rules to be followed, without any personal responsibility or self-reflection. In *Attack Upon Christendom* (1854-55), he suggests:

> Let us collect all the New Testaments we have, let us bring them out to an open square or up to the summit of a mountain, and while we all kneel let one man speak to God thus:
>
> "Take this book back again; we men, such as we now are, are not fit to go in for this sort of thing, it only makes us unhappy." This is my proposal, that... we beseech Christ to depart from our borders. This would be an honest and human way of talking – rather different from the disgusting hypocritical priestly fudge about life having no value for us without this priceless blessing which is Christianity.

Although he could not view himself as an exemplar of the Christian ideal, Kierkegaard could see all too clearly how vast the gap was between Christendom – the alliance of State law and the Christian church – and what it actually should mean to be a Christian. He constantly endeavored to explore how one could be authentically Christian, and in the process to understand how one could be an authentic individual. Part of the problem with Christendom in Kierkegaard's eyes was precisely that it functioned as a regulated crowd that denied any possibility of developing individuality. He saw becoming an individual as something that was only possible by facing the infinite and taking a leap of faith "on the strength of the absurd" (Kierkegaard, 1843). Kierkegaard notes that there is "a fear of letting people loose", resulting from the idea that living as an individual is supposedly easy, and that people must instead be coerced towards behaving ethically. He counters this accusation by noting: "No person who has learned that to exist as the individual is the most terrifying thing of all will be afraid of saying it is the greatest."

Sadly, Kierkegaard's critique did not significantly affect the path of Christendom, but it did greatly influence the French existentialists of the twentieth century, particular Jean-Paul Sartre and Albert Camus, the latter of whom remarks that Kierkegaard's "spiritual adventure" begins "in the chaos of an experience divested of its setting and relegated to its original incoherence" (Camus, 1942). Both Sartre and Camus face down Nietzsche's abyss armed with Kierkegaard's concept of a confrontation between the individual and the infinite – but since neither have Kierkegaard's faith in God, this becomes an encounter between the individual and the abyss itself. Facing an apparently nihilistic universe which seems to offer no stability or objective values whatsoever, the individual in the eyes of the existentialists is left to essentially invent themselves.

The claim of the French existentialists (and Sartre in particular) is that we somehow possess a capacity not just to divide up our series-persons in retrospect, as I was able to do in the discussion of my paper time machine, *but that we can become a new series-person at will.* Simply by willing ourselves to take upon a new identity, we can regenerate freely and without limitation. This extreme claim, as Maurice Merleau-Ponty immediately recognized, was a step too far! No matter how diverse the stories we can tell retrospectively about the people we have been, we are always situated in a specific social context and whatever freedom we may possess "has not the power to transform me instantaneously into what I decide to be" (Merleau-Ponty, 1945).

We are left with Nietzsche's abyss and its apparent threat to the security of both truth and morality – no wonder the logical positivists had to build the Vienna Wall! They needed something to attempt to protect knowledge from being reduced to mere opinion, or as Nietzsche has it:

Against that positivism which stops before phenomena,

> saying "there are only *facts*," I should say: no, it is precisely facts that do not exist, only *interpretations*... (Nietzsche, 1968).

This is the answer to the problem of motive in our murder mystery: the wall was built not with the express intention of neutralizing morality – this was merely a side effect of its construction. Rather, the logical positivists hoped that the barrier might save facts from falling into the crevasse Nietzsche had uncovered where they might be lost forever. But if this account is correct, then we don't have a murder investigation after all – more a case of manslaughter, perhaps even self-defense. It wasn't so much that morality had to be killed, but that facts had to be saved! The Vienna Wall was, in a sense, a defensive fortification constructed to ensure that the facts would remain protected from perhaps the biggest threat to the stability of truth humanity has ever uncovered. Like Hadrian's Wall or the Great Wall of China, the Vienna Wall was a symbolic effort to keep the barbarian hordes at bay – or at least, to make such a show of the need to do so that everyone could feel comforted by the illusion of security it engendered. Morality was never the intended victim – a classic case of mistaken identity!

Revenge of the Relativists

We are getting close to the solution of the mystery of the missing morality. Savaged by Kierkegaard's devastating attack on the moral authority of Christendom, battered by falling into the inky depths of the chasm Nietzsche had exposed, the truth of ethics was left for dead by the philosophers of the early twentieth century who entombed it behind the Vienna Wall, hoping to protect their beloved facts from the threat of eternal meaningless. But did morality expire there in that cavernous hole, alone and dejected on the other side of the wall? Or is there a surprise ending to this strange tale?

When we peer into Nietzsche's abyss we face down the consequences of abandoning faith in *absolute truth*. As long as the truth can be secured – by God, in the old solution, and by a tenuous phantom named Science in the latest incarnation – Nietzsche's abyss remains sealed. But whenever we begin to look at different cultures, whenever we begin to look for something that can survive the diversity of perspectives that we actually encounter in the world, it begins to seem as if nothing tangible could survive. This disaster goes by many names – nihilism, anti-realism, post-modernism – but when people wish to insult those who have made the edge of Nietzsche's abyss their home, the derisive label that is most often wielded is *relativism*.

'Relativist' is only very rarely a title anyone claims for themselves, it is primarily deployed as an insult used to denounce those who would abandon secure claims to truth in favor of infinite uncertainty. If we are going to rescue morality from the chasm, it will be important to distinguish between nihilism and whatever is meant by relativism. Nihilism can be likened to jumping into the hole and seeking a solution within – and sadly there seem to be plenty of intellectuals who think this is the sensible course of action. On the other hand, there are those who stand on the edge of the void and attempt to perform the difficult balancing act entailed in recognizing that there is indeed a crisis here that needs to be addressed – the relativists.

Relativism is taken to be particularly problematic when considering morality, in part because of the assumption that ethics must be understood as the moral law – if all our values are merely relative, nothing like this could possibly be formulated. Moral philosopher Allen Wood (2006) raises this concern when he suggests that if there is no single principle to which moral thought can be traced, it "would spell the end of all moral objectivity, perhaps even of all morality, period." Parfit is willing to accept multiple moral principles, but still cries out fearfully: "it would be a tragedy if there was no single true morality" - morality might be revealed as a mere illusion and any hope of resolving our disagreements would be forever lost.

Yet this is a false dichotomy – it is not a choice between moral law or nothing, and persisting in believing that this is the nature of the catastrophe is to extend the mistakes of Moore and the logical positivists with their silly barrier between supposedly secure facts and infinitely malleable values. We cannot sacrifice morality to save facts, as Nietzsche well knew – either *everything* with a claim to truth is at risk of being swallowed up by the whirlpool or nothing is. So we have two possible courses of action: either we deny the vortex or, as Putnam suggests, we try and steer a safe course around it (Putnam, 2007). Frankly, denial is of little help to us: the contemporary intellectual world is largely committed to the post-modern thesis that our apparent realities are merely social constructs, and in this (relativistic) context even if Nietzsche's abyss were entirely imaginary we would still have to face its consequences! No, I'm afraid under the circumstances we will have to accept the problem and find a way to deal with it, at least for the time being.

Fortunately, as soon as we bite down upon the forbidden apple of relativism it turns out not to be quite as awful as it first seemed. As Midgley has observed, there is a kernel of truth at the center of relativism that we ought to take seriously: no-one comes to the world without a specific cultural background, and there is no conceivable vantage point on any issue that can ignore these circumstances (Midgley, 1991). The fact that we are able to have conversations about issues both practical and abstract is only possible because of the reliability of custom. Our languages are stabilized by usage – we could not communicate at all without this comparative reliability even though, as Ludwig Wittgenstein and others have observed, our words are not markers for eternal concepts but rather practical means of conveying ideas that are always fluid and subject to change (Wittgenstein, 1962).

Language and culture are entangled just as facts and values are – indeed, morality and culture are equally entangled because the communal aspect of morality is not something that we can simply set aside. This intimate involvement between language, culture and morality can be found expressed in the stories that a group of people tell about themselves – their histories, their literature and their rhetoric. All these disparate elements contribute towards a *mythology*, or rather a collection of mythologies, which serve vital roles in coordinating individuals within a collective endeavor like a nation. Some mythologies, especially those we recognize as mythological, are relics of an earlier culture: the ancient Greek legends of heroes and monsters are a great example. However, others still play an active role in establishing the expectations and norms of a society, and are what the mythologist Joseph Campbell (1972) called a *living mythology*. We cannot encounter the world without some kind of mythology, since as Midgley (2003) has noted, our view of the world affects what we pay attention to:

> The way in which we imagine the world determines what we think important in it, what we select for our attention among the welter of facts that constantly flood in upon us. Only after we have made that selection can we start to form our official, literal, thoughts and descriptions. That is why we need to become aware of these symbols.

One of the interesting changes to our mythologies in the twentieth century was our increasing ability to form mythological images *about our mythologies*. As an example of a living mythology, the French philosopher and literary theorist Jean-François Lyotard (1979) laid out an image of post-modernism that remains influential, viewing it as "incredulity" towards *grand narratives* (a term entirely equivalent to Campbell's living mythology). According to Lyotard, we have become aware of the powerful stories that condition our view of the world – narratives such as the progress of history, the infinite capacity of

Science to uncover knowledge, and the possibility of absolute freedom. According to Lyotard's post-modern mythology, we have ceased to believe in these grand narratives. However, as Charles Taylor (2007) has shrewdly observed, Lyotard's apparent myth-busting is really myth-making in a different register. Despite being a "somewhat desperate solution" (Latour, 2010a), post-modernism has become one of the major living mythologies for our day – which is precisely why Nietzsche's abyss seems to loom so large.

Surely if morality fell into something so vast and deep we could not possibly recover it? What could survive such a titanic fall? But let's not be too hasty. It's still not entirely clear *what* fell into the hole, after all, let alone how far it fell. Post-modernist mythology of the kind offered by Lyotard makes the situation seem far worse than it is in practice. Whatever relativists, nihilists or post-modernists may claim, we have not given up our living mythologies – and as Campbell observes, every society establishes its norms precisely by such mythic images or metaphors, since "metaphor is the language of myth" (Campbell, 2001).

It is no coincidence that talk of ethics is saturated with metaphors – we have already seen, for instance, 'the moral law' (a metaphor connecting morality to national legal systems), but there are a vast array of such symbols such as 'rights', 'utility', 'equality', 'fairness', moral 'strength', being morally 'upright' and so forth. George Lakoff (1995) has explored the variety of moral metaphors used by both liberals and conservatives, and demonstrating that our political allegiance is at heart a difference of mythologies. Lakoff is acutely aware of the extent to which metaphor saturates our lives, stating that the way we conceptualize the world – both in terms of thought and action – is "fundamentally metaphorical in nature." (Lakoff and Johnson, 1980).

So we all find ourselves already placed within a mythology, or rather, within many competing mythologies. This is part of what makes contemporary politics so difficult to resolve – wildly different grand narratives attempt to make persuasive arguments *in their own terms,* and thus fail to convince those whose metaphorical background is differently constructed. This causes a lot of confused anger (what spokespeople for the human psyche term *cognitive dissonance*), not to mention accusations of evil and expressions of disgust when these mythologies collide – as they do, for instance, in the minds of those US citizens who are horrified that they live in a State that resists (or endorses!) gay marriage. Contrary to the post-modern thesis that we are aware of our mythologies, these kind of disputes demonstrate how wildly unaware of the grounding of our moral beliefs we all can be when it comes to the issues we care most strongly about.

These clashes between rival mythologies emphasize the apparently insurmountable problems inherent to our disagreements. This is partly why relativism can seem so terrible, and this worry is closely related to Parfit's fear that there might be no true morality: seeing the extent of the differences in moral belief from one culture to the next (or indeed, between one faction and the next within a single culture!) gives us a vertiginous feeling of insolubility. This often goes by the clunky label *incommensurability* in philosophy, but we can use *impossible to compare* as a decent alternative phrase. This issue is particularly problematic since as MacIntyre has argued all our enquiries into the world are tradition-constituted, and all traditions are essentially impossible to compare (Fives, 2008). This leaves MacIntyre open to the accusation of relativism, but Allyn John Fives suggests that this is only true in a trivial sense of MacIntyre: he accepts that cross-cultural moral disputes cannot be resolved by some arbitrary procedure, but this does not count out the possibility that the disputes could be resolved by discussions between representatives of those traditions. Just because traditions are impossible to compare does not mean that dialogue between them is impossible.

Indeed, if there is one clear example of why the insult that is assumed in the term 'relativist' is misleading it can be found in the thought of a philosopher who is often judged the arch-relativist: Paul Feyerabend (pronounced 'fire-ah-bend'). In his essay "Notes on Relativism" he suggests that:

> ...individuals, groups, entire civilizations may profit from studying alien cultures, institutions, ideas, no matter how strong the traditions that support their own views (no matter how strong the arguments that support these views). For example, Roman Catholics may profit from studying Buddhism, physicians may profit from a study of the *Nei Ching* or from an encounter with African witch doctors, psychologists may profit from a study of the ways in which novelists and actors build a character, scientists in general may profit from a study of unscientific methods and points of view and Western civilization as a whole can learn a lot from the beliefs, habits, institutions of 'primitive' people (Feyerabend, 1988).

The reason relativism is perceived as an insult – the reason Fives feels the need to defend MacIntyre from this charge, for instance – is the idea that accepting relativism means abandoning all claims to truth. But Feyerabend is not in any significant way concerned with defending or attacking truth – his interest in relativism is rather in finding a way to advance the idea that dialogue between different traditions, when it is possible, always has the potential to offer something valuable to both parties.

Latour, ironically, sees Feyerabend as not going far enough, calling him "a Protestant, criticizing the religion from within" (Berreby, 1995). For Latour, Feyarabend and other alleged relativists could not resolve the problem they attempted to address because they still treated the disputes as being specifically limited to the question of comparisons between cultures. On the one hand are those committed to absolute truth who claim there is an ultimate yardstick that transcends the specific circumstances of any given culture, while on the other are relativists who are "delighted that there is no such thing!" Whatever their individual claims, both sides agree that "reference to some absolute yardstick is essential to their dispute" (Latour, 1991).

As Stengers (2012) observes, the sign that most relativists are still dealing in absolutes is an appeal to the word 'really', which "marks the polemical power associated with truth". So for instance when some scientist says that ghosts don't 'really' exist, the 'really' is a means of insisting that they are right and others who think differently are "victims of illusions". Crucially, the same is true of the relativist when they insist that "our truths do not 'really' have the authority they claim". In both cases, a claim to have a superior understanding of reality is asserted – either positively or negatively.

Now this is a rather odd consequence of Nietzsche's abyss, don't you think? The chasm supposedly destroyed the secure foundations of truth and reality (hence "God is dead") yet, rather amazingly, anyone who decides to take the side of the relativists against absolute truth can *still* manage to claim to have a better grasp on reality! They alone know that there is *really* no absolute truth and reality. This is exactly the same trick that Lyotard was trying to pull, denouncing grand narratives with his own grand narrative, denying mythology by applying mythology.

What's more, this strategy is not a million miles away from the logical positivist's denouncing of what is 'unscientific' as 'nonsense'. As Stephen Yablo (1998) notes, this use of the word 'really' is "a device for shrugging off pretences" - did you really see a ghost? Is morality really dead? These kind of questions specifically assume that there is some kind of game being played, and ask that we set that aside and reveal what's *really* going on outside that game. But this assumes you know that you are playing such a game, that you have adopted some pretence that you can shrug off. In practice it is not that easy to separate myth and metaphor from fact and value, and the game that we are playing, as Wittgenstein has it, is language itself. Questions of 'real' existence of the kind pursued by the logical positivists, Yablo concludes, fall apart because we cannot divide things into literal and figurative with anything like the ease that had been supposed, because our language is suffused with metaphor. We don't just pretend our mythologies are true, we *live* them.

When moral authority went missing, morality was assumed to be dead, or at least lost. Yet aren't commitments to absolute truth or to relativism attempts to cling onto this very kind of authority, albeit in very different ways? The tacit assumption seems to be that morality is *really* moral authority – that without an absolute truth to secure it, there can be no morality worth having. This seems to be Parfit's fear, at least. But there's another possibility worth investigating, namely that it is not morality that has been lost but *solely authority*. Perhaps this mystery didn't involve a murder at all; perhaps morality just faked its own death because it was tired of the abuses conducted in the name of its long-abused authority...

Meaningful Metaphysics

So in the end it's not clear if anything was pushed over the edge of Nietzsche's abyss, and morality does not appear to be dead after all. Moore and the logical positivists may have been reckless with their Vienna Wall, but they can at least be acquitted of murder. But there is still blood on Nietzsche's hands, if the post-modernists are to be believed, since his "God is dead" can be seen as meaning 'reality is dead' or 'truth is dead'. If we are all embedded within our mythologies, if there is no escape from metaphysics, what is left that can make the claim of being true? Can there be such a thing as meaningful metaphysics, or were the logical positivists correct to denounce everything untestable as nonsense?

Once we get over the vertigo of what Nietzsche's philosophy

revealed, the situation is considerably less dire than it first appeared. We have not, as it happens, lost the truth, only the lazy short cut towards it that would assume any single person or practice could possess the authority of truth alone. It is not that there no truths, but rather that we do not attain them by appealing to absolute foundations of knowledge or morality but rather by examining all the available perspectives that may bear on an issue. This is what I call *perspectival truth,* and like Latour's approach to these issues it recognizes the validity of knowledge and morality without making anything absolute or necessary. It is, of course, a mythology – but it is a mythology of hope when compared to post-modernism's mythology of resignation or even despair.

It might be doubted that truth could depend upon considering different perspectives. David Wiggins (1987) expresses a general objection to this kind of thinking when he writes: "Perspective is not a form of illusion, distortion, or delusion." If multiple observers all view the same statue from different perspectives (Wiggins suggests) and if descriptions of these perspectives can be "reliably collected" then we will have a consistent account of the statue. This much I agree. But it must be noticed that the reliable collection of perspective requires considerable translation. Consider the problems involved if the people describing the statues have no common language (or perhaps worse, one common language that no-one speaks well!). If we could take, say, a set of photographs of the statue, we could be confident of its shape. But if we rely on individual reports, our task will be much more difficult – and even more so if the statue appears differently from different sides. Michelangelo's *David* (1504) does not look like a man when viewed from underneath the plinth. It doesn't even look like a statue when viewed through a microscope. Like Wiggins, perspectival truth suggests that perspective is not a delusion and that when all the necessary translations are conducted, all divisive matters can attain a unity.

The problem is getting undistorted translations.

Perspectival truth is not a new idea: it can be found in the parable of the blind men and the elephant in the Hindu, Buddhist, Jain and Sufi traditions, for instance. For this idea to bring something new into discussions of morality, however, it must be able to do what relativism cannot: it must be able to *include* the perspectives of those who ascribe to absolute truth instead of simply declaring such viewpoints invalid. This is no small task! I confess I have never been able to entirely shake my fear that the alternative to relativism is some kind of cultural imperialism, although Peter Singer (2005) makes a strong case that this anxiety is ill founded: if I live in a culture that places great value on enforcing its morality on others, relativism provides no basis for arguing that this is an error! Furthermore, I am open to Putnam's rejoinder that "recognizing that our judgments claim objective validity and recognizing that they are shaped by a particular culture and by a particular problematic situation are not incompatible" (Putnam, 2002). MacIntyre's view of our diversity of traditions that are internally rational but impossible to compare makes the same point, and stresses the importance of being able to recognize which traditions – which mythologies – are in play in any given situation.

Relativism made it impossible to resist the abyss, since the problem Nietzsche identified was the insecurity of all absolute claims to truth. In the case of ethics, Nietzsche saw that all attempts to defend morality rationally had apparently failed, which as MacIntyre observes is what gave "a certain plausibility" to his proposal to "raze to the ground the structures of inherited moral belief and argument." But as MacIntyre also points out, Nietzsche has the easier task here since for him to succeed all that has to happen is that everyone else fails - "if Nietzsche wins, he wins by default". Post-modernism and relativism hand Nietzsche his victory all too easily, so if we are to retrieve morality from the chasm of meaninglessness it will take a new kind of mythology –

or new ways of understanding the old mythologies. This problem certainly isn't going to be solved by huddling behind the Vienna Wall.

We are no longer in a position to demand that any particular ethic is the sole possible moral stance, but this does not reduce us to the paralyzing ghost world of relativism, which suggested that the impossibility of comparing different ethical traditions meant all we could do was put our hands up and shrug when facing alternative approaches to morality. Relativism recognized a genuine issue – the diversity of moral perspective – but elevated it to an insurmountable problem. Facing the depths of Nietzsche's abyss, a wall dividing fact from value may have seemed to be the best defense, but it just exacerbated the problem on both fronts – facts were presumed to transcend culture, and culture was presumed to lack any basis for comparison. Both these assumptions were mistaken, and with the Vienna Wall knocked down Nietzsche's abyss turns out to be just a narrow crevasse (however deep it might be!), and something we can easily avoid stepping into. Frankly, our traditions cannot be *entirely* impossible to compare since they are all built upon our capacities as humans, and those capacities are something we *also* share – to varying degrees – with many other animals too.

However, even without the wall and the hole, we are still left with those practices we founded on the basis of this dual mistake – in particular, multiculturalism. This promised a tolerance it couldn't deliver because it made different cultures equal only by rendering their moral values interchangeable while forcing a single account of the factual (that composed by mythological Science) onto everyone. This wasn't consistent with anyone's moral values – certainly not with the ideal of equality, since it elevated researchers in the sciences above everyone else, like that caricature of priesthood that pictures the clergy as dispensers of clear answers they simply couldn't have. Illich (1973) is particularly lucid about this political risk of the Vienna Wall:

> The institutionalization of knowledge leads to a... paralysis of the moral and political imagination. This cognitive disorder rests on the illusion that the knowledge of the individual citizen is of less value than the 'knowledge' of science. The former is the opinion of individuals. It is merely subjective and is excluded from policies. The latter is 'objective' - defined by science and promulgated by expert spokesmen. This objective knowledge is viewed as a commodity which can be refined, constantly improved, accumulated and fed into a process, now called 'decision-making'. This new mythology of governance by the manipulation of knowledge-stock inevitably erodes reliance on government by people.

Real researchers do brilliant work, but neither an experiment nor a theory is a magical crystal ball capable of answering any question. The sciences explore ways to get different elements of our world to speak, to turn things into reliable witnesses so that researchers can speak on their behalf. What we learn from this may equip us with new tools that change how our world is comprised, but no-one (scientist or otherwise) can foresee the consequences of creating new technologies – being a spokesperson for something does not and cannot make a researcher into an oracle. The invention of the internal combustion engine, for instance, has radically changed the surface of our planet but no-one at any point, including those who work in the sciences, foresaw the radical consequences of car-based infrastructure, although Illich (1974) certainly tried to warn those nations who had not yet adopted the automobile of the serious costs entailed in doing so.

The divorce between facts and values made it just as impossible to discuss the ethical implications of scientific research as to debate the constitution of our moral values, unleashing twin catastrophes. While we were busy panicking about the size of the chasm on the other side of the wall, the world on our side of the wall was being immeasurably transformed in ways that are becoming difficult to defend as good for anyone or anything. This situation will not improve if we simply change from panicking about one set of problems to panicking about another – environmentalism is a non-religion with a lot to say, but with deaf ears to the objections of its opponents, no matter how salient. In this respect, it is in much the same situation as *all our other traditions*. Whether we are talking about liberals, Catholics, positivists, Kantians, Marxists or conservatives, we can divide the world into those who share a common mythology and thus appreciate objections being raised about some issue or another (marriage equality, abortion, Creationism, torture, inequality, and proportionality, say), and those outside the relevant fictions who cannot understand why this issue should be the locus of such intense outrage – a disconnect clearly marked by changes of terminology (marriage reform, termination of pregnancy, intelligent design, enhanced interrogation etc.).

Let me play at moralist and pronounce an unequivocal moral directive that is not open to dispute: *we must do better*. But let me also play at diplomat and declare our collective uncertainty about *how* we can do better, because it will certainly not come from everyone thumping their tubs ever more loudly. Over this din, we cannot even hear ourselves think, let alone listen to the other voices trying to make themselves heard. Far too much talk about morality has been inanely obsessed with declaring a winner in an ethical contest that necessarily devolves into self-righteousness. When arguments are mounted that purport to be in defense of a particular ethic but that primarily criticize an entirely different ethic, we run into all manner of complications since our inevitable biases disrupt our judgment in *all* human endeavors, including the sciences and philosophy. Criticism itself may be vital to identifying and solving the many problems inherent to different approaches, but we ought to give up our mistaken belief that the flaws we find in other moral systems are the proof of the superiority of our own.

Yet moving beyond the petty bickering of traditions is challenging because our living mythologies, both religious and non-religious, are hidden in the background, and remain that way precisely because we use them to view the world. There is not, as Midgley (1992) recognizes, any way of viewing the world *without* such a mythology to intervene. This is an area perfectly suited for philosophical investigation, and (as noted previously) metaphysics is precisely the branch of philosophy that expressly deals with these kinds of mythologies. Practically speaking, every living mythology we encounter is metaphysical in at least some aspect of its content – even if the extent of that metaphysical commitment is to try to vainly eliminate metaphysics, as the logical positivists thought necessary.

Hostility towards metaphysics is something that even those positivists more moderate than the Vienna Circle tend to harbor. As Allen Wood (2006) remarks, the last "desperate resort" of those whose line of reasoning descends from Hume's is "the accusation that you are committing 'metaphysics'". The problem, as Latour (2004) astutely states, is that "any metaphysics has the disagreeable characteristic of leading to interminable disputes" - which is precisely why it *has* such a bad reputation: "Politicians mistrust it almost as much as scientists do". It is the untestable nature of metaphysical thought that creates the impasse since quite unlike the empirical sciences, which can make aspects of the world speak to us, there is no instrument that can render metaphysics a reliable witness. Yet Wood makes a shrewd point about our inability to eliminate it: we have to dip our toes into metaphysics in order to establish if there are genuine reasons of any given kind, so it would be entirely self-contradictory to claim that there were good reasons to completely reject metaphysics!

We can, however, reject the logical positivists' attempts to erect a cordon around metaphysics and exclude it from consideration, since they could only do so *on metaphysical grounds*. Their attempt to become decisively free of metaphysics required a foundation that could only be situated within metaphysics, and so their position could never be entirely consistent. The same is true of anyone who attempts the same kind of exclusion today, what Latour derides as the 'epistemology police' i.e. those people who claim to have unique authority in matters of knowledge. There is something of the critique of scientific orthodoxy leveled by Robert Anton Wilson (1986) here, and Wilson's term 'the New Inquisition' is even more inflammatory than Latour's! However, I do not want to pursue this issue here, as I have dealt with it in greater detail elsewhere (Bateman, 2012), and besides, the positivist's desire for clarity of knowledge is an ideal worth celebrating, and it is only their over-enthusiastic mythologies that give us these particular problems. Frankly, this isn't a complaint that can be constrained to non-religion, since it is equally true of many of the mythologies peddled by religions.

In both the disputes over the sciences and in the disagreements over the environment, Latour sees the collapse of the mythologies that culminated in the fact-value distinction as a crucial element of the contemporary predicament. The ecological crisis (the poster child of which is climate change) isn't, Latour insists, the sudden emergence of questions about nature onto the political stage, but the unexpected transformation of matters of fact into disputed affairs. This occurs in part for the reasons we have already rehearsed: fact and value cannot be separated, but are intimately entangled with one another. The consequence of this is that metaphysics *cannot be excluded from any question of knowledge*, and as Latour further warns, every question about knowledge will end up necessarily becoming a *political* question once it has been elevated into public discourse.

My approach, however, is to try and stay off the political battlefields until we can address some of the problems in ethics

– and this means exposing our living mythologies *without denouncing them*. Part of the problem, as MacIntyre recognizes, is that it is entirely pointless to denounce someone else's mythology from within your own – and actually, when we try to do this we run the risk of pointing an accusatory finger at other people's metaphysics while failing to recognize the metaphysical assumptions we have to make for this finger-pointing to constitute a denunciation. If you will excuse the resort to a religious reference, Jesus was way ahead of the curve when he declared in Matthew 7:5 that if we want to see clearly how to take the speck of sawdust from our brother's eye, we ought first to remove the plank from our own eye! Those who prefer a non-religious ideal can open any textbook of psychology to the massive section on cognitive bias and find the same warning laid out much more rigorously, but much less succinctly.

This issue of 'denouncing' other people's moral positions is something we frequently encounter in the context of hypocrisy. Oddly, despite the extent to which relativism has established itself in discussions of morality, most people are still extremely willing to accuse people of being hypocrites – it is perhaps the one vice that has been unaffected by Nietzsche's abyss. The trouble with this particular accusation is that it serves to block discussions of ethics rather than to clarify them. If, for instance, somebody raises a valid moral criticism it is a tangential matter whether the person doing so was unable to act on their own advice. Consider Tommy's warnings about heroin – his legitimate concerns are not weakened by knowing he was unable to follow them himself! Indeed, they become all the more urgent because of this. The 'unmasking' involved in declaring someone a hypocrite supposedly ends the discussion, but actually it blocks it from ever beginning. Until you appreciate the mythology, the metaphysics, that someone is living within, you cannot possibly 'unmask' them because you have no genuine access to their reasons for acting.

Metaphysics must be meaningful, because *we all use it to justify what matters to us*. We are one step closer to solving our problems when we recognize that we are all in the same boat when it comes to our living mythologies and their metaphysical uncertainties. All our vessels are afloat on the same ocean, a sea vaster and deeper than we can imagine, but *they all float*. Nietzsche's abyss could not drag all this water into oblivion, it is a mere eddy, although no-one has yet sunk a pylon so deep into the inky depths as to build something on foundations that will be forever secure. As it happens, we never needed that degree of security for our ethics anyway. We should not doubt morality, for it is a wind far stronger than any of us – but perhaps we should try to discover those places where the breeze is blowing all our ships in the same direction.

3

Law and Chaos

Viking Virtues

In June 793 AD, Viking raiders landed at the island of Lindisfarne off the coast of England and came ashore to ravage the monastery that had been sited there for over a century, killing many of the monks, burning the buildings to the ground, and making off with both slaves and loot. It caused an outrage in Christian Europe that was to tarnish the reputation of the Vikings, and Norse civilization in general, for a millennium (Graham-Campbell, 2001). From almost any account of this attack, it seems that a Viking was nothing more than a murderer and a thief operating on a scale that makes most contemporary killers seem small potatoes by comparison. What case could we possibly mount that a Viking could be deemed more moral than a murderer?

Our impression that a Viking must be judged either as bad as, or worse than, a contemporary murderer rests on using our own moral standards as the judge of their conduct – a misleading way to look at any historical era (or indeed, any foreign culture). Obviously if we have faith that our ethical beliefs are right, or even that they lean in the correct direction, then whatever earlier system we examine will be found wanting. Yet even by the standards of contemporary international law, the measure of just or ethical behavior is still the standards of the society in question, at least up to a point. We judge a murderer in our time by our own moral and legal standards because that is the world they live in, but if we want to judge the ethics of a Viking raider, we have to ask about the morality of Norse society at the time that dispatching Vikings abroad was common practice.

Vikings were not a people, but rather a temporary occupation undertaken by individuals from various Norse and Sami territories (i.e. what is now called Scandinavia) that involved sea travel. Not all of these voyages ended in pillaging: at least as many, if not more, resulted in trade or colonization, and the term 'viking' descends from an Old Norse word meaning 'overseas expedition'. The motives for Vikings setting out is a matter of ongoing scholarly debate, but their voyages seem to have come about because their home communities had outgrown their ability to expand by farming at home, and also in part because the despotic Christian monarch Charlemagne had set about converting pagan communities by violence. This created a desire for revenge that might have been the reason for the Lindisfarne attack (Simek, 2004).

Vengeance was an important aspect to Norse life, since their moral philosophy was based on the pursuit of honor and the avoidance of shame, with those who embodied the Norse conception of honor being worthy of emulation and praise, while those whose actions were viewed as shameful being reviled and shunned. As the poet-historian Snorri Sturluson wrote on this matter some time after Iceland's conversion to Christianity: "Valiant men who exert a good influence are called *drengr*" (pronounced 'dreng-ger') and the associated virtue was called *drengskapr* (pronounced 'dreng-skahp-er'), which entailed the qualities of bravery, magnanimity, respect for others, fairness and commitment to personal honor. Self-control was perhaps more important than bravery, since courage was rather taken for granted: a drengr remained composed when facing danger not out of recklessness but because to show fear was counterproductive. Risking death was irrelevant next to maintaining the respect of the community (Short, 1996).

At the opposite end of this scale of honor, a *níðingr* (pronounced 'nee-thing-er') was a reviled outcast and the vice of *níðr* (pronounced 'neeth-er') was despised. The term is sometimes translated as 'shame', and entails treachery, cowardice, oath-breaking or other dishonorable actions, such as killing one's own kinsfolk or defenseless people. This last point is interesting in the case of Lindisfarne – the monks would not have used violence against the Viking raiders, so wouldn't slaying them have been a shameful act given that they were defenseless? On the one hand, this speaks in favor of the idea that this raid was motivated by vengeance, but conversely the fact that the monks *wouldn't* defend themselves might have made them seem cowardly, at which point they would have been beneath contempt. Alternatively, since the monks were outside of the Norse culture these issues might not have applied.

We will never know the truth about this particular matter, but if Lindisfarne was an avenging raid its goal would have been the reparation of the honor of a community that was wronged, not in meting out punishment. Matters of Norse honor could be quite subtle: a thief was considered far worse than a robber, since breaking into someone else's house was a cowardly act, whereas challenging a traveler still allowed for an honorable clash of arms. A killing that occurred at night or in secret would be viewed as murder, but if conducted openly it would be considered manslaughter, a state of affairs attained by declaring it immediately to the next person encountered – with some small deference allowed if that person happened to be a relative of the person killed (Barry, 2008)!

These descriptions of the qualities admired or despised by Norse people goes a long way towards answering the question before us. Vikings were honorable people – certainly within their own communities – and their occasional attacks on outsiders represent a moral grey area, equivalent to questions concerning animal treatment today. Since animals are not, by default, considered part of our moral community (a point to pursue later), they do not automatically accrue the rights we afford other humans – the question of who or what is inside the boundaries of our community being one of the important ambiguities in moral philosophy.

Furthermore, while Viking raiders did take slaves – as they did from Lindisfarne – archaeologist William Fitzhugh notes that "slaves became part of their families... They weren't out to kill everyone in the countryside but rather to find a way to live, to set up shop" (Fitzhugh, 2005). Our contemporary moral mythologies offer strong reasons to condemn human slavery, but the Vikings (and the Greeks and Romans, for that matter) had an entirely different perspective on the practice, which was essentially ubiquitous for much of human history. Recognizing these kinds of differences in moral standards does not amount to conceding to relativism, in particular because the fact that Viking morality differs from contemporary moral systems does not mean they are impossible to compare. There may be no absolute standard by which they can be compared, but this means there are *many* ways to compare different moralities, not none at all.

A contemporary murderer transgresses the moral standards of the society they live in, and are thus deemed immoral, and since murder is considered one of the worst offenses imaginable they are vilified. Conversely, Vikings have been denigrated largely because of a reputation that misrepresents a complex pagan society in which moral respect for yourself and your community was absolutely central. Vikings may have been away from home, but they were still with their kinsfolk and deeply concerned with matters of honor and shame: they were acting ethically, according to the standards of their own communities. But their morality was not in any way based on an appeal to absolute or timeless standards: instead, the Vikings practiced a moral chaos based around honor. With this in mind, our imagined case of the Viking versus the murderer must find for the Viking – even though for many of the monks at Lindisfarne, there really wasn't any difference at all.

I'm claiming that the Viking honor ethic is an example of moral chaos, yet their ethics still involved a concept of law, and the Norse societies were legal-minded – indeed, the English word 'law' descends from Old Norse! This may seem odd: if they used laws, shouldn't they be an example of moral law? Here it is important to remember that the ideal encapsulated in the term 'moral law' involves an appeal to a universally binding morality, and this is something entirely absent from the Viking understanding of ethics. They had laws, but not the moral law as this term is usually meant. It is this absence of universalism that entails moral chaos, since without an absolute standard of ethical truth we are left with an incredible multiplicity of moralities, no matter how legalistic or formalized any given example might seem.

There is a considerable difference between those moral systems that evoke a concept of moral law and those that do not, and it will be helpful to have a means to take into account both approaches. Rather than invent an entirely new terminology for this purpose, I want to take an existing mythology and adapt it for use in moral philosophy. Specifically, I want to take the mythic concepts of Law and Chaos found in the work of the novelist Michael Moorcock and use these to contextualize the face-off between absolute truth and relativism in a radically different fashion. Moorcock read existentialists such as Camus and Sartre in the 1950s and within his novels developed a robust existentialism of his own. Unlike Sartre, however, Moorcock recognizes the contingent pressures that specific situations place upon individuals, and his novels often concern the tremendous difficulty entailed in attempting to change the course of events.

The main purpose of this chapter is to expound Moorcock's mythology of Law and Chaos, and to connect his ideas to contemporary discussions of ethics in moral philosophy. The Vikings serve as a means of putting moral chaos into a specific context, and they make an excellent contrast case since their ethical standards were very different to our own. Once the space of ethics has been adequately traced, I can offer a different understanding of the roots of ethical existence, one that departs from the conventional assumption that rationality lies at the heart of human morality. To get there requires a different way of understanding the relationship between morality, imagination, and fiction, and it is fitting to start by considering the work of one of the most imaginative and influential novelists of recent times.

Moorcock's Mythology

Moorcock's novels occupy a strange place in the literary world. He is most famous (and commercially successful) for his fantasy novels, in particular the Elric series, but he has also achieved substantial acclaim for literary works such as *Mother London,* which was shortlisted for the Whitbread Prize, and the *Between the Wars* sequence, in which a self-deluded narrator provides a uniquely fantastical account of the early twentieth century. Moorcock won the Nebula award for best novella in 1967 for his fantasy *Behold the Man,* in which a time traveler finds himself taking the role of Jesus (a book which most Christians will find offensive), and the World Fantasy Award for best novel in 1979 for *Gloriana,* his sumptuous tribute to Mervyn Peake's *Gormenghast* trilogy, not to mention dozens of other accolades including five lifetime achievement awards. He has been cited as an influence by authors such as Michael Chabon, Neil Gaiman, Colin Greenland, Jonathan Littell, Alan Moore, China Miéville, and Grant Morrison, not to mention inspiring other writers from Moorcock's own generation including Brian Aldiss, Moebius, and Norman Spinrad.

Unusually, while the individual collections of stories follow different protagonists – such as the aforementioned Elric and the cult antihero Jerry Cornelius (who achieved considerable literary fame in the late sixties and seventies) - they also form elements of a greater whole, which can only be appreciated by reading the greater part of the Moorcock canon. This wider framework, which can be collectively referred to as the Eternal Champion mythos, has its own metaphysical themes that are extremely conducive to the exploration of moral law and moral chaos. Although many of his stories are tales of wizardry and wild romance, their thematic content concerns more existential matters, and in particular questions about conflict, imperialism, and human nature.

Some of Moorcock's most celebrated characters, such as Jerry Cornelius and Colonel Pyat, explore existentialist issues concerning our capacity to reinvent ourselves, a point that can be related to the idea of series-persons. In stark contrast to Sartre, Moorcock suggests we cannot change who we are as a matter of purely individual creativity, yet we can and do adapt in response to the demands of the circumstances we find ourselves within. Pyat, the ultimate unreliable narrator thrown amongst the chaos of the mid-twentieth century, takes upon so many different identities, becomes so many different series-persons, that he is unable – in many cases, unwilling – to maintain a coherent narrative account of himself. An anti-semitic Jew who ends up falling in with the Cossacks, the Klu Klux Klan, Italian Fascists, and the Nazi Party, Pyat maintains an idealism that seems entirely disconnected from the practical dimensions of the movements he is swept up within. The reader must search between the lines to appreciate the extent of Pyat's self-delusion, revealing situations that are often hilarious, and sometimes chillingly stark. In one aside, Pyat confesses his lack of control over his own life:

> People judge you too readily. They think you deliberately choose your fate. They do not understand how you gradually slide into situations from which escape becomes impossible. What seems a temporary diversion on your life's road looks, in the perspective of history, like a culmination, an example of your inner evil! (Moorcock, 2006).

The existentialist influence can also be seen quite clearly in the

World Fantasy Award-nominated novel, *The War Hound and the World's Pain* (1981a), in which Ulrich von Bek, an itinerant soldier of the Thirty Years War, is charged by Lucifer to recover the Holy Grail. At one point in the novel Ulrich notes, with characteristic fatalism: "Man struggles in the belief that he can, by dint of perseverance, affect his own destiny. And all those efforts, I think, lead to nothing but ruin." In seeking to recover the Grail on Lucifer's behalf, however, he learns that "one must seek to become human and to love the fact of one's humanity" - and in discovering this, he also discovers the Grail. Upon delivering the cup to Satan, Lucifer remarks: "Man, whether he be Christian or pagan, must learn to rule himself, to understand himself, to take responsibility for himself. There can be no Armageddon now. If Man is destroyed, he shall have destroyed himself."

It is one of the recurring features of Moorcock's novels that I wish to appropriate for my own purposes in this book, namely the endless war between the forces of Law and the forces of Chaos. The essential source of conflict in many of the hundreds of Moorcock novels originates in this tension, although how it is expressed can vary wildly, from vying pantheons of gods in the core Eternal Champion cycle, to competing political pressures in novels with settings closer to our world. When Law and Chaos are viewed as cosmic forces (such as gods), there is also another metaphysical power known as the Cosmic Balance, which strives to retain equilibrium between the two forces, since ultimate victory by either side in this struggle would mean the end of all life.

Chaos expresses unfettered possibility, and in fact within the fantasy novels the stuff of Chaos is the raw material out of which all things are formed. In the short story "The Dream of Earl Aubec" (1964), part of the lands of the Young Kingdoms where the Elric stories are set is dreamed into existence by Aubec from naked Chaos. Within the fantasy milieu, the symbol of Chaos is an eight pointed star, representing possibilities, which Moorcock devised in the 1960s for the Elric stories. There is a beauty to Moorcock's depiction of Chaos in a fantasy context, but it has a savage edge – the gods of Chaos let nothing bind them, and certainly not morality. The other side of Chaos can be found when it expresses itself in historical settings, or in those stories that are set in alternative histories of our world. Here, chaos represents something akin to liberalism, and ultimately anarchy, with a moral relativism that denies any kind of fixed context. The forces of chaos (which are rarely labeled as such in this kind of story) work to undermine the ruling powers and destabilize them, perhaps pushing as far as a return to Hobbes' "war of all against all" (Hobbes, 1651).

Law, on the other hand, represents order and structure. Often, Law initially appears to be beneficent – in the Corum stories, for instance, the protagonist begins by allying with one of the gods of Law in order to defeat the rising tide of the lords of Chaos. However, it eventually becomes apparent that victory for Law means eternal stagnation, and the elimination of all living things (life being far too unpredictable to be allowed free rein in the eyes of the gods of Law!). The realm of Law presented in the fantasy story "To Rescue Tanelorn" (1962b) and elsewhere is a barren wasteland, devoid of features. In the later Elric novel, *The Dreamthief's Daughter* (2001), one such world is described as follows:

> [It] was no ordinary desert. It was all that remained of a world destroyed by Law. Barren. No hawks soared in the pale blue sky. Not an insect. Not a reptile. No water. No lichen. No plants of any kind. Just tall spikes of crystallized ash and limestone, crumbling and turned into crazy shapes by the wind, like so many grotesque gravestones.

The flipside to this is the expression of Law in more familiar settings, where it stands to represent conservatism, and ultimately totalitarianism. The rules, which initially provide justice and stability, become stifling, and when they become wildly out of balance the net result is as horrifying as the worst excesses of Chaos. Heroes in alternatives history stories are often fighting against the forces of Law (which are rarely identified as such in this kind of tale) in order to prevent harm to threatened peoples, or to destroy the ruling political powers – particularly in the *Nomad of the Time Streams* trilogy (1971, 1974, 1981b), considered one of the earliest examples of steampunk, which explores two of Moorcock's perennial themes, racism and imperialism – expressions of Law in the wider mythology of Moorcock's work.

Thus, we can see Law and Chaos expressed at different degrees of metaphor in Moorcock's novels. In the fantasy stories, the Lords of Chaos and the Lords or Law stand for either social and political forces, or in some cases specific political leaders – in the Hawkmoon stories, for instance, the gods of Granbretan are named after British Prime Ministers: The Howling God, Chirshil (Winston Churchill) and the Roaring God, Aral Vilsn (Harold Wilson) to name but two. In the later Elric novel, *The Dreamthief's Daughter*, the Goddess of Law, Miggea is clearly a satirical portrayal of conservative Prime Minister Margaret Thatcher, for whom Moorcock has expressed considerable disdain.

In alternative histories and stories set in our world, Law and Chaos are not explicitly named, but the same political tensions expressed in metaphor in the fantasy novels are still played out within such stories. The conflict between these two political forces – liberalism and conservatism – is the essence of the thematic drive of Moorcock's work, with the core message that people should never permanently ally with one political faction or its rival, since either force can become destructive if left unchecked. Rather, Moorcock urges his readers to be ready to support either side as needed in order to keep these two competing political and social forces in balance.

Moorcock's original inspiration for this Law and Chaos paradigm came from Golden Age science fiction author Poul Anderson, particularly *Three Hearts and Three Lions* (1961), but it was Moorcock's fantasy novels which wove the idea into the heart of the counterculture. The use of Law and Chaos as alignments within the popular tabletop role-playing game *Dungeons & Dragons* (Gygax and Arneson, 1974) owes a debt to Anderson and especially to Moorcock, although most players of fantasy role-playing games are rather unaware of this heritage. Regrettably, recent revisions to this game have eviscerated the original concepts by forcing Law to align with good and Chaos to align with evil – something entirely at odds with Moorcock's mythology.

There is no explicit concept of good and evil in the Eternal Champion mythos, although curiously Moorcock has said that he believes in "tangible good and evil". This can be understood as an existentialist thesis that while our individual actions may be good or evil, the causes we fight for always risk evil no matter how good their goals may appear to be on the surface. In a conversation with Colin Greenland, he expresses his own moral perspective by stating: "I believe in love and stable relationships between individuals. That's the only thing I believe is permanent" (Moorcock and Greenland, 1992). Moorcock thus eschews the traditional fantasy literature approach of ascribing warring factions to the causes of 'Good' and 'Evil', as for instance in Tolkien, where the despicable moral caliber of Sauron or Morgoth is never doubted (Tolkien, 1954-55 and 1977). As Tolkien himself remarked: "the absolute Satanic rebellion and evil of Morgoth and his satellite Sauron" is contrasted in his myth cycle against the refusal of the other powers to take any action at all to oppose them (Tolkien, 1981).

Moorcock's Law and Chaos offer a more sophisticated mythology to explore good and evil in practice. In the Eternal Champion mythos and its related novels, these factions are effectively imaginative projections of the conflict between liberal and conservative political factions that has been going on since at least 1789, when during the French revolution the National Assembly sat the delegates in favor of change to the left of the chamber and those in favor of preserving the traditional order on the right (Gauchet, 1997). Thus Moorcock's Cosmic Balance is a metaphor for something that has long been recognized as a vital aspect of a healthy political system, as John Stuart Mill (1859) attests from the midst of the nineteenth century:

> In politics... it is almost a commonplace, that a party of order or stability, and a party of progress or reform, are both necessary elements of a healthy state of political life... Each of these modes of thinking derives its utility from the deficiencies of the other; but it is in a great measure the opposition of the other that keeps each within the limits of reason and sanity.

This repainting of Left and Right as Chaos and Law follows naturally from the history of the opposition between liberal and conservative views, which has its point of origin in the Enlightenment, the period of history when humanity first begins to imagine itself situated within history and thus starts to invent new mythic images of society to supplant those of the medieval period. As Wood (1999) attests, from the outset, proponents of Enlightenment (liberals) had to contend with conservative opponents who held their enemies responsible for "the moral chaos and spiritual decline of modern society". The idea of order versus chaos has always been the mythological substrate of our democratic politics!

I want to take Moorcock's concepts of Law and Chaos and extend their reference beyond politics, applying them to the kinds of ethical thought that moral philosophers have been discussing for millennia, calling them either *Chaos Ethics* or *Law*

Ethics. Any moral philosophy or system that presumes unconditional truth in some role can be considered a Law Ethic, while any that deny the possibility of an absolute morality can be considered a Chaos Ethic – whether or not this ambiguity rises to the extremes of relativism. This division is not intended to demean or exalt either approach – indeed, precisely the opposite is my goal, for like Moorcock I intend to argue for the beneficial and detrimental aspects of *both* Chaos and Law Ethics. Furthermore, I intend to suggest, as with Moorcock's metaphor of the Cosmic Balance and the notion of political balance that was accepted wisdom not that long ago, we must make use of both these forms of moral thought if we are to have any hope of creating a better world to live in.

A classic exemplar of the Law Ethic is that of the Athenian Stoics, a school founded by Zeno of Citium in the early third century BC. The Stoics believed there was a single standard of virtue, and that the only kind of morality worth undertaking was that which complies completely with it. The Enlightenment philosopher Immanuel Kant may also be taken as a proponent of a Law Ethic (carefully examined in a later chapter), although his moral thought is far from as simple as it is usually presented. Additionally, when Derek Parfit expresses his horror at the idea there might be no single true morality he embodies precisely what the term Law Ethic is intended to capture. Almost all Law Ethics owe something of a debt to Plato, as Isaiah Berlin recognized when he suggested that most moral systems shared a view that "as in the sciences, all genuine questions must have one true answer and one only, all the rest being necessarily errors."

This debt to Plato is not universal, however, since there are exceptions belonging to traditions outside those descended from Greek thought. One example is the Chinese philosophy of Legalism, a term applied in the Han dynasty to the 'School of Law' propounded in the influential Warring States period, around the fifth to the third century BC. Originally, the law was advocated as important for strictly pragmatic reasons, then later it became enforced ideologically in a manner that was effectively an early form of totalitarian rule. Its basis was that the laws of the land would be publically known and promulgated, while the actions and motives of the leader would be shrouded in secrecy – indeed, one Chinese scholar contemporaneous to Legalism called this concealment the "cave of darkness", and lamented the lack of "moral content" in this approach to government (Sato, 2012).

In direct opposition to such Law Ethics are those moral systems that have no role for absolutes, such as the Chaos Ethic of the Vikings discussed at the beginning of this chapter. The exemplar of the Chaos Ethic today is Alain Badiou (2001), who uses the capitalized term 'Ethics' specifically to refer to Law Ethics, and rails furiously against them:

> The only genuine ethics is of truths in the plural – or, more precisely, the only ethics is of processes of truth, of the labor that brings *some* truths into the world... Ethics does not exist. There is only the *ethic-of* (of politics, of love, of science, of art)... it is impossible to speak of *one* Ethics.... The Law (human rights etc.) is always *already there*. It regulates judgments and opinions concerning the evil that happens in some variable elsewhere. But there is no question of reconsidering the foundation of this 'Law', of going right back to the conservative identity that sustains it... it valorizes – throughout the world, and with the complacency of 'intervention' – the gunboats of Law.

While any ethic that presupposes relativism is effectively a Chaos Ethic in my terms, all that is required for a moral system to constitute a Chaos Ethic is that it rejects the axiomatic principle of Law Ethics that there is absolute truth to be found in morality, and thus resists any institutional implementation of its morality. It is this latter point – the resistance to institution – that truly characterizes Chaos Ethics, although in practice even moral chaos rests upon some institutional footing. I shall also put into Chaos Ethics other kinds of resistance to Law Ethics, such as that found in philosophers like William James, who declares "better chaos forever" than an ethical philosophy established in advance, and who further suggests that "the *highest* ethical life – however few may be called to bear its burdens – consists at all times in the breaking of rules which have grown too narrow for the actual case." Both Nietzsche and Kierkegaard can be claimed to espouse a Chaos Ethic, as for that matter can Jesus – which is precisely why Kierkegaard was so horrified by the rigidly institutionalized Law Ethic of Christendom.

This conceit – Chaos Ethics versus Law Ethics – is of course deeply mythological, and could be subjected to any number of salient objections. For a start, there are plenty of ethicists whom it would be exceptionally difficult to force into either 'box', including Aristotle, and also those, such as Wood, whose views on ethics straddle this artificial divide in a way that would make it terribly difficult to force him convincingly into either pigeonhole. Indeed, I tried to get him to admit to being a Law Ethicist in my terms, but only got as far as getting him to admit his commonalities with Parfit, namely "that there are objective truths about what matters, about good and evil, right and wrong" (Wood and Bateman, 2012b). Compare this to his complaint that many an ethicist "behaves as if every moral problem must have a single right answer and as if it is moral philosophy's only job to say what it is" (Wood, 2011). Neither Law nor Chaos will stick to Wood's views convincingly!

These problems need not concern us too greatly, though, as my Moorcock-inspired metaphors are no more problematic than those we already inherit, such as the moral law and human rights, and it is my hope that exploring this additional perspective will help us to better understand what morality is, why we are moral creatures, and how we might use this knowledge to make a better world for everyone. However, even if you accept my claim that there is such a thing as moral chaos, you may find it difficult to accept that there could be something we could meaningfully term a Chaos Ethic. Perhaps because of the assumption that morality coincides with the concept of moral law, or perhaps because of the widespread perspective that ethics must be binding for everyone or else it is meaningful for no-one (a view espoused by, but certainly not invented by, Kant), the idea that a viable system of morality could be constructed without reference to moral law may seem troubling. But if this were so it would be necessary to reject the Viking Chaos Ethic as a moral system at all – and this ancient approach to morality is an example of a kind of moral system that is still very much alive and supporting moral chaos today.

An Ethical Triangle

The Viking Chaos Ethic is an example of what contemporary moral philosophy terms *virtue ethics,* one of three basic approaches to morality that are traditionally viewed as being locked in irresolvable conflict. Before we can engage with any specific moral problems it will be useful to briefly survey these rival positions within moral philosophy, and to contextualize these disparate ethical systems in terms of Law and Chaos where necessary. The three positions in question are what I am calling here (in a slight deviation from the usual terms) virtue ethics, duty ethics and consequentialism, and are characterized respectively by a focus on how people behave, on which rules to follow, or on what outcomes are desired.

In the case of virtue ethics, there can be both Chaos and Law approaches – the aforementioned Stoics, for instance, adhered to a form of virtue ethics that was also a Law Ethic since they presupposed one standard of virtue that all had to adhere to if they were to be deemed moral. Most contemporary approaches to virtue ethics, however, should be considered Chaos Ethics if only as a result of the stark contrast between virtue ethics and its alternatives. Virtue ethicists generally seek to distance themselves from what they view as the prevailing tendency towards Law Ethics, and thus end up on the side of Chaos. Indeed, they are perhaps the primary voices in support of moral chaos today.

Virtue ethics has deep roots, which are conventionally traced back to Aristotle (384-82 BC). However, it would be just as viable to trace their lineage back to the Chinese philosopher Confucius, whose writings in the Spring and Autumn period of Chinese history express another ancient Chaos Ethic. While rules and standards are recognized by Confucius, what is valued in his approach are "ethical connoisseurs" who can tell when discretion demands these rules be ignored (van Norden, 2003). The Legalism that appeared in the following Warring States period is the Chinese Law Ethic that countered this early Chaos Ethic, but which never managed to overcome it entirely. Pragmatically, neither Aristotle nor Confucius can be fairly considered the point of origin for virtue ethics as a practice, since it undoubtedly predates those philosophers who first expressed this kind of moral thought in a written form.

Although virtue ethics certainly has a long history, it is Wittgenstein's student and friend Elizabeth Anscombe who is usually credited with reviving an interest in its practice today with her pivotal essay "Modern Moral Philosophy", which expressly draws upon Aristotle's ethical thought (Anscombe, 1958). She notes disapprovingly the way terms such as 'should', 'need', 'ought' and 'must' have acquired the specific meaning of being obliged or bound by law, and traces this to Christianity "with its law conception of ethics" that built upon the Jewish teachings of the Torah. She thus relates Law Ethics expressly with the concept of *divine command*, the archetype of religious moral law that I could satirize by saying "if God says jump, then jumping is good." However, Anscombe notes that once these influences from sacred law became embedded into European culture via Christianity (or rather, Kierkegaard's Christendom), they could survive the loss of the explicitly religious underpinnings. Those moral systems that are most closely descended from Christianity are often referred to by the term *deontology*, but I shall prefer to call them *duty ethics*. These are chiefly associated with Kant, whose moral philosophy is effectively a secularized version of Christian moral ideals (Wood, 1999).

The other major form of Law Ethic that is espoused today owes its name to Anscombe's seminal essay: *consequentialism*. Rather than promoting virtue ethics, per se, Anscombe's critique sought to excoriate the consequentialist approach to morality, but her objections barely dinted the popularity of those ethics which judge the worth of actions solely by the outcomes that they produce. Consequentialism has traditionally been viewed as being in express conflict with Kantian duty ethics – and indeed, the arguments that have raged between these two rival Law Ethics have produced a great deal of sound and fury for well over a century. However, this has been a three cornered fight, with advocates for virtue ethics, duty ethics and consequentialism all denying the moral worth of rival approaches, while making claims for the superiority of their own methods.

Perhaps surprisingly, I want to suggest that the dispute between these three rival moral systems is rather less problematic than it might first appear, and can certainly be made less troublesome, even if it cannot be resolved outright. The trick is to recognize that whenever we are dealing with ethical situations, choices or decisions, we are dealing with a very definite scenario: an agent acting in a certain way to produce certain outcomes. Whatever the situation, whatever the dilemma, these three elements will always remain the same: an agent, actions taken, and outcomes that result. What's more, while we can learn, derive or devise many different ethical systems, they all *must* entail a focus on at least one of these three crucial elements. This defines an *ethical triangle* inside which all moral discussion must necessarily be framed, with individual ethics varying only in their focus and content.

What I shall term *agent-focused* ethics center upon the nature and characteristics of the person deciding how to act, commonly referred to as their virtues – hence virtue ethics. Conversely, *rule-focused* ethics center upon the nature of the actions, and the obligation or permissibility implied by those actions, referred to as duty – hence duty ethics. Finally, *outcome-focused* ethics center upon the results of the actions, which is to say what happens *after* the actions are taken, referred to as consequences – hence consequentialism. This three-way split mirrors the usual distinctions made between virtue ethics, duty ethics and consequentialism, and builds upon John Laird's (1946) distinction between agent-ethics and act-ethics. As J.E. Leddon (1947) suggests of this two-way split, it shouldn't be thought of as "divergent conceptions of the true nature of ethics, but as supplementary conceptions, indicating different parts of the overall discipline". My renovation of Laird's approach is offered in the same spirit.

Since nothing else is involved in an ethical situation but beings acting, actions taken, and outcomes that result, this represents a complete model of ethical systems (albeit one of many). Of course, individual systems can include elements from any or all of these different approaches – as with Kantian ethics, which as Wood (1999) affirms contains significant agent-focused and outcome-focused elements while being primarily rule-focused. Indeed, we shouldn't think that we can automatically sort moral systems into pigeonholes defined by the three corners of the ethical triangle, since the best ethics will operate in more than one way. Thus Robert Louden (1986) praises Kant's ethical theory precisely because it can "assess both the life plans of moral agents and their discrete acts", noting that "an adequate moral theory needs to do both". (Does an adequate moral theory also need to assess outcomes? This is a question to return to later). However, most ethics will fit more easily into one corner than another, and we can use the ethical triangle to distinguish between three different general approaches.

In an agent-focused approach, such as virtue ethics, the important factors are the qualities of the people concerned, and these qualities will vary according to the relevant tradition. As MacIntyre has observed, there are many different practices that can maintain many different virtues, and most of these are impossible to compare. As a result, talk of 'virtue ethics' should be read in the plural – the many different ethics of virtue – and not in the singular, since there is no one version of virtue ethics. Nonetheless, MacIntyre proposes that there are qualities that are common to any tradition that strives for virtue, specifically justice, courage and honesty. He suggests that any practice that holds some things to be good, and which has standards of excellence, must display these virtues. However, what constitutes justice and honesty, and probably courage as well, can be very different from one tradition to the next:

> Lutheran pietists brought up their children to believe that one ought to tell the truth to everybody at all times, whatever the circumstances or consequences, and Kant was one of their children. Traditional Bantu parents brought up their children not to tell the truth to unknown strangers, since they believed that this could render the family vulnerable to witchcraft. In our culture many of us have been brought up not to tell the truth to elderly great-aunts who invite us to admire their new hats. But each of these codes embodies an acknowledgement of the virtue of truthfulness. So it is also with varying codes of justice and of courage (MacIntyre, 1984).

There are many advantages of the virtue ethic approach – not least of which being that it can be fostered by identifying ethical role models who can be emulated, rather than trying to specify rules or predict outcomes. A common example of an agent-focused ethical practice is embedded in the famous phrase "what would Jesus do?" which holds out Jesus as an ethical role model to be emulated. This example also reveals one of the key disadvantages of this approach – how can anyone actually *know* what someone else would do, let alone a paradoxical figure such as Jesus? Another serious issue is that if one believes ethics and legislation should be related – that is, that the law should be ethical – agent-focused approaches often provide very little guidance. They praise good people, but they do not provide a point of leverage for considering rules of conduct.

Conversely, in a rule-focused approach such as Kantian and other kinds of duty ethics, the regulation of actions is the central element. The way ethical issues surrounding actions are addressed in such approaches revolves around considering which kinds of actions are allowed or permitted, or which actions are required or obligatory. In either case, what results are rules that specify permission or obligation, which collectively denote duties. Duty and rules are equivalent since any rule assumes a duty to comply with it else it is not a rule, and these duties can be wide (allowing significant leeway) or narrow (prescribing very definite restrictions). For instance, not killing humans is supposedly a narrow duty, despite our tendency to find excuses to widen its scope. Unlike agent-focused ethics, rule-focused approaches have the considerable advantage of being amenable to legislative implementation – although this might also be seen as inherently problematic. As Wittgenstein's philosophy cautions, language is never precise enough to express rules exactingly, and a perfect rule-based system of ethics also requires clearly demarked priorities for the many different rules, which risks escalating problems of complexity.

If the term 'rule' is off-putting, it should be noted that when we speak of *rights*, such as human rights, we are actually talking about rules of interaction. Rights place constraints (specify what is permitted) or enshrine requirements (specify what is obligatory). For example, the human right to freedom of belief, one of several liberties protected by the so-called Universal Declaration of Human Rights, is in effect a rule obligating States and individuals to take no action that compromises a person's freedom to choose their own beliefs (or, equivalently, specifying that interference in this right to choose what we believe is not permitted). Anyone who has indignantly declared "I have a right to such-and-such!" is making a rule-focused moral assertion – although all too frequently such claims lack any coherent basis because the declaration was not backed up by any understanding of the duty ethics it presupposes.

Another form of rule-focused ethics must be briefly mentioned, namely the aforementioned Law Ethic of divine command. The Ten Commandments are a classic example of divine command, which presumes that what is good is solely what is commanded by God. If we are to support freedom of belief (and I encourage us to do so), we have to allow people to adopt this kind of ethic whatever we might think of it. Personally, I would suggest that as a Law Ethic for Christians and the like divine command is wildly inferior to Kant's secular alternative, but beyond this I want to suggest that anyone who claims to follow the teachings of Jesus should adhere to a Chaos Ethic consistent with his ministries and not to the law presented to the Israelites by Moses. To choose otherwise would be to value Christendom over Christianity, and thus fall prey to the criticisms justifiably advanced by Kierkegaard.

Finally, in an outcome-focused approach, the important element is the circumstances that are produced by the actions taken. Following Anscombe, these systems are usually referred to as consequentialist, to emphasize the focus on outcomes rather than rules and duties, or the virtues of the agents involved. The most famous consequentialist ethical system is *utilitarianism* (although it is by no means the only such approach), which is usually credited to Jeremy Bentham, with some formative influence from David Hume. According to utilitarianism, whether a particular course of action is right depends upon whether it is for the benefit of the majority, or whether it causes "the greatest happiness for the greatest number" (Bentham, 1776), or whether it causes "the least amount of avoidable suffering for all" (Popper, 1945).

On the surface, this may seem like an excellent approach – shouldn't we judge situations by how things turn out? In practice, this is an exceptionally tall order. Ethical decisions must be made *before* actions are taken, and we human beings have very limited abilities to predict even the overt consequences of our actions, let alone the subtleties. As Nietzsche (1968) quipped in response of what he saw as the naivety of utilitarians: "But does one know the consequences? Perhaps as far as five steps." An additional problem, as Karl Popper recognized, was that as a Law Ethic, utilitarianism carries significant risks since "it is not only impossible but very dangerous to attempt to maximize the pleasure or the happiness of the people, since such an attempt must lead to totalitarianism." There might be such a thing as a utilitarian Chaos Ethic which could sidestep this concern, but no-one has espoused anything like this to my knowledge.

Despite these problems, consequentialist approaches remain popular – particularly with positivists, who tend to assert that pragmatically we have no option but to resort to utilitarian thinking in politics. The moral psychologist Jonathan Haidt, for instance, states:

> I don't know what the best normative ethical theory is for individuals in their private lives. But when we talk about making laws and implementing public policies in Western democracies that contain some degree of ethnic and moral diversity, then I think there is no compelling alternative to

> utilitarianism. I think Jeremy Bentham was right that laws and public policies should aim, as a first approximation, to produce the greatest total good. (Haidt, 2012).

Haidt also cautions that how we actually go about maximizing 'total good' requires that we recognize the complexity of human nature. However, I am far more skeptical than Haidt in this matter: once we recognize our moral diversity, how exactly are we going to produce a *single* measure of total good? A considerable leap of faith is required here if the sciences are expected to offer an answer, since as John Rawls (1971) convincingly argued there is no plausible way of producing instruments that can *measure* happiness or goodness, let alone totalize it. If the appeal of utilitarianism is that it is provides a method of linking morality to numbers, we ought to be aware of how much moral perspective is lost in that translation. As Wood (2011) cautions, the solutions to moral problems "can never be as clear (or as trivial) as the arithmetical fact that five is greater than one".

Although consequentialism is by definition outcome-focused, it is not actually possible to systemize the consequences of actions as such. Rather, what is central to consequentialism is the process of moral *decision-making*. This is related to Robert Louden's (1986) observation that agent-focused ethics (such as virtue ethics) can be contrasted to those moral systems that "focus on discrete acts and moral quandaries" whose interest lies in "formulating decision procedures for making practical choices." Louden, like John Laird (1946) whose distinction he seems to borrow, makes no distinct discussion of consequentialism because what he contrasts are ethics which are agent-focused and ethics with a focus on actions – which is intended to include both duty ethics and consequentialist approaches. The ethical triangle, however, splits these two approaches – and having done so, decision procedures belong primarily to outcomes (although may sometimes be required in a rule-focused approach to establish the priority of one rule over another).

Consequentialism is not just outcome-focused, it is intimately involved with decision procedures. Indeed, Toby Ord's (2005) attempt to rescue consequentialism from its short-comings expressly focuses upon the idea that what is unique and valuable in these moral systems is the assessment of decisions, claiming "we should... follow whichever decision procedure it is that would lead to the best outcome." Conventional forms of consequentialism have generally consisted of assessing situations where numerical measurement can somehow be brought to bear upon ethical content. Utilitarianism originally supposed a "hedonic calculus" (Bentham, 1776) that could measure happiness, but contemporary consequentialists generally recognize the implausibility of this approach. Instead, consequentialist arguments may involve thought experiments counting how many people live or die, or might instead appeal to a number of years of life expectancy – both of which can be found in Parfit's moral philosophy (2011), although he also considers duty ethical arguments.

There is another form of outcome-focused ethics that must be addressed, even though it just barely qualifies as a moral system: the belief that what allows you to judge the goodness of a situation by how good the outcome is *for you yourself.* This is captured nicely in the adage: "That's all very well, but what's in it for me?" This moral stance is known in the literature as *egoism* or ethical egoism, which distinguishes it from the theory of motivation known as *psychological egoism*. As I have argued in *The Mythology of Evolution*, the theoretical form of egoism is demonstrably false, and is certainly not validated by evolutionary science, no matter what you may have heard to the contrary. Similar remarks apply to *psychological hedonism*, which tries to reduce all motivation to seeking pleasure or avoiding pain. As Midgley (1985, 2003) has consistently and cogently argued, the idea that our motives can be reduced in this way without losing vital aspects of the real situation is thoroughly misguided, and the most useful additional remark I can make is to question *why* anyone should think we would get a better understanding of motivation by artificially simplifying rather than by exploring the actual complexities of our behavior...

Theories of motivation aside, the ethical version of egoism is far more problematic than its psychological variants because it *cannot* be proved false, since it is not in any way a testable claim – rather, it is the barely-ethical belief that what we ought to do is what is in our own self-interest. Some moral philosophers have been deeply troubled by the apparent disconnect between morality and self-interest, most notably Henry Sidgwick (1874), who felt his entire ethical project was a failure precisely because he had not been able to bridge the two convincingly. Yet there is no need for such pessimism: self-interest still dictates a significant degree of co-operation, even if it does not necessary extend to anything more moral than that. As a result, if we were somehow able to build a world that would satisfy the conflicting moral claims of other ethical systems, it could easily tolerate a significant number of egoists in the mix. It might be the case, as Parfit suggests, that egoism is best regarded as "an external rival to morality", rather than a moral view, but if egoists will co-operate with others in a way that makes the world better for everyone, it would seem to have at least a minimalistic claim to being a form of morality, however slight.

Egoism and utilitarianism are both consequentialist ethics, since both are primarily concerned with outcomes, and contrasting the former to the latter actually helps highlight why utilitarianism is held to be a desirable moral system: it asks that people treat everyone else's interests with an *equal* weight, rather than valuing your own interests more highly. This may be a tall order, but it is easy to grasp why utilitarianism's striving for equality would be considered morally superior to egoisms self-centered policy. I shall call egoism the *minimal ethic,* because it demands the absolute least that can be expected of anyone who expects to live with others (although there are, as we will see, ethics with even lower standards of care). While I certainly don't want to defend it as good or right, I'm not going to suggest anyone has any proven obligation beyond this minimal contribution. However, I will support Bishop Butler's observation (1726) that the problem in respect of egoism is not that people have too much concern for themselves, but that they have not enough – for what people who claim to be egoists often do in practice is indulge in a self-destructiveness that is simply not in their own self-interest. In this respect, the minimal ethic actually demands *more* from people than they might expect.

One particular example of the minimal ethic being unexpectedly demanding is the famous *tragedy of the commons,* which has been around in one form or another for centuries but received its peculiar metaphorical name from ecologist Garrett Hardin (1968). The 'commons' being referred to are commonly-held grazing land, and the 'tragedy' is that each individual farmer will benefit from grazing all of their cattle on this land, but if every farmer does so the grassland is rapidly depleted and nothing can graze there at all. This, Hardin suggests, is a 'tragedy' in the sense used by Alfred North Whitehead (1926): "the solemnity of the remorseless working of things." The logic of this example presumes that the egoist *must* take advantage, even if knowing that everyone would do the same would be a reason for not taking advantage. I see this as a flaw in conventional economic theory: it is not rational to co-operate in catastrophe, it is either ignorant or stupid. On this basis, I claim the minimal ethic requires a farmer to engage in the discussions required to prevent tragedy from occurring because *this* is truly in their best interest. Again, the motive to act for purely personal benefit is barely moral – but it is far better than what economists usually claim is rational in this scenario.

As is hopefully clear, there are a range of different moral systems from all three corners of the ethical triangle. Because these varying approaches describe the same kinds of situation, there is a capacity for one moral system to be transformed into another – but with a cost! As the Italian proverb suggests, 'all translation is betrayal': what a particular ethic is good at capturing may become distorted when we switch from one focus to another. These issues have been prominent in the academic scuffle between Kantian and consequentialist ethics, with the latter often claiming to be able to absorb the former (e.g. Cummiskey, 1990, Peterson, 2009), and the former steadfastly insisting that something vital is lost when Kant's ethics are converted to an outcome-focused form (e.g. Wood, 2002, Korsgaard, 2004).

This problem equally applies when comparing virtue ethics to other approaches. For example, in the context of translating virtue into a rule-focused approach Fives states that virtue "cannot be reduced to rule-following", and Julia Tao Lai Po-wah similarly claims that "moral judgment involves a sensitivity to context which outruns anything moral rules can establish". Despite the rule-focus of his ethical system, Kant does not actually dispute either of these claims. Although Kantian ethics make especial use of *maxims*, which is to say, succinct formulations of a principle of conduct, Kant had no expectation that applying these maxims could avoid relying on individual discretion. As Wood (2011) clarifies:

> ...Kant insists [morality] can never be reduced to maxims, rules or principles since "one can always ask for yet another principle for applying this maxim to cases that may arise"... the interpretation and application of moral rules or duties to particular cases, always involves a distinct stage of thinking that cannot be made a matter of rules or principles.

To put this another way, that an ethic is rule-focused does not mean that it expects blind adherence to a set of inviolable regulations. Divine command might be a rule-focused ethic that removes human judgment from the equation, but Kantian ethics certainly are not. There is thus an unexpected sense that moral systems that are outcome-focused, rather than rule-focused, might be better exemplars of the absolute truth implied by Law Ethics. In the conflict between Law Ethics and Chaos Ethics, the key question is whether or not there are definite answers to moral questions, and it is often those systems that hope to attain certainty by appealing to mathematics that are most dedicated to suppressing moral chaos.

We now have a sense of both the scope of the problem for contemporary ethics, and perhaps an inkling of how the barriers to productive discourse might be overcome. Virtue ethics, duty ethics and consequentialism are generally taken to represent three different approaches that are essentially impossible to compare. Here, I am suggesting that this apparent hopelessness is partly due to a conflation between Law Ethics, which demand absolute answers to moral questions, and Chaos Ethics that do not. The biggest disagreements in moral philosophy occur over rival attempts to claim ownership of the moral law – particularly the outcome-focused consequentialists trying to wrest the baton from rule-focused Kantians and certain enthusiastic religious groups. Positioned in the context of Law against Chaos, contemporary moral philosophy sometimes seems disproportionately concerned with Law's struggle to reclaim our lost moral authority. To get beyond this blockage, it may be helpful to take seriously the moral demands of Chaos – as proponents of virtue ethics and certain Kantians are already unknowingly doing...

The Clash of Ideals

Although the academic battle between these three competing moral systems has not been the cause of the failure of contemporary politics, it is indicative of the nature of the problem we face. We live at a time when a staggering array of values are on offer, and we can comprehend our political failures precisely in terms of this battleground of ideals. The dimensions of this hopeless collision between rival conceptions of what is good or right or necessary are too vast to catalogue, but it is a simple matter to single out a few judicious examples: the perpetual disagreements between liberal and conservative political factions who can neither understand nor accept the values of their opponents (Haidt, 2012); the desperate fight between corporate-motivated globalism and a strange collection of locally-constituted nationalisms (Saul 2005); the alleged conflict between Science and Religion in a spat between theists and positivists over both the sciences and religious freedom (Bateman, 2012); or the odd dispute between those who defend an illusory 'free' market and those who demand regulation that in practice has never been absent (Harcourt, 2011).

More than a century ago, William James recognized that we were facing a dizzying variety of ideals that "form a maze of apparently inextricable confusion with no obvious Ariadne's thread to lead one out." This crisis only accelerated in the twentieth century, although (as Isaiah Berlin suggested) despite the differing forms of life, the differing moral principles, and the variety of purposes that everyone pursued, there could not be *infinitely* many ideals, since all our ideals necessarily lie "within the human horizon". Tracing the history of our diverse beliefs, Charles Taylor situates the commencement of this accelerating multiplicity of ideals within the eighteenth century Enlightenment, when humanism branched off from the Christianity that had fostered it and became a viable alternative to it. This was the beginning of what he terms *the nova effect*, "the widening gamut of new positions – some believing, some unbelieving, some hard to classify", which pluralized the ideals of the elites in James' century, and of everyone in Berlin's.

Now, in our century, we have to find a way to survive the nova effect, which renders agreement ever more difficult by simultaneously undermining the authority of truth and shattering any hope of consensus. As I have already suggested, if we are going to attain anything close to a better world, we have to begin by allowing that morality is a matter for everyone, irrespective of their mythology, and thanks to the increasing diversification of belief this means accepting a great variety of moral systems – including both Chaos Ethics and Law Ethics, not to mention virtue ethics, duty ethics and consequentialist ethics. Morality is a topic for everyone – for those who follow traditional religion, including theists, non-theists and religious atheists like the Dalai Lama (Smart, 1996); for those who favor non-religion, including positivists, Marxists and enthusiastic environmentalists (Bateman, 2012); for those who know for certain what they believe, for those still making up their minds, and for those who are perpetually agnostic. Additionally, as I also mentioned before, it's important to remember that *accepting* this diversity of belief is not the same as *endorsing* any particular belief – it is merely granting the simple courtesy of allowing each individual to make up their own minds. On my reading of Kant, this freedom was precisely what he thought *constitutes* morality, albeit with some important critical limitations.

To survive the nova effect we may have to make a decisive break from at least one aspect of Kant's thought, and of all the other conventional moral systems too – or at the very least we may have to change the context by which we understand it. The problem I'm referring to concerns the way we think about rationality and about truth, and to get to the heart of this problem means examining the way we think about fiction. To get there, however, I suggest a short detour via the concept of 'rights'. Korsgaard (2012) neatly lays out Kant's position, which remains essential to almost all liberal political ideals, as follows:

> Because human beings are rational beings, Kant believed human beings, unlike the other animals, are able to choose our own way of life. We reflect about what counts as a good life, decide the question for ourselves, and live accordingly. In the liberal tradition, with its strong emphasis on toleration, and its antagonism to paternalism, this kind of autonomy has often been regarded as the basis of rights. We have the basic rights of personal liberty, liberty of conscience, and freedom of speech and association, because each of us has the right to determine for himself or herself what counts as a worthwhile life, and to live that life, so long as the way we act its consistent with a like right for everyone else.

MacIntyre, perhaps the staunchest defender of virtue ethics, will have no truck with this kind of talk, going so far as to suggest that "there are no such rights, and belief in them is one with belief in witches and unicorns." I have to doubt MacIntyre's claim here, not least of all because I have many pagan friends and hence have no reason to suspend belief in witches, but he goes further declaring that natural rights and human rights are *moral fictions*, as is the concept of utility that underpins the utilitarian ideal. On this point, I have to say that MacIntyre is *absolutely right* – Kantian ethics and utilitarianism are indeed founded on moral fictions! But this is in no way a reason to abandon these moral systems since *every ideal we adopt is necessarily a moral fiction.*

What blinds us to understanding this is the conventional way that 'fiction' and 'fact' are positioned as diametric opposites. It is presupposed that either something is fact or it is fiction, but this presumption is incredibly premature. In *Imaginary Games* (2011) I expanded Kendall Walton's make-believe theory (1990) from its point of origin in representative art to include games, and from there to our social beliefs. In *The Mythology of Evolution*, I used Walton's related *pretence theory* to demonstrate that thinking of fact and fiction as opposites was incredibly misleading. *Fictional*, in Walton's theory, means 'prescribed to imagine' - so for instance we can say that it is fictional in Moorcock's Eternal Champion series that Law and Chaos are kept in check by the Cosmic Balance. This means that when we read one of these books, we are expected to imagine that this circumstance is true – indeed, 'fictional' means the same as 'fictionally true' in Walton's pretence theory.

Yet as I note in *The Mythology of Evolution*, the prescription to imagine we associate with fiction is in no way constrained to works of fiction. When we read a newspaper story describing an event happening elsewhere in the world we are equally prescribed to imagine what we read – it is just we are *also* prescribed to imagine that what we read is *true*. Walton says "what is true is to be believed; what is fictional is to be imagined" but I say "whether it is fact or fiction, it is to be imagined; if it is authorized as a fact, it is *also* to be believed true". Rather than truth and fiction being opposites, we can understand that truth emerges from a certain kind of fiction, that some stories – the *authorized stories*- consist of true fiction. The reason the contents of newspapers are taken as true accounts is precisely because newspapers (provided we trust them!) have the authority to declare that the prose they contain is factual. Just like those stories that are solely fictional, we imagine what we read in a newspaper – but we also imagine that what we are reading is true.

It is important to appreciate that in putting the relationship between imagination, fiction and truth in this way, I deviate not just from Walton, but from the majority of philosophers who have discussed imagination. Gregory Currie and Ian Ravenscroft (2002), for instance, develop an astoundingly rigorous account of imaginative capacities, but they maintain the philosophical party line that thinks about beliefs as 'tracking truth', as Tamar Szabó Gendler puts it (2008b). For Currie and Ravenscroft, fictional stories work by "mixing up beliefs and imagining and seeing what results". Their point is that we bring along our beliefs about the world in order to "fill out what the story tells us". I completely agree that this happens. But in my terms, the beliefs in question are just *another kind of fiction*, a fictional model of the world that 'aims' at being true. (This is not so far from Currie and Ravenscroft, in that they recognize that imagination is not a kind of belief, but that the two share "a multidimensional space".) The merit of my approach is that it defuses problems involved in understanding belief, albeit at the cost of blurring fact and fiction. It is precisely this blurring, however, that will help us understand the role of imagination in morality.

In this light, MacIntyre's attempt to dismiss Kantian ethics and utilitarianism on the grounds that they are moral fictions is farcical – yes, they are ideals, which are evidently things we imagine and thus necessarily moral fictions, but this has no bearing whatsoever on their truth. What would make Kantian ethics true, or utilitarian ethics true, would depend upon whether those moral fictions were authorized as facts. But precisely the problem that contemporary moral philosophy has struggled with is that *morality entails facts but is not purely factual*. As Putnam notes, facts and values are entangled – but this entanglement doesn't allow us any way to establish that one moral ideal is true and another false; at best, it allows us to establish certain moral facts *if* we apply a given ideal. Who could possibly authorize one ideal or another as being true?

Korsgaard, reciting Kant's perspective, has an answer – *we do*. Because we are rational (Kant claims), we are able to choose our own way of life, and thus we are able to choose our own ideals, our own moral fictions. Yet I want to dispute this assumption that rationality is the important point here. It is not because we are rational (if indeed we *are* rational!) that we can choose how to live, but because we are *imaginative*. Imagination, not rationality, is the bedrock of morality, although this metaphor fails because imagination is not something that offers firm foundations. Rather, I would say we are afloat on a sea of imagination, our moral fictions bobbing gently upon its surface, and this vast ocean is wide enough to sail an armada of ideals upon it.

This is not to deny that rationality – whatever that might be – has some role here. One of the fascinating things about studying fiction and imagination has been that we naturally defend *consistent* fictional worlds. When the purely fictional stories we read don't stack up, it mars the quality of the imaginative experience. As Hume (1757) noted, this is especially true of deviations in moral content, which we naturally resist. Currie and Ravenscroft make the point that we find it far easier to vary our beliefs in imagination than to vary our desires, which helps make sense of why moral deviations can be harder to imagine: as ideals, our moral fictions are about what we wish for the world, not about what is authorized as truth. The latter we are happy to imagine differently, the former is more challenging – you *could* imagine that genocide was morally acceptable, but who would *want* to imagine this? Who could desire such a world?

Although we are not equipped with the capacity to imagine contradictory content about the world we live in, we can sometimes imagine things that would otherwise be nonsensical provided we do so within the fictional worlds of stories (Gendler, 2000). But because our imaginings *about our world* are governed by rational constraints, we have the option to switch from rationality being the grounding of morality to viewing our moralities as proceeding from our imaginative capacity, of which our rationality is merely one aspect. As Nietzsche's abyss warned us, rationality is not as solid a foundation as had been hoped, but within our imagination it is an indispensible guide between good sense and nonsense.

Returning to MacIntyre's prophetic declaration concerning moral fictions, we have yet to demonstrate that virtue ethics also entails fiction. Fortunately, MacIntyre does it for us! Developing his account of virtue, he makes the claim that there is no way to possess virtues except as part of a tradition, and that all practices which maintain a concept of virtue trace back to what he terms "heroic societies". He specifically refers to ancient Greece, but my previous example of Viking ethics operates in a substantially similar fashion. In these cultures "the chief means of moral education is the telling of stories" and furthermore "every particular view of the virtues is linked to some particular notion of the narrative structure or structures of human life." Thus virtue and narrative – which of course, is a form of fiction – are intimately connected:

> The narrative therefore in which human life is embodied has a form in which the subject – which may be one or more individual persons, or, for example, the people of Israel, or the citizens of Rome – is set a task in the completion of which lies their peculiar appropriation of the human good; the way towards the completion of that task is barred by a variety of inward and outward evils. The virtues are those qualities which enable the evils to be overcome, the task to be accomplished, the journey to be completed... man is in his actions and practice, as well as in his fictions, essentially a story-telling animal. He is not essentially, but becomes through his history, a teller of stories that aspire to truth.

Oh the irony! In attempting to praise virtue ethics and condemn all other points on the ethical triangle, MacIntyre instead allows all ideals to be united through their necessary engagement with the central imaginative activity of human life – story-telling. The only salient difference between the moral fictions of virtue ethics and those of consequentialism and duty ethics is that virtue ethics depends upon its fictions for both its propagation *and* its substance. But this does point out a significant advantage of agent-focused ethics that its rivals cannot claim: by depending upon stories rather than logical and mathematical systems, we can expect them to be considerably easier to teach and learn.

This switch of focus in morality from rationality to imagination is part of my wider project to offer a philosophy of imagination as an alternative way of looking at the world, a project that began with *Imaginary Games*, continued with *The Mythology of Evolution*, and which concludes with this book. While most philosophers talking about imagination make clear and useful distinctions between alternative mental states such as perceiving, remembering or believing, I treat all these activities as different forms of imagination in order to offer a story about life that is also a story about the development of imagination. In my sense of the word, our ancestors first acquired the ability to imagine very basic things about their world – when an amoeba senses food I will say it imagines (in a very primitive way!) that there is food around and responds accordingly. As the next chapter discusses, from this early perceptual form of imagination our ancestors later acquired a kind of proto-belief and proto-memory, then the form of imagination we call belief, and finally make-believe, which is perhaps the most sophisticated imaginative capacity so far. Without our ability to make-believe, without moral fiction, it's not entirely clear that human morality would be any different from the morality of other animals.

With imagination positioned as the pivotal element of morality, we can finally dispatch relativism and close off Nietzsche's abyss. Relativism suggested that there was no possibility of one way of life being understood by another, but as our stories and legends show this just isn't the case! I can indeed learn about ancient Greece from *The Iliad*, about ancient China from *Romance of the Three Kingdoms*, or about Victorian London from the novels of Charles Dickens. As Berlin notes we can "by the force of imaginative insight" come to understand "the values, the ideals, the forms of life of another culture or society, even those remote in time or space."

Similarly, as Gendler (2000) observes, we can 'export' certain fictional truths from stories – and indeed, for certain stories it is *difficult to avoid doing so*. This offers another solution to Hume's problem about our reluctance to accept stories whose moral assumptions we find offensive. If the moral content of a story was always as isolated from our lives as relativism suggested, we would not have to worry about imagining something we might otherwise find morally offensive, such as ethically-justified genocide. It would be locked away in another world forever. But we cannot *avoid* exporting fictional truths from stories, and as such it becomes far harder to want to imagine moral propositions that we find objectionable – they will not remain comfortably locked away in the fictional world of the story after all.

We quite naturally move between our fictional worlds, but as we do so our ethical standards – as reflecting our desires for the world we live in – travel with us, packed safely away in our 'moral suitcase'. We can try on other values, but there is a limit to what kinds of ethical clothing we are willing to experiment with, something that is set in part by the specifics of the moral practices we are participating in. The post-modern mythology thus transpires to be the ultimate example of fearing monsters under the bed – the fact that we can recognize the *extent* to which narrative and fiction affects our view of the world never placed us under any significant limitation. Only the odd belief that we had to be strong and resolute and reject all illusions left us paralyzed. Once we welcome back our dependence upon our imagination, morality is successfully salvaged – battered, bruised, but substantially intact.

What of the battle between Law and Chaos? Recall that in Moorcock's metaphysics 'Law' stands not only for absolute truth but also for conservative political ideals, while 'Chaos' stands also for liberal political ideals, and the anarchic pluralism this unleashes. The conflict is in part between individualism (Chaos) and tradition (Law), which as MacIntyre states has long been taken as the enemy of individualism. To resolve this we need to do much better than dismissing tradition out of hand, especially since *all* our moral ideals are instituted as traditions, as for that matter is each of the sciences. When we make tradition our enemy, we are exceptionally selective about *which* traditions we denounce, and this is especially true of those who are supposed to see further – our intellectuals.

In philosophy, for instance, there has been a long-standing conflict between two rival positions, conventionally called realism and idealism, although the latter camp periodically changes its name and focus. 'Realism' attempts to see the world as it 'really' is, predicating the contents of an objective reality to be discovered. 'Idealism' claims that we cannot access this objective reality, and must content ourselves with the models of that world that we construct with our minds instead. But these aren't really opposites, they are intimately related metaphysical positions: as Emmanuel Lévinas (1974) remarked: "Neither realism nor idealism, twin brothers, have the birth-right." Latour relates this to the way nature (realism) and society (idealism) are deployed in support of the erroneous fact-value distinction, and urges that we "secularize" this mythology. I wholeheartedly agree. Realism is Law to idealism's Chaos, and we don't get one without the other.

There is, as Latour remarks "no need to make a big fuss" about objective reality, since we all live in it. Realism – like the various Law Ethics – tries to draw confidence from focusing on objectivity, while idealism – like the many Chaos Ethics – tries to blunt this certainty with cautionary warnings. In morality, the same dispute is just as likely to be rendered by other terms, as in Derek Parfit's (2011) astonishingly detailed and rigorous defense of 'cognitivism' (Law) against 'non-cognitivism' (Chaos). Whichever mythology is being defended, be it realism or idealism, cognitivism or non-cognitivism, conservatism or liberalism, Law or Chaos, the problem is the same: the limitations of rival metaphysics are not necessarily reasons for accepting *your* metaphysics, and you are far more likely to recognize *other people's* untestable metaphysics than you are to recognize your own.

This problem in philosophy is a microcosm of a far larger problem in intellectual circles. As Haidt and Graham (2007) report, academia leans wildly towards the left of the political spectrum, and when discussing conservative ideals researchers all too easily dip into self-righteousness and contempt. We are, as Haidt (2012) remarks, bound to "political teams that share moral narratives" - and once we have accepted a particular narrative, we "become blind to alternative moral worlds". Narratives, fictions, metaphysics – whatever terms we use, the problem is the same: an unnoticed double-standard in our attitudes towards the diversity of ideals. Unfortunately, becoming aware of this bias transpires to be no defense against it. For example, despite calling for a political armistice Haidt displays a blatant prejudice against the Kantian tradition and attempts to dismiss the entirety of Kant's views on the grounds that he may have been autistic – a despicable insult to both Kant and autistic people. Even those who are pushing for a ceasefire continue to mount attacks!

This war is what we call politics, and the only plausible solution must be somehow *prior* to the political: it may have to be ethical. It might be the case, as MacIntyre laments, that there is "no rational way of securing moral agreement in our culture", but perhaps this doesn't mean there is no way to *imagine* moral agreement. Part of the problem, as both MacIntyre and Latour recognize, is that our commitment to pluralism, to multiculturalism, does nothing to help – it simply serves to brush the extent of our disagreements under the carpet. Our basic concept of toleration is merely willful ignorance: we don't want to listen to what the others say, let alone attempt to understand what they believe. But have we even *tried* to genuinely communicate with each other? Perhaps we have been so busy waiting for answers to be developed by experts that we have failed to notice that the really big problems we are facing don't need ingenious technical solutions, they need consideration, discussion, and commitments from *everyone*.

Whether our politics have failed us, or we have failed politics, our situation isn't going to improve without a major change in our approach. Politics to MacIntyre is little more than "civil war carried on by other means". Wood (2008) admits that "no argument about ultimate value can be expected to convince everyone". Midgley (1984) laments that the world is "riven with feuds, quarrels and misunderstandings which are not at all in the interest of most of those engaged in them". Latour (1991) declares that "denunciation and revolution have both gone stale". We have fought each other to a standstill! Let us lay down our arms for a while and take better stock of our situation. If the moral law cannot save us, perhaps we can try moral chaos.

4

Wild Ethics

Mosquitoes, Mice, and Me

In the weeks before I started work on this book, my wife and I discovered our house had been colonized by field mice. I'm not sure how they got into the house, but most likely it was through the old metal grate above the cellar drain since we have certainly acquired two extra residents this way in the form of a pair of frogs. The frogs are most welcome to make their home in our basement since as insectivores they are allies in my lifelong battle against mosquitoes, but the mice were rather less gracious house guests.

We had been harboring suspicions that there were mice living in the walls for quite a while – the occasional scratching behind a skirting board, and my mother-in-law's declaration that she had seen a mouse on the kitchen counter. I investigated after that report, but since I could find no droppings I dismissed it as a false sighting – without any spoor, it's hard to pursue the hunt. But when I discovered that a bag of dog treats stored in a basket had been chewed away to mere fragments leaving only a tattered bag of mouse droppings, the ambiguity fell away and we knew we really did have unwelcome visitors.

The situation escalated when I walked into the kitchen one evening to find six stunned eyes staring back at me: it seems our rodent squatters had been busy, as there were suddenly juvenile field mice at work in almost every room of the house. Many of the new arrivals were spectacular unconcerned by our presence. One evening, while dozing off on the sofa, a pair of them repeatedly climbed a power cord up to the shelf where the dog treats had been kept and scouted around unsuccessfully before scurrying down and off into the corner again. Our original mouse would never have been so careless – only my mother-in-law's soft footed approach had managed to startle her the first time!

My wife and I, with occasional help from our toddler son, mounted a number of spirited attempts to corner mice, but we frequently underestimated their talents – they can not only climb almost anything, but they can jump more than a foot, and squeeze through holes of absurdly small diameter. Several humane traps utterly failed to capture anything, although I eventually found a metal device that seemed promising and eventually yielded success when deployed tactically: noting the routes the mice were regularly moving along, I positioned the trap in that path and sure enough they stumbled into it. This proved a productive strategy, and I began to catch mice, releasing them far from our house.

In addition to my regular household routines was added a new duty: driving to the nearby nature reserve to release captured mice. It all felt slightly absurd – especially doing so one night at midnight – but hanging over me at all times was my consenting to my wife that if we were unable to remove them ourselves we would have to call in professionals to poison them. This did not sit well with me. Although I did not become a vegetarian as a result of animal cruelty concerns (my horror at the resources squandered in raising cattle for meat had proved sufficient motive), I have always strived to be compassionate in my dealings with *every* creature I encounter.

Well, *almost* every creature. All my life, mosquitoes have sought out the deep echo of my heartbeat and feasted upon my blood. They leave me with itchy welts and a resentment towards an insect some say has been responsible for more human deaths throughout history than any other cause. Indeed, as Christine Korsgaard quips, "collectively speaking, the mosquitoes may get us yet" (Korsgaard, 2012). Because of this vendetta, I kill any blood-sucking bug I find at home. The sentence for even *looking* like a mosquito in my house is death.

What interests me about my feud with this particular insect, and my forcible deportation of mice, is what this says about my relationship with other living things, and also what this might imply about everyone else. As I say, I am a vegetarian by diet, and by intention kill no animal. I do, admittedly, make some compromises – my dog food is not vegetarian, for instance, a situation about which I am conflicted, and I own a few pairs of leather shoes. Still, farm animals are at less risk from me than from me than from most other humans, although I certainly fall short of vegan moral standards in my dealings with livestock. You might say that I aim to minimize the deaths of other creatures that my own life will cause, while recognizing that I cannot have no impact at all. In the most extreme perspective, after all, my being alive at all is taking food away from *something*.

However, when it comes to dying at my own hands, the mosquito is the only animal subjected to my vengeful wrath. I have used almost every weapon that can be found around the house against them – shoes, newspapers, jets of water, even an improvised flamethrower made of an aerosol canister – and I feel nothing but the satisfaction of getting rid of the irritating pests whenever I do so. Although I would draw the line at some insane plan to eradicate all mosquitoes (perhaps by a viral agent or genetic engineering), I do not otherwise feel any moral obligation towards those insects that resemble mosquitoes. Yet I feel moral obligations not to kill every other creature, at least directly. I would never expect anyone else to feel or behave the same way as me on this, yet I do consider my moral stance in this matter to be defensible, or at the very least more tolerable than the alternatives.

How can this be? How can I defend my own ethic of death when it directly conflicts with everyone else's so flagrantly – whether we're talking about the meat-eater's slaughter of livestock, or the vegan's cries – elevated to an anthem by

Morrissey and Johnny Marr – that 'meat is murder'? These disputes may seem trivial, but they are indicative of much wider issues in ethics that we need to pry open and examine carefully. In the case of my leniency towards field mice, other people could certainly accuse me of being unethical – after all, if you call mice pests (or worse, agents of disease) you can claim I have a duty to stop them from breeding, to end their lives for the good of everyone who lives around me (or around where I release them in the wild). You could also claim that I have a duty to the field mice to end their lives *humanely*, which is to say, painlessly, but few will take my side and feel obligated to mount a rescue attempt for the mice, and those that do will have strong ideological reasons for making such a case.

The presumption of a moral law requires a clear right or wrong on such issues. Indeed, the most frequently repeated aspect of Kant's moral system is his concept of *ethics as universal*. This, as we will later see, is only a very small part of Kantian ethics, but it also happens to be the part with the most commonly accepted, intuitive meaning. As Derek Parfit (2011) notes of two of Kant's ways of expressing the idea of *universal ethics*, they "develop the ideas that are expressed in two familiar questions: 'What if everyone did that?' and 'What if everyone thought like you?'" We who live in societies whose moralities have an intimate familial relationship with Kantian ethics are well accustomed to thinking in these terms, even if we are not consciously aware of Kant's ethical system as such.

Parfit – ever the revisionist – also offers this updated version of one of Kant's formulas for universal ethics: "It is wrong to act in some way unless everyone could rationally will it to be true that everyone believes such acts to be morally permitted." On this wording, I am wrong to try to rescue the field mice, since there are people – exterminators, for instance – who rationally believe what I am doing is wrong. "What if everyone did that?" they can say. "We'd be overrun with mice, food would be eaten up by the hordes of mice and it would be a catastrophe. People could starve to death!" Indeed, this scenario is not entirely idle, although as will become clear it is not much of a risk today.

In ancient Egypt, the agricultural boom provided by the regular seasonal flooding of the Nile led to huge storehouses filled with grain, which inevitably attracted mice that – given the immense all-you-can-eat buffet that had been laid on for them – proceeded to breed into apocalyptic numbers. Indeed, the association with plagues and Egypt that the Bible has helped solidify likely has its roots in this kind of natural history. Fortunately for the Egyptians, the mice attracted their traditional predator – a kind of wildcat that was delighted to feast upon the mice, but left the grain alone. Cats are socially territorial, and as Donald Engels (1999) suggests of the above episode in Egypt's history, the cats:

> ...would soon strike up associations (if not exactly friendships) with the humans and come to regard the area around their homes as their own. Thus it was just as much a factor of the cats adopting the humans in their territory, as the humans adopting the cats.

Cats saved Egypt from starvation, and indeed from other disasters as well! The Greek historian Herodotus (circa 440 BC) tells the tale of an attempted Assyrian incursion into Egypt that was foiled by a plague of mice that ate all the invaders bowstrings. The Egyptians, who lived closely with cats, avoided this catastrophe and thus possessed a major tactical advantage against their aggressors, allowing the home team to win a decisive victory. The esteem for cats felt by Egyptians can be felt not only in their honoring of the cat-goddess Bastet, but in the practice of mummifying the cats of the wealthy so that they might join them in the next life.

Here my tale of mice and me takes a strange turn, because

while I worked hard to escort the mice safely off my property before time ran out and they faced extermination by poison, if my wife and I lived with cats at the time we would never have had this problem. We had both lived with feline friends growing up, but I was nervous about having a cat in this particular house because of its proximity to two major roads – having lost many cherished pairs of whiskers to cars growing up, I found it difficult to commit to bringing one into this particular place. Yet there's an obvious and strange contradiction in my behavior here, for if we had cats *they* would have certainly killed the mice, and not painlessly either – almost every cat lover has had the unpleasant experience of watching as their beloved kitty tortures and eventually kills a small rodent for its own amusement.

I have to compare the feelings I have about having a hypothetical cat who would have slain these rodent interlopers to the feelings I had when an attempt to capture a mouse with my weapon-of-choice (a pint glass) went disastrously awry. I keep a store of peanuts in the kitchen because I have a lifelong love of squirrels, both the red squirrels that are native to Britain and which I grew up with on the Isle of Wight, and the invading grey squirrels that thrive in the British parks and countryside. I often leave some nuts in the garden, and at times have fed both garden birds and visiting squirrels by hand, when I have had the time to build up sufficient trust.

One day I came into the kitchen and heard rustling from the shelf where I kept the peanuts – a cubby hole I had thought impregnable to mice because there was no viable approach. Yet there in the wooden recess was a mouse who had somehow defied my expectations and leapt from the microwave oven onto the shelving unit and found a rich store of tasty nuts. Armed with my trusty pint glass, I attempted to scoop him up, but he leapt from the shelf onto the work surfaces, and from there to the floor. I fell to my knees and brought down the pint glass to ensnare him – but I must have misjudged my angle because although I successfully caught him inside, he began to twitch and shudder. I must have struck the glass edge against his tiny skull and caved it in, and after a few horrible moments he was still. Even now, a long time after these events, I cry when I think about killing that mouse, even though it was an accident and I had what I believed were his best interests in mind as I attempted his capture.

Hence the strange paradox of the mice. Killing the mouse upset me – still upsets me – yet if I'd had a cat, watching it slay the mice would have been unpleasant but it would not have reduced me to tears. I have seen many a vole, mouse and similar critter abused and mangled by many a cat, and even if my sympathies were aroused in these cases, what I mostly felt was mild disgust at the gory spectacle. *I've never shed a tear for a mouse before that day that I killed one by my own hand.* There is a temptation to dismiss this observation as trivial – obviously we feel greater emotional connection to our own circumstances than to those of others, but this issue really isn't as simple as it first seems. I have cried for plenty of entirely imaginary beings in books and movies, and I have also been reduced to tears imagining the circumstances of people whom I have neither contact with, nor plausible means to do so. The question of what arouses our sympathy deserves a philosophical treatment that goes beyond and beneath our initial instinct to dismiss its importance. Indeed: that dismissal may be the most significant aspect of this entire mystery.

What's more, the day before the exterminators came to unleash their toxic weaponry against our visitors, I had another chance to capture one of the baby mice with a ceramic receptacle. The mouse in question had been poking around our shoe pile, and I was able to maneuver her into a corner and thus imprison her under a coffee mug until I could safely transfer her to something suitable for her journey to the nature reserve. The relief I felt, knowing I had saved her from the poison – even though it was exceptionally likely she would die in the fields as a victim of a fox, a cat or even just the bitter cold of winter! I find it very difficult to defend my behavior as rational – yet I do not have much difficulty defending it as *moral.*

Here once again is an example of what I am calling moral chaos. Law Ethics have terrible difficulty dealing with our relationships with other animals, although I greatly admire the work Korsgaard (2004, 2012) has performed in demonstrating that Kantian ethics can be made compatible with a concept of 'animal rights', and may indeed require such extension to remain consistent with itself. If I am to defend my actions and responses in the case of the mice – not to mention the mosquitoes – I will need a Chaos Ethic to do so. The purpose of this chapter is to investigate what moral fiction or ideal could possibly provide a justification for calling my relationship to the mice 'moral'. But before we can explore the nature of that morality, we must consider the morality of nature, and this is no small topic.

Having suggested we can view imagination as the key to morality in the previous chapter, there are immediately questions to be resolved about the degree that both moral and imaginative experiences extend beyond humanity. If we accept imagination as the necessary basis for morals, does this mean other animals cannot be moral because they are not imaginative? As I hinted previously, I want to take exactly the opposite tack and suggest that other creatures are not only moral but also imaginative, albeit in radically different ways to us. Only after humanity's relationship with the other creatures has been carefully examined can we fairly consider what was moral about my trying to save the mice from a doom I myself brought upon them. This peculiar adventure requires that we recount the four billion year journey life has taken through moral chaos.

Morality Before Humanity

Can there be morality before humanity? Not only do I claim there must be, the case for this once unthinkable assertion becomes ever stronger the more that the spokespeople for animals study their behavior. Ethologist Marc Bekoff and philosopher Jessica Pierce collectively make a case that there is indeed a kind of morality found in non-human animals – what they call *wild justice* (Bekoff and Pierce, 2009). Indeed, as Peter Singer (2005) has remarked, justice is not a human invention, but originates in animals that preceded our species. Bekoff and Pierce are careful to distinguish between morality as it is experienced by humans and the more general kind of moral intelligence that wild justice denotes, but nonetheless argue that drawing a line at humanity to demark the boundary of morality would be a gigantic error:

> Eleven elephants rescue a group of captive antelope in KwaZula-Natal; the matriarch undoes all of the latches on the gates of the enclosure with her trunk and lets the gate swing open so the antelope can escape. A rat in a cage refuses to push a lever for food when it sees that another rat receives an electric shock as a result... A cat named Libby leads her elderly, deaf, and blind dog friend, Cashew, away from obstacles and to food. In a group of chimpanzees at the Arnhem Zoo in The Netherlands individuals punish other chimpanzees who are late for dinner because no one eats until everyone's present... Do these examples show that animals display moral behavior, that they can be compassionate, empathic, altruistic, and fair? Do animals have a kind of moral intelligence? Yes, they do.

If we have morality before humanity, an obvious question to ask is: how far back can we go and still find something like morality? Rather than attempt to draw a line and claim 'No Morality Beyond this Point', I want to leave this question entirely open and pursue a rather different strategy, using the living mythologies of the sciences to trace the connectivity between the capabilities of the earliest forms of life and the abilities of animals today in order to show that humanity does not represent the beginning of morality, but merely its most sophisticated expression thus far. What's more, the reason that human morality exceeds that of the other animals is not because we are 'more moral' than other creatures – it would be just as easy to make the converse claim – but simply because our powers of imagination outstrip everything else in the living world.

Our story begins some 4,600 million years ago, when our planet coalesced out of the gigantic cloud of dust that was the remnant of previous stars that were themselves made up from the dust of previous stars (Heger and Woosley, 2002). Such is what the astrophysicists, the spokespeople for the stars and planets, report on the basis of our theories of physics and a vast number of complex computer simulations (Lyra et al, 2010). In fact, this nebular hypothesis was originally developed in the eighteenth century – and it was Immanuel Kant (1755), building on the work of Emanuel Swedenborg, who advanced it! The details of this theory have swayed back and forth a little over the last few centuries, but for the most part it is clear that the stars and planets are becoming ever more reliable witnesses to their origins as our physical theories increase in sophistication. Stars, planets, rocks, water... all these things had to be in place before we could get to what we have chosen to call life.

The spokespeople for the rocks use radiocarbon dating to suggest that life as we understand it appears to have begun on our planet sometime between 3,850 and 3,650 million years ago – and indeed argue furiously with one another over who has the more reliable witness in this matter (Tenenbaum, 2002)! Those who speak for the microbes report that something truly amazing happened just a few hundred million years later: the first cell appeared (Koch and Silver, 2005). Everything alive on Earth today is related to one of these early cells, a concept captured in the dry phrase 'Last Universal Ancestor' (Theobald, 2010) and rendered in Darwin's original speculations with more poetic prose suggesting that "probably all the organic beings that have lived on the earth have descended from some one primordial form, into which life was first breathed." (Darwin, 1859). Whatever else we can say on behalf of our primordial ancestor, we can at least say it was rather similar to contemporary bacteria, and that *every living creature you have met, seen or read about is related to it.*

Some truly remarkable things happened between 3,500 and 1,500 million years ago – and as Lyn Margulis (1970, 1994) correctly predicted, it all happened because of unprecedented co-operation between single celled organisms (although it's hard to find reliable witnesses to help establish timings). Firstly, two different kinds of cell formed an unlikely partnership creating a different kind of bacteria with a tough double cell wall (Lake, 2009). Next, although there is some dispute about this, two cells partnered together to create a new kind of organism which divided its labor, so that everything associated with managing DNA could be delegated to what is termed the nucleus (Margulis et al, 2000). Then, another cell joined the party and took upon the management of energy production in what is called the mitochondria (Thrash, 2011). Finally, and perhaps as a direct consequence of this previous union, this remarkably sophisticated alliance of cells began to find new ways to group together beyond forming mere colonies of identical cells. Thus around 530 million years ago we reach what is called the Cambrian explosion and the first wild experiments with the kind of multicellular life that would lead ultimately to every moral creature that ever lived.

Thus we have gone from a world without life, to simple chemical replication, to cells, to bacteria, to complex cells, to life as we know it. In the sense we usually use the word, imagination does not apply to our single celled ancestors (and our unthinkably distant cousins, the bacteria who are even now the most successful organisms that ever lived). However, I want to extend this term so that we can reasonably claim that the origins of imagination lie with the single-celled creatures by coining the slightly clumsy term *premagination*. According to the spokespeople for microbes, "most organisms – even bacteria – can sense sound, light, pressure, gravity, and chemicals" (Parkinson, 2002). When an *E.coli* bacteria swims towards glucose, I want to say it does so because it imagines (in the most primitive conceivable sense) that it is heading in the right direction – or at least, it *premagines* this. My only purpose in saying this is to extend our understanding of imagination *across the entire pre-history of life*, so that we can better appreciate both our connectivity with our ancestors, and the extent to which we exceed their capacities in a few crucial ways.

How do we go from the primitive perceptive capacity of bacteria and their kin to the incredibly versatile capacity for fiction and make-believe that humans possess? It may be helpful to work backwards through the varying degrees of imaginative capacity, connecting each to the earlier form of imagination it has developed from. In the case of make-believe, the immediate predecessor is straight-forward belief. Tamar Szabó Gendler (2008b) offers a simple summary of the philosophical concept of belief, suggesting that whatever it might be it can be recognized by its inherent motivation to 'track truth'. Belief offers a model of the world, one that is sensitive to observations of it such that the content of someone's beliefs, all things being equal, will be subject to revision if contrary evidence is encountered. I have suggested that for humans this sense of belief – the attempt to imagine what is true about the world – is effectively a *special case* of make-believe. In both belief and make-believe, we imagine a state of affairs – belief is characterized by an additional constraint, namely that what we believe is also imagined as true (Bateman, 2012).

However, if we turn our attention towards other animals it becomes less clear that we can distinguish make-believe from belief so easily, because the classic examples of make-believe – children's games, toys, and, following Walton's make-believe theory (1990), novels, plays, movies, games, and representational art in general, do not manifest in any obvious way. I am willing to leave open the question of whether dolphins, dogs, ravens and so forth can make-believe in some sense (and indeed, in the case of dolphins and dogs their games *could* be understood in this way), but perhaps a bigger stumbling block is that philosophers have been rather reluctant to accept that such animals can *believe*, let alone make-believe. Just over a decade ago, Alasdair MacIntyre (1999) found it necessary to argue against the prevailing trend in philosophy that assumed that language use was a requirement for belief, and thus that (for instance) a dog who has seen a cat run up a tree and waits at the bottom for it *does not* believe there is a cat in the tree.

MacIntyre, drawing on work by John Searle, argues that the attempt to exclude other animals from belief obscures the way human belief frequently depends upon pre-linguistic capacities that it is unproblematic to connect to the behavior of other species. Philosophical objectors have assumed that belief is the same as the ability to articulate propositions, which is indeed a linguistic capacity. But this confuses the kind of determinate beliefs that can be discussed in propositional logic with belief in general, which is seldom as clearly defined as logical statements. That humans (and, I might impishly add, computers) can manipulate logical propositions is not a reason for denying belief to other animals – if anything, this kind of complaint obscures the fact that human belief rarely if ever operates on stringently logical grounds. MayIntyre makes exactly this point: even when we *can* express propositions in language, we still rely upon a more basic kind of indeterminate belief that we have been capable of since our childhoods, long before we could talk. This pre-linguistic belief is something we clearly share with certain other animals, and our more complicated faculties in connection with belief depend upon this earlier form.

We lack reliable witnesses that might allow us to say how old this more general imaginative capacity of belief might be, but given that we can connect it to many of the social mammals (such as dogs and dolphins), and also to the more cognitively adept birds (such as ravens), we can broadly suggest that it appears either sometime during, or soon after, the time of the dinosaurs. Yet if this supposition is even close to the mark there are a vast range of creatures that were out behaving in various different ways *without belief*. So it would seem we need to connect belief to its preceding imaginative faculty, whatever that might be, or we will have difficulty explaining the actions of crocodiles, fish, and frogs. As long as we can find a plausible candidate for this earlier link in the chain of inheritance, we can set aside questions such as whether or not it makes sense to talk of crocodiles believing.

Gendler (2008a) offers a wonderful term for that form of responding to the world that predates belief, calling it *alief*. She terms it 'alief' because it is "*a*ssociative, *a*utomatic, and *a*rational" and because we share this capacity with "nonhuman *a*nimals" being "developmentally and conceptually *a*ntecedent" to other cognitive capacities. I prefer the alphabetical obviousness of the connectivity between alief and belief, since clearly 'a-lief' comes before 'b-lief'. Gendler's work on alief addresses a number of presumed paradoxes in the philosophical literature that had struggled because of the limitations of thinking either in terms of belief alone, or in terms of only imagination (in the sense of make-believe). But while Gendler (2008b) suggests that some cases of alief do involve imagination, alief itself is recognizably distinct from both belief and make-believe. Alief is a kind of proto-belief, something I have discussed previously and connected to the limbic system (Bateman, 2011), that part of mammal brains that dates back at least as far as the ancient amphibians (Bruce and Timothy, 1995).

Examples of alief in nonhuman animals mentioned by

Gendler include frogs who lap up a bouncing BB pellet as if it were a fly *and do so every time, never learning it is not food,* and puppies responding to the strange young dog in the mirror in front of them. Broadly speaking, aliefs can be understood as "an innate or habitual propensity to respond to an apparent stimulus in a particular way (Gendler, 2008b). On this definition, aliefs probably predate the limbic system as such, since the behavior of fish also seems consistent with Gendler's concept for alief. Although she offers a very precise formula for categorizing aliefs, here I will stick to a simpler form that is parallel to the way we talk about belief, a form she recognizes but generally avoids for reasons of imprecision. In this loose way of talking about alief we can say that when a school of fish suddenly changes direction because one fish spots a threatening movement, the scared fish alieves there is a threat and the rest of school alieves in turning to maintain formation.

Alief is the 'missing link' between premagination and belief, thus completing this lineage of imaginative capacities across billion of years of life. The amoeba doesn't alieve anything, because premagination is simply stimulus and response, while alief entails a basic kind of representation as well as emotion-like states such as fear or desire. Fish, frogs and reptiles have aliefs, but presumably lack beliefs since these entail a model of the world that is (as far as we can tell) beyond their ability to imagine. Conversely, dogs, dolphins, and ravens have both aliefs and beliefs – and these may clash in many situations. When I walk my dog past the pet shop where he was once terrified by an attack from a larger dog he recoils in fear every time, even though the shop in question has long since closed and the dog lives elsewhere. Even when he can see that the shutters are closed and there is no possible risk, his fear does not abate: we can say that he alieves he is in danger, even though he has no corresponding belief.

Notice that although these imaginative faculties build upon

one another, they are never superseded. If my wife takes a flash photograph of me in a dark room, my eyes dilate because of a premagined change in lighting conditions, I alieve a threat as my limbic system arouses in a fear response (perhaps registered consciously as surprise), and as soon as I have had a chance to work out what's going on I believe I have been photographed. I might also make-believe that I look good in the photo, if only to allow myself to feel better about what is sure to be an embarrassing picture. Although we have the most sophisticated imaginative capacities of any species we know about, the cells, organs and other collective functions of our bodies inherit the complete suite of older forms such that we possess the full range of imaginative faculty.

As the degree of imagination increases there comes a point where a creature not only imagines simplistic aspects of its immediate environment, as with premagination and alief, but further imagines that *it is something that matters*. As Korsgaard (2004) puts it: "The strange fate of being an organic system that matters to itself is one that we share with the other animals." On the scale of imaginative capacities I have sketched, this certainly happens when creatures can believe, although perhaps animals can alieve they matter too. Either way, this capacity to value oneself – which is vital for the kind of moral thinking we now take for granted – extends far beyond humans. That said, as my earlier discussions of my emotional relationship with mice highlights, we seem to be able to take this far further than other creatures, and we tend to do so more often than they do, albeit perhaps only because we have the luxury of well-domesticated animals to indulge our imaginations for something other than personal survival.

Korsgaard suggests that our moral values rest upon our instinctive endorsement of the kinds of good we are inclined to pursue by virtue of our animal heritage. She recognizes that this 'animal good' depends in turn upon the sort of good that applies to plants, and that this similarly depends upon "the general, functional capacity for having a good". But this raises a potential challenge to this way of thinking: if this sequence of dependencies is plausible, why shouldn't we think that an implication of our endorsement of personal concern can be extended to a concern for *everything* that has a good? To this, she suggests that "at the risk of being thought a complete lunatic", this prospect is still tempting, since there is no particular reason to think that 'moral standing' is a strictly black and white concept – it might instead have varying degrees and kinds.

She goes on to note that we respond to the moral needs of plants, since "a drooping plant in need of a drink seems to present us with a reason to water it", and notes that when we see a sapling growing in a rock face that seems to beggar belief that any plant could be there, we are inclined to (if you'll excuse my pun) root for it. In a similar vein, Mary Midgley (1978) remarks that our natural sympathies reach out far beyond humanity, noting that "we rejoice in the mere existence of plants and lifeless bodies – not regarding them just as furniture provided to stimulate our pampered imagination." Returning to Korsgaard, she fearlessly pursues her argument to its logical conclusion:

> Or could it even be that we have duties, not only to our fellow creatures, but to our fellow entities? Granted, it sounds absurd to suggest that we might have duties to machines, yet still there is something in the far outer reaches of our normative thought and feeling that corresponds even to this. A general discomfort in the face of wanton destructiveness, a tendency to wince when objects are broken, an objection to the neglect or abuse of precision tools that isn't rooted completely in the idea of economic waste...

Korsgaard considers that it would be easy to dismiss such a feeling as resulting from "a kind of animistic imagination" - we imagine that a tool "feels the badness of being broken" - but she asks that we query what it is that evokes this imagined animism, proposing that it could be "a distant form of respect for functional identity", something we share not just with plants and animals but with *everything*. She ponders whether "we should treat every kind of thing in accordance with its nature... with the kinds of good and bads to which it is subject." She doesn't mention these extended consequences of her argument in order to endorse them or insist upon them – but she makes it clear that she doesn't consider such conclusions completely absurd. Neither do I.

There is something about looking at morality before humanity which leads me inevitably towards thinking about *morality beyond humanity*. As Joanna Zylinska (2009) challenges us to consider: should we respect a carrot? Should we respect a bacterium? These are not idle questions: genetic engineering raises the challenge of whether editing the genome of a vegetable or single-celled organism is something we would wish to endorse, and respect for other forms of life is entailed in moral resistance to this technology. That something is not a moral agent as we understand it is not a de facto reason to exclude it from moral *consideration*.

As a recent debate between plant ethicist Michael Marder and animal ethicist Gary Francione brought to light, it is not so clear that we can draw an unequivocal "line of moral considerability". Marder argues directly for the ethical consideration of plants, at least in terms of methods of cultivation and the possibilities of reproduction. Although resistance to genetically modified crops has primarily been motivated by uncertainties and fears, there is a moral argument that can be made on behalf of cabbages and carrots, and indeed Marder *does* advocate on behalf of plant ethics. Although he is not asking for bacteria ethics, he doesn't consider it absurd, suggesting "we should certainly not reject the possibility of respecting communities of bacteria without considering the issue seriously." It is this wider consideration in the domain of ethics that has been conspicuously absent in moral thought since the Enlightenment.

The more the issues are examined, the clearer it becomes that there must be more to morality than humans respecting humans. The development of imaginative faculty across the history of all life allows us to consider the corresponding landscape of morality across all living things, and the "animistic imagination" that Korsgaard alludes to further implies that our moral concerns could apply to things as well as beings. This is a point that will have to pursued in a later chapter, but for now we are at least one step closer to understanding the moral chaos between the mice and me. To flesh out this rough sketch will require that we begin to seriously consider the morality of the other animals.

The Morals of Cats

A close friend of mine had his life saved by his cat when a fire broke out on the lower floors of his apartment building. He was asleep at the time, and the smoke alarms in the building were not working for whatever reason. It seems his cat was out in the night air, stalking some small creature or other, but when the blaze began he came back into the building and rushed over to my friend's bed, meowing forcibly until he awoke from his deep slumber to find himself in a smoke-filled room. The two friends escaped the building together, although just a year later the cat sadly passed away, possibly in part as a result of smoke inhalation. It may be tempting to dismiss this story as an oddity, but Eugene Linden has collected hundreds of anecdotes of pets rescuing humans that are remarkably similar to this one (Linden, 2000).

There are powerful mythologies in circulation today that seek to exclude cats, and indeed many other animals, from moral agency. Some of these stories simply underestimate the talents of our close relatives, some involve strong ideological commitments that would attempt to undermine any attempt to understand animals *as animals*, preferring (in the most common form) to interpret behavior as something caused by genes. As I have argued elsewhere, this mythic image is utter nonsense, and misrepresents genetics as much as it slanders the animals themselves (Bateman, 2012). While a little caution is required to avoid what is termed anthropocentric thinking, or in simpler terms, confusing animals and humans, for much of the last few hundred years the *opposite* mistake has been made: intellectuals have consistently failed to recognize how *alike* other animals are to humans.

Midgley has been insightful on issues such as these, and her first book, *Beast and Man* (1978), marks a turning point in philosophical discussions about animals. She notes when we are making comparisons or distinctions between humanity and other animals, we are severely limited if we look solely at the other primate species, such as the great apes:

> Primates do not have big cooperative enterprises, nor therefore the loyalty, fidelity and developed skills that go with them. Nor do they have fixed homes and families. But the hunting carnivores do. And neither apes nor wolves have anything like the human length of life, nor therefore the same chance of accumulating wisdom and of deepening relationships. But elephants do. And no mammal really shares the strong visual interest that is so important both to our social life and to our art, nor perhaps needs to work as hard as we do to rear our young. But birds do. This is why it is vacuous to talk of "the difference between man and animal" without saying which animal.

She also makes a crucial point about our ability to understand emotions, a point which applies beyond the narrow confines of humanity. Philosophers of mind have been incredibly timid about private experiences, and extremely reluctant to suggest that recognizing emotions allows us to say something about private experience. I discussed this issue at some length with the philosopher Gregory Currie, who seemed entirely reluctant to give any objective weight to our capacity to recognize the meaning of an emotion, even though doing so would have solved a significant problem in one of his projects. Yet as emotions researcher Paul Ekman (2003) has decisively demonstrated, we share all our core emotional experiences with *every other member of our species*.

Midgley, writing over three decades ago, long before reliable witnesses had been made to speak on this matter, already sensed that we were being too timid when it comes to our emotional experiences, observing:

> Solipsists apart, most of us would be ready to accept that we can know something about human feelings. Ought we to hesitate about extending this ability to our contacts with animals? Do we really not know what they feel? ...The species barrier is, in itself, irrelevant. Members of one species do in fact often succeed in understanding members of another well enough for both prediction and a personal bond. Nothing more is necessary.

In the intervening years, the situation has become far clearer, and it is now quite absurd to apply relativism to our relations with our close relatives and pretend that we cannot understand them – on the contrary, we understand them all too well because we share a great deal of common ground in terms of our emotions. One of the most surprising reports from the spokespeople for molecules has been the quite unexpected revelation that all of the chemicals of human neurobiology (i.e. neurotransmitters) had appeared some 1,000 million years ago, and all of the receptors that go with them had appeared by some 800 million years ago – long before anything like animal life as we think about it was on the scene (Walker et al, 1996). Although the functions of these chemicals often differ from species to species, the common toolbox from which all emotions spring is truly ancient.

Emotions are an essential aspect of our moral lives, and Midgley (2003) makes the point that anyone who had only a theoretical interest in morality, who didn't feel disgust or outrage when considering slavery and torture, for instance, would have "missed the point of morality altogether". Emotional experience is vital to animal morality because creatures like us and our distant relatives, as Korsgaard (2012) attests, *experience firsthand* their own good or ill. But animals also experience *other creatures'* good and ill through experiences that combine imagination and emotion. Empathy is not uniquely human, although humanity certainly seems to be able to take it further than the other animals, and Bekoff and Pierce stress that if we consider empathy as something more than just imagining another being's perspective, we find it present in a wide variety of different mammals – including the domestic cat.

Yet of course the cat can be incredibly cruel, as I mentioned earlier in the context of mice – how can this be squared with the idea that cats are also capable of empathy? It is important to recognize here that the capacity for empathy carries with it no requirement that it will always be in play – indeed, if it did, most animal species would be unable to live, since a significant aspect of animal life is the necessity of preying upon other beings in order to live. The cat is an excellent example, since feline biology is simply not able to synthesize all of the chemicals it needs to survive, and in the wild it doesn't have to since the prey it feeds upon will meet all its nutritional demands.

As Bekoff and Pierce suggest "moral agency is species-specific and context specific", and for the most part non-human animals are moral agents solely within their own communities. In the case of my friend's cat, he was a part of his cat's moral community – indeed, he was the center of his cat's community, and not just because he was an easy source of food. They were true companions. This capacity to desire companionship seems to be far more ancient than the spokespeople for animals have previously claimed, as David Attenborough's loving tribute to the lives of reptiles demonstrates in terms of the community between frogs, the brief intimacy shared between snakes, and the grief of a lizard who has lost its partner (Attenborough, 2008).

However, those who speak for the great double helix molecule DNA attest that something amazing happened some 200 million years ago, near the beginning of the age of dinosaurs and precisely at the arrival of the mammals – something that has made a significant difference to animal empathy ever since. Oxytocin, a chemical that had been around for an estimated 700 million years and is found in both invertebrates and vertebrates (Gimpl et al, 2001) began to develop a powerful new role in securing bonds between parents and children (van Leengoed et al, 1987). What began as a heightening of parental instincts became something that enhances trust (Baumgartner et al, 2008), and although this has mostly been studied in the context of a single species, there are good reasons for believing that this powering-up of compassion at the dawn of mammals extends *between* species as well. Those who speak for molecules confirm that levels of oxytocin are elevated among humans who relate with dogs (Nagasawa et al, 2009), among dogs who live with humans (Handlin et al, 2011) and indeed in *all* interactions between humans and other animals, on both sides (Beetz et al, 2012).

It is lamentably difficult to turn up enough reliable witnesses for events in the distant past – thus far, we have methods to allow the molecules of our genetic inheritance mechanisms to speak, and to allow the rocks to speak, but in the latter case the rocks only remember a little about those creatures that died as they were forming. We may discover additional windows that open onto the past, but I doubt the situation will improve beyond the point whereby we must speculate a little in order to tell stories about the times before storytellers. In the case of the arrival of mammals, I don't want to go beyond the barest account of what must have happened, but taking all our currently available reliable witnesses we can at least say that the appearance of mammals and the transformation of oxytocin to its new role (effectively, heightening the compassion of mammals) are nearly contemporaneous events, at least in terms of time as the rocks record it.

Those who speak for the fossils report that one of the earliest mammal ancestors remembered by the rocks was a small shrew-like creature, known as Morganucodon or 'Glamorgan tooth', after the place in Wales where it was first found (Kühne, 1949-50). It must have done well for itself, since its fossils are found in rocks all around the world. This animal was the direct ancestor of you, everyone you know, and every dog, cat, horse, elephant, whale, dolphin and so on and so forth – every mammal that gives birth to live young, and every marsupial like the kangaroo and platypus. It lived around 205 million years ago, just as the dinosaurs were beginning to take over the multi-cellular world. (Remember that the bacteria, then as now, were the most prosperous forms of life).

Now a shrew and a mouse are rather similar animals – is the reason I was able to feel such strong feelings for the mice in my house connected with my ancestry? After all, my family tree includes animals just like mice if I go back as far as Morganucodon and its immediate descendants. This could be a part of the puzzle, but it cannot be the whole of it, for the cat is just as related to Glamorgan tooth as I am, and cats have no difficulty treating the mice as playthings with no concern as to whether they live or die. But there is something here that we ought to note: we humans (on the whole) find it *easier* to relate to mammals than to reptiles. We relate well to birds, a separate lineage, but tend not to find chicks as cute as we find puppies and kittens. When we compare creatures whose form predates the reptiles – invertebrates like crabs and lobsters, insects, spiders and scorpions, jellyfish and starfish, or even vertebrates like fish, frogs and newts – our capacity to emotionally connect tends to recede. There is a sense that our ability to bond with other animals increases the more the face of the other animal approaches our own in terms of its composition and features, at least as a general trend among our species.

It's important not to get confused by what the spokespeople for molecules report – don't think, for instance, that oxytocin *causes* you to act compassionately. A simple comparison reveals why this would be an error. When another driver cuts you off on the road, you get angry, but the cause of your anger *isn't* the chemical that underpins the emotional experience of anger (what's called norepinephrine). Rather, *what you experienced* is the cause of your anger, and the chemical is just the molecule involved in transmitting your emotional experience around your body. Parts of your brain trigger the chemical in response to an assessment of the situation, and the cells in your body then respond appropriately to this warning flag of a possible impending fight. Similarly, my compassion for the mice was not *caused* by oxytocin but by my experience of relating to the mice – oxytocin is simply the molecule that my body uses internally during my experiences of trust, intimacy and friendship. That said, were it not for the oxytocin I would not have that experience, but the same is true of anger and norepinephrine and we should not mistake messengers for messages. Nobody would think that the cause of redundancy was the letter that informs you of it.

The bonding that oxytocin underpins cements our recognition that the social life of mammals is grounded upon the parental instinct. Hobbes' "war of all against all" ended long before humanity came onto the scene, as Midgley recognized long before the DNA had testified in this matter:

> Creatures that have to deal with helpless and demanding young must be capable of genuine kindness and tolerance. This makes it possible for fellow-adults to tap these resources if they behave in a childlike way. Thus, courting birds continually approach each other with gestures typical of nestlings, and inferior creatures do the same with dominant ones. And mutual relations can be formed, in which both parties can, on occasion, play both roles. It is at this point – long before the emergence of primates – that nature ceases to be Hobbesian. Friendship becomes possible. And it is on such a foundation (however unsuited to human dignity) that the serious business of social life is actually grounded.

Despite the common picture of the cat as a solitary animal, cats can and do form friendships. In Athens, my wife and I noted that it was not just the street dogs who had banded together into packs for mutual support. Sometimes cats form friendships of the most unlikely kind – with dogs, horses, squirrels, rabbits, mice, even dolphins in rare and odd occasions. Some of these species are what we would think of as the cat's natural prey, but given the right circumstances, and an appropriate encounter, the cat's imagination is sufficient to make friends with almost any creature. Nonetheless, cats do not make friends as easily as some other animals! As the nineteenth century French Romantic Théophile Gautier quipped: "It is difficult to obtain the friendship of a cat. It is a philosophical animal... one that does not place its affections thoughtlessly."

Cats are great illustrations of morality at the outer limits of Bekoff and Pierce's wild justice, which testifies to the morality of non-human animals. Drawing from examples taken from a wide variety of animals, they divide wild justice into three clusters: co-operation, empathy and justice. The first of these, co-operation, includes reciprocity, trust, self-sacrifice, as well as punishment and revenge. The second cluster, empathy, includes sympathy, compassion, caring, helping, grieving, and consoling. Finally, the justice cluster includes sharing, equity, fair play, and forgiveness, as well as indignation and retribution. Some of these words may not *sound* very moral – punishment and retribution for instance – but they are intimately connected with conceptions of justice, both in humans and in other animals. In terms of the three clusters, cats are passable at co-operation, show a few inclinations towards justice, and are perfectly capable of empathy, although they are far from the most sympathetic of animals.

Because cats are moral creatures but are not especially prone to compassion, we might reasonably ask: is the morality of cats the minimal ethic? This is the term I am using for egoism, a moral stance that is primarily a form of prudent self-interest. There is something to this claim that the morals of cats are minimal, although it is worth noting that what the minimal ethic might represent for a human is *not necessarily* what the minimal ethic might be for another animal. Because of our talent for imagining, we can have prudential concerns about all manner of issues that are simply never on the menu for cats. Still, part of what people find admirable about cats is precisely their ability to project an aura of self-sufficiency. It often seems that they do only what they want, although what they want often includes a desire for companionship and affection. Whether or not we feel cats are a fit to the minimal ethic, feline morality definitely leans towards it, and thinking this way might make it easier to accept their amoral cruelty when they play with small creatures.

Play, according to Bekoff and Pierce, is a key part of the picture that wild justice paints of the moral lives of animals, since most animals do not play with other animals the way that a cat plays with a mouse, or an orca plays with a seal: these encounters are playful only for the predator, since they are fatal for the prey! However, most animals must reach an agreement *before* playing, since play entails co-operating and behaving fairly. When fairness breaks down, play becomes impossible. Bekoff and Pierce remark that "unfair play is an oxymoron, and this is why play is such a clear window into the moral lives of animals." It is in this concept of fair play that they find justice most definitely expressed, remarking that "if we define justice as a set of social rules and expectations that neutralize differences among individuals in an effort to maintain group harmony, then that's exactly what we find in animals when they play."

The Dutch primatologist Frans de Waal (1996) has shown a particular interest in animal morality, and suggested upon reading John Rawls' *A Theory of Justice*: "I cannot escape the feeling that rather than describing a human innovation, it elaborates on ancient themes, many of which are recognizable in our nearest relatives." De Waal observes that rules and order among animals ultimately derive from hierarchical organizations, within which the subordinates play close attention to the dominant animals (who, incidentally, often take responsibility for protecting those animals beneath them in the hierarchy). He suggests that not every social rule is established via these kinds of dominance rituals, but that this is the general prototype for how a rule becomes a rule among animals – by being enforced by the higher ranked animals. Without the hierarchy, rule-following becomes impossible:

> Without agreement on rank and a certain respect for authority there can be no great sensitivity to social rules, as anyone who has tried to teach simple house rules to a cat will agree. Even if cat lovers fail to see a nonhierarchical nature as a shortcoming – on the contrary! - it does place their pets firmly outside the human moral realm. Evolved as solitary hunters, cats go their own way, indifferent to what the rest of the world thinks of them.

This actually overstates the image of the domestic cat as a loner, since as I've already noted cats are far more social than they are usually given credit. Putting aside their numerous relationships with humans and other animals, they communicate with other cats in their territory via scent markings in a way that some spokespeople for cats interpret as social interaction (Leyhausen, 1978). But de Waal's general point remains: cats lack a respect for authority and a willingness to accede to a hierarchy, which makes them very bad rule-followers. They may have their morals, but they do not form moral systems of the kind we tend to call ethics. For these, we have to look to more social creatures.

The Rules of Dogs

For the first two years of his life, my black Labrador dog was not allowed onto any of the furniture in the house. Instead, we gave him a dog bed in most of the rooms we hang around in, which he will happily use to curl up and take yet another nap. When he turned three, however, we decided to let him onto our bed as a special treat, which he found both confusing and thrilling, spinning around excitedly with his back legs almost folded under his body. What surprised me about this, however, was that having been invited onto our bed, he then felt free to go onto our bed at other times, such as when I was working at my desk. He did not begin to climb onto other beds, nor onto the sofa – only onto the bed that we had invited him onto. It was not that the rule not to climb upon the furniture had gained an exception, but almost as if he had simply learned a new rule 'you can jump onto this particular bed'.

If cats show us a minimal morality for mammals, dogs and wolves demonstrate the extent to which ethical codes are possible without the complex imaginative powers of our own species. Partly this is because dogs, unlike cats, are excellent rule-followers – something they share in common with humans. Vilmos Csányi (2005) observes that human hierarchies, unlike most other animals with hierarchical societies, seem to include both humans and rules in the order of rank. Even those in charge are still expected to follow the rules. Csányi seems to believe that the dogs have inherited this capacity to respect rules from us, which is possible although I'm not sure where we could find a reliable witness for this. There are puzzles here worthy of exploration.

From the outset, the concept of following a rule is much more problematic than it first seems. Wittgenstein (1962) called it paradoxical that we could even hope to follow a rule: "no course of action could be determined by a rule, because every course of action can be made out to accord with the rule." Wittgenstein's interest in rules was part of his investigation into the way we use language, which he insightfully suggested could be understood in comparison to games: when we name an object in most situations, it is a cue for the person listening to hand it to us, or to look at it, and so forth. Because these kinds of games that language-use can be compared to depend upon the context of other people, Wittgenstein denied that it was possible for someone to have a *private language*. He noted that "To think one is obeying a rule is not to obey a rule. Hence it is not possible to obey a rule 'privately'" - if this wasn't so, then *thinking* you were following a rule would be the same as obeying it, which is clearly not the case when an individual has misunderstood a rule. Consider the case of Tennessee drivers who fail to indicate: they may *think* they are following the rules of the road, but they are mistaken.

Saul Kripke picked up Wittgenstein's argument and generalized it to the concept of rules, suggesting that there could be no such thing as *private rules*. Exploring this issue, Kripke suggests that when we say a child has mastered the rule of addition, this is precisely to say that we can entrust them to engage with (say) a shopkeeper in the same way that we do. He adds that "our entire lives depend on countless such interactions, and on the 'game' of attributing to others the mastery of certain concepts or rules, thereby showing that we expect them to behave as we do". The inescapable conclusion is that rule-following is a *social* activity, and precisely the reason that cats are bad at it is that they are too aloof, too independent, they are not sufficiently embedded into a social hierarchy that they can accede to its authority, and this inevitably means they are no good at following rules.

As Peter Lamarque (2010) reports, Wittgenstein and Kripke's philosophical investigations "moved into the mainstream of both ethics and aesthetics" making rule-governed activities a hot topic among philosophers. Lamarque recognizes that at the core of the private rule and private language discussions is the notion of a *practice* which can ground a certain activity, the purpose of which is revealed in social interaction. Taking the issues in the context of the entirety of Wittgenstein's work, Lamarque cites Thomas Morawetz (1978) to suggest that the relationship between games and rules is only a special case of practices - "we need to invoke practices in order to understand the possibility of having games". Practices require a background of understanding to work, and this background is socially constituted. Bartosz Brożek (2012) makes the same point: rule-following has to be understood as a *communal* practice, and further suggests that this ability develops from the more basic capacity to imitate.

Now in the case of dogs, this rule-following capability cannot (as Csányi suggests) have been acquired from humans, although it almost certainly has been *heightened* by this association, because dogs have plenty of practices that they enact with one another, and they share these with their closest relatives, the wolves. In particular, the rituals of play – the submissive bowing of the head, the raising of the tail – are things that most dog-relatives share. A juvenile wolf will even attempt to play with a coyote, which is more often a prey animal for wolves, precisely because they share common body language – they share the same practice in respect of play. Living with humans may have expanded the range of practices that dogs can take on, but they were already primed to do so, precisely because they are a social species.

It is this ability to share practices among a social group – which need not be species-specific – which forms the basis for the systematic forms of morality that we tend to call ethics. An ethic is a practice, and as such can always be *expressed* in rules, although some practices may become badly mauled by this kind of representation. This is the essential tension between agent, rule and outcome-focused ethics in a nutshell: the nature of the practice that forms the core of any given ethic is what gives that ethic it's most distinctive qualities. The imitation of moral role-models for virtue ethics; the upholding of the rules for duty ethics; and decision-making for consequentialism – everything inside the ethical triangle depends upon certain practices to make the relevant moral claims meaningful. There is no morality without practices, and practices depend upon a capacity for imagination that sets limits to the moral fictions available for any given creature.

Cats, I would suggest, can conduct something close in form to agent-focused ethics, even if this does not rise to the complexity of virtue ethics. Dogs can do this as well, but have the additional capacity to engage in rule-focused ethics, at least within the context of their own 'pack'. Outcome-focused ethics, however, require a degree of imagination not found outside of our species as far as we can tell – the capacity to mentally simulate future situations to an extent that this might be used to reach a moral decision. These three forms of ethics form a kind of continuum, from that which requires the least imagination (virtue ethics), through that which requires a considerable social imagination (duty ethics) to that that requires the most imaginative speculation (consequentialism). It does not follow from this that consequentialism is superior to virtue ethics – actually, the opposite conclusion is just as defensible. We will return to this point later.

The rules of dogs, like all rules, are socially instituted practices. The core of such practices for dogs and wolves are dominance hierarchies, which are essential to both mammal and bird societies – and these involve another practice, namely simulated aggression (Midgley, 1983). Aggression is rarely aimed at killing another animal, and is much more commonly about securing space. But aggression is common to all animals that establish dominance hierarchies. It seems that "species incapable of mutual attack do not, apparently, ever find the occasion to become friends" (Midgley, 1978). It is important to understand that such hierarchies can be deeply contextual – an animal low in rank in one context could still be high in another, and being low in a hierarchy can also mean that you are protected by those above you. Midgley notes the relationship between these hierarchies and justice:

> ...the lot of subordinates is not especially oppressive. Dominant members in general really do protect them by coming forward to help them when danger threatens, whether from outside enemies or from other members of the group. In the latter case an interesting and very common pattern is for low-ranking members to be rescued from middle-ranking ones by those higher still – a situation that clearly holds part of the material for human justice and government.

Thus we return to wild justice, and specifically Bekoff and Pierce's justice cluster. Wolves express the justice cluster far better than cats. Robert Solomon (1995) suggests that wolves have "a keen sense of how things ought to be among them", paying attention both to individual needs and the needs of the pack as a whole. Those wolves and coyotes that won't play fair find themselves unable to get others to play with them. They co-operate closely in their hunts, and share the kill according to their social order. Wolf morality is both agent-focused and rule-focused, reflecting a code of conduct that is never articulated except by actual practice, and which guides all the animals within each pack. "Wolves are agents only within this context", Bekoff and Pierce suggest, and the boundary of their community is the boundary of their moral world – their *home community*, as I will put it, is comprised solely of wolves. What happens outside this is of limited moral relevance to the wolves, and when they prey upon an elk, Bekoff and Pierce propose that this should be taken as amoral, "not subject to condemnation or accolades".

Without disputing its essential amorality, I shall call this predator-prey relationship the *predator ethic*. We must consider it carefully if we are to understand not only what goes on between different animal species, but also what goes on between humans and other animals – not to mention humans and other humans. The rules of dogs expands upon what could be found in the moral of cats – and just as wolves are moral agents only within their home community, so it is with cats. The practices of morality are always situated within a specific community, which also means that pragmatically there are always exclusions to any applied moral standard (a point to be explored in the next chapter). What the predator ethic brings to light is that there are radically different ethical standards *outside* any given home community – and in this space of exclusion, it becomes much harder to call what happens *moral*. We are now in a far better position to begin to think about not only my relationship with the mice in my home, but about humanity's relationship with all those many species that have the misfortune to be judged vermin.

Worse than Predators

When the shrew-like Glamorgan tooth was around, 205 million years ago, it was undoubtedly a prey-animal for many other creatures around at the time. With respect to its predators, its moral status was that of prey, which implies a relationship *worse than* that of the minimal ethic of egoism in so much as the minimal ethic implies co-operation for mutual self-interest. Predation cannot meet this requirement in terms of individual animals, although a case could be made more abstractly: as I suggest elsewhere, when the fox preys upon the rabbit, it gradually refines the possibilities inherent in the rabbit, to the benefit of rabbits in general (Bateman, 2012). If it seems confusing that we can specify ethics that are worse than the minimal ethic, remember that egoism is minimal solely *within* a given community of beings, possibly even just within a community of humans. It is the minimal required for living together – it is not the lowest ebb of moral concern by a long shot, since anything *outside* of any given home community can be subject to far worse standards of care.

Is the predator ethic still an ethic? Yes, because it is still a moral system of some kind. Indeed, it not only designates some creatures as prey, it also excludes certain creatures from being preyed upon – wolves, for instance, do not eat other wolves; the expression 'dog eat dog' speaks more to humanity than to canines. It is tempting to call the predator ethic the 'Cthulhu ethic', since H.P. Lovecraft's horror mythology is very much about putting the reader face-to-face with creatures of immeasurably greater power and unthinkably less concern for human life – hence the endless implications of horrific jaws, maws, claws, fangs, and tentacles, all images of predators from the perspective of their prey. I suspect Michael Moorcock (1987) is onto something when he suggests that Lovecraft appeals to us most when we are depressed because it is only then that the hopelessness of his fictional world matches our own melancholy.

For the next two hundred million years, those descendants of Glamorgan tooth that remained mouse-like were subject to the predator ethic in their relations with a great many other animals. Only in the last century has the situation for mouse-like animals become significantly *worse*, as humans went beyond using cats and traps for killing mice and began to deploy poisons as well. Mice, rats, and so forth are deemed vermin, and as such are considered to have either *no moral status whatsoever*, or at best are deemed not to deserve a painful death and are thus treated 'humanely' (which in the case of vermin means 'killed painlessly'). This use of 'humane' makes it sound as if the mice get a better deal from us than from cats by focusing on *how they die*. But the cat leaves open the possibility, at the very least, that an artful mouse might survive. Once humanity begins deploying poison to manage vermin, the mouse is effectively excluded from living *anywhere that humans live* – which is to say, just about everywhere, with the notable exceptions of those mice kept as pets or laboratory test subjects. From life under the predator ethic they become subject to the *extermination* ethic, which goes beyond simply having no moral judgment on how to treat an animal and demands their death as morally necessary.

Human relations with other animals are at their most positive with those animals we share our homes with – such as cats and dogs, and those pet mice that are excluded from consideration as vermin. The status of these animals is legally equivalent to slavery, since they are deemed property, although for individual cats and dogs the situation is usually far better than this. (Actually, this has often been true of slaves, human or otherwise: as came up in discussion of the Vikings, those taken as slaves would still be a part of the family, although many of those captured by Vikings would have been sold for money). However, in the case of livestock – animals who are raised for food – the situation is worse than that of pets and may be better or worse than the predator ethic depending upon the conditions they are kept on. Battery chickens, for instance, live in a state of squalor that must be judged far worse than the conditions of wild poultry subject to predation, and might even be judged worse than it would be under the extermination ethic if living in appalling conditions is judged worse than a 'humane' death. Thus at the lowest ebb of humanity's compassion for other animals we find the *exploitation* ethic – just as deadly as extermination in the long run, but far beyond the euphemistic niceties of 'humane' treatment.

As can be seen, our moral relations with other animals are generally not something we should be proud of – for the animals affected by it, the extermination ethic represents a situation at least as bad as the predator ethic, and given the sheer *scale* of the solution offered to vermin it is pragmatically far worse than predation for those animals who fall under its deadly remit. The exploitation ethic adds to the assurance of death the certainty of a life barely worth living. It would not be hard to judge life in the wild as superior in every way for the animals concerned, even though being killed and eaten by a predator is far from a desirable occurrence. We can and should ask questions about our relations with other animals precisely because we seem to have failed to notice just how badly we treat them. As Zylinska recognizes, our ethical stances toward other forms of life are "often violent", even in some cases "inevitably violent" - we may have the *capacity* to engage emotionally with vastly more and different kinds of creature than the other animals can, but we do not exercise this capability very often. It remains an open question whether we should.

Midgley (1978) suggests a pragmatic acceptance of humanity's instinct to place its own concerns ahead of other animals, noting that all animals are embedded within conflicts of interests and within such disputes "we have to take sides, and are entitled to put our own species first". She suggests that this is something all species have to do, since no animal subsists without killing some others, if only by out-competing them for food. We cannot avoid harming other animals (including humans), but Midgley stresses that we ought to recognize that such injuries *matter*. We should attempt to avoid doing so whenever no adequate reason can be found to justify it. In later thoughts on the subject, she develops the idea that the home communities of humans often include other animals, albeit usually with a lower status than the humans within that community. Midgley uses the imagery of a set of concentric circles to suggest that we all develop very *different* moral communities, with different beings included at different 'distances' from the center points of our individual moral worlds (Midgley, 1983). The cat-lover's moral community contains cats, and the dog-lover's moral community contains dogs, for instance.

What is practically included in these varied communities is not a matter of rational decision: it is "purely social and emotional, and a lot of it is mere chance." For almost as long as humans have been around, they have chosen some animals to accept as friends – and different societies have chosen very different animals to welcome in this way (Midgley, 2003). Part of what makes our species so unusual is precisely that we befriend other animals on a scale that surpasses every other creature on our planet (Midgley, 1983), and as a result our home communities are constituted in a great many different ways, with different creatures at different metaphorical distances from the centers of our worlds – no wonder Donna Haraway (2003) calls us a 'companion species'.

Indeed, as well as accepting many more different creatures into our home community, we also have many more circles of care because we can imagine relating to many more different kinds of being and also imagine relating to beings we never actually meet. We can say that as well as our home community, almost all of us also have an *outer community*. We may act in preference for those creatures within our home community (our family, pets, and friends, for instance), but there is less of a sharp termination at the edge of our concern. For many of us humans, our outer community (in theory at least) extends to include all humans and has done ever since the legal abolition of slavery.

When it comes to humanity's relationship with other animals, those that make it into our home communities often get well-treated while the composition of our outer communities is extremely ambiguous and vast numbers of species are subject to the extermination or exploitation ethics. The minimal ethic, which supposedly marks the boundary of human morality *towards humans*, requires *nothing* in respect to other animals, and before the twentieth century the majority of moral systems in common usage had essentially no moral position on non-humans (at least outside of those parts of the world with influence from religious practices such as those of the Hindu, Jain, and Buddhist traditions).

In Richard D. Ryder's famous phrase, popularized by Peter Singer, we humans are 'speciesist' - we are prejudiced against other animal species (Singer, 1975). This rhetoric has done much to mobilize defenders of other animals into political action, while simultaneously hindering their cause by alienating the vast majority who have (unsurprisingly) not been persuaded by blanket accusations of prejudice (Zamir, 2007). This has, in fact, been the pattern of almost all contemporary political movements surrounding moral disagreements, a theme that we will return to in the next chapter.

Morality as Hesitation

In my encounter with the mice at the beginning of this chapter, I found myself compelled to act against what I felt was the rational course of action, and more than this I felt that what I was doing was the only course of action I could defend as *moral*. This conclusion seems to outstrip everything moral philosophy has to offer – even Midgley's image of our home communities as a set of concentric circles doesn't seem to quite apply to the mice since I never thought of them as part of my home community, as I do my dog, my family or my neighbors, nor even really as part of my outer community like humans living in (say) Tibet whom I've never met but still care about abstractly. But then perhaps my outer community is quite a bit more accommodating than most people's – after all, the only creature I definitively exclude are the mosquitoes, which I can and do kill. And even in respect of the mosquitoes, I *still* have some distant circle of care set aside for them, as I would not wish them extinction.

To conclude this discussion of wild ethics requires that I attempt some kind of justification for calling 'moral' my attempt to rescue the mice from a poison I myself summoned. This is rather implausible under a Law Ethic, but even as a Chaos Ethic it is a difficult question. It stacks up badly under consequentialism, which is far more likely to assess the costs of letting vermin live as outweighing any emotional desire to save them, and the contrast case if I had a cat in my house makes the rule-focused approach equally unlikely to bear fruit. It seems I need some kind of agent-focused ethic to defend what I did, and compassion does not, in and of itself, seem sufficient to the task, although it has to be part of the explanation. What kind of virtue could it possibly entail?

In a messy but extremely insightful paper, Émile Haché and Bruno Latour (2010) develop a distinction between *moralism* and morality that will help resolve my problems in respect of the mice – although it will in turn throw open a veritable hornet's nest of new problems. They propose a pair of orthogonal axes for examining moral issues – in the first dimension, a concern for the range of *distributions* of beings that are capable of having moral relevance for us, and in the second dimension, a range of *intensities* that are produced in response to those beings. They seek to make a distinction between a 'moralism' that draws a hard line between humans and other entities and a 'morality' that attends more to the second dimension than the first. What they call 'moralism' is attentive to the first dimension – the distribution of beings – but ignores the second. Conversely, they advocate a morality that attends to *both* dimensions, but is more attentive to the second dimension – the intensity of feelings evoked by such beings.

They are particularly scathing with their accusation of 'moralism' in the context of a quote from French philosopher André Comte-Sponville, who asks "Which is worse: to slap a child or to gouge out a cat's eyes?" and concludes that while the cat can be something moral theory thinks about, it is not a moral creature because it cannot ask such questions – questions such as "Which is worse: to scratch a child or to tear a mouse apart?" Comte-Sponville concludes: "Cats have no morality, nor any words with which to realize it." Against this stance, Haché and Latour accuse Comte-Sponville of refusing to even consider or investigate the cat as a possible moral creature – in his writing, the cat doesn't "have an opportunity even to meow". It is not allowed the chance to become a reliable witness in its own case: "The author speaks in place of his cat, not in its name. He does not lend it his voice as a trustworthy spokesman for a puss he knows well but speaks in its place on the grounds that it has nothing to say on the matter."

Haché and Latour approach these issues with the suggestion that we need to be more sensitive to the capacity for other entities to evoke responses in us – that we need to cultivate a moral *sensitivity* towards our fellow creatures in place of the dismissive attitude that places a boundary at the human and treats everything outside as necessarily excluded from the moral world, essentially by definition. Equipped with clearly defined moral systems, we speak and act with moral confidence that allows us to *ignore* a whole range of things that are excluded from moral consideration – specifically other animals, and indeed, the rocks and other inanimate elements of our world. This is what they condemn as moralism. Against this, they suggest that we can judge whether morality is present in a situation precisely by how much we pause in our encounters with other entities – indeed they suggest that this *hesitation* "may be said to define morality".

The *hesitation ethic* that Haché and Latour suggest asks that we not presuppose what may or may not be involved in the good. It asks instead that we hesitate in the face of our encounters with other things – yes, even with the rocks! - in order to discover for ourselves what might be morally good. That an animal lacks the depth of our imagination is not enough to exclude it from morality, as Bekoff and Pierce's wild justice demonstrates. Even that something *cannot* feel is not enough to eliminate it entirely from moral consideration, as Korsgaard foreshadowed in her talk of our reluctance to break tools. Shall we grind all mountains into gravel simply because they have no feelings? No, even the mountain may be involved in what is good, as with the rivers that spring from the meltwater from Kilimanjaro, bringing water where it otherwise could not be found. When we hesitate in morality, *nothing* is definitively excluded from consideration.

This morality of hesitation is a virtue ethic – or perhaps just a virtue, although we lack a synonym with clear overtones of goodness for it, since to hesitate is not always virtuous. As Haché and Latour point out, it is the virtue of having *scruples,* since a scruple is precisely a feeling of doubt or hesitation regarding which is the right course of action. Sadly, 'scrupulousness' has not maintained this sense of the merits of uncertainty, and has become little more than a synonym for righteousness, hence I suggest sticking with 'hesitation' and using *hesitancy* as the title for the virtue in question. We can contrast this moral hesitancy to indecisiveness or irresoluteness. To hesitate in the relevant sense is to resist judging in advance what we can or should morally respond to. Conversely, indecision carries the implication of not knowing what to do, which may also be moral but may not involve scruples, and irresoluteness is simply a failure to stick to what one has chosen to do. To be hesitant need not imply being irresolute, although someone who was uniformly resolute about their behavior could not display the virtue of hesitancy.

This ethic of hesitation is clearly a Chaos Ethic in the terms I am developing, for it is entirely uncertain of its own content or implications, and Haché and Latour's indictment of moralism is clearly an attack on Law Ethics. However, there must be more to this situation than simply praising the moral chaos of the hesitation ethic and condemning the certainty offered by the moral law. If this were not so, Haché and Latour would fall prey to the accusation leveled against them by Stephen Mulhall (2009) in his response to their paper: if sensitivity to other beings is the alternative to the limitation of morality to humans alone, there aren't two dimensions at work here at all but just one – moralism versus moral sensitivity.

The point Mulhall perhaps misses is that while Haché and Latour only need the distribution axis *in this case* to demonstrate the insensitivity of a purely humanistic ethics, the twin dimensions of distribution and intensity are intended to be far more general than their paper has space to explore. For example, Wood and Kosgaard's different approaches to other animals open up questions concerning distribution of moral status, but do not significantly attend to questions of intensity, while Midgley opens up both the distribution *and* the intensity to scrutiny in her account. But all three hesitate in their relations with other animals – they just do so in different ways. As Tzachi Zamir (2009) suggests in his response to Haché and Latour's paper, there are different kinds of moral responsiveness at work in sensitivity to other beings on the one hand, and in concerns about the distribution of moral concern on the other.

What Haché and Latour condemn as moralism are the current exclusions implied by what I am terming Law Ethics, but their account leaves open the possibility of a Law Ethic that still hesitates. If morality is hesitation, in the sense explored here, a Law Ethic may hesitate over its allocation of moral concern just as much as I hesitated over my treatment of the mice – indeed, Korsgaard's attempts to bring other animals into the scheme of Kantian ethics strikes me as just such a hesitation. It is easy to condemn as heartless those who are not open to the intensity of an encounter with other beings, as I was in the case of the mice, but I balk at the suggestion that they are morally wrong to do so. Actually, it seems to me precisely the case that my hesitation over the mice was not as helpful to the plight of mice as Korsgaard's attempts to extend the moral law to encompass other animals, including mice. Her arguments may yet extend the home communities of others to include mice; my hesitations only saved a few mice from being poisoned. We were both, I would claim, acting morally – but in very different ways.

Perhaps surprisingly, the responses to Haché and Latour's discussions of this ethic of hesitation have been most damning when they have come from those who claim to fight on behalf of animal ethics. Zamir (2009), for instance, complains that making an appeal to sensitivity is pointless since it can speak only to those who are already won over by the claims of other animals. "One begins by responding to particular animals, leaving unparticularized billions to be slaughtered, maimed, and maltreated," he complains. This is the claim of a supporter of a Law Ethic that renders its distribution of moral concern very differently to the mainstream views, but it is a view just as at-risk to moralism – specifically the moralism that allows an animal activist to emotionally abuse a fellow human on the basis of the perceived harm to other animals they have caused (although Zamir does not endorse this kind of behavior).

This brings to light the more general issue: those who are fighting for animal ethics do so, almost without fail, under the banner of Law. Although prepared to ditch the rhetoric of 'speciesism', Zamir is quite explicit in his support for a rigorously argued ethic that will end the mistreatment of animals, but I cannot for the life of me understand why he thinks his strategy can be successful while Haché and Latour's Chaos is doomed to fail. If the elevation of the human to the center of the moral stage under the influence of ideals of equality failed to prevent the atrocious treatment of humans by other humans, how is a re-imagined moral law going to prevent the dreadful treatment of other animals by humans? As Mark Rowlands (2009) remarks in his response to Haché and Latour: "the same insensitivity... is also characteristic of our dealings with our fellow human beings." The problem of insensitivity, as Rowlands recognizes, isn't constrained to our failed relations with other animals – it is also at the heart of our failed relations *with other humans.*

Haché and Latour's concept of sensitivity has something to offer morality, whether we are considering other animals or just other humans. It is the idea that even at the boundaries of our outer communities, whether we are talking about humanity as an abstract whole or some wider collection of entities, we cannot afford to be entirely deaf to the cries of those who are excluded. In *The Politics of Nature,* Latour suggests two roles for those concerned with morality: the *moralist* and the *diplomat.* The diplomat is tasked with dealing with the uncertain task of negotiating between different groups of beings – including humans, other animals, and inanimate entities such as cars and concrete – in the attempt to work out what the best of all possible worlds might be. This path, which I suspect I am walking, requires the ambiguity of Chaos Ethics. The moralist, on the other hand, is charged with the uncomfortable knowledge that every solution offered will be imperfect and will need to be immediately replaced with something better. Someone or something is always excluded – and the moralist feels an outrage on behalf of what falls between the cracks of our societies that drives a never-ending process of reform. "For the moralists, we can never call it quits." (Latour, 2004). This path, which Kantians like Wood and Korsgaard are walking, benefits from the confidence of Law Ethics.

However, in the context of animal ethics, which is to say the attempt to expand humanity's outer community of care, it is far from clear that moralists can be successful. As Timothy Costelloe

(2009) alludes, there might be "limits to how far beings different in kind can be brought into the same moral universe" - even if we passionately believe in ending the horrors of factory farming and support campaigns for the ethical treatment of animals. Wood and Korsgaard have the advantage of a Law Ethic that shares significant presuppositions and intuitions with most humans – in part because Kant's moral mythology has become a significant part of our contemporary world via conceptions of rights. Zamir's approach to animal 'liberation' is primarily outcome-focused, but it is still a Law Ethic – he comes as a moralist to demand better treatment for those animals we mistreat. But the disregard of other animals he and others argue against comes about in part because of a Law Ethic that prioritizes humanity via ideals such as equality, and Law Ethics rarely if ever replace one other because different visions of the moral law are always built upon rival premises. Slavery could be legally abolished *because Christians appealed to other Christians within the same Law Ethic,* not because one Law Ethic replaced another. This option is not available for animal ethics, and as a result it may ultimately fall to the diplomats to use Chaos Ethics to renegotiate relations, rather than moralists to furiously demand change.

Let me close this discussion by returning to the relationship between myself and other animals. I cannot quite square my actions in respect of the mice with the thought that if my family included a cat, I would have been spared all my Hamlet-like hand-wringing and moralization since my cat would simply have killed the mice, and that would have been that. But my sensitivity to the mice would not have ended just because my decision to accept a cat into my home community made it difficult to allow mice into my outer community – I would have grieved for the mice after the cat had mauled them just as I grieved after I accidentally killed one with a pint glass. But I suspect my feelings would have been weaker in this case, as the bystander charged with burying the corpse rather than the person found guilty of 'mouseslaughter'. Many of my friends who live with cats still feel sympathy for the small rodents their felines kill, and some have even endeavored to rescue mice before their cats find them.

The enigma of my emotional response to the mice is no longer mysterious in the light of sensitivity and hesitation. As Korsgaard foreshadowed, we humans possess an imagination capable not only of viewing ourselves as something that matters but capable of viewing *anything* as something that matters, and this is coupled with a capacity for compassion that also exceeds what other animals seem capable of – perhaps precisely because our imagination allows us to morally relate to a far wider range of entities. But despite these capabilities we usually do not exercise them, in part because to do so for all the animals that humanity interacts with would be to be endure exposure to the horror of the exploitation and extermination ethics. Those that argue for animal ethics, like Zamir, Rowlands, and Mulhall cited above, often do so from a position of acute awareness of *what* is being ignored – as can be felt in Zamir's teeth gnashing over the billions of animals that are "slaughtered, maimed, and maltreated". The intense sense of injustice that arises from imagining horrific situations that are already happening has extreme importance to a great number of apparently insoluble ethical situations, and not just in connection with other animals: we will meet it again in the next chapter when we are ready to face down the issue of abortion.

In my situation with the mice, I came face to face with the gruesome consequences of the extermination ethic, and because I did so personally, in an encounter with the actual animals, my emotions were all the more aroused. It is possible that I am particularly sensitive (in Haché and Latour's sense) to other beings, since they have always engaged my imagination, interest and compassion. Wherever I have travelled in the world, I have related to squirrels and birds and foxes, to frogs and lizards and snakes, to fish and squid and lobsters, to dragonflies and spiders and scorpions, and to humans almost as varied in habit and lifestyle as the other animals I have met! My house growing up was always a menagerie, and my exploration of the world has always been a disclosure of the incredible diversity of life that shares this planet with us. I, like many other humans, experience an unusual intensity of emotion in my encounters with other beings because of this sensitivity, and this is especially so when the encounter involves other animals because my outer community has always contained – despite the terrible tensions this evokes! - all of humanity *and* all the other animals too.

Well, all the other animals, except for the mosquito. I kill mosquitoes because they are entirely excluded from my moral community. We use words like 'vermin' and 'exterminate' to express our willingness to kill those creatures that lie beyond our threshold of care, and revile those who would take a similar view on other humans – or at least *say* that we do. Our relations with other animals (and with other humans) change as our ideals change, as our mythologies change to reflect the new worlds we are constantly creating and destroying. Morality is not static, but that does not render it a mere illusion, as Nietzsche's abyss seemed to threaten. Wild ethics have been developing for four billion years, and our species is only a recent addition to the moral world. We live among many other beings, and since our relations with the other creatures are both diversely composed and forever in flux, the scope and implications of morality – like the constitution of our home and outer communities – are subject to perpetual change.

5

Moral Horror

Unmarriage

Marriage has been steadily losing popularity for some time now. A great many of my friends are in long-term, committed relationships, but few are married. Having children makes no difference in this respect: they continue with the now-ridiculous relationship roles of 'boyfriend' and 'girlfriend' even though they have obviously made a long-term commitment to one another. They are, to my mind, already married in the practical sense. They have just refused to ratify it publically because, as far as they are concerned, they see no reason to elevate an entirely personal matter to the level of the community, or they denounce marriage as the State interfering with their private affairs. I call friends in such situations 'unhusband and unwife', and the state of being in a relationship that is eerily similar to marriage yet is not ratified as such 'unmarriage'.

In the eyes of many conservatively minded people, unmarriage and single parent families are often seen as indicators of the decline of the morality encapsulated by the phrase 'family values'. Say what you will about such conservatives, on the issue of marriage they have remained remarkably consistent. Those that have a strong view on the topic would like men and women to get married before having children (or even before having sex), and they would like *only* men and women to get married. The liberal overreaction to this position is that whoever opposes gay marriage must overtly or covertly be homophobes – it's essentially impossible for committed liberals to understand why anyone would want to preserve a traditional institution that dates back millennia for the sake of the institution itself.

Labeling conservatives 'homophobes' is a way of dealing with the incomprehensibility of alien morals by mentally distancing those who hold them – much as conservative Christians sometimes deal with liberal political campaigners by labeling them 'Godless'. Of course, liberal intolerant tolerance applies to far more than just the defenders of traditional ideals of marriage and conservative bigotry is in no way limited to gay people, but in the context of unmarriage this entrenched hostility offers a particularly interesting window into the nature of contemporary moral conflicts. In the first place, it is one of the clearest examples of a contemporary clash of ideals since different conceptions of both equality and marriage are entailed in the dispute over marriage reform. In the second place, it is a quintessential example of cognitive dissonance.

Whenever someone has to deal with two radically different ideas or values, the result is a state of intense discomfort, known by spokespeople for the human psyche as cognitive dissonance (Festinger, 1957). Imagining that those people whose beliefs strongly conflict with our own are radically different from ourselves is, researchers suggests, one of three standard ways of alleviating the painful confusion associated with this kind of internalized conflict. The other two are to persecute those who embody the problem, or to adopt the relevant alien perspective (as with peer pressure). In other words, when facing a point of view that we cannot comprehend or that clashes with our own fundamental beliefs, we either exclude those who hold those views from our outer community or we attempt to join *their* community by abandoning our old mythology and accepting a new one.

Although cognitive dissonance is discussed in a variety of situations, in the context of morality I want to focus upon those situations where the discomfort is so intense that it manifests as fear, anger or hostility. I shall call this *moral horror,* which means nothing more than intense cognitive dissonance caused by contemplating radically incompatible values. Moral horror occurs around almost all of the major political battlefields that are moral in focus, including abortion, suicide, war, capitalism, and of course, gay marriage, and it happens to people on *both sides* of such disputes. It is a cause of great problems, but it is also a source of great possibilities, since I am doubtful that slavery could have been abolished or that women could have won the vote were it not for the moral horror that powered the outrage necessary to precipitate change.

There is, alas, still considerable prejudice against trusting emotions, resulting in part from the contrasting of emotional experience to mental experiences – heart versus mind. It is assumed that the mind is reliable and the heart is not, although having explored metaphysics and the authority of Science this already seems like a suspicious assumption! It is important to remember that moral emotions, as Sabine Roeser (2010) points out, are themselves a source of reflection and of rationality – they relate to the kinds of complex narratives we tell about ourselves, which is to say, our personal mythologies. The experience of indignation, Roeser notes, means having both a feeling *and* a judgment, and cannot be reduced to an emotion responding to an initial mental verdict: "Forming the judgment and having the feeling go hand in hand". Our moral judgments are always mental *and* emotional at the same time, and I do not share Peter Singer's faith that our moralities would be improved by a Vulcan-like suppression of emotions (e.g. Singer, 2005).

The moral horror of conservatives in the face of gay marriage is quite understandable once it is recognized that the institution of marriage is what puts the 'family' into 'family values'. Whatever tries to change the meaning of 'family' intolerably distorts the moral world of someone whose home community is built upon an ideal of family life, of parents and children, but also grandparents, cousins and so forth too. This particular family ideal is not identical with the other family ideals that have been passed down the various (mostly religious) traditions that practice marriage, but it is considerably closer to its antecedents than the opposing ideals that are used to defend marriage reform. That *different* ideals are in conflict here, rather than different versions of the same ideal, is a key point that is often overlooked.

A great many liberally minded people don't care one jot about marriage, which is why they often prefer unmarriage to the traditional alternative. The sole reason marriage has come to matter to such people is because commitment to the liberal ideal of equality engenders moral horror when anything is approached from a perspective of asymmetry. Thus despite being fairly cool on, or even openly opposed to, the institution of marriage, a great many liberals suddenly care deeply about *gay* marriage, because they believe everyone has a right to enter into an archaic legal and religious arrangement, even though they themselves don't actually believe in it. Questions concerning what a family is or should be are irrelevant to this issue from a liberal perspective, which is solely concerned with what seems to be a serious inequality.

Unmarriage demonstrates the hilarious nonsense in the contemporary liberal approach to marriage: as far as it applies to themselves, it is antiquated and of no importance. But tell any liberally-minded person that there's some minority who isn't allowed to do it and suddenly it's an outrageous affront to human dignity! While there are perfectly principled ways of defending this apparently absurd disconnect, there is still something disturbing in this attitude whenever it is manifested through knee-jerk accusations of homophobia and other kinds of intolerant tolerance that steadfastly refuse to even acknowledge that opponents might be defending *different* ideals. 'We must have equality!' the liberal battle cry demands, 'except you: your ideals oppose our ideal of equality and therefore you do not get to be treated equally.' It is important to appreciate that the specific ideal being applied here – equality of opportunity in the context of marriage – is of a fairly limited kind, and is certainly not exhaustive of all the possible ways of understanding an equal status between people.

Of course, the conservative attitude towards marriage is often just as incoherent as its liberal counterpoint, but at least in such cases there is a genuine concern about marriage as an institution, something their political opponents cannot seem to fathom. If it is tempting to scoff at all this talk of 'institutions', it is worth remembering that equality, autonomy, and freedom are *also* institutions, political and moral institutions that have emerged in their contemporary forms from the Enlightenment, for all that they have far older roots. Even if it is difficult to accept that freedom is an institution, there is no way of understanding human rights as anything but institutional, as with any matter of law – as with marriage itself. Indeed, it is worth reflecting that, as Ivan Illich (1973) remarks in passing, "marriage laws are no less purposely shaped social devices than road networks." Whatever traditional marriage might *seem* to have been, it has changed over the centuries, and will continue to do so. However, enacting lasting institutional change requires forging new visions of ideals, and sadly for gay marriage no-one can be bothered to do the groundwork.

Unlike many conservatives I support gay marriage because, unlike most liberals, I support the institution of marriage. When two adults are willing to make a commitment to one another founded upon their mutual love, we should support them and help them to celebrate it publically. It should not matter what flesh those two souls inhabit if their love is genuine. It is a far bigger injustice to force such lovers to remain unwillingly in unmarriage than to allow them to marry, whatever their respective genders. Liberal voices have failed to decisively win the argument in favor of gay marriage precisely because they have not made the story about the deep love that exists between committed (gay) partners. Instead, they all too often try to make it about equality, because that's *their* sacred value, and that way the argument seems pre-empted: no further discussion required. This is an appallingly self-defeating way to approach any problem.

If it seems that conservative Christian opposition to homosexuality makes it essential to turn a moral disagreement into a political war, it is worth reflecting that the meaning of a sacred text is *always* subject to new understandings. Leviticus, the book which records the social codes of the Israelites from at least 2,500 years ago, clearly takes a dim view of homosexual acts between men, but the same text also takes a dim view of men who see women that are menstruating, the wearing of garments made of more than one kind of fiber, and the acquisition of tattoos – yet no Christian to my knowledge has declared nylon-polyester clothes an abomination. Furthermore, Leviticus quite clearly endorses the ownership of slaves, something almost no-one advocates today no matter how old school their religious beliefs might be. The vague gesturing at Leviticus that conservative Christians occasionally resort to is shorthand for a very different kind of argument: 'we've always done it this way'. But whatever aspect of religious life is being considered, it is never the case that contemporary practices are directly continuous with the traditional practices they descend from. The maintenance of a tradition *requires* a continual renewal of its institutions.

Slavery ended in the United States because too many Christians were unable to reconcile the practice with their belief in the essential dignity of all people. Slavery ended, despite the fact that Leviticus endorsed it. It didn't matter what the Bible said, because deep down, Christians – even many conservative Christians – have a sense of right and wrong that is rooted in their theology, and that theology is always subject to change. The very essence of Christianity is founded upon this renewal – as anyone who has read and understood the epistles of Paul must recognize. However, no-one is open to persuasion while they are in the grip of moral horror towards what is being proposed. This makes it all the more important that campaigners for change (on any issue) try to *align* moral horror with their cause, and thus create something closer to a consensus on the relevant issue.

This chapter explores the relevance of moral horror to ethics, and particularly its troubling relationship with ideals of equality. Part of my aim is to expose those raw nerves that cloud our judgment of others when they disagree with us on the most emotionally charged of issues. I led off with gay marriage with the expectation that most readers of this book will be inclined towards liberal political views, and my strident rhetoric will hopefully have triggered your own moral horror, giving you a hot flush of righteousness. I could do the same for those inclined to conservative politics just by mentioning abortion. Although these topics are political, our interest in moral horror is ethical – it is what lies under the floorboards of the various political positions that requires scrutiny. Indeed, for much of the rest of the book we must move amidst the political and attempt to discern the ethical, in part by uncovering the sources of moral horror. Recognizing this experience may help us address the problems it creates, but it is also important to appreciate that moral horror isn't something we must seek to eliminate – it is part of our existence as humans, and an essential part of morality.

The problem with moral horror, and particularly in the context of equality ideals, is that too many people expect their own gut responses to transfer to other people. Yet this can never happen when the mythologies in play are radically different, and the outrage ends up blocking dialogue instead of solving the problem in question. This is precisely what we saw in the previous chapter in respect of those most fervent defenders of the moral status of other animals. In situations such as these, we distance ourselves from those who do not share our disgust and anger, and commit to opposing them, closing down any possibility of mutual understanding. Extreme voices dominate the public dialogue, while moderate voices are either unheard, or never speak out. In politics as war, the major issues are all too often collisions between different mythologies, battlefields where two very different manifestations of moral horror collide. In such situations, change becomes all but impossible and intolerant tolerance, or outright bigotry, is the unfortunate residue.

Fictional Values

What motivates us in morality is our pursuit of ideals, and it is these ideals that are colliding in the wake of Charles Taylor's nova effect, the unprecedented diversification of beliefs as expressive individuality offers ever more positions within and between the established traditions. These ideals entail imagination because they are all moral fictions – we bring them to life in our minds through the same kind of mental faculty that allows us to follow the narrative of a novel, pretend that a movie depicts events that actually happened, or dismiss what happens in the context of a game as 'just a game'. Gregory Currie and Ian Ravenscroft (2002) stress the continuity in our imaginative faculty, and distinguish between *recreative imagination* that allows us to imagine other people's mental lives and the *creative imagination* that produces innovation. It is recreative imagination that is intimately connected with our relationship with fiction.

Fiction is a collaborative activity – although we think of the author of a book as the one responsible for stating how everything is in the story, the readers of fiction are still greatly involved in the creation of the imaginary worlds within which these stories take place. They have to be, as so much of the detail of these worlds is left to inference. The practice of reading novels has a close relationship with the practice of writing novels, and storytelling has always involved a certain complicity between the speaker and the listener. As Currie and Ravenscroft draw out, what happens via imagination when we relate to fiction is closely tied to the recreative imagination, which allows us to conceptualize the interior mental world of others – it seems we could not have one without the other, since all stories depend upon this capacity to imagine entering the minds of others.

Michael Tomasello, a researcher specializing in the great apes and small children (and particularly in the similarities and differences between them) has suggested that humans are "the world's experts at mind reading", and that we possess a capacity to share intentions that may be unique among the animals (Tomasello et al, 2005). The great apes may have creative imagination, but they seem to lack recreative imagination, and thus the capacity to engage in activities that require sharing of intentions (Currie and Ravenscroft, 2002). Apparently it's not that the apes don't know that other apes have intentions, it's just that they seem to lack a desire to *share* them, except in very clearly defined tasks, centered upon specific objects (Tomasello, 1999). According to Tomasello and his associates, the capacity to share intentions is the origin of institutional facts like money, marriage and government.

Whether or not Tomasello speaks for reliable witnesses in this matter, the institutional facts he mentions are precisely the kinds of things that depend upon recreative imagination, or to come at the same thing from a slightly different direction, they all depend upon fiction (Bateman, 2011). Don't mistake this for a claim that these things have no objective value, however – as Peter Lamarque (2010) astutely observes, the value of a chess piece is constituted by the practice of the game of chess *and is objective in that context*. Similarly, while money may be (as I like to say) a fictional representation of value, that value is objective *in the context of currency exchanges*, precisely for the reasons Lamarque mentions: the practice (in this case, the practice of using currency to represent value) establishes the relevant value, and anyone who participates in that practice can and does recognize the associated value. Similarly, that marriage depends upon fiction – namely, the prescription to imagine the union of two individuals – does not make the marriage any less real, although it *does* mean that the preservation of that marriage is at risk when the underlying mythology wears thin.

Morality also depends upon fiction, and specifically upon what I have called moral fictions or ideals. As William James (1891) puts it, the "elementary forces in ethics" have nothing in common "apart from the fact they are ideals." Whatever the situation, there is always, as James warned, a 'pinch' between the ideal and the actual; the moral fiction cannot remain unchanged when it is forced out of the imagination and into the world. Great movements, as Isaiah Berlin (1988) suggests, begin with ideas in people's heads about how the relations between humans "have been, are, might be, and should be", and these are the "substance of ethics" - but as Hannah Arendt (1958) warns, no-one can be entirely sure what these movements will do when they actually come out of the imagination and into the world. The very word 'ideal' carries with it a warning about the discrepancy between what we imagine and what actually happens when we act upon it.

Although we cannot avoid using our imagined ideals as a source of guidance, there are always risks when fiction is deployed in this way. In philosophy and the sciences, for instance, thought experiments are often used to demonstrate points or explore new perspectives – consider Einstein's chasing of a beam of light, Schrödinger's Cat, Plutarch's Ship of Theseus, or Descartes' Evil Demon, the modern form of which is the Brain in a Vat, or perhaps those holodeck stories in *Star Trek: The Next Generation* that cast doubt over our ability to tell what is real. Daniel Dennett cautions that while thought experiments can be "wonderful imagination grabbers" we should be aware that "they're not arguments, they're stories. Instead of having a conclusion, they pump an intuition" (Brockman, 1995). However, thought experiments are perhaps the most fun aspect of philosophy, which is perhaps why Dennett, after originally pouring cold water on the validity of thought experiments with the derisive term 'intuition pump' (Dennett, 1984) has continued to use thought experiments throughout the rest of his career.

While there is always a place for more rigorous philosophy, I fear the philosophical traditions would be sorely impoverished if they were to lose all of their colorful imagery. What's more, thought experiments can have direct moral consequences. Indeed, Tamar Szabó Gendler (2007) suggests that it is part of the role of philosophy not only to attempt to ascertain what morality demands of people, but to provide "resources that enable him or her to make the perspective shift that the moral stance requires at the moment of moral decision-making." She suggests this is precisely the role played by some of the most famous thought experiments that have been offered by moral and political philosophers over the centuries, such as John Rawls' 'veil of ignorance'. I heartily agree with Gendler's claims: as Stephen Yablo has persuasively argued, we will never divest language of its metaphors (Yablo, 1988) and we certainly won't gain extra clarity by pretending that we can. Rather, we should make use of those metaphors and ideals that capture our best understanding of what is good – we should, in other words, use the best moral fictions we can to guide our mythologies.

It is worth noting that although 'great movements' have given rise to changes in the living mythologies that underpin our fictional ideals, for the most part it is not that the new mythologies create *new* ideals so much as they shuffle the moral deck and invite a re-deal. Mary Midgley (1991) identifies a number of original moral creations, such as the Christian elevation of charity above vengeance and the contemporary exaltation of freedom, but maintains that in each case a *new* value or ideal was not created:

New words were indeed sometimes used, and old words

> given rather different senses. But this does not involve the creation of new items, any more than the use of new words in the physical sciences involves the creation of new matter. What arises is a shift in attitude, in ways of thinking. The innovators have simply brought forward an existing ideal that they thought had been underemphasized and have shown good reason why it should have more attention as against other ideals, with which it had come into conflict.

Precisely because of the connection between fiction and morality, one of the chief ways that these kind of shifts in ideal can come about is via the arts, and particularly through literature. It is no coincidence that so many religious traditions are sustained by the reading of their great books, whether we are talking about the Bible or the Bhagavad Gita. Even among the non-religious, though, stories and morality are intimately connected. Anna Sewell's *Black Beauty* is not just a novel from the perspective of a horse, it is an invitation *to imagine the world from the perspective of a horse,* and in so doing to reconsider the moral dimensions of animal cruelty (Sewell, 1877). Both the novelists and the philosophers of the nineteenth century seemed to recognize the power of literature – indeed James felt the moral philosopher had to ally with the dramatist, and as Midgley (1984) warns, any conception of the arts that plays down its role in sustaining and renewing morality represents a profound betrayal of this aspect of human life.

For Alasdair MacIntyre, the connection between literature and morality has especial relevance for virtue ethics, which he views as being dependent upon a conception of "human life as a narrative unity". This notion of narrative unity is part of the living mythology of virtue ethics as MacIntyre describes it, in which what is good for an individual is conceived of in the context of their entire life story – an approach diametrically opposed to the concept of series-persons I introduced in relation to my paper time machine. Narrative unity asks that we view the many people we have been as stages in the life of one person, which is indeed the usual way we understand ourselves. Only in such a context, MacIntyre suggests, do the virtues truly have meaning (or, to echo Lamarque, only through the practice of telling life stories do the virtues attain objectivity). MacIntyre suggests there is even a virtue that has no meaning whatsoever without this capacity to imagine the entirety of a human life as one story, namely integrity (or constancy). He cites Kierkegaard's remark that "purity of heart is to will one thing" (Kierkegaard, 1938) to express the relevant ideal: that the concept of a life with purpose depends upon the ideal of narrative unity, of a coherent 'life story' that could be judged as purposeful.

This has a consequence for the series-person concept defended by Derek Parfit (1984), since it is entirely incompatible with this concept of narrative unity. If we think of ourselves solely as different series-persons, we risk lacking integrity since we can disown the series people we were in the past, and thus do not need to take responsibility for them. Parfit seems to view this positively, as a way of being more lenient to those who made mistakes in the past, as well as suggesting that by thinking of series people we can be more conscious of how our actions in the present affect who we will be in the future. There is some merit to this way of thinking, especially given our general difficulty in seeing beyond the present with any clarity – thinking that we have duties to our future series-persons might help us take better care of ourselves, for instance. Nonetheless, we should be cautious whenever we set aside the coherent narrative we tell about ourselves, since *this is the story that tells us who we are*, our own personal living mythology. We should not wish to repeat the mistakes of those existentialists who imagined we could simply re-invent ourselves at will.

Like narrative unity in MacIntyre's account of virtue ethics, all of our ideals are elements of living mythologies. These generally lie in the background of our awareness, where we use them constantly to evaluate situations ('that's not fair', 'she had no right to do that') without usually being aware of where the ideals come from. To make progress in moral philosophy, it will be helpful to conduct some excavation of our ideals – to expose the moral fictions, and establish where they came from. In some cases, the living mythology that sustains an ideal is the same as that which created or discovered it, in others the mythology has changed but the ideal has remained the same, and in still more cases the ideal retains its moral force but it has become entirely divorced from its native mythology.

For Kant (1785), the ideal of equality is founded upon the concept that those beings that are capable of setting themselves anything as an *end* (that is to say, as something to be attained, a goal) have an "absolute worth", which he terms 'dignity'. Allen Wood (1999) explains that this dignity is "a value that cannot be compared to, traded off against, or compensated for or replaced with any other value" - and it is from this line of thought that we get contemporary conceptions of human rights (Demenchonok, 2009). For Kant, this capacity to set any end is part of "rational nature", which he also associates with a capacity to form the representation 'I' - that is, to think of yourself *as yourself* (Kant, 1798). For me, this is not a question of rationality, but a question of *imagination*. I do not want to pre-empt the question of which other beings are capable of thinking about themselves in this way, but neither do I want to deny that humans are more imaginative than most other creatures, and that this might have consequences worth teasing out.

Christine Korsgaard (2004) expresses Kant's approach by noting that because we are rational, we implicitly endorse the principles upon which we choose to act. In conventional Kantian imagery, those principles are 'willed' as if they became universal laws. It is this endorsement (or legislation) which generates value in Kantian ethics – in the living mythology espoused by Kant, it is our acts of *valuing* that are the source of all value, not the other way around. (In Lamarque's terms, the practice of valuing our actions makes the value of our actions objective). Wood supports this interpretation of rationality as the source of value in Kantian ethics – and suggests that this leads to a claim concerning human equality, since as an absolute and unconditional value (an end-in-itself), rationality provides no means for the comparison of those that possess it other than placing them on precisely the same level.

From equality, we can reach other ideals – as when John Rawls (1971) uses Kantian equality as his inspiration for his ideal of 'justice as fairness'. However, we have to be particular careful when we talk about ideals such as equality and fairness: even though we may use the same word, we aren't always using the same mythology. Jonathan Haidt (2012), while prone both to passing judgment in situations where he has no reliable witness *and* to criticizing others for the exact same fault, is at least a trust-worthy spokesperson for conservative values when he is contrasting them to liberal values (not coincidentally, the topic he has spent the most time studying). He notes that "everyone cares about fairness" but cautions that there are *two distinct ideals of fairness.* On the political left, fairness implies equality (as it does with Rawls). On the political right, however, fairness implies *proportionality* - "people should be rewarded in proportion to what they contribute, even if that guarantees unequal outcomes." These two moral fictions – *fairness as equality* and *fairness as proportionality* – both express an ideal of fairness, but it is not even remotely the same ideal in each case.

In this respect, Haidt is correct to criticize Rawls for being misled by his own ideals – but he goes astray in suggesting that Rawls failure was not empirically testing his proposed ideals, as was indeed later carried out, confirming that Rawls assumptions were in error (Frolich et al, 1987). The flaws in Rawls' concept of distributive justice were identified by philosophers just three years after Rawls' first published *A Theory of Justice*, and over a decade before any researchers were inspired to investigate (Nozick, 1974): in both cases, shouldn't Rawls be praised for encouraging further exploration of these ideas? No matter how mistaken Rawls may have been in his specifics, formulating his concepts in his own particular way allowed for all sorts of further explorations, both philosophical and empirical. Researchers no doubt wish philosophers were more like them when it comes to research (Haidt's criticism of Rawls), just as philosophers wish researchers could be better informed about philosophy (my criticism of Haidt) - but no-one expects virtuoso violinists to be good at playing the flute, nor great flautists to be sublime violinists. There are plenty of different instruments in the orchestra, and somehow they still manage to make great music together.

Fictional values lead to real conflicts – genuine problems that do not lend themselves to easy solutions. This is particularly disastrous, as MacIntyre incisively recognizes, when the rule-focused ideal of rights descended from Kantian ethics comes into collision with the outcome-focused ideal of utility that has become the organizing principle behind almost all major bureaucracies, from government to industry and beyond. The impossibility of comparison between two very different traditions – incommensurability – raises its ugly head once more:

> ...protest is now almost entirely that negative phenomenon which characteristically occurs as a reaction to the alleged invasion of someone's *rights* in the name of someone else's *utility*. The self-assertive shrillness of protest arises because the facts of incommensurability ensure equally that the protestors can never lose an argument either. Hence the *utterance* of protest is characteristically addressed to those who already *share* the protestor's premises. The effects of incommensurability ensure that protestors rarely have anyone

> else to talk to but themselves. This is not to say that protest cannot be effective; it is to say that it cannot be *rationally* effective and that its dominant modes of expression give evidence of a certain perhaps unconscious awareness of this.

Arendt (1961) offers an additional problem of a similar form, namely that liberalism "measures a process of receding freedom" while conservatism "measures a process of receding authority" – and both complaints are accurate since "we are in fact confronted with a simultaneous recession of both freedom and authority in the modern world." But in the fifty years since she wrote that, the battle between Law and Chaos that is encountered in the political conflict between conservatives and liberals has ranged far beyond this particular front, and now takes in so many issues it has come to be judged as entirely insurmountable – a conclusion often made by insisting that political opponents 'cannot be reasoned with'.

Within the nova, the clash of ideals seems irresolvable because (as MacIntyre puts the matter) everyone proceeds from different premises. We are all working within very different living mythologies, which support different versions of the same ideals and validate entirely different conclusions about what must be done. If this Gordian knot is to be untied, it will not be by any quick fix – if we simply cut it open, we will just start fighting about who gets the biggest rope fragment! Rather, we need to look at what the knot ties together and work out how we might potentially retie it without making the same mistakes. Something like perspectival truth – the idea that truth emerges from comparing different points of view – is required to allow for the kind of discussions that relativism made impossible, since acknowledging that different traditions offer alternative perspectives still allows some room for identifying mistakes. Even more importantly, it allows that disparate viewpoints might converge on common ground. When it comes to disputes like equality versus proportionality in the context of finances, or equality versus family in the context of marriage for that matter, finding where our ideals intersect helps suggest a way forward.

Equality as Exclusion

Larry Temkin (1986) remarked that there were very few moral ideals more widely discussed, yet less well understood, than that of inequality. Considering how central to moral and political discussions claims of equality tend to be, it would be tempting to think that this was something we fully comprehend, yet as the distinction between fairness as equality and fairness as proportionality highlights, there are so many different ways of misunderstanding similar ideals. Furthermore, there are genuine complexities concerning the questions of fairness as equality: as Midgley (1983) jokes: "Inequalities above one's own level tend to be visible: those below it tend to be hidden." This is more than just a good one-liner though – there is "a real conceptual difficulty involved." We all tend to complain about inequality precisely when we are the ones being treated 'unfairly', and tend to be significantly slower at spotting those situations where it is *us* that are getting more than our fair share.

It is this kind of problem that encourages advocates for fairness as equality in the United Kingdom to point fingers at the British Royal Family more readily than they notice how many of their goods are produced in sweat shops or as the result of other unfair trade practices. But even a clear focus on those below our level of income can render the equality ideal problematic: most Africans live on indescribably less than most US citizens, but the solution to this problem (in so much as it is viewed as a problem) cannot be to elevate the African nations to the wasteful standards of the US lifestyle – this would just make a bad situation worse. Besides, as Illich (1973) recognizes, there is something terribly misleading about a perspective that would judge those nations rich in convivial community as 'underdeveloped' and those where "living has been transformed into a process of ordering from an all-encompassing store catalogue" as 'advanced'. In facing Africa with the equality ideal, it can be argued that we in Europe or North America or Australasia need to be *more like the Africans,* and need to avoid making them more like us.

Much contemporary discussion about morality is predicated on moral fictions concerning the equality of human beings, but by framing the discussion expressly in terms of *equals* complications are always generated when considering those entities that are not deemed equal. The ancient Athenian citizens declared themselves equal – but only by excluding women, children, slaves and everyone outside their particular city-state from consideration. We differ from the Athenians only in those things we choose to exclude before evoking our appeals to equality. The concept of *equality as exclusion* I am suggesting here can be brought into clear focus by returning to the question of our relationship with other animals.

A human who lives with a cat may consider her an equal, but the other humans around are highly unlikely to grant the cat equal moral status! From the point of view of the law, the cat is equivalent to a slave, it is defined as property even though in practice the way it is treated will be far better than what faces livestock. Appeals to equality *always* depend upon a concept of exclusion: to judge some set of beings as equal implies inequality between those beings and everything else, yet it is only by making such exclusions that an equality ideal can be brought to bear on a situation. By asking about the more subtle and complex moral relations we hold with other animals first, we not only get a glimpse of morality outside of the box of equality, but we might better understand the moral fictions upon which equal status is claimed, and perhaps also understand why the appeal to equality manages to fail so often.

In connection with other animals, appeals to equality aren't going to work under any circumstances. Suppose the minimal ethic requires any human to respect all humans, if only as a means of securing mutual benefits such as property. We will struggle to extend this bubble of equality to include other animals, even those that are close to us in certain respects (such as monkeys, wolves, dolphins, and ravens, all of which display intelligence and a moral perspective). It certainly isn't going to be reasonable to offer equality to clams and cucumbers, much less bacteria and slime molds. As Zylinska suggests, the "so-called post-humanist critique" asks us to question our belief that we are the top of the pile and can exploit everything without restriction (Zylinska and Bateman, 2009). It seems quite implausible to expect to solve these kinds of problems with an appeal to equality (although, as we shall eventually discover, there may yet be a way to do so).

Zylinska makes reference to the *great chain of being*, an ancient moral fiction that guided ethical thought for Plato and Aristotle in classical Athens, throughout the medieval period, and up until the Enlightenment. It is a simple concept: all of life can be arranged in a strict hierarchy, with God at the top, divine beings such as angels directly beneath, royalty as the top of the earthly part of the chain, then through the nobility, to peasants, wild animals, trees, plants, and down to the rocks themselves at the bottom of the pile. A similar imagery can be found in China, but it has always been balanced by alternative mythologies that do not express hierarchy (Hu, 2005).

Where this fiction still echoes today, God and royalty tend to have been ousted from the top, leaving the whole of humanity now enjoying the top of the heap. As Slavoj Žižek (2012) quips, the contemporary version of this is the food chain, "the great chain of eating". Plant ethicist Michael Marder makes the same connection between the idea of a food chain and the great chain of being, and makes the further suggestion that it is no longer enough to tinker with the relationships between humans and animals – the whole notion of a hierarchy of moral status needs questioning (Marder and Francione, 2012). This leads him close to the kind of secular animism being espoused by Bruno Latour and others of similar ilk, a view that also resonates with Korsgaard's point about our reluctance to break tools. The moral fictions of the food chain are not a sufficient revision of the great chain of being, all things considered.

In this respect, the term 'top predator' demonstrates how the chain of being's inherent logic of ranked superiority still echoes today, albeit in a degraded fashion. We tend to imagine top predators such as lions or sharks as 'ruling' their relevant environments – hence the expression 'King of the Jungle' (despite the fact that lions actually live on the savannah). But this way of thinking is a rather questionable scientific mythology, and obscures numerous pertinent dependencies and vulnerabilities (Bateman, 2012). Top predator or not, the situation of lions is far more precarious than the grazing animals they prey upon, who must necessarily outnumber their predators by several orders of magnitude. All predators depend upon their prey in a fashion that is obscured by the residual imagery of the great chain of being.

Much of Enlightenment philosophy can be understood as attempts to shatter this old fiction, and the equality of humanity was the key replacement mythology. The cost of this switch in dominant moral fiction from the great chain of being to equality is twofold: firstly, in the great chain of being it was at least established that humans *have a relationship with other animals, rocks and the environment* for all that this relationship was decidedly biased in favor of the human. Secondly, changing the focus of morality to equality – a mathematical concept – invites a thoroughgoing replacement of moral thought with algebraic calculations. This is indeed where utilitarian ethics seem to commence, and because mathematical truth is at root a form of logical truth (Yablo, 2002) turning to algebra to solve moral problems seems to promise an elevation of moral truth to a new plateau of rigor. The dreadful costs of this transposition are explored in the chapter that follows. In both cases, what is added in the move beyond the great chain of being is the concept of a *person* as a holder of equal status, and in both cases it is solely humans that are traditionally taken to be persons.

While the moral fictions of equality successfully elevated the relationship of human to human by deeming all humans to qualify as persons, it did so in part by drawing a hard line between humans and other animals, and attempts to cross back across this border then seem to threaten all the hard-won gains of the equality ethics. Wood (2008) is keen to defend Kant's concept of dignity and stresses that it *need not be constrained to humanity,* stating that any claim that humanity gets its special status as persons solely because it happens to be *our* species "seems no better than regarding as persons only those who share our nationality or religion or skin color." His point is that if other animals – elephants or dolphins, say – showed our degree of rationality (or, in my terms, imagination) - they would *also* qualify as persons. But I suspect that the required evidence for this state of personhood would be an ability to engage with *us* in moral discourse – and this might pragmatically have the same effect as restricting personhood to our species.

In practical terms, Wood is not far from Midgley's perspective discussed in the previous chapter – they offer different justifications for humans preferring their interests to those of other animals, but they both accept that we will have to place our interests above those of our fellow creatures in many situations. Wood, following Kant, offers an objectively-reasoned Law Ethic approach in respect of which animals qualify for dignity, while Midgley offers a Chaos Ethic, acknowledging the immense diversity of animals that different traditions have chosen to exempt from being 'merely' animals. Cats, dogs, and horses, for instance, get special treatment in Europe and North America, while cows and elephants get special treatment in India. Still, both Midgley and Wood also feel a strong pull towards the fair treatment of animals, whatever that might happen to entail. Wood, for instance, is keen to stress the sheer *ambiguity* of our moral judgments in the context of animals who are quite different from us:

> ...when we are unsure what our stance on the pain of some being is, because it is a being whose nervous system is very different from ours, we would seem to have lost our moorings. The line separating callousness from excessive sentimentality seems extremely hard to draw. Those who think anything is obvious here, or that it can be settled empirically in any easy way, seem to me very much mistaken.

Coming at these issues from a Kantian position related to (but distinct from) Wood's, Korsgaard (2006) suggests that the fact that our pre-frontal cortex – a part of the brain intimately involved in decision-making – is more developed than other animals gives us access to powers of judgment and rational thought that provide an *awareness* of the justifications for our actions. It is this capability, she suggests, that separates humanity from other animals, and it is this that we can use to ground our special moral status. Lacking this, other animals cannot participate in moral legislation, although Korsgaard (2004) stresses that this certainly doesn't mean that we never have reasons to extend moral and legal protections to the other animals.

Korsgaard's approach offers a version of Kantian dignity grounded in the sciences (something Kant, as staunch supporter of the value of the empirical sciences, would very much have approved of!). But I don't want to follow this line of reasoning, for a simple reason: it is overly concerned with decision-making. The part of the brain Korsgaard refers to is indeed more developed in humans, and as a result we are capable of making very complex mathematical decisions. But mathematics is not the center of human experience by any stretch of the imagination. Furthermore, the neural structures that are involved in decision-making show dominant usage solely among the most geeky of people – mathematicians, scientists, programmers, and of course, analytic philosophers. Other humans *can* use this faculty, but they rely much more on *other* neural structures in their lives.

Placing too much value on the pre-frontal cortex is to make Plato's mistake of enshrining the Philosopher King on a pedestal above everyone else (Plato, 380 BC). The King of the Nerds is not even capable of ruling *other nerds* (who anyway would not agree with him sufficiently to grant such impertinent authority!). Whatever kind of world we are trying to make, we men and women of geekdom will make excellent spokespeople for those things that cannot speak without the sciences, and we will make insightful advisors on difficult issues, including moral dilemmas, but you cannot seriously expect us to be in charge. We geeks are just too locked up in our own over-developed imaginations. Other skills, far beyond number crunching, are *essential* to any conceivable image of a better world.

However, whatever my disagreements with Korsgaard in the context of human brains, I do not disagree with her assessment that, unequal or not, when we treat those beings that are excluded as entirely exempt from moral concern it allows the most terrific injustice to be perpetrated on other animals. As she suggests, you only have to look at what actually happens in factory farms or experimental laboratories to recognize the horrors unleashed by the suggestion that animals have no moral status at all:

> So long as there are profits to be made, and the tantalizing prospect of expanding the human lifespan by experiments on the other animals, to tempt us on, there will be people who will do anything – anything at all, no matter how cruel – to a

> captive animal. And the rest of us will be guilty of benefiting from these acts whether we want to or not. That's not going to stop because the human race is suddenly someday going to have some giant collective humanitarian impulse (Korsgaard, 2012).

Korsgaard argues that the only way we can protect ourselves from an unjust relationship to our fellow creatures is to grant them legal rights, a view that she develops from Kant's argument that "respecting the rights of the other animals is something that we owe to ourselves" (Korsgaard, 2012). But we need to be careful not to place too much stock in the idea that legal reform can substitute for moral reform – in many areas where equality as exclusion is an issue, the problem is not with the law, as such. Consider, for instance, discussions of intersectionality in feminism (e.g. Garry, 2012), which recognizes that the feminist tradition has been overly focused on the concerns of white, middle-class women, while the concerns of other identities have been marginalized. The feminist campaign has pursued equality for women, but only by excluding a great deal of matters pertinent to other identities that are extremely relevant to a great many women.

The unfortunate point here is that feminist ideals are just as likely to fall prey to the problems of equality as exclusion as any other moral fiction. Sunera Thobani (2007) has criticized the conventional view that what is often called 'the West' has a unique subscription to women's equality. She suggests that "the non-west" is all too frequently presented as being rife with violence against women and gender oppression. Practices that evoke moral horror in a 'western' feminist – such as forced marriage, dowry death, honor killings and so forth – are taken to be essential characteristics of 'non-western' cultures, while the kinds of violence or discrimination that occur in 'the West' are "never popularly defined as emblematic of western cultures".

The result is yet more intolerant tolerance, this time in the form of a mythology of superiority whereby 'western' feminists expect to come to the rescue of poor, oppressed third world women.

This problem exceeds that of gender equality issues, and extends to questions of race and religion. Thobani suggests that the "unrelenting public exaltations of the west in popular culture" are also wed to an "interminable maligning of Muslim men as hate-filled misogynists and Muslim women as abject victims and hapless dupes." Perhaps worse, this mythology is then used as a justification for the detainment, exportation, or harassment of refugees and immigrants, and the simultaneous legitimisation of a foreign policy that conducts war under the auspices of cultural rescue. She is forced to conclude that while the emergence of the concept of a citizen with rights and entitlements is celebrated as an emblem of Enlightenment equality ideals, this has been attained by the devastating exclusion of others against whom unlimited indignities can now be unleashed.

By recognising these problems with the ideal of equality I do not intend to undermine the achievements of the Enlightenment, nor to suggest that the equality ideal is untenable. It might be impossible to attain equality in practice, but we should not withhold our support for a worthy moral fiction just because it is practically unobtainable. Perfect freedom is an ideal we shall never attain, but it can still influence our morality in positive ways. We might, however, need to be more discerning about our criticisms of inequality, and especially careful about the moral horror we feel in the face of the lives of others whom we do not adequately understand. Equalities always come at a price, and we cannot afford to remain ignorant of the cost of exclusion.

Killing Humans

In facing down the problems of inequality and moral horror, the most contentious issues, the most fractious attempts at debate, surround questions of killing humans. It is not surprising that questions of death are the site of a terrific clash of ideals, but what is astonishing is that almost *everyone* today advocates killing humans, with the key differences concerning the circumstances under which we will advocate it. Broadly speaking, the forces of Chaos defend killing humans in the cases of abortion and euthanasia, while the forces of Law abominate both yet support killing humans in the cases of war and capital punishment (although this is at best an approximation for what is actually a labyrinth of complex and contentious issues).

It is prudent to begin by considering abortion, if only because it is far easier to recognize moral horror in this context than in some of the others. To someone who sees the commencement of the human life process in terms of an unborn child, abortion is the murder of innocent child-to-be – the very concept causes moral horror for obvious reasons. But equally, to one who sees the early life process as a physiological state inside the body of a woman and not (yet) as a person, the rhetoric deployed against abortion *also* causes moral horror – especially in the light of the fact that many such people know friends or relatives who have terminated a pregnancy, and the framing of their loved ones as child killers is inevitably offensive.

More than any other moral issue, it is abortion that has driven a wedge between liberals and conservatives in the United States. There is no more contentious issue in contemporary metaphysics, and as with any purely metaphysical argument it cannot be resolved solely through discussion because, as Korsgaard (2012) attests, there is no fact of the matter as to when an embryo or fetus becomes a person. Since the mythologies involved are unlikely to change, it is very difficult to see how the abortion debate could be resolved. Latour (2004) suggests that this "painful debate" might be addressed by an "experimental metaphysics" that puts terms on the table for open discussion, but even then it is far from clear how such diplomacy might be conducted in practice.

Parfit (2011) notes that the mythologics concerned hinge upon how the phrase 'a human being' is deployed. On the one hand, a fertilized egg is alive and a member of the species homo sapiens – hence, it can be argued, it is a human being. Parfit suggests this is like the claim that when the first green shoot emerges from an acorn, it is already an oak tree (albeit a very small one). On the other hand, we could say that a sprouting acorn is *not yet* an oak tree, and an embryo is not yet a human being. Parfit does not offer a solution to this impasse (it is not clear that there is one to be offered), but observes that borderline cases like these help show the limits of the assumption that acts can be shown to be wrong in an "all-or-nothing" way. This is a rare case of Parfit arguing against Law Ethics: he suggests that if every act either must or must not be wrong, then "must it not be similarly true that every man must either be, or not be bald?"

The Vatican is a major voice on the issue of abortion, because on this as with so many issues it adheres rigidly to its own Law Ethic and (at a formal level, at least) refuses to allow for exceptions under any circumstances. The political theorist Bhikhu Parekh, who was appointed to the House of Lords in the UK in 2000, has provided a rare balanced perspective on the Catholic stance to abortion. He suggests on this subject:

> When the Roman Catholic Church insists on the sanctity of human life and rules out all forms of abortion, it is clearly being absolutist, unworldly, unrealistic, and oppressive. However, is also serves the vital function of affirming an important value, nagging our consciences, requiring us to reflect publicly and critically on our moral practices, and forcing us to consider issues we would happily prefer to suppress or ignore. We might, and in this and other matters should, challenge and even reject the Church's views, but this does not detract from the fact that its voice deserves to be

heard with respect.

Parekh challenges the Catholic position, noting (among numerous other arguments) that if the Catholic Church can think in terms of a just war, it should also be able to think in terms of a just abortion. He also observes that while it is free to ban abortion for its followers, it has no right to force this value upon society as a whole – and if it insists on behaving otherwise, then liberals may attempt to force their value of equality of the sexes upon the Catholic Church, requiring the ordination of female priests and even female Popes. Perhaps his strongest argument on this issue is that "banning abortion damages human dignity as much as and to an even greater degree than allowing it" (Parekh, 2000).

The comparison between war and abortion draws attention to a strange peculiarity concerning the morality of killing humans. While liberals generally believe individuals have a right to abortion and euthanasia, conservatives generally believe the State has a right to execute prisoners and wage just wars. It seems everyone agrees in killing humans, we just differ over who and how. It is striking in this respect that if you believe in a right to suicide, abortion is generally unproblematic, and that conversely opponents of abortion are also in the main against suicide. Certainly it is clear that if ending your own life is acceptable in all cases, then abortion no longer presents a moral barrier – suicide would end the life of both the mother and the child-to-be. Under an ethical system that permitted this, abortion could be the ethical choice: if it is despair over the pregnancy which motivates the mother to kill herself, terminating the pregnancy may seem like a morally acceptable outcome.

Because the majority of abortion opponents are operating within some form of Christian ethics, the converse usually holds – both suicide and abortion are abominated, because human life is afforded a sacrosanct status. However, for some reason the majority of conservative Christians in the United States do not extend this status to the condemned. Liberals object to the death penalty not because they are against killing humans (they generally support at least two forms of killing – abortion and euthanasia) but because they are horrified by the number of innocents that are executed by the State, or because they do not believe that the State should have this power over life and death. But again, *everyone* believes in killing humans. The difference is in what kinds of killing evoke moral horror.

My understanding of contemporary opposition to abortion was improved immeasurably when a strange set of coincidences in my own life revealed to me an entirely different situation that brings about moral horror, namely the declawing of cats. This is a fairly common procedure in the United States, although there are many vets who refuse to conduct it and there is far from a consensus in that nation concerning its moral status (Patronek, 2001). For those who live with cats, this procedure is an affront to all they hold dear, as can be clearly seen from any internet search about cat declawing. What struck me about this topic in particular is the way that opponents of cat declawing talk about the procedure – it wasn't just that they are obviously experiencing moral horror, it is that their arguments move in ways almost directly parallel to the opponents of abortion. In both cases, the standard response to cognitive dissonance – distancing those who believe differently by imagining them to be radically different kinds of people – is very much in evidence. Terms like 'barbaric' and 'horrific' can be found in great abundance in discussions of either practice.

I do not mean to compare cat declawing to abortion in terms of the moral status of either – beyond not wishing to be personally involved in either, I don't wish to take any specific stance in this regard. But I do want to make the claim that in both cases, and in many others involving moral horror, what facilitates the state of angry confusion is an imaginative extension of a person's actual home community to the imagined situation under consideration. Thus the cat lover facing the horror of declawing imagines *their own cats* having their claws and associated bones amputated, just as the opponent of abortion pictures *their own children*, whether real or in an imaginary future, having been killed in the womb. This is not necessarily a conscious superposition, but it is emotionally potent all the same. If this claim is correct, it is no wonder that the sense of moral horror in these situations is so intense!

Similarly, and conversely, the defenders of war and execution *avoid* moral horror by excluding the relevant victims from their home community. The enemy in war is inhuman; the criminal is a monster – equality as exclusion expressed solely by exclusion. Since these excluded other people are viewed as not equal, not innocent, perhaps not even human ('savage monsters' or 'vicious beasts'), killing them is not a problem. Conversely, the opponent of war imagines that the enemy is still part of their outer community, or imagines the criminal as if they were someone they know, or feels for the plight of an innocent who has been condemned to death. It is no help to attack this exclusion as the root of the problem, however, since an equivalent exclusion occurs with abortion – the fetus is not yet a child, it is excluded from equality. It is only by making such exclusions that we can defend killing humans in *any* of these situations.

The terrible irony of all these instances of killing humans is that the moral horror that opponents of abortion, euthanasia, war, or execution experience can become a cause of cognitive dissonance in those who accept one or more of these practices, thus allowing *the opponents themselves* to be distanced, marginalized or ignored. As a result, it becomes impossible for dialogue to proceed on any of these issues because at no point is there a consistent image of a common community. The variety of ways that equality can manifest as exclusions becomes in itself a barrier to any kind of productive debate. All these cases are in desperate need of greater hesitancy – both in terms of the relevant victims, and in terms of our moral assessment of those with contrary views on these issues.

The Duty to Die

Both a right to die and a right to life are evoked as a bulwark against the moral horror of unthinkable killing, but neither comes close to the ideal of death that we most desperately need to acknowledge. In the case of euthanasia, the purported 'right to die', conceals an issue that is potentially more serious than any of the others, for all that it is rarely discussed. This particular topic is less about killing humans and more about what we will or will not tolerate within our vast medical bureaucracy. An advocate of euthanasia may want to allow someone whose quality of life is terrible, or will become terrible, to end their life through technical means but this obfuscates their background assumption that medicine exists to *extend human life as long as possible.* This remit is taken – by nearly everyone, irrespective of their stance on euthanasia – as unlimited, and this is another worrying case of cyberfetish that we are all caught up within. It's not unreasonable for people to *want* to live forever – but it would be utterly unreasonable for them to actually do so! It is not our right to die, but our *duty*.

Medical research is not only concerned with finding cures to specific ailments, it also has a wider and more general goal in mind, namely the unlimited extension of human life. This, it is presumed, would be something good that is worth striving for – a moral achievement. But this is a grotesque misunderstanding of life and death and the ethics of both, since to develop technology with this end in mind *must be unethical,* irrespective of which moral system is in play. Whether we consider virtue, duty or consequence, there is no ethical argument that can justify the permanent circumvention of death, as becomes apparent if the question of longevity is examined carefully. We each get to live many lives as many different series-persons, but one of these regenerations is always fated to be our last. Immortality technology is perhaps the most immoral proposition that anyone ever takes for granted, for its advocates forget (either naïvely or knowingly) that death is not only a fact of existence, it is our inevitable obligation.

To defend my claim that there is a duty to die without resorting to some foundational claim that could be disputed, I must show how every approach inside the ethical triangle must reject the alternative – that it is morally permissible, or even desirable, to strive for immortality. I do not have to show that living a long and happy life is wrong, which is just as well as I do not believe this. What I have to show is that dying is good or right, and that refusing to die would be bad or wrong. Fortunately, I don't need to worry about the nihilist who has chosen to leap headfirst into Nietzsche's Abyss, since they have already abandoned morality and thus excluded themselves from our ethical discussions. It is only those who are able to make moral claims that can be subject to ethical constraint, but of course, there are many ways to make such claims.

The consequentialists may seem to be the biggest problem, since most do not recognize any concept of 'duty' and thus it may seem impossible to prove an outcome-focused duty to die. However, the essence of a duty can be seen as having overwhelming reasons to do something, and equally powerful reasons to refrain from doing something, and consequentialists *do* accept that morality can make these kinds of demands. As it happens, an analysis of consequences is the *easiest* way to demonstrate the duty to die. Each day that passes on our planet some 360,000 humans are born and some 150,000 die (Ecology Global Network, 2013): universal immortality would eliminate the latter reduction and thus significantly amplify the rate of growth, accelerating every associated social and environmental crisis. With the compound effects of population growth, the number of humans on our planet would grow exponentially towards imminent catastrophe. This is not an acceptable outcome.

For virtue and duty ethical approaches, it is sufficient to recognize that being alive places a burden upon the world we live in to sustain us, as it does in the case of all animals and plants. This cost is something that we pay for in part by eventually dying and leaving the way clear for others to come after us and enjoy what we have enjoyed. Techno-immortality would disrupt this by forging cyberimmortals who would live, not forever, but for radically extended life spans, many more regenerations than are currently possible. The details of the technology are unimportant, and it doesn't matter if we're talking about extending the longevity of a body or transferring consciousness between them. However it is approached, this dream of living forever is incompatible with freedom in general and reproductive freedom in particular, for if we continue to breed at the same time as we acquire immortality technology the Earth would rapidly become an unsuitable environment for human life, not to mention many of the other species we share the planet with.

For anyone who recognizes an obligation to future generations of humans, the duty to die is straightforward – for all that there may be a powerful emotional desire to resist the idea. A typical way to elude the implications of techno-immortality is to suppose that everyone will want it and thus would willingly give up procreation to get it. This seems like a plausible fantasy only if you fail to recognize how widespread the ideal of family is in the contemporary world, and it is not sufficient therefore to *blame* those who imagine a future with children for the problems that would be unleashed by an utterly undesirable technical solution to human mortality. This would be like blaming a careful cyclist for getting run over by a reckless car driver. It won't do to push back the problem further by imagining, for instance, that we will escape the Earth and colonize the universe, thus giving humanity near-infinite space to expand into. Perhaps someday we will extend our presence beyond this planet that birthed us – but as Lynn Margulis (1998) has warned, this will not happen if we cannot solve our problems here first.

We are left with a small number of remaining positions that can resist the duty to die. Firstly, the minimal ethic (or egoism), which is founded purely upon self-interest, which collides with the duty to die as a tragedy of the commons – if we all try and take too much from the limited pool of resources that are available, we will all lose out. So it is with a technological triumph over death: if everyone has it, no-one has it, since there is no world that can support an ever-growing legion of immortals. In fact, population problems were precisely the context in which Hardin originally raised the tragedy of the commons. He made the prescient observation that there was no technology that might "rescue us from the misery of overpopulation" (Hardin, 1968). As I stated before, the minimal ethic asks only that people act in their self-interest: in a tragedy of the commons like this one, it is not in *anyone's* self-interest to bring about catastrophe.

Secondly, there are those who would advocate some specific vision of immortality that would circumvent the problems – for instance, by enforcing a choice between reproductive capabilities and immortality, or by restraining the technology to the privileged few. Such an approach would not work in most contemporary duty ethical approaches, since it violates ideals of equality, but a virtue ethical or outcome-focused approach might plausibly defend something like this at the cost of equality or anything like it. This is a rather small concession, though, since the radically unequal society it posits can be defended only on entirely selfish grounds. To demand immortality thus entails abandoning morality.

This putative technology of immortality, which we can only hope will prove entirely impossible, is at best difficult to defend as moral and at worst irrevocably catastrophic. Even the extended human lives we are currently offered by medical bureaucracy are problematic, although at least in this limited context it is more plausible that some workable solution might be found, perhaps by forging new ideals of family and procreation and thus accepting that having an unlimited number of children is no longer a feasible proposition. Cyberfetish is a monstrous insanity when it infests our perfectly normal fear of dying and seems to offer a way that we might avoid our own end. We sometimes seem to have run away from the terror we feel facing our own deaths solely by focusing upon arguments over *killing* – such as abortion and euthanasia – and ignoring our duty to die, our necessary stepping aside and handing over this world to each new generation that follows us.

This problem has been growing for some time, as Illich (1975) attests, and stems in part from the substitution of the doctor for the priest in the rituals of death – an appealing replacement in so much as the latter is sometimes erroneously believed to be able to *prevent* death rather than merely being able to postpone it. A fear of "unmedicated death", Illich reports, was first felt by those elites of the eighteenth century who rejected a belief in an afterlife and refused religious assistance. Today, it is so widespread it affects both religious and non-religious alike in those countries where the medical bureaucracy has taken root. Prior to the Enlightenment, our notion of self identity was based, in a manner not unconnected to MacIntyre's link between virtue ethics and narrative, upon the completeness of a person's life span, where death was viewed as the end of a whole. Today, the medical mythology glosses death as a mere interruption of the chain of events that makes up our personal stories, an accidental end to the succession of series-persons that we become, a sequence which we implausibly believe can go on indefinitely.

We have lost the recognition, once universal, that we all *must die*, and with this we have abandoned the art of both suffering and dying that were once cornerstones to human existence. This is not, despite how it may at first seem, a mark of progress, or if it is then progress cannot be seen as a measure of positive achievement. Whereas societies previously taught each individual how to deal with suffering, healing, and dying, now the medical bureaucracy claims authority over all three aspects of life. Suffering and dying (Illich suggests) are now treated as "malfunctions from which populations ought to be institutionally relieved." Under the welcoming wing of the doctor's care, contemporary humanity has unlearned how to accept suffering as part of their experience of life, and instead learns "to interpret every ache as an indicator of their need for padding or pampering." We have lost our faith in our *ability* to die – something we are all capable of doing, and shall indeed eventually do – and it is this in part that has made euthanasia ("the right to be professionally killed") into a major contemporary issue.

Illich summarizes the problem when cyberfetish collides with medicine as follows:

> Medical procedures turn into black magic when, instead of mobilizing his self-healing powers, they transform the sick man into a limp and mystified voyeur of his own treatment. Medical procedures turn into sick religion when they are performed as rituals that focus the entire expectation of the sick on science and its functionaries instead of encouraging them to seek a poetic interpretation of their predicament or find an admirable example in some person – long dead or next door – who learned to suffer.

For all that religion is sometimes criticized for salving people's fear of death, we do not honestly face down the extent that today it is medical science that is the omnipotent ointment for this particular anxiety, being deployed by both religious and non-religious individuals in this role. When this deceptive surrogacy collides with cyberfetish, it takes us towards a fantasy of techno-immortality that is anathema to children, families, and any kind of hope for the future. In the polar extremes that contemporary politics are framed within, to be in support of eternal life is to be *against children*, and even those with no desire to procreate ought to recognize how vital children are to moral living. We forget, sometimes, how set in our ways we become, and how hard it is to change once we reach adulthood. Children, conversely, always bring the possibility of change back into play in a liberating, powerful way. As Arendt (2005) suggests, birth creates new possibilities for us, and we are "constantly dragged into what is unpredictably new by the spontaneity of each new arrival." This is not something we should want to give up, especially if we hope to change the world for the better!

One final example of equality as exclusion may serve as a warning here. Although we should take care when we think about future people, since they currently exist solely in our imagination, we can at least say that to advocate techno-immortality is to exclude *almost all future humans* from equality. Even as it stands, our ongoing industrial degradation of the living conditions on our planet produces an inequality between current and future generations that is unforgivably vast. My son or his children might grow up in a world without giant pandas, snow leopards, black rhinos, chimpanzees, orangutans, Bengal tigers, Indian elephants, loggerhead turtles, bluefin tuna, or blue whales – the largest animals that ever lived. That this might happen because of our collective failure to come to terms with cyberfetish is a scandal no-one wants to talk about. Techno-immortality is the heroin of cyberfetish, and we owe it to the people of the future to kick this addiction while it is only a fantasy.

We do not need to establish a right to die, because we already possess a *duty* to die, a responsibility to give way to the generations that follow us. This duty is inherent in being a living being

– it can be denied only by rejecting the concepts of duty, of virtue, and of good consequences, that is, by abandoning morality entirely. There are certainly some odd orthodox science fiction mythologies around that can envisage a future of techno-immortality, but anyone who lets themselves be fooled by these dreams of undying is as naïve as the most credulous religious follower. We have a severe problem with the human population that fortunately we can all help solve by eventually dying, something that I'm pleased to say we all will eventually do, whether with or without the 'help' of doctors. Our dying won't fix all our problems, but our refusal to die would only make the situation intolerably worse. Although we face moral horror when we consider the killing of humans, this might yet help us imagine a better world where such killing is reduced or even eliminated, assuming we can get our fears collectively aligned. But if we face horror at the thought of our own inevitable death, the only ethical solution is that most challenging of moral demands: acceptance.

6

The Tragedy of Bureaucracy

Institutional Evil

It was quite rare during my wild years to feel that I was not in control of my life, but I have this feeling more and more often as I use the internet today. While working on this book I have frequently run internet searches for papers that relate to my topics, and when I am out-and-about I send myself emails to remind myself to check various points when I am back working on the manuscript. Yet when I go to the search engine to explore, or check my email, there is a red box with a number that pops up, inviting me to look at notifications in a social network. This is something that I don't want to do most of the time – it's a drain on my time, and the majority of notifications are trivial and not worth the disruption. Yet I also have a fairly compulsive streak, and often click on the box even though it's not what I want to do. As a game designer I know full well that the red box is intentionally *designed* to prey upon our instincts, to encourage us to take an action whether or not we want to do so. I am being manipulated against my will by an organization I have no capacity to influence.

The red box is linked to the social network Google+, the search engine I use is Google, and my email is handled by Google's Gmail service. I switched to Gmail on the recommendation of a friend, and I do love the sense of being liberated from the tedium of having to maintain my own email system. What I did not appreciate in making this switch was how much power I was giving a *transnational corporation* to influence my own behavior, as with the siren song of the red Google+ notifications box. Of course, I could leave the social network and delete my profile – scarcely a day goes by that I don't think about doing this – but I have remained, even though I largely feel blackmailed into doing so. Since my blogs rank well on Google's secretive algorithms I gain something of value from them, which becomes clear as advertisers constantly offer to pay me money to link words I have written to commercial sites. Since Google have made Google+ part of their ranking system, they effectively threaten me with obscurity if I withdraw from their network. Google leaves me feeling more trapped than drugs and alcohol ever did. My own cyberfetish is revealed in my constant failure to resist technologies that undermine my own autonomy.

Google famously adopted the phrase 'Don't be Evil' as its unofficial motto, and indeed uses this slogan throughout its official code of conduct (Google, 2012). Inevitably, as it has come into conflict with other people's moral values this adage has been thrown back in their face, whether the issue is freedom of speech in China, prioritizing its own products above its competitors in search results, or forcing competitors out of business by offering excellent free tools it later abandons. Throughout all the criticisms of Google in recent years that have challenged their claim to eschew evil, few seem to have doubted that Google *could* have maintained their ethical stance, whether or not they actually did. A bigger question is not whether Google has managed to avoid being evil, but whether any sufficiently large institution *could* avoid causing evil – and this is far from clear.

Since the early twentieth century, the institutions that have been the target of the most vociferous complaints have largely been the organized religions. Writing almost a century ago, Bertrand Russell expresses the view of many people today when he says of religion "I regard it as a disease born of fear and as a source of untold misery to the human race" (Russell, 1930). Reading Russell, you would think that all that was holding the world back from utopia was the existence of traditional religions, a view that I find incredibly naïve for it to have been held so dogmatically by a thinker who is so generous on so many other issues. I am far more convinced by Mary Midgley's (2003) suggestion that "the evils that have infested religion are not confined to it, but are ones that can accompany any successful human institution."

Midgley's remark bears directly upon the question of whether Google could plausibly avoid being evil, but before we can begin to answer this we either have to resolve what we mean by the word 'evil' or find another way of approaching this question. This is a tricky situation, because even with the Vienna Wall knocked down and Nietzsche's Abyss revealed as deep-but-not-wide we still have no clear way of approaching the concept of evil. Perspectival truth allows for diversity in ethics because it recognizes that what is good cannot be specified too narrowly, but the word 'evil' carries with it a deeper and darker connotation – we cannot get to that concept simply by inverting conceptions of the good. If we view evil as simply the absence of good, it will describe all manner of situations that no-one really considers evil – no-one thinks that a broken hammer is good, but equally no-one would call it evil. There is something stronger about the way we use 'evil' - something that is likely to evoke moral horror.

When the national army and Hutu militias in Rwanda murdered half a million Tutsis in 1994, something truly dreadful happened that seems to deserve the name 'evil', but does this mean that the civil war that scourged that African nation for the previous four years was not evil? It killed as many people. Either way, it is events such as these that seem to be the clearest examples of evil as it is typically understood, and it is notable that in both cases we are talking about *institutional* evil. No individual can commit genocide – it takes an organization to commit something so terrible. This is not to absolve individuals of responsibility for their involvement in tragedies, but it is to acknowledge that the greatest disasters humanity has caused were not possible without the complicity of a great many people.

Clearly, as a company whose business has primarily been based around search algorithms it is implausible to suggest that Google could be responsible for the kind of genocide that savaged Rwanda. This makes a promise to 'not be evil' seem fatuous – what kind of thing could Google possibly be doing that would constitute evil as I just sketched the concept? According to Google CEO Eric Schmidt: "Evil" is what Google co-founder Sergey Brin "says is evil" (McHugh, 2003), reflecting the extent that a single person dominates the assessment of the ethical impact of this corporate institution. Interviewer Josh McHugh notes that the only consistent moral term that Brin deploys is "useful", suggesting that the interpretation of Google's 'Don't be Evil' maxim is shaped primarily by "a worldview where usefulness is the paramount virtue." This makes it seem that the utilitarian's moral fiction of utility is what shapes Google's moral universe – but if this is so, we have excellent reasons for doubting that Google's motto makes ethical sense since we are inundated with institutions that focus upon utility yet have few if any reasons for believing that what they typically do is morally good.

We can, however, say one thing about Google that sets it apart from other institutions striving to be useful or to maximize utility: *someone* inside Google is serving as a moral compass. The reading of that compass may be flawed, of course, but at least with Google we see a large organization that makes *some* concession towards thinking about how a corporation might act ethically. I am not, on the whole, convinced that this is enough to defend Google from the myriad problems it inevitably causes, especially since a billion people use the company's products and they are all utterly powerless in relation to it. But in a world where most other large institutions have *only* utility to guide them, I can at least hope that Brin somehow makes a difference internally to what Google does, for all that I do not see it in their relationship with me. I find myself manipulated and betrayed by

Google's software at every turn, but then, the situation is not significantly different with (say) Microsoft's software.

Large institutions like Google pursue utility, often measured in monetary terms, but they largely fail to act morally in relation to individuals. Even if we set aside the question of how a corporation deals with its customers, most generally fail to act in ways their *employees* would deem good. In both cases these failures occur in largely two forms: failures of management, in which a hierarchical power structure treats subordinates as expendable resources, and failures of bureaucracy, in which a pre-established set of rules remove any possibility of free thought or moral action. Whichever kind of institutional immorality we're addressing, it rests at heart in a failure to relate to people as people – the kind of dehumanized thinking that is summed up poignantly in the phrase 'human resources'. This is not an evil like the Rwandan genocides, it is something far more shallow and paltry. It is merely *petty evil* that corporations and other bureaucracies cause on a daily basis, the willful disregard of the moral treatment of individuals in pursuit of some definition of utility.

Bureaucracies excel at petty evil, because they are organized in such a way as to judge their actions in an entirely outcome-focused, consequentialist way, but without the consequentalist's commitment to maximizing good. Utility to Jeremy Bentham was a means to approve or disapprove of actions according to its tendency to "augment or diminish the happiness of the party whose interest is in question" (Bentham, 1789). The bastard child of utilitarian utility is institutional utility, since it has no concern of happiness at all and assesses only the self-maintained goals of the organization in question. For most corporations, this is money, and for almost all large organizations it is efficiency. We live in an age of efficient nightmares, where giant institutions pursue their own conceptions of productivity in utter disregard for their wider effects on people, beings, or things.

Alasdair MacIntyre (1984) has been a scathing critic of the petty evil of contemporary organizations. He is particularly skeptical of the concept of managerial effectiveness, calling this "one more contemporary moral fiction and perhaps the most important of them all." However, the belief in the effectiveness of managers is not a moral fiction in my terms, since it is not an ideal. It is rather an institutional mythology – the story that justifies a manager's claims to an authority that rests entirely upon the chain of command of the organization in question. This is one more relic of the great chain of being: we may now deny the authority of kings, but who is in a position to deny the authority of the CEO? MacIntyre, however, views the hierarchical structure of corporations and similar institutions as deeply counter-productive.

At the core of MacIntyre's critique of managerial effectiveness is the inherent contradiction between creating an institutional bureaucracy that can make the activities of employees and customers predictable, and the responsiveness to problems that allows organizations to obtain their goals. He suggests that "organizational success and organizational predictability exclude one another", such that the attempts to manage "necessarily routinize, suppress intelligence and flexibility" and ultimately turn employers against the managerial chain of command, either covertly or overtly. I would add to MacIntyre's objections that vertical chains of command serve to isolate those in the upper strata from the facts at every other level making the head of large organizations unable to offer reasonable guidance for those who actually do the work, and thus squandering the inherent intelligence that is embodied in an institution's staff. The mythology of managerial effectiveness presumes that the best decisions are made by those who are completely unaffected by those decisions. From the perspective of utility as money it might be argued that this claim has some plausibility, but if happiness or effectiveness are to be taken into account it is absurd to imagine that the great chain of corporate command offers anything beyond a counterfeit authority.

The other side of the petty evil of institutions, bureaucracy, has been savaged by Hannah Arendt (2005). Considering the Marxist regime in the U.S.S.R. she observes that the institutional arrangement was "supposed to be no-rule", where everyone would be equal and no-one would be in charge. In fact, it could not achieve this questionable ideal and transpired instead to be "rule by nobody, that is bureaucracy", which Arendt describes as "a form of government in which nobody takes responsibility". This is indeed the source of most petty evil – the rules and procedures of an organization are arranged so that *no-one has responsibility,* and relationships with people outside of the institution are frequently arranged to give the greatest chance that they will simply go away, since there is no-one who can actually act freely in any given situation governed by the bureaucracy.

For Arendt, tyranny and bureaucracy are remarkably close, since in both no adequate account can be given. Furthermore, the bureaucratic "rule of nobody" is a danger that is always present when an ideal of universal equality is applied. Bureaucracy makes everyone equal by making everyone equally powerless and irrelevant. The equality of bureaucrats "means nothing other than that no man is free" and the anonymity of bureaucratic rule is no less despotic because 'nobody' is exercising it. "On the contrary", Arendt warns, "it is more fearsome still, because no one can speak with or petition this 'nobody'." Thus our institutions – corporations, governments, organizations – insulate themselves from responsibility for their actions, leaving only blinkered ideals of utility to guide their activities.

It is this blind, anonymous despotism that is the tragedy of bureaucracy, using 'tragedy' once again in Alfred North Whitehead's (1926) sense of "the remorseless working of things." In some situations, perhaps, an institution *intends* to be a law unto itself, but in many cases bureaucracy is tragic precisely because it aims to help, but cannot. When government bureaucracy reacts to the latest political furor by cranking out legislation constructed to respond to the perceived problem, it inevitably and tragically fails to render the necessary assistance and instead piles higher the endless interference of red tape. Ironically, red tape was historically introduced to distinguish important matters, whose papers were bound with it in order to mark them for discussion, but it has come to stand for the tragedy of bureaucracy itself (Kaufman, 1977). As long as we expect a central institution to mediate and unify our diverse values, we will be stuck with the problems of petty evil. Perhaps more worrying is the capacity for the anonymity of bureaucracy to facilitate the starker kinds of evil.

Google may not commit evil in the wider sense, but like any similar company it cannot help but commit petty evil. Indeed, since it does not care for the individuality of its customers (you could further argue that it *cannot* care about them as individuals, because of the problem of scale) it cannot help but systematically implement policies that unleash untold and unseen acts of petty evil upon vast numbers of the people who are dealing with it. The internal bureaucratic procedures of all large organizations are immunized to interference from the outside, which means they are ignorant of the feelings, thoughts and desires of those it is affecting. In many cases, these efficient bureaucracies isolate themselves entirely from human contact by hiding behind robot gatekeepers, whether software designed to 'answer questions' on a website (which can only actually provide pre-set answers) or phone systems designed to provide a layer of insulation between internal operations and the outside world.

What's more, the petty evil of institutions is far from constrained to industry – it is the essence of contemporary government. Politics in ancient Athens could just about involve discussions with everyone because the citizens only numbered a few tens of thousands. In a nation of tens or hundreds of *millions* of citizens, the idea that government can represent the moral community of its citizens becomes implausible – there is no single moral community that *could* be represented. Under such circumstances, MacIntyre warns, government can only become "a set of institutional arrangements for imposing a bureaucratized unity on a society", since there is little or no hope of obtaining moral agreement on any issue. This is why contemporary politics is reduced to a kind of war, and thus cannot be an elevation of morality as Isaiah Berlin (1988) had believed. But in the absence of consensus, MayIntyre warns, "the nature of political obligation becomes systematically unclear." This is, in part, why so many people today become entirely disengaged with politics, a problem also addressed by Chantal Mouffe (2005).

I am for the most part an optimistic individual, and I believe – quite implausibly – in the goodness of humanity. As a result, I refuse to accept that these efficient nightmares are the best that we can do. Furthermore, it seems to me that our best hope for overcoming the petty evil of bureaucracy, and institutional evil in general, is to change our understanding of utility such that it is no longer monomaniacally obsessed with efficiency and profit. Such a change asks for pioneering new work in moral philosophy, and in this case the responsibility for change rests largely upon the shoulders of those whose moral systems lie in one particular corner of the ethical triangle: the consequentialists. Exploring the problems of outcome-focused ethics is the theme of this chapter, since it is consequentialist reasoning (primarily of a utilitarian kind), that animates our bureaucracies, and if our institutions are to be improved it may take a new kind of consequentialism to do it. But before we can work this minor miracle, we need to appreciate how imagination can distort our understanding of the morality of outcomes, and for this we need to look at one of the most famous thought experiments in the history of moral philosophy.

Off Your Trolley

The trolley problem is a moral dilemma originally proposed by the virtue ethicist Philippa Foot (Foot, 1967). 'Trolley' is another name for a tram or streetcar, and the basic form of the trolley problem goes something like this: *You are the driver of an out-of-control trolley which is rushing down a track towards five workmen. You can flip a switch to divert your trolley down a different track where there is a single workman. Should you flip the switch?*

Have a think about this problem before reading on. Would you flip the switch, killing the single person tied to the other track, or would you do nothing, killing the five on the trolley's current track? What would you choose to do, and why would you choose that particular course of action?

Now consider a variant on this theme proposed by Judith Jarvis Thomson (1985) that goes something like this: *You are standing on a footbridge and see below an out-of-control trolley rushing towards five workmen directly in its path. Also on the footbridge with you is a fat man, and if you push him off he will bring the trolley to a stop, but will die in the process. Should you push the fat man?*

According to Thomson, everyone she has asked about the basic trolley problem agrees it is acceptable to flip the switch, while nobody believed it was permissible to kill the fat man. When I put these problems to the readers of my blog, I found a much greater diversity of responses! The majority felt the same as Thomson's respondents – flip the switch but don't kill the fat man. Others replied that they could not justify taking any action at all, or suggested that being willing to flip the switch but not kill the fat man was "analogous to eating beef but being unwilling to slaughter a cow", or intimated that the situation would depend upon if they knew any of the people involved, or simply interpreted the dilemmas as irresolvable and refused to accept their terms (Bateman, 2007b). For myself, I concluded on the basis of trolley problems that we all use some kind of outcome-focused moral reasoning when all other considerations fail – but a few years later I was to read something that caused me to radically reconsider my stance on this.

Before exploring my change of heart, I want to look at the way trolley problems have begun to creep into discussions of moral psychology, and specifically Joshua Greene's "The Secret Joke of Kant's Soul" (2008) which purports to provide scientific evidence that duty ethics are wrong and outcome-ethics are right. Greene reports on 'brain scan' (fMRI) results obtained from subjects in response to various trolley problem thought experiments, principally the two cited above, which we can call Trolley and Footbridge respectively. In thought experiments involving direct harm, like Footbridge, Greene claims 'emotion' centers light up on scans, while in impersonal cases he claims 'cognitive' centers light up. Greene alleges that the former quintessentially entail duty ethics considerations, while the latter involve basically consequentialist decisions, and uses this to argue that our emotional reactions, having allegedly evolved in different contexts to those we face now, cannot be trusted and therefore duty ethics is suspect and consequentialism is the only moral approach that survives scientific scrutiny.

The trouble is, *no part of that argument makes a lick of sense or is based on viable research*. Greene is entirely lacking in reliable witnesses in this case, as examining just a handful of the papers that have offered rebuttal to his paper reveals. Colin Klein (2011) demonstrates that the fMRI inferences are badly reasoned, since none of the brain areas Greene identifies are specific to either emotion or cognition, and suggests that the weight of research does not favor a dual track model of moral cognition involving discrete 'emotional' and 'cognitive' modules, but a *single* network involved in imaginative self-projection (which is to say, Currie and Ravenscroft's recreative imagination). Sabine Roeser (2010) raises similar concerns, and also points out that Greene's arguments are self-defeating since he states we can't derive a 'moral ought' from a 'neural is' but then does *exactly this*. Richard Dean (2010) is one of several people who have demonstrated that even if the core experiment held up, it *wouldn't* be evidence against any salient form of duty ethics, and Guy Kahane (2010) makes the point that if the kind of evolutionary debunking that Greene attempts were plausible, it would undermine the cognitive judgments just as much as the emotional ones! Perhaps more worryingly, John Mikhail (2013) points out that all the thought experiments used, if treated as *legal* cases, would fail to absolve the actor of blame for the murder that they would have committed.

Indeed, if we were to take Greene's case seriously, we could easily conclude precisely the opposite: the fact that most people *would* consider flipping the switch but *not* murdering the fat man shows how easy it is to act immorally when the circumstances are de-personalized. On this reading, Greene's work arguably sheds light on why Stanley Milgram's (1963) famous electroshock experiment was accepted unquestioningly by so many of its test subjects, despite asking them to conduct torture: the experimental protocol de-personalized the people that the subjects believed they were electrocuting. It looks suspiciously as if the key reason Greene believes he has constructed a case against duty ethics is that he has a *prior* commitment to consequentialism (admitted later in his paper), a position that leads him into making quite troubling claims once they are considered carefully. However, I don't want to get bogged down in 'unmasking' - I believe in Greene's sincerity, if nothing else. This paper is mostly of interest to me not because of its misguided faith, but because of its assumptions about the trolley problem.

Roeser contends that in predicating the superiority of utilitarianism both Greene and Peter Singer, who specifically endorses Greene's views (Singer, 2005), treat trolley problems as if they had clear solutions simply by always assuming the outcome-focused solution trumps the duty ethical solution. This kind of short-circuiting of the moral issues allows Greene to conclude that people are morally right both to flip the switch *and* to murder the fat man, and thus something has gone wrong (Greene and Singer believe) when we are ready to kill an innocent by flipping a switch but not by pushing someone off a footbridge. This conclusion should trouble us *far more* than Greene's concern that emotions might 'interfere' with moral judgments, since it asks that we believe that murder can be justified solely by desirable outcomes. When Singer suggests that "there are no morally relevant differences" between Trolley and Footbridge, he bases his argument for killing the fat man on the claim that the death of one person is "a lesser tragedy" than the death of five. But the *murder* of one person might be a greater tragedy than the death of five, and any moral system that cannot see why this distinction should matter risks replacing morality with an inhuman concern for numbers.

Singer and Greene seem unaware of just how much their arguments rest upon appeals to evolutionary mythologies of a rather questionable kind (Bateman, 2012). Both try to argue that our emotional judgments cannot be trusted because their purported evolutionary histories undermine their validity, while our cognitive judgments transcend the circumstances of their development. Kuhane (2010) makes the point that even if it was plausible to debunk certain specific judgments in this way (and neither he nor I are convinced of this!), what was undermined would not fall into clear lines such as 'emotion' versus 'cognition' - rather, such arguments would cause a "truly radical upheaval in our evaluative beliefs". If the evolutionary histories of our faculties had these kinds of implications, we would have reason to doubt our cognition as much as our emotions, but rather fortunately such histories cannot even be *derived* from the available evidence, much less provide a basis for 'disproving' moral feelings.

Besides, there is no need to accept the rather simplistic view of emotions Greene advances, since those who speak for emotions contend that they entail cognitive aspects anyway. The idea that we can entirely separate thinking and feeling lacks plausibility. As Currie and Ravenscroft remark in connection with the work of neuropsychologist Antonio Damasio, emotion is inescapably important to rational decision-making. Indeed, it makes no sense to view emotions as being "at odds with rationality", since the evidence we have clearly demonstrates that emotions "are a vital ingredient in practical reason". If our emotional capacities have been damaged, it becomes incredibly difficult to make *any* kinds of decision, since without hints from emotions regarding "the appropriateness of a proposed course of action" we become "lost in endless consideration of possibilities" (Currie and Ravenscroft, 2002).

What forever changed my own view of trolley problems was an essay by Allen Wood in Derek Parfit's *On What Matters* (Wood, 2011). For much of volume one of this book, Parfit relies upon thought experiments very similar to Trolley and Footbridge in order to advance various arguments, and in his invited response Wood offers a savage critique of trolley problems, exposing just how far from morality they take us. Part of the problem, right from the outset, is that the way a question is framed can significantly alter the answer people will tend to give – something that has a well-documented effect on poll results (Lakoff, 2010). What makes this far worse in the case of trolley problems is that we are typically deprived of important, morally relevant facts that we *would* generally have if the thought experiment were actually happening to us. As a result – like pollsters skewing the wording of questions to favor a specific response – trolley problems encourage us to *ignore* moral principles *because they have been stipulated away*. What's more, these kinds of thought experiment also specify our certainty on matters that we could not possibly be certain about in practice, thus inviting conclusions that follow from the premises of the trolley problem *but which could not be as decisive if we actually faced an equivalent situation.*

Consider what happens if we use our imagination to re-incorporate elements that were stipulated away in the original trolley problem. As Wood points out, the kind of transport systems we are talking about are either the responsibility of public agencies or are run by private companies that are regulated with a view towards public safety and the prevention of loss of life. It would be considered a scandal if the lives of workmen were endangered *at all* while working on the lines, and the question of five lives or one would never enter into the relevant moral deliberation at all. As Marc Majcher half-jokingly observed when I posed the trolley problems on my blog:

> Don't throw the switch, don't push the fat man. Let the trolley hit the five people in either case – the magnitude of the tragedy will bring the specter of horrific runaway trolley accidents into the public eye, forcing the trolley operators to implement and enforce stricter safety regulations, preventing untold trolley-related deaths in the future (Bateman, 2007b).

The kind of fictional situations that the trolley problems ask us to ponder can be *imagined* but they are not really *conceivable* in practice – they are absurd comic book fantasy conundrums, entirely removed from life as we actually live it. We only have to add back in a few of the consequences that the wording discreetly covers up to really appreciate how insidiously horrific Greene's assumption of the 'correct' solution to the trolley problems must be in practice. As Wood notes, were we to actually face such a situation ourselves and decide to take no action, we might well torture ourselves for years to come over whether there was something we could have done to save the five. But this is still a more desirable outcome than killing the fat man, which would certainly (as Mikhail attests) have ended in our conviction for murder, not in our being hailed as a hero. Would even the workmen, whose lives are endangered, wish to be saved if it meant the sacrifice of an innocent to do so?

To make matters worse, very small changes to these imaginary scenarios radically alter the responses that people offer. As Tamar Szabó Gendler (2007) reports, psychologist David Pizzaro conducted research that varied the description of the Footbridge trolley problem in ways that shouldn't, in principle, affect the moral judgment entailed but in fact radically altered people's responses. For instance, when asked to push a man named Chip Ellsworth III off a bridge to save the members of the Harlem Jazz Orchestra, subjects were much more willing than when asked to push a man named Tyrone Peyton off a bridge to save the New York Philharmonic. Gendler suggests that what might be at work in these strange responses could be overcompensation for racist tendencies – the people tested were more willing to murder someone who sounded like a rich white guy to save musicians who were likely to be black than to murder someone sounding like a poor black guy to save an elite orchestra of predominantly white and Asian performers.

As Wood attests, the correct response in most trolley problems must be indeterminate since the only significant moral issue they raise is how such a situation might have been permitted to arise in the first place. We should be troubled not so much by the trolley problem, but by the seriously disturbing idea that there are people who expect us to judge *solely* by the immediate results of an action, ignoring all other factors as morally irrelevant. Indeed, trolley problems sometimes include the caveat that 'there are no other relevant facts' beyond those described – such a stipulation, Wood suggests "cannot be regarded as either theoretically neutral or morally innocent."

Ironically, neither Thomson nor Foot (who proposed the most commonly discussed trolley problems) believe that these problems must be decided on the basis of numbers of lives lost –

but there are consequentialist moral philosophers who *do* make this kind of claim, and perhaps more worryingly there are influential people in our world making decisions on precisely this kind of logic. This point returns us to Elizabeth Anscombe's paper from which the name 'consequentialism' originates, since part of her original criticism was precisely that:

> ...the point of considering hypothetical situations, perhaps very improbable ones, seems to be to elicit from yourself or someone else a hypothetical decision to do something of a bad kind. I don't doubt this has the effect of predisposing people – who will never get into the situations for which they have made hypothetical choice – to consent to similar bad actions, or to praise and flatter those who do them, so long as their crowd does so too, when the desperate circumstances imagined don't hold at all (Anscombe, 1958).

I suggested above that one conclusion we might plausibly draw from Greene's experiments, broadly construed, is that we are more willing to act in ways we would ordinarily judge as immoral when the relevant situations are presented in a depersonalized form, as with Milgram's disturbing experiment. Wood concedes that there are "extreme and desperate situations", such as war or natural disasters, which might require us to "coldly and grimly" weigh the benefits and harms of a particular course of action. But significantly, such decisions are only made *when there is no recourse to humanizing social institutions*, such as those that protect the lives of workmen on tram lines. That trolley problems help us to think in such rational-but-dehumanized ways is, Wood concludes, "a powerful argument against using trolley problems in moral philosophy."

However, I do not believe Wood goes far enough in this regard, since these kinds of thought experiments are causing even more trouble in moral psychology! Greene's strange conclusions about the trolley problem are only one example of the kind of work that empirical researchers are conducting that fail to produce reliable witnesses. Jonathan Haidt has made a lot of strident claims on the basis of a variety of experiments that use extremely suspicious thought experiments, particularly in the context of what he calls "moral dumbfounding" (Haidt, 2001). For instance, Haidt offers a thought experiment we can call Incest in which a brother and a sister decide it would be "interesting and fun" if they were to try having sex with each other. They use two forms of birth control and although they enjoy the experience "they decide not to do it again." They keep it a secret "which makes them feel even closer to each other." Haidt then reports that the undergraduates faced with this situation "immediately say that it was wrong" but are unable to provide reasons for doing so. This is the alleged moral dumbfounding.

Haidt claims that "the story makes it clear that no harm befell them", but does not appreciate the cost of using such stipulations as the framework for investigation. Wood's objections to the trolley problem apply just as much to this scenario, which stipulates a purportedly neutral outcome that strains plausibility. As Daniel Jacobson (2012) suggests, it is a mistake to presuppose that stipulating that no harm is done removes any legitimate moral reasons for concern. He goes on to provide objections compatible with a variety of ethical systems, including consequentialist approaches, which would justifiably condemn the situation in Incest. The problem is that the thought experiment describes behavior which is recognizable *dangerous*, and then pretends that this doesn't matter because it is stipulated that the problems that could have happened did not occur. As Jacobson suggests, the danger in Incest is that the people involved "do irreparable harm to their relationship as siblings", and this is "hardly an insignificant matter". Stipulating away this outcome does not change the risk that was involved.

After taking into account a range of additional concerns,

including the likelihood that young undergraduates were not the best choice of test subject for this experiment, Jacobson offers a rather different reading of Haidt's conclusions:

> ...the subjects are not *dumbfounded* by these cases so much as certain (extremely intelligent) psychologists and philosophers are, rather, *stupefied* by their moral theories. To be morally stupefied in this fashion is to be rendered unable to see obviously good reasons, because you are in the grip of a theory too narrow-minded to accommodate them.

By stipulating away almost all the relevant information necessary to morally interpret them, trolley problems and similar thought experiments radically distort the situations they present, brushing serious issues under the carpet and sometimes making it seem as if the answers are as simple as the logical truth that five is greater than one. Precisely what makes real moral dilemmas agonizing is that the truly difficult problems for morality do not have such easy answers, and presenting them as if they were trivial cases is a clear sign of moral stupefaction. This conclusion doesn't just bring trolley problems into question, it presents a serious challenge to any form of outcome-focused ethics that attempts to reduce moral concerns to mere calculation, as traditional forms of consequentialism such as utilitarianism had always endeavored to do, and as the efficient nightmares of bureaucracy attempt on a daily basis.

Calculating the Good

A lot of recent work by consequentialists such as R.M. Hare, Amartya Sen, Samuel Scheffler, Peter Railton, David Brink, and John Broome has focused on demonstrating the flexibility of consequentialism, showing that it can be made to accommodate moral concerns traditionally associated with other moral systems. But as Benjamin Sachs (2010) has argued, this flexibility is a "double-edged sword" for anyone who wants to argue that consequentialism is superior to its alternatives. To make their case, Sachs suggests that consequentialists must either show that the best alternative moral systems fail to accommodate some "Compelling Idea" or that they fail to embody some "Desirable Quality". The former option is undermined by the very flexibility its proponents have demonstrated: the capacity to translate agent or rule-focused aspects into consequentialism cannot possibly show that consequentialism involves a Compelling Idea that could not be translated into other moral systems. Sachs allows that there may yet be a Desirable Quality associated with consequentialism – but it seems to me that this must be its amenability to mathematics, which is also a double-edged sword for the reasons discussed above.

This is another of the disasters that contemporary moral philosophy brought upon itself: the attempt to suture the degree of certainty possible in mathematics into morality, where no such certainty is attainable or desirable. It is easy to appreciate why proponents of consequentialist moral theories felt that what they were doing was worthwhile – if there were a mathematical form of morality, definite answers could be attained and with them all sorts of putatively positive programs could be launched. But as both Rawls and MacIntyre recognize, traditional utilitarian mathematics could never work because, as Rawls objects, there is no way to measure pleasure and pain in a manner conducive to summation and, as MacIntyre objects, the concept of 'the greatest happiness for the greatest number' is "a notion without any clear content at all" that can only be used ideologically. Note, however, that despite savaging utilitarianism, MacIntyre praises influential utilitarian John Stuart Mill, calling him an "exemplar" of virtue as he understands it. Whatever problems a particular moral system has, it can *still* inspire its adherents to do good in the world.

Beyond these specific problems with utilitarianism, the grail of moral certitude that mathematics seems to hold out for ethics has a more pragmatic problem. The usual complaint leveled against the popular forms of outcome-focused ethics is expressed in the accusatory adage 'the ends justify the means', which carries with it the implication that the ends *should not* justify the means. Unfortunately, this claim is nonsense – as Wood (1999) points out, the meaning of the word 'means' is precisely whatever is used to achieve an 'end', so it is *always* the case that the ends justify the means: "once we have decided, all things considered, what ends we should be pursuing, they will always justify the means to them". Ends are goal states we aim to achieve, and means are the methods we use to achieve them, so 'the ends justify the means' is a very poor complaint to level, being necessarily true. The problem it seeks to illuminate, however, is extremely relevant to consequentialism, namely that having a worthy end (such as the utilitarian 'greatest happiness for the greatest number') *doesn't* justify any and all means. Perhaps we should revise this complaint to say that 'the goodness of ends cannot justify the immorality of means'.

The problem with utilitarian theory, and much of consequentialist ethics in general, is that by aiming for mathematical solutions to ethical problems it all too frequently circumvents moral discourse rather than enriching it. As Latour suggests: "After short-circuiting sciences and politics, utilitarianism creates an impasse over the proper contribution of morality. It would be hard to do worse!" The problem is not outcome-focused ethics, though, but the sheer magnitude of the effort made to insist consequentialism is right and its alternatives are wrong, that is, to forcibly defend consequentialism as a Law Ethic. In this regard, the contrary attempts to prove that virtue or duty ethics are the correct morality (by, say, MacIntyre and Rawls respectively) have been equally misguided. The way forward might involve nothing more than accepting that even if there were an absolute truth behind morality, *more than one Law Ethic might be required to fully express it.* This would certainly be the case if – as seems likely – our moral systems were always flawed, since even if there were a perfect Law Ethic, there would be no way for us to get at it directly.

None of this discussion is intended to discredit consequentialism as a moral tradition – it is clear that there are many people for whom this form of ethics is the one that speaks to them most powerfully, and as MacIntyre's praise of Mill's virtue attests, the ideals of outcome-focused ethics are just as capable of motivating change in the world as any other system. Indeed, in the case of animal ethics, I suspect it is no coincidence that consequentialists like Singer (e.g. 1975) have been major voices: from the abstract mathematical perspective that utilitarianism and its cousins propose, it becomes very difficult to ignore the suffering of animals, since however you are going to construct your moral accountancy, the pain of animals is impossible to wipe clean from the ledger. In this regard, consequentialism has offered significant pushback against the human-centered moral traditions – but this benefit has nothing to do with Law Ethics. Indeed, by presupposing that consequentialism was necessarily a Law Ethic (albeit not expressly in those terms), the arguments for animal ethics that have been advanced were *weakened* because they spoke not of a pressing moral issue that everyone needed to consider more thoughtfully *from within their own moral tradition,* but rather of a presumed requirement that everyone convert to consequentialism. The persuasiveness of this approach is understandably limited.

Fortunately, the situation seems to be improving. Parfit (2011), in his attempt to offer a systematic approach that bridges between duty ethics and consequentialism, recognizes that we don't need to establish actual numbers to be thinking about whether one outcome is better or worse than another, as well as recognizing that you don't have to be a consequentialist to care about the consequences of actions. Furthermore, Toby Ord (2005) notes that no outcome-focused ethicist actually expects morality to be attained by "naïve calculation", since there is a general recognition that it is impossible to calculate which actions will cause the most good. Rather, the consensus among contemporary consequentialists seems to be that we should make our decisions in whatever way will lead to the best outcomes. Ord admits that this kind of comment tends to appear solely as a small note in most books about consequentialism, but suggests that once this is accepted in could entail that "a consequentialist should eschew calculation altogether" in favor of a more rigorous focus upon determining *which* decision procedures will lead to the best outcomes.

However, the encouraging noises from moral philosophers in this regard must be contrasted against the endorsement of consequentialism from outside philosophy, such as Haidt's suggestion that democracies have "no compelling alternative to utilitarianism". This view entails that governments must deploy utilitarian moral systems *despite the impossibility of doing so.* According to Ord, "no prominent consequentialist" has argued against following the best decision procedure as the method likely to produce the best outcomes, but this *decision ethic* is radically different from the utilitarian ideal of 'the greatest good for the greatest number', especially when it entails the farcical assumption that it is possible to calculate goodness according to some formula. If the moral tradition of consequentialism doesn't support naïve calculation of the good, as Ord suggests, we should be especially concerned about the fact that a great many of our bureaucracies still try to justify their activities in precisely this way.

Within organizations, utility is the principal moral fiction that is deployed, purportedly to determine the best courses of action. But of course, there is no way to actually calculate what is good, not to mention no consensus understanding of what even *qualifies* as good, so decisions are made primarily about whatever can be quantified in a suitably mathematical form – and money is far and away the easiest measure in this regard. Even when other numbers are available, the justification for their application is unlikely to align with the moral perspectives of those affected.

Consider the case of the highway bypass, where the number of road users who will benefit is weighed against the number of residents who are being relocated and this calculation is deemed to provide justification – as if the convenience of motorists were somehow equivalent to the emotional security of residents. I saw the effects of this particular application of utility when my wife's grandparents were forced to move away from the house in Kentucky that they had lived in for over fifty years. Under the doctrine of eminent domain, they had no choice but to accept the money offered to them and relocate. Their new house was bigger and better appointed than their old one, to be sure, but they were *miserable* there and ultimately ended up moving back into their old house when it transpired that the route of the new road didn't actually require the demolition of their old home. As a strictly utilitarian calculation, the convenience offered to drivers on the new road was supposed to trump the happiness of an eighty-year-old married couple – but I find it impossible to call any aspect of that calculation *moral*.

This draws attention to Parfit's observation that there are forms of consequentialism that don't seem to be moral perspectives at all, and that could be seen as external rivals to morality. One of these (as already mentioned) is egoism, the minimal ethic, which only barely seems to qualify as an ethic. The other is any kind of consequentialism that expects people to sacrifice their own purportedly lesser good for the greater good of others – the ideal that allegedly was in play during the displacement of my wife's grandparents. Parfit allows that adherents to this kind of consequentialist ethic might be "strongly motivated and often moved to act in ways that prevent or relieve suffering", but suggests that "they may be doubtful whether any acts are duties, or mustn't-be-done, and doubtful about blameworthiness, and about reasons for remorse and indignation." For him, this casts doubt on whether we should think of these ethics as being moral systems at all.

I don't want to take as strong a line as Parfit in this regard, since it seems to me that even those ethics that advocate sacrifices for the greater good still merit consideration as moral systems, just as I'm claiming the minimal ethic does – albeit just barely! It might be the case that consequentialism (like egoism) risks confusing moral reasoning and prudential reasoning, but for the best examples of outcome-focused ethics there is still a moral ideal at work, often one that genuinely hopes to alleviate suffering. But when I consider situations like the forced displacement of my wife's grandparents, I do not see anyone acting to prevent or relieve suffering, but rather suffering caused in the pursuit of convenience. I find no *greater* good of any kind in the construction of this additional road, although there is of course the deeply *lesser* good of slightly shorter journey times and the temporary relief of congestion.

If 'the goodness of ends cannot justify the immorality of means' we should be especially wary of situations such as this whereby suffering is caused in the pursuit of ends that are only trivially good, if indeed they are good at all. While I am not willing to follow Parfit in denying to consequentialism the status of moral system, I do contend that when we let institutions make decisions using the ideal of utility this will all too frequently cause harm, and the bypass example is only an exceptionally minor case in this regard. We cannot calculate what is good any more than we can produce a number to meaningfully evaluate a tragedy, and we should be wary of all attempts to reduce morality to mere mathematics. Bad utilitarian decisions are moral failures for everyone concerned – and consequentialists, with their moral commitments to both better outcomes and superior decision-making, should be just as outraged as everyone else.

Hesitant Bureaucracies

What I have tried to sketch in this chapter is the connection between consequentialist reasoning and the appalling moral blindness of our bureaucratic institutions. It is not my purpose to deny the moral value of outcome-focused thought, but rather to discredit the suturing of mathematics into morality as if the numbers were all that mattered. As mentioned in the previous chapter, we have to be careful to recognize those situations in which the cherished intelligence of nerds is conflated with (and reduced to) the ability to render a situation in numbers. If we accept perspectival truth, we have to allow that there are many ways to imagine what is good – and we also have to accept that few of these ways can be reduced to a calculation.

There is a possible solution to the problem of the petty evil of institutions that is worth considering, for all that it may prove difficult to implement in practice. The relationship between individual humans and a bureaucracy they operate within today is parallel to the relationship between individual cells and an organism they operate within. In both cases, the individual components are oblivious to the wider picture and continue with whatever activities are appropriate to their small piece of the puzzle. Only when there are macro-scale problems do the individuals begin to feel the wider problems. Ordinarily, the organism or the bureaucracy (and these are very similar concepts in certain respects) isolates its elements from any awareness of what is going on.

Compare this to other kinds of group activity among animals, such as the flocking of birds or shoaling behaviors among fish. In these cases, the individual creatures act in concert with the group but without any kind of hierarchy. Each is able to make a judgment about what to do in any given situation based upon what it knows about the other animals around it. Hence birds stay in formation by watching the birds flying in front of them – although of course, somebody has to be in the lead. In the case of shoals of fish, however, the sense of a leader has gone entirely since there are many fish at the front edge of the formation. If the typical human bureaucracy is arranged with a vertical chain of command that echoes the great chain of being, flocks and shoals are arranged horizontally, with responsibility distributed throughout, in a manner that is closer to ideals of equality.

There have been considerable efforts to move towards a more horizontal and less vertical form of bureaucracy in recent years, although it is often mounted within conventional concepts of utility. For instance, Frank Ostroff (1999) argues for horizontal organization because it is "tailor-made for helping a company reach its competitive peak." However others have made claims for horizontal organization that stress an ability to promote care both within the institution and between it and the outside world. Jody Hoffer Gittell and Anne Douglass (2010) have proposed what they call *relational bureaucracy*, a horizontal conception that preserves the sustainability and ease of replication associated with formal institutions and couples it with a relational or network approach based upon shared relationships. The core to this concept, much like a flock or shoal, is that individuals are bound to others through reciprocal relationships that occur between worker and worker, worker and manager, and worker and client.

In relational bureaucracy, those who work for the bureaucracy are linked together through shared knowledge, common goals, and mutual respect. The goals of the organization are pursued, but not in ignorance of the needs of those working for it. Rather than a management structure descended from the great chain of being, Gittell and Douglass propose abandoning 'power-over' and substituting 'power-with', which is to say replacing hierarchical command with a more equitable form of representation. The entire concept is based around maintaining a personal touch, so that rather than Arendt's rule of nobody the organization distributes responsibility and authority practically via a network of relations. They caution of the need to avoid "the unintentional adoption of formal practices that put people into rigid boxes rather than connecting them with each other". Something like relational bureaucracy offers a way to imagine future institutions that are less prone to petty evil because they are built upon reciprocal relationships and mutual respect rather than the unthinking enforcement of a pre-existing structure of rules.

Ultimately, the need to renovate older institutional forms – and with it the ongoing renovation of the mythology of the great chain of being that still lurks behind so much of contemporary thinking – can be seen as the necessity of creating *hesitant* bureaucracies, in Haché and Latour's sense. Recall that the hesitation ethic is based upon rejecting a previously established certainty in favor of pausing in the face of moral problems in order to reflect upon them. Relational bureaucracies, and other such institutional renovations, offer ways to encourage hesitancy by substituting reciprocal relationships for blind rules. This is an attempt to bring the Chaos of hesitation into the Law of bureaucracy, and of course finding a balance between the two is never easy. But it is only by striving for a balance between the two that we can achieve anything truly moral.

However, a certain caution is required in thinking about these renovations to the bureaucratic form. While Gittell champions caring institutions, she sometimes seems to be less than clear on what it is she is asking for. She remarks in a panel discussion that she imagines that Google combines relational and bureaucratic forms "quite well" (Rynes, 2012). Yet there is no conceivable way that Google can be involved in the relational co-production between workers and clients that is encouraged by Gittell and Douglass' approach, since Google has 30,000 employees and a billion clients (Warman, 2011). This makes the ratio of workers to clients roughly the same as the size of the company – 30,000 to one. It is self-evident that this massive disparity will not lend itself to a "flexible, emergent response to clients", and instead must fall into the traditional bureaucratic and professional space of "emotional neutrality, emotional detachment, and professional 'power-over' the client" (Gittell and Douglass, 2010). Google has no choice but to do things *for* its users, it cannot work *with* them, it certainly cannot have 'power-with' them. It may hesitate internally, but it cannot do so in its relations with the rest of the world.

If co-production is ethically desirable, Google – and any other institution with a gigantic client-to-worker ratio – is at best morally flawed and at worst inherently immoral. Google itself would of course deny this suggestion and in part because its moral compass, Sergey Brin, may still believe it is possible to calculate the good. There is no need to invoke virtue or duty ethics to undermine this obsessive outcome-focused approach to morality since as already noted *even the consequentialists admit that calculation cannot supplant morality*. Meanwhile, Brin and his company *avoid* the ethical consequences of their transnational bureaucracy by evoking the authority of Science via numerous research programs that are believed to alleviate them of any further responsibility. As Lazlo Block, Google's head of 'People Operations' states, the corporation has "a large enough scale so that when we run experiments, they're statistically valid" (Manjoo, 2013). No doubt. But statistical validity has no bearing on the morality of the specific questions asked, and the consequentialist sea-change should make us extremely cautious of all claims to calculate the good, no matter how statistically significant they may be.

I may criticize Google for bordering on immorality, but paradoxically I genuinely believe in their commitment to ethical business – it is just that Brin and his associates radically underestimate what a moral industry would need to do and be, and perhaps fool themselves into believing the sciences can alleviate their responsibilities to individuals *as individuals*. Of course they are far from alone in this – statistics has long been bureaucracy's chief tool for suppressing individual dissatisfaction and unhappiness beneath the democratic mythology of majority rule. To single out Google as an unethical corporation would be absurdly unjust – other transnationals are far further from 'power-with' either their clients *or* their employees. My reason for focusing on Google was to demonstrate that even *with* a moral commitment, any bureaucratic form that draws upon the mythology of the great chain of being risks immorality in so much as autonomy is deemed morally desirable, and invoking the authority of Science against this is merely an excuse for disempowerment, not a solution to it.

Bureaucratic reform, however desirable, cannot resolve all the troubles of contemporary institutions, especially since many of the problems result from the sheer *scale* of the bureaucracies involved. As Ivan Illich warned, when an enterprise grows too large "it first frustrates the end for which it was originally designed, and then rapidly becomes a threat to society itself" (Illich, 1973). This issue aside, a corporation that allows for the hesitation ethic is at least conceivable, in part because the satisfaction of customers is already an accepted part of the ideal of utility deployed in business. The situation is not equivalent in politics: for governments, the *dissatisfaction* of a significant number of constituents is presumed to be an inevitable consequence of majority rule, and this immunizes governments from hesitation when they appear to have a popular mandate. This mythology of 'the public interest' or 'the good of the people' becomes a justification for implementing policies of convenience, as in the case of the highway bypass – situations complicated by the complicity of those who benefit from such actions.

In the context of governmental organizations, hesitant bureaucracies may make the process of dealing with the institutions more bearable, but without substantial reform directives will still be drafted and implemented on the old vertical model of authority, and thus dominated by the residual mythology of the great chain of being. Isn't the usual reason we vote for one political candidate over another precisely their claim that they can force a policy we desire onto everyone, even those who do not want it? It is not clear we are willing to give up the conflation of the political leadership with the wider bureaucracy that underpins governmental institutions. This is a conceit that allows the praise or blame for any government action to accrue almost entirely to its figurehead, while simultaneously alleviating many voters' sense of responsibility for what governments do. 'I voted for the other guy' is an excuse that plays into MacIntyre's concern that we have obfuscated the concept of political obligation: we can now talk about our governments as if we, the people purportedly represented by them, held absolutely no responsibility for what they do. In such circumstances, the concept of political representation has become meaningless.

Furthermore, governments have generally presumed that the only people they need to take into account are their own citizens, and that their obligations extend only trivially to the citizens of other nations. Human rights legislature may seem to ground a moral commitment from governments to all humans, but these statutes have not been ratified by all countries, and perhaps more worryingly, are not honored by many of the countries that did. For all that we may vilify the transnational corporation for its inability to hesitate and its inevitable petty evils, the idea of hesitant governments seems even more unobtainable, and in part because nations have mythic stories they can use to gloss over the worst imaginable atrocities. If we wish to put a stop to the efficient nightmares of the twentieth century and end the tragedy of bureaucracy it will be necessary for citizens to find ways to hold their own governments morally accountable.

7

Rights and Wrongs

National Insecurity

The year before my wife and I were married, we had to conduct a rather difficult international relationship. In order to spend time together, I ended up entering and re-entering the United States under the visa waiver scheme, which permitted me to stay for up to three months provided that I then left for at least a month. Although what I was doing was legal, I was aware that I was skirting the boundaries of the immigration system and that it might eventually become a problem – as it did in the year 2000, the fourth and last time that I landed inside US borders claiming a visa waiver. The staff at the airport swept me aside into a small room where I waited with a Spanish woman whose passport had accidentally been through the washing machine and a Chinese woman who didn't speak any English. There, we waited, uncertain whether we would be permitted to enter the country or if we would be unceremoniously deported back to the nations we had departed from. Thankfully, luck was with me and I was eventually allowed to complete my journey.

I often think about that small room when I am travelling abroad, because although I was not at any particular risk at that time I was nonetheless for a short period of time caught between two stumps. I had left the United Kingdom, but not yet arrived in the United States, I was in the no man's land that saturates the cracks between nations, figuratively sailing in international waters without a flag. I had faith that, as a British subject, nothing was going to happen to me. But if my name had been something a little less English, if my travel history had more recently entailed African nations, and if I had been travelling just one year later, my situation could have been utterly different. For the 'crime' of having a Muslim name and having visited a nation on an official list of suspicion, citizens of the United Kingdom otherwise no different from me have been taken away and indefinitely detained with no legal jurisdiction, no access to representation, and no human rights of any kind.

Jamal Udeen Al-Harith was not as lucky as I was. A fellow resident of Manchester, Al-Harith had been born Ronald Fiddler but changed his name in 1994 when he converted to Islam. Like me, he was pursuing an international relationship in 2000 – in his case, with a woman living in Australia. Whereas I married my lover, he broke up with his around the time I was exchanging vows. Later, he travelled to Pakistan on a backpacking trip, and from there wanted to visit Iran. His truck was stopped near the Afghan border and Taliban guards, seeing his British passport, arrested him as a spy. He was later 'rescued' by US troops who found him among many other foreigners in a jail in Kandahar, and initially released him. But he was not to leave Kabul, since he was later arrested as a 'suspected enemy combatant' and transferred to the detention camp at Guantánamo Bay (Forbes, 2004).

Al-Harith was eventually released without charge two years after his spurious arrest, becoming the first detainee to describe the conditions inside Camp X-Ray and Camp Delta on the island of Cuba. He described to the British newspapers how prisoners were shackled for up to fifteen hours a day in 'cells' that were little more than wire cages with concrete floors, offering no privacy whatsoever. Guards known as the 'Extreme Reaction Force' gave punishment beatings in response to even the pettiest breach of rules. Worse, inmates suffered brutal humiliations as part of a systematic application of psychological torture intended to force confessions: devout Muslims who had never seen a woman without a veil were tormented by prostitutes who had been paid to touch themselves, in one case smearing menstrual blood on the face of a prisoner (Prince and Jones, 2004).

Such treatment is expressly forbidden by international law for prisoners of war, but the detainees of Guantánamo Bay are only 'suspected enemy combatants' and not afforded such protections. They should, therefore, have been protected by the civil statues of human rights legislation – but instead they were told they had no rights. "They actually said that - 'You have no rights here'" Al-Harith told reporters after his release. "After a while, we stopped asking for human rights – we wanted animal rights". While in Camp X-Ray, his cage was next to a kennel housing a German Shepherd dog with an air-conditioned wooden house and green grass for exercising upon. Al-Harith half-jokingly asked the guards: "I want his rights". They replied: "That dog is a member of the US army."

Human rights, something the United States had been instrumental in ratifying internationally after the horrors of World War II, supposedly guard individual freedoms. In the twenty first century, these legal protections have been savaged by the rhetoric that "national security trumps human rights" (Ignatieff, 2002). But this is not about the security of nations – as Al-Harith demonstrates, those who have their rights withdrawn need not be a threat of any kind, they only have to *seem* like they *might* be a threat. This is not about the rule of law and it is not a matter of national security at all, it is national *insecurity* – the paranoia that demands a *suspension* of the law to prevent imagined threats from striking in a make-believe future. National insecurity elevates the biases that constantly undermine individual morality to the scale of the nation, allowing moral and legal commitments to be simply brushed aside as inconvenient.

Although the horrific consequences of being excluded from law and due process come into clear focus in the squalor of Guantánamo Bay, this *state of exception* as Giorgio Agambens (2005) has called it, has long been a normal aspect of democratic government. The state of exception is an extremely troubling moral fiction, or rather, an *immoral* fiction – a mythology of chaos-within-law embodied within the sovereign's capacity to suspend constitutional law because of a pressing crisis. Because the leader of a nation has been given the authority to declare a state of war in response to an emergency, thus suspending national law, the power of presidents and prime ministers rests in part upon the state of exception. This helps explain why, Agambens suggests, the twentieth century sees war metaphors becoming integral to the political vocabulary. In his epic depiction of Europe 'between the wars', Michael Moorcock (2006) similarly notes how Mussolini deployed just such a rhetoric to motivate Fascist Italy, a theme also discussed by Elizabeth Nelson (1991). Whether it is a war on drugs or a war on terror, the image of war sanctions the state of exception.

Thus national insecurity fuels an outcome-focused ethic that is so far from morality it does not even clearly lie inside the ethical triangle, a prudential paranoia that excuses violation of any and all moral systems as strictly necessary. The moral limbo of the state of exception is "exemplified by camps and prisons, such as Guantánamo Bay, Abu Ghraib, Belmarsh, the secret prisons and dark sites of CIA. In these camps, the legal exception becomes the rule" (Douzinas, 2007). It might be the case, Agambens suggests, that a temporary and controlled use of the political power to suspend law could be consistent with democratic constitutions – but when the state of exception becomes the norm, it can only lead to the "liquidation" of democracy. For all that nations appear to be grounded in Law Ethics, the state of exception reveals that a grotesque parody of Chaos Ethics manifests on the international stage – and there is nothing morally good about this.

The connection between mythology and the state of exception is horribly parallel to the exposure of the fallacious morality of the trolley problem. When the judge Richard Posner argues that torture should be used to obtain information if it would stop "the detonation of a nuclear bomb in Times Square", he falls prey of Allen Wood's condemnation of misleading thought experiments, and of Elizabeth Anscombe's recognition that improbable hypothetical scenarios can be used to justify terrible actions. The stipulations of Posner's imaginary threat are not plausible occurrences in the actual detention of suspected terrorists: there is no bomb in Times Square, and even if there was it is exceptionally unlikely that military personnel would uncover this fact in a way that would guarantee that one person could be tortured to prevent it detonating. At Guantánamo Bay, torture was not conducted to stop tragedy, tragedy was enacted by torture to stop nothing more than the application of human rights to victims who desperately needed their protection.

Here is equality as exclusion in all its ugly brutality, as Dousinas (2007) and Thobani (2007) argue. Since the universality of human rights is the core of their claim to justice, they must necessarily become *meaningless* if they protect solely wealthy white men. As Thobani forcibly argues, nationality and citizenship have been reconfigured around the mythology of "Muslims as the global enemy" such that citizenship is no longer a protection since it can be nullified without trial or edict, throwing anyone suspicious – meaning any Muslim – into the moral limbo of the state of exception. That they can be imprisoned with impunity is not even the worst of the suffering unleashed against those whose only 'crime' is being Muslim in the wrong place at the wrong time, since armed drones now offer the capacity to terrorize the innocent and assassinate with placid impunity.

On the morning of 17 March 2011, for instance, a drone was deployed to fire missiles into a bus depot in the town of Datta Khel in a mountainous region of northwest Pakistan that borders Afghanistan. According to the public account by US officials, everyone killed in this attack was an 'insurgent'. However, according to eye witnesses, the Pakistani military, and investigators for the Associated Press, most of the people killed in the attack were civilians who had come along to a tribal meeting in order to settle a dispute about a nearby mine. They had even notified the Pakistani military of the event ten days earlier. Roughly four of the forty people slain that day were Taliban fighters, while at least twenty four civilians have been named as victims of the attack, while others who died that day may never be known by name (Stanford, 2012).

There are thousands of other similar stories coming to light. In a statement offered to a Senate Judiciary subcommittee on Human Rights, Farea Al-Muslimi accused the United States of waging a "war of mistakes" by using drones to conduct what are euphemistically called 'targeted killings'. Al-Muslimi lives in a remote village called Wessab in the mountains of Yemen and was a recipient of a scholarship from the US State Department to study English. Six days before presenting his testimony, his town was struck by a drone attack that "terrified thousands of simple, poor farmers." His fellow villagers called and texted him after the strike asking why the United States was attacking them, why they were "trying to kill a person with a missile when everyone knows where he is and he could have been easily arrested?" Al-Muslimi reports that "what radicals had previously failed to achieve in my village, one drone strike accomplished in an instant: there is now an intense anger and growing hatred of America" (Al-Muslimi, 2013). Even if there were not a moral case against drone attacks, there would still be an inescapable prudential argument against such counter-productive terror.

As if the internment camps were not grotesque enough, those who have their rights stripped from them by fiat can now be blown up by soldiers acting upon bad intelligence with questionable authority – even in situations where an arrest would be entirely plausible. This is not only a horrific injustice to the victims, but also a terrible dishonor to those brave souls who risk their lives to protect those ideals the United States purports to stand for. The state of exception not only validates unjust internment, it brings the extermination ethic humanity has unleashed against other animals into its dealings with other humans. It is exactly as Nietzsche (1886) warned: "He who fights with monsters should be careful lest he thereby becomes a monster." We do not, as Derek Gregory (2006) reminds us, have to accept this state of affairs: "there is nothing ineluctable about the triumph of the security state or the generalization of the space of exception." If we wish to maintain the story that we are moral beings, we must resist national insecurity or risk voiding morality in its entirety.

Even if the state of exception is an unavoidable element of the concept of sovereign power, which is a matter for debate, the state of exception cannot be used to destroy the conditions for morality itself without undermining the authority of the national leader – the great chain of being is broken, after all, and our presidents now rule *in our names*. If human rights are moral, if they express (even badly) a baseline for the ethical treatment of humans by other humans, their nullification by the state of exception represents a far greater threat to morality than Nietzsche's abyss ever could. This raises a demand for us to better understand the notion of rights, and to achieve this we have to examine the ethical thought of the philosopher whose work paved the way for contemporary human rights legislation: Immanuel Kant.

Communal Autonomy

There have been few books of ethics as widely read as Kant's *Groundwork for the Metaphysics of Morals* (1785), and none that are as widely misunderstood. Asking Kantian scholar Allen Wood about this, he replied that "the first fifty times I read the Groundwork I did not understand it at all, but accepted many of the common errors, because they were easy to commit and had become hallowed by generations of misreading by others" (Wood and Bateman, 2012a). Part of the problem is that Kant is notoriously hard to read, and part of *this* problem is because Kant's writing is really quite terrible. I once presumed that this was simply an issue of translation, and that it read more poetically in the original German, but a German reader of my blog assured me that, no, "Kant's writing in German is pretty much unreadable" (Bateman, 2007). Indeed, as Parfit amusingly remarks:

> It is Kant who made really bad writing philosophically acceptable. We can no longer point to some atrocious sentence by someone else, and say 'How can it be worth reading anyone who writes like that?' The answer could always be 'What about Kant?'

Another part of the problem with the *Groundwork* is that it is intended to be the first of several volumes exploring its theme, but is usually read on its own. As the title itself specifies quite clearly, it is supposed to be read as a foundational piece for a future work entitled *The Metaphysics of Morals* (1797) – a book which is ironically quite easy to read, especially for something written by Kant! A still further problem is the order in which Kant chooses to present his key ideas. The *Groundwork* is written as a progression from a broadly common sense starting position to a deeply philosophical end point – and it is only in the context of these later sections that what Kant intends becomes clear. All too often, however, both proponents and critics of Kant's moral philosophy focus excessively on the first phase of the project, which entirely distorts the purpose of Kantian ethics, the most comprehensive duty ethics tradition in the world today.

It is important to understand that the project of Kant's *Groundwork* is an attempt to achieve some kind of *understanding* concerning what morality might be, and in particular what first principle might ground it. Kant was not looking to dictate some arbitrary system of moral rules, as he is sometimes presumed to have done. To be sure, when Kant does talk about specific duties he seems awfully uptight – but then, we're talking about an eighteenth century pietist Christian, whose view of the world is very different to anything around today, even those Christian sects in the US whose theology is close to the eighteenth century in character. Liberals looking back at Kant's specific moral claims may be shocked at how conservative he seems, as for example when he suggests that if all the prisons were to be closed down it would first be necessary to execute all the murderers (Kant, 1797). However, within Kant's own time, his views were most definitely liberal and, perhaps more importantly, much of what passes for liberal thought today descends from ideas developed most thoroughly by Kant. This is not to suggest that Kant is the architect of contemporary liberalism, since many other voices were involved in this discourse, but if all talk of 'rights' today were to be grounded philosophically rather than simply assumed, it would be impossible to do so without turning to Kant.

Not only an exceptional philosopher, Kant was also extremely active in the sciences. I mentioned earlier his role in the proposal of a theory of stellar evolution that is still used by astrophysicists today, to give just one small example. He was particularly active in anthropology (although this was a very different field in his day) and indeed his lectures on this subject were hugely popular – in terms of "attendance, interest, and accessibility" (Jacobs and Kain, 2003). It was Kant's view that it was impossible to explore ethics without studying human character, and although he never left his native town of Königsberg (what is now Kaliningrad) he read everything he could lay his hands on that might inform him about humanity, and he was as well-versed with the customs and peculiarities of the human world as anyone in his time could hope to be. As Tamar Szabó Gendler (2011) suggests, philosophers with an interest in human judgment have "always made use of the best empirical psychology of their time" – in Kant's case, he also *contributed* to that field directly.

In the *Groundwork*, however, Kant's exploration is expressly metaphysical since he is seeking to find a principle capable of grounding the moral law. As this implies, Kantian ethics from Kant's perspective is expressly a Law Ethic, but it is so because Kant believes that the moral law is something shared by *every* human, irrespective of their cultural differences – which is precisely why he believes there must be an underlying principle to be discovered. This point comes across most clearly for me in a footnote of a later work expressing surprise at the idea that there could be different religions:

> Difference of religions! A strange expression, as if one were to speak of different kinds of morality. There may indeed be various means which have been used in the course of time to promote religion, - but they are mere subjects of learned investigation, and do not really lie within the sphere of religion. In the same way there are many religious works – the Zend-Avesta [of Zoroastrianism], the Hindu Vedas, the Koran etc. - but there is only one religion, binding for all men and for all times. These books are each no more than the accidental mouthpiece of religion, and may be different according to differences in time and place (Kant, 1795).

Thus for Kant, as for contemporary Unitarians, Sufi Muslims, members of the Bahá'í Faith and so forth, at the heart of the different religious traditions is one religion, and equivalently at the heart of the different moral practices found around the world lies one morality – the moral law. But Kant, in a quintessentially Enlightenment move, refuses to see this law as being blindly passed down the great chain of being from God, through various intermediaries, down to lowly humanity, and instead seeks to understand morality as being founded upon human *freedom*. Part of Kant's political goals, particularly in the later *Metaphysics of Morals*, is precisely to justify the transition from autocratic monarchies to representative democratic institutions that Kant's contemporaries were already experimenting with. In other words, Kant sought to shatter the great chain of being and offer a new mythology of human equality.

The core of Kant's revolutionary moral mythology is the final formula of the moral law that he presents: the Formula of Autonomy, or "the idea of the will of every rational being as a will giving universal law (Kant, 1785). This idea combines the key elements of two earlier formulas he gives, the Formula of Universal Law, and the Formula of Humanity, and indeed he expressly states that these are really just different formulations of the same law. This has caused a great deal of confusion, since the three formulas clearly say radically different things! Wood (2006) clarifies, and rectifies some mistranslations, in stating that it is the final formula that "unites and sums up the others" and thus should be regarded as "the definitive formulation of the principle of morality, insofar as there is one". Kant calls this principle the *categorical imperative*, but by this he simply means that morality is the one thing that is not dependent upon whichever goals we happen to have set (which thus imply hypothetical imperatives) - by its very nature, the demands of morality as Kant construes them are necessarily 'categorical'.

As I understand it, the Formula of Autonomy expresses the concept of *communal autonomy* that is crucial to the way we understand ourselves as individuals who are united in collective endeavors such as democracies. On the one hand, we have the freedom of individuals to set our own ends – to *will* those ends as Kant would say. On the other hand, however, we have to make allowances for the *different* ends that our fellow individuals will. Willing something is not the same as desiring something, though, since it entails a sense of commitment beyond just wanting. To will something in Kant's terms is to be determined to actively work towards its enactment, which involves both an ambiguity as to whether it will indeed happen and a certainty about whether you actually want it to happen. What we want can change from moment to moment, but what we will changes only rarely.

As a trivial example of the distinction between wanting and willing, I may want a single malt whisky, but I cannot will one. On the other hand, I *could* will that I founded a distillery that ferments single malt whisky, although that seems like a lot of work that I would rather someone else did on my behalf (which is why I don't *will* that, even though I might imagine it). Conversely, I *did* will that I write this book, and indeed I am fulfilling that commitment now by writing this book. According to communal autonomy as Kant sees it, because I willed the writing of this book, you were obligated to me (at the absolute least) not to block me from doing so. Note that my willing the writing of this book doesn't obligate you to read it – and importantly I *can't* will you to read it, because I can only will my own ends, not yours.

However, this concept seems to immediately present some difficulties. What if I will to take all your money? After all, that doesn't ask you to will anything and is something that anyone might want to will for themselves. Kant disposes of problems like these with his first formulation, the Formula of Universal Law, which asks that we act only in ways that we could will to be universal laws. Clearly I cannot will it to be a universal law that anyone could take everyone else's money, since this leads to immediate contradictions (everyone would want to take everyone's money, so there could be no money). This is the idea of *ethics as universal*, which we encountered earlier.

Kant presents this as essentially the common sense view of ethics, which is why he presents it first in the *Groundwork*. Sadly, too many people took this as meaning that the Formula of Universal Law, and not communal autonomy, was the core of Kantian ethics – which radically underestimates Kant's vision of the categorical imperative of morality. Worse, as Wood (2002) remarks, many people have attempted to use Kant's first formula as "an ethical sausage machine" to mechanically crank out rules of action, which entirely misses the point of Kantian ethics. The idea of universal ethics is key to how Kant views the Formula of Autonomy working in practice, since if there were not some framework for common moral agreement there could be no communal autonomy. Kant presumes (not unreasonably) that we require some mutual ethical framework if the kind of co-operation he envisages is to become even remotely possible. For Kant, only a Law Ethic could be universally binding, and thus only a Law Ethic could ground morality.

Mutual Respect

It should be clear from what has already been said that Kant's moral system is indeed rule-focused, and that it is radically different from all other duty ethics approaches. The 'rules' of the categorical imperative do not dictate specific injunctions ('thou shalt not'), but instead provide a framework for reasoning about morality abstractly. As Wood (2008) explains, the fundamental principle of morality that Kant expounds doesn't even necessarily provide answers to the important ethical questions, but it *does* allow practitioners to orient their values when thinking about such questions. Rules are not the entirety of Kantian ethics, however, since his system also touches upon the other corners of the ethical triangle. They are agent-focused in so much as "the duty to develop one's moral character is the linchpin of Kant's entire system of duties" (Louden, 1986) and outcome-focused in so much as they value the goodness of ends above conformity with duty, although Kant's proposed duty to promote the happiness of others is certainly not a duty to maximize collective happiness in a utilitarian sense (Wood, 1999).

Precisely because it is primarily rule-focused, Kantian ethics can sometimes imply different moral conclusions to those that everyday moral judgment might sometimes offer. As a simple example, consider the case of a commuter who steps off the train with a ticket that is valid for the whole day but who isn't planning to travel any further and so generously decides to give the ticket to another commuter waiting in line, thus saving them the cost of travel. On the surface, this seems like a nice thing to do – but it violates ethics as universal, since it allows the second traveler to avoid paying their fair share of the cost of running the transport system. What looks like mutual benefit in the context of the two travelers seems differently when viewed from the perspective of *all* travelers.

However, this makes it sound as if Kant's moral system is as removed from the particulars of life as the already-rejected utilitarian 'naïve calculation', so it is worth remembering that ethics as universal is only one facet of the categorical imperative. Despite the previous example, co-operation for mutual benefit is precisely what Kant seeks to encourage, and the second formula aims to elucidate the proper relationship of one person to another. As the Formula of Humanity as End in Itself (or just Formula of Humanity) expresses: "Act so that you use humanity, as much in your own person as in the person of every other, always at the same time as end and never merely as means" (Kant, 1785).

There has been much disagreement concerning what the phrase "merely as means" is supposed to imply, but actually this formulation is extremely intuitive. For me, it is expressed quite effectively in the concept of *mutual respect*, which asks that we always take into account the individuality of other people, and never ignore their own capacity to will ends. Importantly, hiring someone does not violate this principle provided the job they are doing is what they will that they do for work or is consistent with whatever they will. Conversely, an employer that pays low wages, pays no benefits and insists upon long hours is taking advantage of their position of power and violating mutual respect *and* ethics as universal, since no-one could coherently will to be treated in this way.

Mutual respect asks for a different way of relating to others, one in which our capacity to set ends is taken to be deserving of a special dignity. Indeed, for Kant this dignity is inherent to all "rational beings", and not just humans, and he views this dignity as having an absolute worth that grounds the value of all other things. For me, as I have already established, this capacity has less to do with rationality and more to do with our imaginative capacities, but the point remains the same: because we can imagine ends that we will, we become a source of value for ourselves, as can any being with sufficient imagination. What's more, if we accept the idea that this dignity – whether of rationality or of imagination – is absolute, it follows that all beings that possess it have *equal worth* (Wood, 1999). This is precisely how Kantian ethics ends up with a moral fiction of equality, equivalent to the more mathematical equality ideal of the utilitarian that 'everybody counts for one, nobody for more than one'.

However, whether we consider rationality or imaginative faculty to be the critical factor, it is clear that without some kind of revision Kantian equality will include only humans and other animals with a comparable capacity to set ends. Depending upon your preferred approach within the ethical triangle, this is either a boon or a bane – for those arguing for animal ethics, the focus on rational beings is usually perceived as a significant deficit. Indeed, Kant tends to see duties towards animals as something that emerges indirectly from our duties towards other humans, leading Tzachi Zamir (2009) to allege that Kantians would be fine with someone secretly torturing stray cats in a cellar provided the torturer does not then proceed to torture humans. However, this is certainly an error since the concept of virtue Kant elucidates in *The Metaphysics of Morals* (1797) entails that a secret cat torturer would fail both in Kant's conceived duty to aim for self-perfection *as well as* being more likely to be cruel to other humans. As for other Kantians, I have already noted Korsgaard's (e.g. 2004, 2012) extension of Kant's system to other animals, which rests on the idea that animals qualify as ends-in-themselves and thus should not be treated merely as means under the (in this context, oddly named) Formula of Humanity as End in Itself.

Frankly, whether we are dealing with duty ethics or consequentialism, the question of moral relations with other animals can proceed only by modifying or discarding the relevant equality ideals – and this entails significant costs in both cases, since as is hopefully becoming clear we are still securing our democracies upon these particular moral fictions, albeit badly. We need to be especially careful when criticizing other people's moral systems precisely because we are most likely to be mistaken when we are away from the familiarity of our own ethical neighborhoods. If I may parody Zamir's erroneous assertion with an equally ludicrous counter-accusation, what is the rate of exchange between humans and mice for a utilitarian animal ethicist? Is it acceptable to murder a human if ten thousand mice will live? Yet such barbs are unworthy of philosophers, especially since consequentialists no longer adhere to naïve calculation and Kantians have far more diverse moral beliefs than other ethicists tend to expect. Kant's formula for mutual respect calls for us to accept diversity in the ends we collectively will – and that in turn might require us to accept *different* moral systems. No-one said Kantian ethics wasn't challenging!

Mutual respect is essential to communal autonomy, since only if we have at least a minimal respect for one another can we hope to align our ends. If the ideal of communal autonomy seems farfetched, if the ideal of mutual respect seems too optimistic, it may be worth reflecting upon what we discovered by considering morality before humanity. Each of us – every human, every dog, every cat, every mouse, and every mosquito – is comprised of vast numbers of individual cells, relatives of the bacteria, who collaborate to form these grand communities that operate on a scale of life that a single celled organism cannot hope to imagine. They do not co-operate in communal autonomy, however, for each cell does not set its own ends as such. Rather, these wonderful colonies are organized into a system of, if you will, communal heteronomy – they are collectively swayed by forces beyond their recognition. Yet still, they make it work somehow, no matter how strange and improbable it may seem. Next to this miracle, communal autonomy and mutual respect among humans should not seem beyond possibility.

Along with his various formulas of the categorical imperative in the *Groundwork*, Kant always provides an alternative formulation which is more metaphorical in nature, in the sure knowledge that it will help capture the imagination. These moral fictions are consistent with the content of Kant's system but offer a more vivid imagery that helps express the core of each formulation. Of these metaphors, the one that has the most impact is that offered for the Kantian 'master principle', the Formula of Autonomy – the *realm of ends*. This ideal, as Wood (1999) attests, is effectively a secularization of the Christian ideal that all humans are the children of God – indeed, another translation of the same term is 'kingdom of ends', which Korsgaard (2004) identifies as equivalent to the Kingdom of God on Earth. In the realm of ends, moral laws are viewed as having been legislated by everyone and for everyone, the individual autonomy of all is respected, and each is free to set their own goals provided they can align with the conditions of the realm itself. Kant recognizes the difficulty in attaining this state, admitting that it is "merely possible" (Kant, 1785), but stresses the unlimited value in striving for it.

To qualify as a 'realm' in Kant's sense, all the ends everyone has willed must neither conflict nor compete with each other, forming "a mutually supporting system" (Wood, 2006). To belong to the realm of ends, therefore, we would have to set ends that could conceivably belong to this common community, and avoid adopting ends that could not be part of it. Kant sometimes considers the realm of ends as something close to an ultimate goal for morality as he sees it. Indeed, at the end of his anthropology lectures, Kant suggests that it might be possible to progress towards greater good but that this could not be attained by "the free agreement of individuals" but only by "a progressive organization of citizens of the earth... as a system that is cosmopolitically united" (Kant, 1798). Wood (2006) notes in this regard how very different Kantian ideals are to utilitarian ideals, since the realm of ends affords priority not to human satisfaction and welfare, but to securing human community and harmony.

I confess, one of the key reasons that Kantian ethics appeal to me is that I have *always* seen morality this way myself – as an exercise in mutual respect and communal autonomy – and for this reason the realm of ends speaks to me in a way that resonates with how I try to live my life. Yet this also gives me significant problems, since I struggle with the concept of moral law, being far more comfortable with moral chaos. But how could there be a realm of ends built upon chaos? Kant's image of the realm of ends depends upon universal law to provide its solid foundation. My chaotic realm of ends could not rely upon this, or at least, it could not appeal to it in the way that Kant does. But then, Kant's lawful realm of ends is "merely possible" and I cannot know that my chaotic realm is impossible, so perhaps, just perhaps, there is a possibility here that may yet be explored...

Are Rights Wrong?

Kant's work in ethics and political philosophy builds upon a tradition of natural rights, the culmination of which are our human rights agreements, what Edward Demenchonok (2009) has called "the universal achievement of our civilization". Alasdair MacIntyre compares natural rights with unicorns, and there is a sense in which this comparison is apposite – the unicorn, after all, was mistakenly deduced from the horn of a narwhal, so there *was* an animal with a single horn it just *wasn't* a horse. In a similar manner we might say that while natural rights assumed a mythology that we are in no way obligated to accept, human rights do not depend upon this metaphysical foundation since they are *agreements*, promises that governments have made to their citizens, and are thus objective only within that context. But this recognition brings to light some rather disturbing aspects of the way human rights are currently deployed, and exposes another of the many disasters of contemporary moral philosophy.

Our chief witness for the prosecution in this affair is Alain Badiou, who I have already identified as the exemplar of Chaos Ethics today. Badiou demands nothing less than the immediate disbanding of the International Court of Human Rights, declaring that it "is clearly prepared to arrest and try, in the name of 'human rights', anyone, anywhere, who attempts to contest the New World Order of which NATO (i.e. the United States) is the armed guard" (Badiou, 2001). This criticism sounds odd while we think of rights as beneficial protections, and it is necessary to understand that Badiou sees human rights legislation as a horrific bastardization of Kant's intentions:

> What essentially is retained from Kant (or from an image of Kant, or, better still, from theorists of 'natural law') is the idea that there exist formally representable imperative demands that are to be subjected neither to empirical considerations nor to the examination of situations; that these imperatives apply to cases of offence, of crime, of Evil; that these imperatives must be punished by national and international law; that, as a result, governments are obliged to include them in their legislation; that if they do not, we are justified in forcing their compliance (the right to humanitarian interference, or to legal interference).

At the heart of this accusation is the idea that rather than Kant's communal autonomy, which demands our mutual co-operation, what has been retained of the Kantian project is solely the ethics as universal, compounding what Wood (1999) affirms is the most basic error about Kantian ethics. Yet Badiou's invective cuts deeper than this, for he is not interested in rescuing Kant's moral thought but in undermining *everything* that is taken for ethics today. Badiou's condemnation targets what he terms 'Ethics' with a capital 'E', which can be understood by what I have termed Law Ethics. He views Law Ethics as a presumed ability to discern Evil (also with a capital 'E'), inferring a consensus on what is "barbarian" and thus defining good as "what intervenes visibly" against this pre-defined Evil, stating that: "Law itself is first of all law 'against' Evil."

Rather than espousing something good worth defending, Badiou argues, human rights have somehow become the basis for nations to act in appalling ways on the grounds that they are fighting Evil. Hence it is acceptable to invade another nation in order to bring it the wondrous gift of human rights – something Kant (1795), incidentally, expressly forbade as immoral – while simultaneously *denying* those rights to those that are held in custody. Rather than serving as a counterbalance resisting national insecurity, human rights become its core propaganda. This is the danger Badiou identifies in a Law Ethic whose concept of good is defined only as a negative reflection of Evil, and the reason that he condemns the entire institution of human rights, root and branch. The moral fiction of Evil has become the justifying principle for evil. Instead of agreements capable of "cementing a global consensus" human rights have placed the politics of emancipation in a fragile state and left us all at the mercy of "the unrestrained pursuit of self-interest" and "the universality of unbridled competition."

Against this Law Ethic founded on opposition to Evil, Badiou proposes something quite different – an *ethic of truths*. But despite how this may sound, this is not a form of relativism – indeed, Badiou is equally critical of post-modernism and anything else that would deny claims to truth, insisting that "all truth is strictly *eternal* and impossible to reduce to any relativism" (Meillassoux, 2011). However, 'truth' for Badiou has an almost completely different meaning from how this term is usually understood, for he sees knowledge and truth as being radically distinct. In this way, Badiou's answer to Nietzsche's abyss is perhaps the most novel and surprising – he accepts that our relationship to truth must be constructed, but denies that this proves that there is no eternal truth. Instead, he sees truth as emerging through four (and, rather oddly, only four) truth procedures – amorous love, the arts, the sciences, and militant politics.

As we have come to recognize, knowledge is far more fragile than it first appears, and indeed is always open to future amendment. As such, Badiou denies that knowledge is the exemplary figure of truth, since he demands of anything claiming the name of truth that it must be eternal. He embodies knowledge in the iconic figure of the encyclopedia, which claims to capture truth but which is, of course, always subject to revision. (This is all the more true of the Wikipedia, although this is a far better aggregator of trivia than it is a model instance of an encyclopedia). Against this, Badiou claims that truth itself is almost impossible to recognize as such, but that it can become briefly discernible for a passing moment in what he calls an *event*. The event is a rupture in the current circumstances caused by an awareness of what is missing from those circumstances – a glimpse of the void inherent to any given state.

Truth thus punctures the existing order, exemplified by the encyclopedia, and although the truth itself is eternal and objective, those that encounter the event have only their subjectivity to make sense of it. This concept of truth is not something that can be *understood*, because to understand it would require putting it into the categories of knowledge that are already established, and Badiou's truth by definition *exceeds* whatever is captured by the categories of the encyclopedia. This approach owes a debt to Plato, highlighted by Badiou's recent audacious reimagining of Plato's *Republic* (Badiou, 2013) and made explicit by his stated aim to "found a Platonism of the multiple" (Badiou, 2000), since his entire philosophy proceeds from (of all things!) mathematical set theory.

Provided those who encounter the event can remain loyal to it, they have a chance to introduce that truth into the state of the world. This fidelity to an event is a key part of Badiou's ethics, indeed, it is practically *the entirety* of his ethic of truths, which he terms a "*persevering* ethic" and that he summarizes by the imperative "Keep going!" (Badiou, 2001). In this sense, Badiou's ethic of truths is agent-focused, and could be seen as a highly peculiar form of virtue ethics except for its commitment to the event of truth rather than virtue, as such. But whereas virtue ethics emerges from its ties to institutions that form part of the established order, Badiou's ethic of truths is always fundamentally opposed to the established order, his political truth process in particular is *always* resistance. Politics, for Badiou, cannot mean parliamentary democracy, which is obsessed with public opinion, it must mean commitment to eternal truth – and the political mythology he leverages for this is always that of equality.

By maintaining fidelity to truth as the focus of his moral thought, Badiou creates a Chaos Ethic for the militant, the revolutionary, the imaginative genius, and the lover, for all those who forsake the established order for a new truth they have encountered. Those who can maintain their fidelity to an event will find themselves in a position of struggle "achieved precisely through enormous effort." In this regard, calling Badiou's approach a Chaos Ethic after the terminology of Michael Moorcock is particularly apposite, since Moorcock's heroes repeatedly strive to break cycles of repetitive history by their own tremendous exertion and struggle. For Moorcock, as for Badiou, the only viable way of disrupting the injustice of empire is by militant resistance, and both recognize that it is equally possible for this opposition to run spectacularly awry.

Badiou identifies three specific forms of Evil, all of which distort the fidelity to truth he places at the heart of his ethic of truths. Firstly, there is 'simulacrum' (or 'terror'), an "appalling imitation of truths" that acts as if it is founded upon universality but that becomes "terror directed at everyone". This evil involves genuine fidelity, but to a *false* event – an event that does not involve the eternal aspect that Badiou associates with truth, it lacks "universal address". Badiou sees the ethic of truths as directly in opposition to this terror, claiming that "every invocation of blood and soil, of race, of custom, of community, works directly against truths". Fidelity to a simulacrum, therefore, works to promote the private interests of a given nation, race, or community *against* universality and eternal truth. Badiou gives the example of the Romanian revolution of 1989 as a case of simulacrum, but there are no shortage of examples of uprisings that ended in sustained terror (Badiou, 2005), and the theme also appears frequently in Moorcock's alternative history novels (e.g. 1971, 1974) where it is expressly associated with his key themes of racism and empire.

The second Evil Badiou identifies is that of 'betrayal', to give up on a truth in the pursuit of self-interest. Here, someone who has been exposed to the eternal truth of an event eventually convinces themself that it didn't happen, that the event *never happened* and that the person transformed by it *never existed*. Betrayal in Badiou's sense is more than mere renunciation, for he insists that it not possible to simply 'renounce' an eternal truth. He says of this that it explains why it is that former revolutionaries must declare that they were "lost in error and madness", and equally why those who give up on love can no longer understand *why* they thought they were in love. The defeat of the ethic of truths at a crisis point presents itself precisely as a betrayal, and this is "an Evil from which there is no return" (Badiou, 2001).

Lastly, Badiou talks of 'disaster' as the third form of Evil – to believe in the total power of a truth such that it becomes absolute, and so comes to organize Evil. The problem here is that the power of eternal truth is *situated,* it is encountered through the event and then must be maintained by fidelity to whatever truth is thus revealed. In disaster, the truth is elevated to an absolute principle that can no longer possibly relate to whatever was revealed by the event. The truth of the event has a power to change the meaning of the language used, to bring the terms of discussion closer to the truth, but it cannot hope to settle such matters permanently since Badiou's truth is something that can be encountered solely as a process. There is always something unnamable about a situation, and the principle of disaster is to demand and require that this be named. Disaster tries to end discussion by making truth absolute, but the power of a truth, Badiou suggests, is also necessarily a powerlessness. When the truth is instead used to make something absolute and total, something beyond dispute, the process by which the truth can transform a situation is irrevocably destroyed – hence the disaster.

It is in this sense, I suggest, that Badiou's critique of human rights *fails* to demonstrate that human rights are wrong. What Badiou *does* show is that contemporary pursuit of human rights on the international stage has become a simulacrum, a source of terror, and simultaneously a disaster in so much as it assumes the absoluteness of its principles. Yet human rights are institutions we have formed *and are still forming* through our communal autonomy (to what limited extent we have managed to embody this truth). It is indeed a disaster when human rights are taken to be absolute, since then it seems both plausible and necessary to *force* human rights agreements onto others. Yet no-one can justifiably be compelled by violence into promising to defend liberty

– to suggest otherwise is the most dangerous kind of contradiction.

The criticism that Badiou raises needs to be taken seriously, however, because even if we have no interest in his Chaos Ethic, it must be recognized that a genuine Kantian ethic, a genuine consequentialist ethic, a sincere virtue ethic must *all* deny what is being done in the name of human rights, even – especially! - if they wish to defend human rights. As Mary Midgley (2003) suggests, whatever doubts we may have about rights, the fact that those who are oppressed so frequently turn to the language of rights to express their situation demonstrates that it serves as "a kind of intercultural dialect that everybody understands." In this sense, human rights are eternal truths in Badiou's sense, or rather, the process by which we come to understand such rights contains truth. But as Midgley observes, the language of rights is just one part of our moral repertoire, and we cannot afford to let our enthusiasm for human rights lead us to ignore our many other ideals, much less can we use it to justify national insecurity.

The ethic of truths, the radical Chaos Ethic of truth-as-process, endeavors to "ward off Evil" by striving for fidelity to eternal truths that we can only encounter subjectively. Under its imperative to "Keep going!" it offers virtues of discernment ("do not fall for simulacra"), courage ("do not give up"), and of moderation ("do not get carried away to the extremes of totality"). Unlike Law Ethics, it cannot expect to "submit the world to the abstract rule of a Law", and neither can it struggle against an externally specified Evil. Rather, it recognizes that Evil itself occurs as the "underside, or dark side" of the very truths it seeks to foster (Badiou, 2001). Evil might thus be prevented by fidelity to a truth that cannot be known – but *this* process is something we usually refer to by another name: *faithfulness*.

This word, which nowadays has acquired a decidedly negative reputation in intellectual circles, is so intimately connected with religion that the contemporary backlash against faith traditions makes it practically heretical for me to even *say* it, much less mean it. Yet Badiou's ethic of truths asks precisely for faithfulness to the event – his is a non-religion of faith despite the entirety of his philosophy being positioned against traditional religion. Badiou's core objection in this respect is that his philosophical ruminations on set theory convince him God is an impossibility, since "the One is Not" (Badiou, 2011). Actually, this atheological argument is far from convincing, since set theory *also* renders Badiou's event entirely impossible and yet his philosophy depends upon it, a point noted by Peter Dews (2008) and others.

Badiou borrows his term 'fidelity' from the sphere of love and relationships, where 'faithful' is less tainted by the accusation that it denies reason – although anyone who has sustained a marriage successfully for many years may be far less quick to jump to assumptions about the virtue of rationality and the vice of faith. I've only been married for twelve years, but I would never for a moment suggest that my marriage has been sustained by reason! If what Law Ethics have in common is their commitment to absolute truth, and with this a commitment to the rationality that derives or approximates this truth, then perhaps what Chaos Ethics have in common is precisely what Badiou invokes with the word 'fidelity': faithfulness, with all the potential irrationality that might entail.

Otherness

When talking philosophically about faithfulness, the figure who inevitably stands out is Søren Kierkegaard. As already mentioned, much of Kierkegaard's life and work was tasked with trying to undermine Christendom, the vacuous perversion of the Christian tradition into a rule-governed, nationalistic enterprise. A parallel aspect of his philosophy was an attempt to discover how it was possible to be an authentic individual, something he suggests necessarily requires a leap of faith (Kierkegaard, 1843). Although it is rarely noted, MacIntyre points out that Kierkegaard's work owes a positive debt to Kant, suggesting that "it is in Kant's honest and unpretentious German that Kierkegaard's elegant but not always transparent Danish finds its paternity." Indeed, when Kierkegaard argues against an ethics of the universal, stressing the individual's necessity to be true to God, it is to Kant's concept of ethics as universal that he clearly refers. MacIntyre also notes that Kierkegaard's paradigm of the ethical is marriage, "a state of commitment and obligation through time, in which the present is bound by the past and to the future." Ethics, faith, and marriage are intimately connected in Kierkegaard's philosophy.

In recent years there has been a certain resistance to Kierkegaard among intellectuals that stems in part from the understandable hostility that most positivists have towards the very idea of 'faith', which is viewed as inherently negative. Faith is also usually contrasted to reason, which is presumed to be devoid of faith. Yet as Badiou's discussion of fidelity demonstrates we would be unwise to consider faith as a vice given that any act of commitment to any worthwhile cause (including a marriage) is necessarily an act of faith, and this is just as true of the commitment to reason and rationality as it is of anything else. Much of the hatred poured out against faith traditions from both intolerant positivists *and* from rival faith traditions does not distinguish between fidelity to the values of a tradition and blind faith in absolutes – two radically distinct concepts of 'faith'. Kierkegaard was keen to note in this regard that when it comes to individuals with 'blind faith' they *cannot* embody faith since they act with a certainty that denies the doubt inherent to faithfulness – as Charles Taylor (2007) remarks, very few religious believers are this untroubled about their faith.

In a quintessential Chaos Ethical move, Kierkegaard (like Foucault after him) recognized that purportedly dispassionate reason was all too often a cover for self-interest, and that any claim that we can have access to an absolute point of view (as Law Ethics tend to presume) was a fantasy with very sketchy foundations. It was this that caused him to argue against Kant's view of ethics as the universal – even though Kierkegaard's moral philosophy is strikingly dependent upon Kant, as MacIntyre attests. Indeed, despite the apparent gulf between Kant's Law Ethics and Kierkegaard's Chaos Ethics, the connections between the two philosophers run deep. Ronald M. Green has written a wonderful "detective story" that exposes not only the extent to which Kierkegaard's work was built upon Kant's foundations, but also shows that Kierkegaard's contradictions between morality, reason, and faith are mirrored, point-for-point, in Kant's work (Green, 1992).

In some respects, it is surprising how long it took Badiou to get around to discussing Kierkegaard (Badiou, 2009), since it has long been apparent to students of both philosophers how much Badiou's theory of the event resembles themes the Danish philosopher was exploring a hundred and fifty years earlier. Badiou even seems to recognize this commonality in remarking that Kierkegaard thinks and understands matters in a similar manner to him, although he of course is unable to endorse Kierkegaard's philosophy in its entirety because of the theological gulf between them. Badiou's friend Slavoj Zižek has been relentless in his amusement at the tacit religious themes that lurk in Badiou's philosophy, and explicit in drawing a connection between Badiou and Kierkegaard, although only ever in passing (e.g. Zižek, 2004). No matter what differences there might be, it seems these two Chaos Ethicists belong together in some ill-defined sense.

Caught between Kierkegaard and Badiou in many respects is another ethical philosopher, Emmanuel Lévinas, who was raised in a traditional Jewish community in Lithuania before joining Strasbourg University in 1924 as a philosophy student. As Lee

Braver (2012) notes, Lévinas' work took inspiration in part from Kierkegaard, as well as from Kant, and especially from his mentor Edmund Husserl. Badiou *despises* Lévinas' ethical philosophy, complaining that it sheds no light on any actual situation to think in the terms that Lévinas proposes (Badiou, 2001). I am less keen to dismiss Lévinas, in part because my discovery of his work proceeds through the work of Joanna Zylinska (2009) - and the face revealed to me in her ethical thought, while certainly descending from Lévinas, does not appear to suffer from the criticisms Badiou raises.

It is important from the outset to appreciate that the ethic that Lévinas espouses isn't a system of values, and contains no suggestion of adherence to laws or inner principles (Valevičius, 1987). It is not so much an ethical system as it is a way of thinking about morality, although it still qualifies as an 'ethic' in the broad sense I am using and Lévinas philosophy can be used as the basis for moral systems (Wu, 2007). Unlike other philosophers, for whom ethics usually depends upon philosophical work in other areas, Lévinas insisted that ethics were *primary* in philosophy, believing that moral notions could be explained by the fundamental phenomenon of the face of the other (1963). 'Face' should be understood in this context not as the literal visage – eyes, nose, mouth and so forth – but the aspect of another being that we encounter. Although in Lévinas' writing the other is always another human, in Zylinska and with the *otherness ethic* in general, the face we encounter could be anything at all – even a creature with no face! When I stare at a limpet clinging to a rock at Steephill Cove, what I encounter is the 'face' of the limpet, in Lévinas' terms, even though a limpet has no face to speak of.

This experience of encountering the face of the other is prior to conscious reflection in Lévinas' account, and leads to a kind of guiltless responsibility whereby we are "responsible without being culpable" (Lévinas, 1983) for the other that we encounter. This responsibility can never be absolved, and is prior to any action that might be taken. Responsibility in Lévinas' account is not therefore something you owe to yourself so much as it is something you hold for the other that you encounter: "The I before another is infinitely responsible" (Lévinas, 1963). Thus, according to Lévinas, we are all responsible for those that go hungry in our world in a way that is more fundamental than the way we are responsible for our own actions, because the ultimate source of our (unenforceable) ethical obligations is our need to ameliorate the suffering of the other, and in this regard, we must inevitably flounder against the scope of the problem.

In terms of the relationship between imagination and ethics, Thomas Cottle (2002) offers a fascinating perspective on the human experience of the otherness ethic, noting that the way we encounter other humans is generally through the story they tell us. But in this we always risk misunderstanding, since we tend to interpret such stories in our own terms. Thus we step away from the encounter believing the other to be "dead wrong, pigheaded, dogmatic, outrageously ideological, or outright mentally ill". Yet still, the trace of the other (as Lévinas puts the matter) is there in the story they tell us, the *narrative* becomes the other for us, "as direct as the meeting of eyes". What's more (as my paper time machine suggested) *we are all infinite narratives*, yet we tend to encounter others as just "that one telling tale". The challenge that Cottle develops from Lévinas is thus to respond to the words of the other human whose story we are told, because the story I tell of myself will struggle to maintain that I am a good person if I do not. This has some commonalities with MacIntyre's description of virtue ethics, with its stress on narrative unity, and of course both are effectively agent-focused.

Lévinas' approach to ethics has acquired quite a following among certain intellectuals, but it has not been immune to criticism. Wood (1999) expresses a certain disdain for the "mystical worship" of the other in a footnote, but this is nothing compared to the scorn heaped upon the otherness ethic by

Badiou. As an initial criticism, Badiou contends that in order to make his ethics work, Lévinas has to appeal to a principle of otherness that transcends experience, and this principle is "quite obviously the ethical name for God" (Badiou, 2001). In this regard, Badiou's critique is rather flat, since no commentator on Lévinas' work would deny that this was how Lévinas saw the matter, and it is certainly not something that is concealed in his work. However, Badiou here entirely ignores the effort Lévinas applies towards emptying his approach of any explicit religious content to leave only moral experience behind. Defenders of Lévinas need not accept this particular criticism from Badiou at face value, although neither can they entirely ignore it.

A far more troublesome complaint is Badiou's suggestion that infinite otherness is both self-evident *and uninteresting*, since infinite difference is entailed in all experience. For Badiou, the cornerstone of Lévinas' approach is "nothing more than the infinite and self-evident multiplicity of humankind, as obvious in the difference between me and my cousin from Lyon as it is between the Shi'ite 'community' of Iraq and the fat cowboys of Texas." But this latter concern does not seem to have as its target the Lévinas-inspired otherness ethic so much as it aims its barbs at the multiculturalism we have already exposed as troublesome. It's far from clear that Badiou's polemic attack on liberal ideals of difference is wisely directed at Lévinas. Indeed, Badiou seems to simply *assume* that these kinds of problems stem from the otherness ethic, despite no aspect of this politically correct charade being proposed by Lévinas or (as far as I can tell) anyone else in the ethical tradition that follows from him.

The point of focusing on the encounter with the face of the other in Lévinas is certainly not to advance anything like what Badiou excoriates in his savage remarks against so-called respect for difference. Rather, Lévinas key point is that ethics begins with the acceptance of the ethical demand that the face of the other presents us, a demand that he frequently summarizes in the Abrahamic commandment "Thou shalt not kill" (e.g. Lévinas, 1974) - and it is precisely here, in the decision *not to kill the other*, that Lévinas claims ethics *begins*. In this regard, if we are going to connect the otherness ethic with something else it would not be liberal intolerant tolerance, but Haché and Latour's ethic of hesitation, which is perhaps why the proponents of otherness have so frequently been open to extending it to other animals, despite Lévinas himself rarely leaning in this direction.

Suppose we accept Lévinas suggestion that ethics begins when we decline to kill – what kind of ethics springs from this stepping point? Lévinas does not develop a specific system, having been more intent on offering new foundations, but if we use Lévinas' moral fiction of encountering the face of the other and use it to interpret Kant's categorical imperative, what results might help shed light on both. Our responsibility for the other, Lévinas claims, stems from the other's infinite difference from us, and this can be seen as the source of Kant's formula of mutual respect: to treat another being as a means to our ends would be to ignore the face of the other, and thus refuse to be ethical. As long as we recognize the other's face, and the unenforceable obligation this represents, we have mutual respect for the other.

Joanna Zylinska raised a query to me in this regard, in that core to Lévinas' ethics is the idea that it is one-sided and non-mutual. She notes: "it doesn't even matter whether the other will reciprocate or not, because this obligation – to respond, and be responsible – is solely mine" (personal correspondence, 2011). However, Kant's second formula seems to be compatible with this stance. Consider his original wording: "Act so that you use humanity, as much in your own person as in the person of every other, always at the same time as end and never merely as means" (Kant, 1785). Although this formula leads to mutual respect, it *begins* with the obligation for the individual to treat the other as an 'end-in-themselves'. Kant and Lévinas are not so far apart on this point, as Feng-Wei Wu (2007) attests, and in an interview Lévinas even states that Kant's Formula of Humanity is close to his concept of the other.

Furthermore, since even through inaction we allow the suffering of others to take place, we inherit a guiltless responsibility whereby we have an ethical duty towards the other in all its faces. Thus the needs of others (at least in the sense of curtailing their suffering) become *our* needs – which is Kant's formula of communal autonomy, provided it is constrained to dealing only with the alleviation of suffering. In many respects it may even be possible to push this analogy further. Kant characterized this particular formula as follows: "Act in accordance with maxims of a universally legislative member for a merely possible realm of ends" (Kant, 1785). This viewpoint is very different to that of Lévinas, but both philosophers were gesturing in the same direction – to a communal engagement in well-being (the realm of ends) rooted in the inescapable responsibility of the individual. As Wu remarks in this respect: "Lévinas shares much of the goal of Kant's moral enterprise."

All that remains is Kant's first formula for the categorical imperative: ethics as universal. But if our ethical duty is for the other and not for ourselves, as Lévinas asserts, this duty by definition *must* be universal, since we are all the other for every other (we are all someone else to someone else). However, Lévinas recognizes along with Kierkegaard (1843) that there is an inescapable conflict of interest in this universality: in any given moment, we have responsibility for everyone else but we can only act responsibly towards a particular other, so to behave ethically is paradoxically to fail in our duty in some subtle sense. (Zylinska suggests this is also the moment when politics enters into the ethical domain). This circumstance does not alter the duty – it does not alter the universality – it is simply a recognition of its problematic limits. Besides, for Lévinas the need to respond to the other is "unconditional and infinite" (Wu, 2007) - a universality rooted not in moral law but in moral chaos.

Thus when Lévinas' moral fiction of the face of the other is used to interpret Kant's concept of a categorical imperative, the three distinct formulations that Kant proposes appear as consequences of Lévinas' approach of situating ethics as a responsibility without culpability resulting from our response to that other face. From the perspective of Chaos Ethics in general, it is worth noting that Lévinas' approach also allows for Kierkegaard's overturning of the necessary priority of the universal, asking that the urgent needs of those we encounter weigh above even our conception of the moral law (a theme prefigured in the parable of the Good Samaritan). Lévinas is therefore revealed not only as a Chaos Ethicist, but also as arguably offering a different path towards the realm of ends, the communal autonomy that lies at the heart of the ethical for Kant. Ever the epitome of Law Ethics, Kant himself would not approve, and neither would many Kantians, but it does not weaken their core ideals to suggest that there could be more than one way to attain them. Although Lévinas does not expressly offer a Kantian Chaos Ethic, he at least hints that such a thing might yet be attainable.

The Dishonor of Nations

Returning to the issues with which this chapter began, we are now in a position to appreciate the brutal irony in the way national insecurity is publically defended by appeal to a Law Ethic, even though it manifests via the state of exception and thus through immoral chaos. The whole purpose of the human rights legislature was to offer a Law Ethic that could transcend national concerns. As stated by Eleanor Roosevelt, who chaired the United Nations commission that drew up the so-called Universal Declaration of Human Rights in 1948: "We stand today at the threshold of a great event both in the life of the United Nations and in the life of mankind. This declaration may well become the international Magna Carta for all men everywhere" (Roosevelt,

1948). In this historical moment was the fulfillment of Kant's dream of bringing morality to international politics, sketched in *Toward Perpetual Peace* (Kant, 1795). As Roosevelt herself stated: "Man's desire for peace lies behind this declaration." Alas, fear and anxiety were to unravel this hope half a century later; imagined terror has trumped promises of justice.

There are so many betrayals of the hope of human rights that it is difficult to know where to begin, but perhaps the most extreme cases are the abominations resulting from indiscriminate drone attacks. On the moral question of the deployment of drones in war, defense analyst Bradley Strawser (2010) has provided the general form of the argument: if the war is just, its soldiers have a duty to use the best equipment available in order to defend themselves. However, even he concedes that this argument is about how drones *should* be used, not how they are *actually* used, which he admits entails military actions that are "morally questionable or outright impermissible." The deeper problem with the drones doesn't lie in their specific qualities, but in the way they bring into focus the vast gap between the mythology deployed to justify war (the just war doctrine), and the kind of warfare currently being waged. As Strawser argues, it's no good complaining at the asymmetry of the drone attack since how can you view as 'fair' a fight "between an F-22 pilot flying at altitude delivering a precision missile and a tribal warrior wielding a rocket-propelled grenade?" The asymmetry problem was long since hurdled by our cyberfetish for war machines.

What is amazing about drones is that they finally bring this aspect of cyberfetish into clear focus, since many of us find something deeply disturbing about these robotic weapons. But it is not this specific technology that is a problem from the perspective of war but rather the idea that there is a moral obligation to develop ever-better weaponry and defenses for the waging of war, a position that Strawser openly defends, albeit with qualifications. He does so on the basis that we have a moral obligation to protect a just warfighter, and I do not disagree. But this cannot possibly overwhelm our obligation to avoid deploying our soldiers in an *unjust* war, and it is far less clear that it is possible to know the justice or otherwise of any contemporary armed conflict. If 'our' side has sanction to use robotic weaponry to murder civilians, then the war it is waging is *no longer just,* no matter what circumstances are claimed for its onset.

I found it very challenging to write letters to a friend of mine who served in the second Gulf War. He had been born in Denton, Manchester, but later moved to live in Denton, Texas – weird coincidences having always been his stock-in-trade. After the events of the early twenty first century, he signed up to serve in the U.S. armed forces because he didn't want to stand idly by and do nothing – a surprising development, since in my wild years no-one had been a greater hedonist than him! His fellow soldiers couldn't quite understand why a college graduate with a career in computing was there in the desert alongside them, since enlistment for most had been something of a last resort (for all that they held the services in great respect). I wrote to him despite my opposition to this war, because I wanted to support my friend through difficult times. But what do you tell someone who, having made a willing sacrifice of duty, begins to doubt the justice of their cause? I told him what I had learned from *Henry V* (Shakespeare, 1600): "if the cause not be good, the king himself hath a heavy reckoning to make..." He had to have hope for the people of Iraq, whatever the providence of the war itself.

For all my opposition to the way that the U.S. Military has been deployed, and for all that I am inclined to pacifism, I still believe in honorable military service. This ideal only doubles the tragedy of Guantánamo Bay and the horror of civilian drone attacks, since as well as the terrible costs to their victims there is the additional price paid by the honor and respect of the men and women who risk their lives to defend ideals their own nation is now too frightened to uphold. Not only a betrayal of Eleanor Roosevelt, but the breaking of the promises of a nation: the true expense of the war on terror is incalculable. All those politicians – Republicans and Democrats, Presidents, senators and congressmen – who have brought such grave dishonor upon the military institutions of the United States should be ashamed that they lacked the courage to defend moral law against their own cowardice. It can only be immoral to blindly sacrifice not only strangers and foreigners you had sworn to treat as equals, but friends and family you have unwisely dispatched into harm's way, all in the pursuit of a safety your own actions render unobtainable.

The problems of bureaucracies explored in the previous chapter are escalated when they are occur in national organizations in part because it is much more difficult to persuade nations to hesitate. By their very nature, a State embeds a certain bias towards its citizens and against those of other nations – but as earlier discussions of home communities have stressed, this need not devolve into immorality. However, it is exceptionally likely to do so when a country forms a bureaucracy *incapable* of hesitation. This is the essential problem with 'intelligence' organizations and the justifications for war – the state of exception is used to justify a failure to hesitate, and thus immorality becomes implicit in military bureaucracy. This is by no means necessary – it is entirely conceivable that a nation could instill in its military all the values that it wishes to defend domestically: neither Spartan hoplites, nor Viking raiders, nor Chinese tiger generals would have accepted that attaining victory was worth dishonorable conduct.

Furthermore, and as a simple matter of fact, it is *not* necessary that armed forces kill – weapons technology *need not* focus on lethality. Somehow, we constantly forget that we could choose to channel our technological developments away from those things we abhor. Yet even accepting this possibility, there is always a risk in funding the institutions of war since such organizations counterproductively escalate what they are meant to eliminate (Illich, 1973). As Hannah Arendt (2005) stated of the arms races of the mid-twentieth century, the conditions that international cyberfetish engenders now suggest that Kant's statement that "nothing should happen in a war to make a later peace impossible" has been turned upon its head so that "we live in a peace in which nothing may be left undone to make a future war still possible."

National insecurity is personal bias elevated to the stage of Statehood. Within the ethical triangle, there is no way of evoking the state of exception that does not render it toxic for morality because it depends at heart upon the exceptionalism that all ethics necessarily seeks to curtail. Whether we come to the problem via Lévinas' otherness ethic, Badiou's ethic of truths, or Kant's communal authority, national insecurity is categorically *wrong*. Badiou may reject human rights, but he would not and could not do so to defend the horrors of Guantánamo Bay or the despicable and cowardly use of armed drones for the murder of innocents. On the contrary, the detainment camps are Badiou's simulacrum and terror since they exalt the citizens of the United States above others; drone attacks are his disaster, because they take national insecurity to be an absolute truth; and the state of exception is his betrayal because the United States were acting faithfully to the truth of Kantian ethics when they instituted human rights, and have now been depressingly unfaithful to this tradition.

Yet it is only with Lévinas that our quandary in respect of national insecurity becomes truly moral, and not merely political, because in the unlimited responsibility for the other we all bear the shame of permitting the state of exception that allows for such terrible abuses of our fellow humans. As someone who was himself subjected to the state of exception during World War II,

Lévinas is perhaps the most fitting spokesperson for the catastrophic failure of morality inherent to internment camps. He was fortunate that he was wearing a French uniform and thus was treated as a prisoner of war, since the alternative was unthinkably worse, yet still he writes that he and his fellow prisoners were all but invisible to everyone in and around the camp – except for one dog who treated them as men, the "last Kantian" in a nation that had abandoned ethics for terror (Lévinas, 1990). When Al-Harith wished for the rights of a dog at Guantánamo Bay, he might just as well have wished that the dog had been the arbiter of his rights: it seems as if he would have received better treatment.

8

Ethical Things

Speaking for the Sun

The year that my son was born, my family travelled to Devon to visit my aunt. While we were there, we took the opportunity to go hiking, something we have long enjoyed. Some of our favorite destinations for hikes are the stone circles that dot the landscape of the British Isles. Although Stonehenge receives star billing among these prehistoric landmarks, there are well over a thousand such monuments, all differing in size, number and composition of stones, and even in shape. Whereas the henge is characterized by its arch-like constructions, most of the stone circles are far simpler, consisting of little more than tall stones positioned in an elliptical or circular formation. Although the British stone circles are some five thousand years old, they are not the oldest that have been found – those at Göbekli Tepe in Turkey are at least twelve thousand years old (Scham, 2008), for instance.

I discovered that there was an unusual example on Dartmoor known as Grey Wethers, which consists of two stone circles positioned as neighbors just a short distance apart, and we resolved to hike to them. With my baby strapped to my back and my wife and dog by my side, I attempted to navigate the moors to get to our ancient destination. However, our first attempt was unsuccessful – we came on a trail that was so untraveled as to be effectively unmarked, and came up against seriously swampy ground that made progress impossible. Examining the maps more carefully, I discovered an alternative route that took us over the top of one of the peaks of Dartmoor, connecting up with an access road through a forest that took us right to the edge of the grassy plateau where the stones stand. On our second expedition, we arrived at Grey Wethers amidst a dense mist, and stood at a site that millennia hence was obviously of great importance to the humans of that time.

How are we to understand the relationship between Grey Wethers and the humans that constructed it? They are no longer around, these ancient peoples, and these twinned stone circles are all that remains of their world. Archaeologists can study the site, but their investigations create further mysteries without resolving those we already have. Obviously Grey Wethers was constructed, and we can get a sense of *why*, in the sense that we can understand reasons for wanting to track the position of the sun, of tracing the passing of seasons. But I cannot get back to the world of the people who built Grey Wethers any more than they can join me in my world. Even if the rocks themselves could speak, they could not tell me about those people that moved them there, those who placed them in such carefully constructed configurations.

It is all too easy to be misled when thinking about the lives of ancestral humanity. There is a commonly recounted story in circulation that recapitulates August Comte's mythology of progress, placing the makers of fetishes as a first stage, and the replacement of religion by Science as a final stage (Comte, 1830). You can get a sense of this perspective from Brian Cox's description of the Thirteen Towers, a row of stones upon a ridgeline at Chankillo in Peru that functions in many respects like a stone circle:

> Chankillo still works as a calendar because the sun still rises in the same place today as it did when these stones were first laid down... You can almost feel the presence of the past here, you can imagine what it must have been like, thousands of citizens stood here to greet the sun, which was almost certainly a deity, almost certainly a god. What a magnificent achievement, probably one of our earliest attempts to begin to

> measure the heavens. Over the millennia that desire to measure what's going on in the skies has led to modern astronomy and the foundations of our modern civilization (*Wonders of the Universe,* 2011).

Actually, the Thirteen Towers are only about two and a half millennia old, and so a long way from being a first attempt to measure the passage of the sun (Ghezzi and Ruggles, 2007), but Cox's soliloquy here is insightful not for what it reports but for the mythology that underpins it. Although he clearly has appreciation for the people who built the Thirteen Towers, his admiration is positioned within the story that what they were doing "has led to" contemporary sciences and civilization – the achievement of the ancient Peruvians is to be understood as a stepping stone towards our own greatness. This is Comte's positivist mythology in the form it most often manifests today, which entails a kind of time-travelling intolerant tolerance – the accomplishments of prior civilizations are to be understood as crude attempts to push towards *our* achievements.

Standing at Grey Wethers, I certainly did not feel this sense of temporal superiority that is implicit in Cox's account. On the contrary, I felt not only the admiration he and I share for the astronomical skills on display – mapping the heavens using just stone tools, with considerable accuracy – but also a sense of wonder and respect for the men and women who not only built Grey Wethers, but also made it a part of their lives. We can only guess at their mythologies, but we need not do so by looking down our noses. Whatever religious practices occurred at Grey Wethers, they surely involved a ceremonial celebration of the seasons. Who could honestly say that the winter rituals that took place at Grey Wethers were inherently inferior to the way we last celebrated Christmas or similar festivals? Who is even in a position to judge?

There is still a remnant of the condescending attitude that the

British and other Empires held towards 'primitive' cultures behind the implicit denigration of prehistoric monuments. I find them more impressive than the glass and steel monstrosities we build today, and have great respect for those who built them, even if there is very little I can uncover about how they lived. We are no more separated from these early settlers than we are from remote tribes today, and there are few if any reasons to believe our contemporary cultures are inherently superior to these other forms of human life. That we are even tempted to claim otherwise is another manifestation of cyberfetish, and shows how this also connects with intolerant tolerance.

The fetish being that which is constructed by human hands but imbued with divine attributes, we can say that Grey Wethers and the Thirteen Towers were fetishes for those that built them. Yet they also measured time, and formed the basis for a seasonal calendar with great relevance for agriculture – the rocks allowed the sun to speak. These ancient monuments were both fetish *and* fact. The impulse of the positivist and others of similar disposition is to denounce the fetish and praise the fact, but to do so is to fall prey of Isabelle Stengers' 'curse of tolerance' (2003): the makers of Grey Wethers *believed* the sun was a god, but we *know* it is just a ball of hydrogen fusing into helium.

Bruno Latour (2010c) raises similar problems in the context of Catholic Portuguese explorers meeting tribal humans on the western coast of Africa, around what is now called Guinea: "Covered with amulets of the saints and the Virgin themselves, they accused the Gold Coast Blacks of worshipping fetishes." The term 'fetish' is actually derived from a Portuguese verb meaning 'to do' or 'to make', and the concept comes with an accusation: "You can't say both that you've made your own fetishes and that they are true divinities; *you have to choose*: it's either one or the other." As Latour quips: "Too bad the Africans did not return the compliment. It would have been nice to see them ask the Portuguese dealers if their own amulets of the

Virgin had been made by hand or had fallen directly out of the sky."

Latour sees these encounters as essentially the origin of the division into belief and knowledge that is captured in Stengers curse of tolerance, the fetish being the icon of belief and the fact being the emblem of knowledge. What makes a fact both 'factual' and 'true' is an appeal to its autonomy from humanity - 'it doesn't matter what we believe, the facts remain the same'. Conversely, fetishes and beliefs are 'merely fabricated', and thus dependent upon their makers. This is the historic root of the Vienna Wall that would attempt to divide facts from values, or knowledge from belief – the fetish is precisely why the metaphorical wall was constructed, what was kept outside and denied any claim to truth.

The essence of Latour's approach is to deny all the distinctions that the Vienna Wall implied, and in particular this strange concept that only something that is not constructed could have a claim to be a fact. Our scientific facts are not, despite the positivist mythology that claims otherwise, unconstructed – they are not simply revealed, like a divine vision. Indeed, if they *were* merely revelations *we would not trust them*. It is precisely the difficult work of construction within the sciences, and especially within the scientific laboratory, that Latour has studied anthropologically. It is scientific constructions that currently authorize a fact as truth, an authorization that is always contingent and subject to future revisions. This is why it is as misleading to contrast fact and fiction as it is to contrast belief and knowledge – facts are *also* a kind of fiction, the kind that has the authority to claim truth (Bateman, 2012).

In an attempt to break down the division into fact and belief, Latour offers the term 'factish' as an amalgam of the concept of facts and fetishes, throwing together elements that were previously neatly sorted into different kinds. For Latour, "lactic acid ferments, divinities, black holes, tangled genes, apparitions of the

Virgin, and so on" are factishes – they are constructed (in a laboratory, in a ritual, within a tradition), but they are also factual, they are sources of knowledge, they are authorized as the kind of fiction which is also fact. His goal is to point out that even today we continue to make fetishes – especially in our laboratories – and treat them as having an autonomous existence. The theory of quantum mechanics is imagined to be something revealed by the universe, and its origins as a mathematical construction by Niels Bohr, Werner Heisenberg and others in the 1920s are to be ignored, brushed under the carpet as irrelevant unless Bohr and Heisenberg are to be praised for delivering this revelation to humanity. What an oddly religious account of the hard work of scientists!

For Latour, the concept of a 'factish' helps level the playing ground a little, to block the curse of tolerance by taking away the basis for keeping beliefs and facts separate. It is a stone thrown against the Vienna Wall and all the similar divisions that parallel it. However, it has not proved enormously successful in this role, in part because it is frequently misunderstood and in part because positivism is as incapable of dealing with the mythology it embeds and requires as any religious tradition is of staring its own mythology squarely in the face. Our own mythologies are always something more than they seem to others – and with good reason, since we would be driven mad or reduced to relativism if we had to smash our own icons *even while we were still using them!*

Grey Wethers is as much a factish in Latour's sense as any scientifically constructed concept like neutrinos, space-time or chemical affinity. It is a fetish, in that it is constructed – much as a neutrino detector, a space-time model, or a chemical reaction must be constructed in (or with) the laboratory. But having been so constructed, it is also factual – facts about the movement of the sun, but also an array of facts about the people who built Grey Wethers. Just as I have spoken of those who speak for animals (ethologists), those who speak for the rocks (geologists), and those who speak for the microbes (microbiologists), so I can speak of those who spoke for the sun using a stone circle as their tool. The druids of Grey Wethers, for want of a better name for these ancient scientist-priests, were speaking for the sun as much as our contemporary researchers speak for the sun and everything under it – and many of the things they could say remain just as true today as they did back then, as Cox correctly observes.

But if I imagine these druids solely as conveyers of calendar facts, I will do them a grave disservice – whatever it was that they said, they did not only speak for the sun. The astronomical aspect of stone circles was never the only factual element that could be associated with them – this was a mistake caused by projecting our mythologies onto a prehistoric world we can no longer communicate with. The facts of Grey Wethers are part of the mythologies of those for whom it was an inescapable part of life, and these facts are now lost to us. But if we understand why Grey Wethers is a factish, we can better understand the parallel with those facts we now manufacture today – and perhaps escape the strange idea that autonomy can be constrained solely to the minds of individuals. Instead, we confer our autonomy onto our creations – and in so doing, we cease to be in perfect control of our technology.

This returns us to the discussion of guns, drugs, and cyberfetish with which the book began. Rather than morality as something we can constrain to beings, or even to just human beings, there is a sense that things are "morally charged" and "play an important role in our moral agency" (Verbeek, 2009a). We are trapped between two competing and contradictory mythologies – the "myth of the Neutral Tool under complete human control" that declares that 'guns do not kill people' and the parallel "myth of the Autonomous Destiny that no human can master" that declares that 'drugs make addicts' (Latour, 1994).

But between these two absurd extremes, something happens between things and beings *that is affected by both.* "You had wanted only to hurt but, with a gun now in hand, you want to kill," Latour suggests. "It is neither people nor guns that kill. Responsibility for action must be shared", and this means we have to take seriously the implications of ethical *things*.

Talking to the Mountain

Part of what Derek Parfit pursues in his gargantuan *On What Matters* (2011) is a valiant attempt to bring to a close the endless disputes between Kantians and consequentialists that have littered the last century of moral philosophy by suggesting that the apparently deep disagreements between them are not as divisive as has been assumed. Through my own metaphor of the ethical triangle, I share Parfit's goal – but I also hope to take it considerably further. Burying the hatchet between the tradition founded by Kant and the tradition founded by Jeremy Bentham and John Stuart Mill is part of the problem, but a much smaller part than perhaps Parfit takes into account. As Mary Midgley (2003) suggest, the attempts to reduce moral philosophy to a "tribal battle" between these two camps "is a shallow and futile evasion" of the real problems. Concluding the first volume of his tome, Parfit writes:

> If we and others hold conflicting views, and we have no reason to believe that we are the people who are more likely to be right, that should at least make us doubt our view. It may also give us reasons to doubt that any of us could be right. It has been widely believed that there are such deep disagreements between Kantians, Contractualists, and Consequentialists. That, I have argued, is not true. These people are climbing the same mountain on different sides.

Parfit's metaphor here is powerful, bringing to mind as it does images of teams of mountaineers trying to scale the summit of a difficult mountain. This mountain is the moral law, or perhaps moral progress, and for Parfit, those in the tradition of Kant and those in the tradition of Mill are simply trying to scale the summit from different routes while sharing the same task – to conquer the mountain. It is telling that Parfit decides not to mention or engage with virtue ethics at all – the traditions that he sees as "climbing the same mountain on different sides" are those of Law Ethics. When morality is viewed as moral law, it is easy to set virtue ethics aside because it is part of the messy world of Chaos Ethics – hard to summarize, let alone rationalize. Perhaps the virtue ethicists are on a different side of the mountain, or maybe they are too busy learning to live beneath the mountain and thus have not been attempting to scale it at all...

Thinking metaphorically about mountains and mountaineers suggests something else missing from our conventional line of thinking that it could be fruitful to consider. The humans may try to conquer the mountain, but it is the mountain that will be there long after the mountaineers have returned home with their gallant stories of epic trials and eventual victory. George Mallory famously said his reason for climbing Everest was "because it's there" (Anon, 1923), but this is at best only half the story. Even if the mountain is only a thing, it is never entirely mute and inanimate – certainly not for the mountaineers in the process of climbing it! The mountain is not a neutral component of what happens upon its rocky crags and steep traverses. If we could talk to the mountain, what would it have to say about those little humans that insist upon traversing its dangerous slopes?

The Law Ethics traditions that Parfit does try to bring together are the major inheritors of Enlightenment ethics, not just Kantian and consequentialist ethics, but also the Contractualist tradition that emerges from the idea of the 'social contract'. This moral fiction came to replace the old mythology of the great chain of being, and specifically the part of this fiction that grounded the divine right of kings, from which European monarchies had based their rule. As Mary Midgley (2003) suggests, the social contract was "a typical piece of Enlightenment simplification" with the worthy goal of resting political authority upon the consent of the governed. But because this moral fiction is based upon the notion of an agreement in the manner of contract, it could never specify duties to outsiders – whether human or otherwise.

But perhaps it is too hasty to suggest that the Enlightenment disposed of the great chain of being, since it was primarily the links in that chain between God and royalty that were undone by the social contract tradition (which Kant participated in). The notion of the equality of humanity, whatever merits it may have when taken in isolation as a moral mythology, had the unfortunate side effect of preserving the rest of the great chain from humans 'downward'. Rather than eliminating the mythic great chain of being, humans were simply elevated to the peak position! As Zylinska observes, we still maintain "a belief that the human is situated at the top of the 'chain of beings'" and we use this to bankroll a whole range of exploitative attitudes towards other animals, to forests and rainforests, and towards our planet as a whole (Zylinska and Bateman, 2009). The more we recognize this problem, the less convinced we can be that social contracts are the metaphor we need. As Midgley (2001) remarks of this fiction: "when we come to such chronic non-litigants as the rain forest and the Antarctic it fails us completely." If all our duties were the consequences of contractual agreements, how could we plausibly have duties towards such things?

Korsgaard (2004) has offered something of a response to this concern in the context of animals, by recognizing that Kant's arguments extend to all beings that are aware of their own interests, but this argument only goes so far. Consequentialist defenders of animal rights like Peter Singer face a similar problem: if we are going to ground our concerns on the capacity to suffer, we aren't going to be able to offer an argument for defending rainforests. All manner of moral traditions can of course make arguments in favor of protecting forests and other ecologies, but such contentions largely fail to offer a new moral mythology, and just as the Enlightenment required the remaking of moral fictions, so too does our present situation. As Latour (1994) suggests: "if inventing myths is the only way to get on with the job, we should not hesitate to invent new ones." Without either renovating our existing moral fictions or devising new alternatives, we will fail to get a grip on the increasingly desperate situation our planet is facing as a result of our unchecked expansion and exploitation of everything the chain of being says is ours to use – which is just about everything!

It will not do to expect Science to save us by identifying the correct answers to our problems, because not only do we not know which questions we should be asking, but the sciences are not a source of definitive answers in anything other than extremely marginal cases like gravitation and optics. Rather than the great achievement of the sciences lying in the alleged certainty they have brought about reality (as positivist mythologies often entail), the incredible expansion of the scientific programs in the wake of the Enlightenment has revealed just how complete our *uncertainty* must be. While research has led to a bewildering expansion of technological capacity on the one hand, it has also created sheer *bewilderment* on the other. In debates *between scientists* over climate science, evolution, moral psychology and so many other fields it is clearer than ever that the idea that we can turn to mythic Science to answer all questions for us has either failed or, even more likely, was never plausible to begin with. The idea that the sciences were only concerned with brute facts, and that only research that could present facts was truly scientific, involved a metaphysical contortion that was always waiting to bite us back, as indeed it has today when we can no longer count upon the sciences to deliver facts because all the relevant facts have instead become *issues* (Latour, 2010b).

Yet if the sciences cannot hope to address the problems inherent in our never-discarded mythology of human superiority over all other life, what other options are there? It will hardly satisfy positivists or those with no specific commitments to suggest that religion is going to provide an answer, and since our politics is now an entrenched battleground between rival ideologies there would seem to be no help there either. The answer – and it comes as a surprise to philosophers as much as anyone else – might involve turning to the only part of philosophy that is prepared to address irresolvable uncertainty, namely metaphysics. As I have already suggested, this is really our only option since it is the clash of rival mythologies (so presciently predicted by Nietzsche) that is at the root of all our political impasses.

Yet this call for philosophical aid cannot be for philosophers to impose truth upon everyone else, and thankfully there are no metaphysicians left who would buy into such a preposterous plan anyway. Since the chain of being was always metaphysical, it will take metaphysics to dismantle it completely – but it will not then fall exclusively to philosophers or scientists or any other specialist field to replace it. Whatever the replacement process will entail, it will need to somehow involve *everything*. It must involve the mountain at least as much as it must involve mountaineers.

Alas, the great chain of being has never been broken, but at least we are gradually able to admit that this mythology is no longer workable. As Latour (2004) recognizes: "Nothing can line up beings any longer by order of importance." What's more, in the growing recognition that we have a problem that needs to be addressed in our relationship to other animals, to trees and forests, to rocks and stones, and to the planet as a whole, we are finally *regaining* a mythology that helped our ancestors survive for tens of thousands of years: animism. This idea is heretical to many positivists, since it flies in the face of a commitment to view the world as comprised of inanimate matter that does nothing but respond to the agency of conscious beings – a fiction installed as part of the Enlightenment's reforms. Yet what Latour's work has repeatedly revealed is the extent to which we misjudge the involvement of things in what actually happens – the split into subjects and objects, which Kant helped instantiate via his critical philosophy, has the unfortunate side effect of obscuring the intimate relationships between people and things.

The division into subject and object, mind and matter, conceals the incredible abundance of hybrids situated between the two (Latour, 1991) - what Donna Haraway draws attention to under the name *cyborg*, saying that we are all "theorized and fabricated hybrids of machine and organism; in short, we are cyborgs" (Haraway, 1991). The essence of what in Latour's work goes by the name of actor-network theory, and what in philosophy is discussed as object-oriented ontology, is a very simple premise: that things are not passive, but have an effect on beings just as beings have an effect on things, that everything that happens in our human world *involves and entails more than just humans*.

As Latour succinctly observes (1994), it is wrong to say that "man flies" because "Boeing-747s do not fly, airlines fly", or in other words, 'flying' is something possible only by an "association of entities that includes airports and planes, launch pads and ticket counters." Similarly, we misjudge the mountain if we do not recognize its role in being climbed by mountaineers – it is, after all, the only thing that *must* be involved in every attempt on the summit. Rather than action being a simple property of conscious beings, action is something that is *only* possible as a result of an association of things. Need I point out, this was *always* the case, even before humanity: there is no way to understand our single-celled ancestors without also considering water, and water had as much influence on the development of life as the replicating chemicals that are sometimes singled out for special attention.

I have called this new mythology *secular animism*, to stress its relationship to far older living mythologies that sadly were gradually eliminated, first by religious prejudices and then later by scientific prejudices. Latour (2010b) also recognizes this connection, suggesting that if we are to solve the problem caused by the breakdown of absolute truth in the sciences, we must "tackle the tricky question of *animism* anew". Similarly, Stengers (2012) has suggested a pressing need to "reclaim animism". The problem is, far too many positivists have committed wholeheartedly to the denouncement of anything close to animist thought by adopting a metaphysical view of the world consisting of inanimate matter that simply responds to the actions from a cause. Yet as Latour is quick to note:

> ...every consequence adds slightly to a cause. Thus, it has to have some sort of agency. There is a supplement, a gap between the two. If not, there would be no possible way of discriminating causes from consequences. This is true in particle physics as well as in chemistry, biology, psychology, economics, or sociology. ...consequences overwhelm their causes, and this overflow has to be respected everywhere, in every domain, in every discipline, and for every type of entity.

Thus although no-one espousing secular animism is suggesting that 'the mountain has a mind' (much less a soul!), there is still an important and generally overlooked sense that the mountain has an influence in every situation involving it, and this is akin to conscious agency in so much as the rocks do have an ability to affect those situations they are involved in. In the wake of chaos theory, no-one would suggest we can predict the outcome of a landslide or avalanche with precision, yet oddly we resist thinking of the rocks themselves as having been involved in the process that determines their final positions. The dual notions of mind and body subtly encourage us to think of all consequences springing perfectly from mind alone, matter simply behaving as a faultless machine to execute what has been decreed – as if the universe were just one giant computer, waiting to flawlessly execute the program offered by consciousness! Or to compound the error, mind is dismissed as mere illusion and matter alone is given the role of the emperor of causality. Our repeated failure to make the world behave as perfectly as either of these strange scenarios implies has somehow not been evidence against these rather absurd ideals.

This rejection of dualist notions of mind and body, or equivalently 'nature' and 'society', has tangential support among those scientists who advocate theories of mind such as enactivism (Varela et al, 1991) that recognize the difficulty of separating thought processes from the physical environments they occur within. We only have to briefly consider the effects that technologies have had on the world to recognize the entanglement between beings and things: can there be anyone who is foolish enough to believe that our road systems, with their inability to handle the traffic we force into them, can be attributed entirely to human decisions and not *also* to the essential characteristics of both the automobile itself, and the human-car cyborg that is the car's sole mode of operation? If we want to resist allowing the humble car this capacity to have been involved in the actions that secured its central role in our terribly confused infrastructures, we must instead heap all the madness onto humans alone – in this choice, secular animism is hardly as insane as the alternative!

Kant, as Latour (2002) observes, "imagined human beings in command, putting its categories to work on a raw material without rights", and as Latour admits this was not so unreasonable in Kant's day since "human beings had hardly started to scratch the earth"; they could live or die without significantly impacting the other beings and things they shared the planet with. Today, however, we can see what Kant could not possibly have anticipated – the complete breakdown of the ancient idea that moralists can set the ends, while technologists can supply the means. The technologies we are now inescapably embroiled within have not simply provided new means, they have *"changed the end in changing the means"* - to the extent that it is no longer plausible to consider technology purely as a means to an end. Latour gives the example of nuclear power, and the strange way that we go from entirely failing to notice the power it has supplied, to panicking about the problem of storing waste that will be around *longer than our species has been around*. Never mind *means*, nuclear power goes from invisibility to political crisis without ever changing its essential form!

The technologies we are now ceaselessly inventing create "complete uncertainty about the relations of means and ends." When 'technology' meant ovens, ocarinas, and oars, it may have seemed plausible to view humanity as masters – but we can no longer expect certainty about innovations today since it is increasingly clear that technology *"forever* escapes mastery." To continue with Latour's example, no-one is in a position to truly promise that nuclear waste can be safely stored on the vast time scales this technology invokes – how could they, when the scientific theories required to make the relevant calculations are both young and perpetually subject to revision in the light of new research? We can make estimates, but we can hardly expect them to remain unchanged. Indeed, our most basic experience with technology in the last century has been to discover time and again that some new miracle is really a blight – consider asbestos, DDT, and thalidomide, as just three easy examples! As a result, we cannot afford to think solely in terms of beings, let alone just human subjects. We have accelerated the creation of a world where we cannot afford to lose sight of the many and varied *things* we have added to it – all without any conceivable possibility of disclosing the full consequences of having done so.

Reforging the Chain of Being

This renewed necessity to consider things *as well as beings* has especial importance for our moral fictions, and hints at a possible solution to the aforementioned problem of how to get past a contractual understanding of duty. The problem with the social contract was that this metaphor struggles when dealing with entities like rainforests or mountains that we may intuitively recognize duties towards but which are denied moral status by our existing mythologies. Latour's innovative approach knocks down not only the Vienna wall between facts and values, but the Kantian wall between subject and object thus "forcing us to reconsider the premature and rather strange confinement of the moral dimension to humans alone" (Haché and Latour, 2010). He draws heavily from Stengers *cosmopolitics,* the gradual assembling of an ecology of practices, which she states is expressly opposed to Kantian cosmopolitanism. Both Stengers and Kant agree in the pursuit of a 'good common world', but Stengers aims to *slow down* its construction, since it could only be rushed along by assuming a Law Ethic, and hence moral or political answers that are knowable in advance, the authority of which might then be used to crush dissent (Connor, 2010).

Recently, Latour has taken to calling the project he, Stengers, Haraway and others are involved in *compositionism,* the gradual composition of the *common world,* the best arrangement that might be constructed out of the disparate needs of everything contained within it. This takes up the Enlightenment search for universality without believing that the universal was "already there, waiting to be unveiled and discovered" while also taking up the legacy of relativism in its recognition that this common world "has to be built from utterly heterogeneous parts that will never make a whole, but at best a fragile, revisable, and diverse composite material" (Latour, 2010b).

The compositionist project is incompatible with the old idea of nature as something fixed in advance, and it is equally incompatible with the concept of critique, in so much as this *also* assumes an absolute truth in its claim to 'uncover' the truth of a situation. So many previous idealistic projects that pursued a common world on the basis of a Law Ethic have run aground on the problem that they all assumed that what was good could be *imposed* upon everyone for their benefit. Compositionism, on the other hand, is based on the alternative view that the good common world could only possibly come about through the painstakingly gradual process of composing it, a process that might never be complete. It involves a careful balance between Law Ethics and Chaos Ethics, very much in the spirit of Moorcock's philosophy.

But there is something ironic in Latour's proposal when its details are compared to the situation we face in terms of still being trapped within the mythology of the great chain of being. In *Politics of Nature* (2004), Latour attempts to develop a prototype for how political institutions might allow for this slow composition of a good common world, which he refers to in this book as *political ecology*. What he offers is a bold vision, but one that is not so idealistic in practice, since it depends only upon those skills and competences we already have. Throwing away the old distinction between facts and values, he suggests a political process consisting of two powers, each with two distinct phases, each entailing both matters of fact and matters of concern rather than separating out facts and values into two divergent camps. These two new powers form the basis of an imagined cycle of political activity that would aim to ensure the involvement of all relevant things within all discussions that potentially affect them.

The first of Latour's two powers is the 'power to take into

account', which concerns how beings and things are consulted. This begins by asking that we do not artificially limit our consideration of whatever might be relevant in any given situation, that we don't let existing theories or prejudice limit the kinds of things we might need to take into account. This reflects the situation of faithful scientists, who never assume they have the answers and always believe there is something else to be taken into account. Later, consultation is extended to those involved in discussing the topic in question, requiring that every being and every thing associated with the subject matter will be consulted (either directly, when appropriate, or by scientific instrumentation). This power to take into account thus allows humans, animals, trees, mountains, and everything else to have a voice in matters that relate to them, albeit with scientists serving as spokespeople for those things that do not have the capacity to speak for themselves.

Secondly, there is the 'power to arrange in rank order', which is concerned with how hierarchical relations will be instituted. This begins by ensuring that whatever new issue is being discussed can be squared off against whatever had already been decided and promised previously. Although it entails creating a hierarchy, this hierarchy is tentative and always subject to revision, and necessarily involves compromises and accommodations between those who came forward during consultation. Once the matter appears to be settled, it can be instituted as a means of closure. Certain issues where agreement can be attained thus become accepted into the common world as stable institutions and do not need to be questioned again outside of extreme circumstances. Institution completes the cycle of political ecology by allowing the discussions to come to an end – even though the cycle then begins anew as soon as it is ended.

Now the irony here is that it is all but impossible to consider Latour's apparently new concept of the 'power to arrange in rank order' and not see within it an echo of the ancient concept of the great chain of being! Sure, it is no longer a rigidly specific, fixed-for-all-time order of priority, but still, in creating hierarchies and then instituting them, Latour's political ecology is expressly concerned with reforging the great chain of being in an endless process of composition and re-composition. No wonder that Latour sometimes sees his work as an attempt to cancel out the entire 'Modern' movement of the last three hundred years, from the Enlightenment until more or less now! Instead of shattering the great chain of being once and for all, Latour suggests we engage *everyone and everything* in establishing how the new chain of being will be forged, and that we prepare to reforge it again and again, in the infinite pursuit of a better world for all.

There is, however, a crucial difference between the ancient moral fiction of the great chain of being and the new priorities that political ecology is tasked with negotiating. The great chain of being was linear, static and universal – but the rank order that Latour discusses can involve huge situational variances. It certainly will not always rank humans above other beings and things: that Norwegians or Japanese fishermen are human will not authorize them to fish any species to extinction, for instance. Rather than a chain, the apt metaphor for political ecology's eclectic hierarchies might be a web. Perhaps even this is too organized a structure to capture the subtleties of the approach, but it makes it clear that the result will not simply be an ordinal sequence. The choice of a web also reflects the corresponding nuances in the scientific fictions of the food chain and the food web – the latter of which intentionally foregrounds the interdependencies that were hidden in the metaphor of a chain.

Latour's philosophical challenges create problems for contemporary morality since the separation into ends and means that follows from Enlightenment thought in general, and Kant's critical philosophy in particular, has become impossible to honestly sustain. For Kant, human subjects were the site of moral agency, and objects were simply means for the execution of their willed ends. But as secular animism reveals, *nothing is merely a means*. There is an inescapable friction between technology and morality when considering the relationship between means and ends that Latour (2002) summarizes when he suggests: "Of course, the moral law is in our hearts, but it is also in our apparatuses." One of Latour's favorite examples of this is his filing cabinet that will not allow a drawer to be opened until all the others are closed – binding his behavior more than any other 'moral' law he could mention!

Latour states that *both* technology and morality disrupt the relationship between imagined ends and practical means. In the case of technology, we cannot simply treat things as means because *everything* involved in *anything* has its own not-insignificant effect on what transpires, effectively preventing any attempt to completely master our tools. But in the case of morality, we are constantly called to interrogate the situations of life in order to uncover their own necessary needs, which again denies the possibility of laying down once and for all a hierarchy that will declare some things means and other ends. For instance, when we treat medical technology as merely a means for prolonging human life, we obscure the complete reconfiguration of our concepts of humanity that these techniques unleash. Combining morality and technology, as Latour offers as a pun, is to discover "*the end of the means*".

To be sure, as Peter-Paul Verbeek (2009a) reflects in connection with Latour's work, this is a difficult perspective to conceptualize, since that which has no intentions seems to lack moral relevance, let alone moral agency. But Verbeek makes it clear that Latour is *not* suggesting that things are moral agents, since he always addresses agency as something expressed by a network of relations. Thus things *affect* the agency of beings without being agents themselves. The crucial point is that things have *moral relevance,* since they "help to shape human actions and decisions". Verbeek paraphrases Kant in saying "ethics without subjects is blind, but without objects it is empty."

Verbeek goes on to stress that what is needed is not a new morality – since our existing moral systems of virtue ethics, duty ethics and consequentialism are just as applicable as they ever were – but rather the recognition that the humanism of the Enlightenment needs radical supplementation to make it plausible again, since "the human can only exist in its relations to the nonhuman". We need to move beyond Enlightenment humanism, but this would not mean giving up the human – it would entail finally starting to understand what this signifies. As Verbeek puts the matter: "by approaching the human as more-than-human it becomes possible to adequately give shape to the respect for humanity the humanist tradition has rightly been defending for so long."

The net result of this realignment of our moralities does not marginalize humanity, it allows us to see what had for so long been obscured – that humanity was always entirely dependent upon everything other than the human for its continued existence and for any possibility of flourishing. The early animist mythologies never lost sight of this, which may explain why those who upheld these moral fictions managed to subsist for tens or even hundreds of thousands of years. But the advent of Modernism in the Enlightenment, with its centrality of the human subject as expressed in Kant's critical philosophy, obscured these debts and linkages, and made humanity seem above and beyond the world it was within. This new mythology was always a path to annihilation as long as it denied our dependence upon everything that had been marginalized as 'objects'. It is not because secular animism is asking us to consider our morality in terms of both beings and things that it is important for ethics, it is because it reveals that any plausible morality *already* required this.

The Parliament of Things

In *We Have Never Been Modern*, Latour characterized an early form of his political ecology as a *parliament of things* (Latour 1991) - expressing the idea that secular animist ideals can help things *as well as beings* into political representation, to give them their chance to influence how these experimental new hierarchies might develop. In Latour's concept of a spokesperson and Stenger's concept of a reliable witness the tools we need for such representation are already available through the sciences, which by their very nature give a voice to that which cannot speak, as the etymology of the names of the various scientific specialties attests. Latour's parliament of things is related to, but also more than, Molly Scott Cato's concept of a 'parliament of all beings', a thought experiment she deploys to stress the unlikelihood that the rest of the creatures with whom we share this planet would consent to (in her example) the building of a nuclear power station (Cato 2009, 2011). Cato asks that we give a voice to the other living things – Latour asks that we give a voice to *all things*, something Kant's philosophy (with its specific focus on humanity) could not possibly have allowed.

Yet in stressing the break with Kant's *critical* philosophy (with its distance between subject and object) we may have concealed the ways in which Latour's proposal *aligns with Kant's moral philosophy*. Doesn't Latour's parliament of things have something of the ring of Kant's realm of ends about it? At times, Latour himself is tempted to draw from Kant's ethics to make his points, and he even concedes that what he calls 'diplomats' are "charged with what the later Kant called 'the kingdom of ends.'" The key difference between Kant's and Latour's approaches lies in part in the tentativeness expressed in Haché and Latour's ethic of hesitation, which is contrary to Kant's confident calculations of the moral law. Interestingly though, Haché and Latour recognize that despite helping create the 'break' with the natural world, Kant *still hesitated* in the face of his awe of nature (Haché and

Latour, 2010, Kant, 1790). Latour even spells out the parallels between his work and Kant's ethics explicitly:

> We can define morality as *uncertainty* about the proper relation between means and ends, extending Kant's famous definition of the obligation "not to treat human beings simple as means but always also as ends" - provided that we *extend it to nonhumans as well,* something that Kantianism, in a typically modernist move, specifically wanted to avoid... What if equality asks us to take responsibility for nonhumans without knowing in advance what belongs to the category of simple means and what belongs to the kingdom of ends? What if the Republic becomes at once a very old and very new form of the Parliament of things? (Latour, 2004)

So is the parliament of things just an extension of Kant's realm of ends? Some Kantians may be doubtful of this claim, and understandably resistant of the parallel being made. Even if they follow Korsgaard in allowing the notion of an end-in-itself to be extended to other animals, nothing in Kant's approach could possibly justify a rock being considered an end-in-itself. Of course, Korsgaard also remarks about an "animistic imagination" allowing us to judge, for instance, the breaking of a tool as something bad, and this may be seen to open the door for all sorts of further nonsense, but there's a limit to how far these arguments will take us. Secular animism may extend the concept of *agency* to allow influence from things without consciousness, but it cannot comfortably extend moral judgment to anything but beings.

However, these concerns turn out to be of little relevance, since without any fancy tricks it is easy to show how the parliament of things *just is* the realm of ends, or at least it is a possible form of it *now,* since when Kant was writing he had good reasons for imagining the realm of ends in very different terms. Consider the following: what is represented in the parliament of things? Everything. But *who* represents in the parliament of things? Only the humans, sometimes on behalf of themselves, sometimes as spokespeople for other humans, sometimes as the spokesperson for another kind of being or thing. So in both the parliament of things and the realm of ends we are talking about a united community of humans, and since the realm of ends requires us all to take into account the ends of *all* others provided they do not destroy the possibility of the realm itself, *the representation of other beings and things is guaranteed provided some human ends entail them.* This is precisely the situation we are facing: given our growing recognition of our utter dependence upon the other beings and things for our continued existence we now *must* accept non-human ends as being entailed by human ends.

Hence the parliament of things can be understood as the realm of ends viewed from a particular perspective – the realm of ends seen in the light of our current ecological predicament. Of course, the details of Kant's ethical system and Latour's political program diverge in a great many ways, but their core ideal remains identical. For Kant, a cosmopolitan relationship between different nations could be made possible by taking what was necessary in national law and elevating it to international law. This was a sensible plan from the perspective of the Enlightenment, since Kant could already see that the self-interest of nations would need to be constrained by wider agreements if there was to be any hope of peace (Kant, 1795). He could not have foreseen the extent to which the tremendous disparity of power between nations today would undermine the idea that all countries might be bound by one law, or even by their own promises. The shortest route up Parfit's mountain is completely blocked, but it is not that Kant's Law Ethic failed, it is simply that we failed to live up to its high standards.

Yet all is not lost since there have always been many roads to the realm of ends, and nobody – least of all Kant – ever expected it to be easy to reach even a practical kind of utopia. Stengers (2003) recognizes that the parliament of things is indeed utopian, and suggests it is "nothing more than an empty dream" if it doesn't help us work out *why* it is only a utopia, if it isn't "a learning opportunity for resisting what today opportunistically frames our world." The key difference of focus between the realm of ends and the parliament of things is that the latter implies many different traditions – old and new - "that gather around issues and must invent their interrelations", as well as the creation of new traditions, namely 'interest' groups that can represent "ignored dimensions of issues and situations". This difference, however, is one that the realm of ends can easily absorb – indeed, it must do so as soon as this requirement becomes a human end to be incorporated, which clearly it has. Stengers sees the core distinction between Kant's moral fiction and Latour's lying in the requirement for the parliament of things that insists that no-one taking part "can introduce themselves by establishing conditions – take it or leave it – from which the possibility or impossibility of agreement would follow." I differ from Stengers solely in seeing this requirement as being utterly Kantian in spirit.

Given the value of the prize to be won, Latour's parliament of things is an option worth considering, especially since it is compatible with virtue ethics, duty ethics and outcome-focused ethics, and requires nothing more than what we already have. But whereas the original plan traced out by Kant allowed for a certain rapidity in establishing the institutions of right, Latour's political ecology or Stengers' cosmopolitics cannot be rushed. Indeed, if these projects are to be done properly it will take time and patience, because it involves weaving together a great many different threads, and there is no absolute pattern available to offer a template for the final tapestry. Whatever Latour may think about his proposal, I cannot help but see it as a continuation of the Kantian moral project, albeit at the expense of the Kantian critical project. Besides, the moral dimension was *always* the important one, even for Kant himself.

With this in mind, I should like to submit some additional formulas modeled on Kant's categorical imperative. Firstly, a new kind of animistic respect expressed as a revision of the Formula of Humanity as End in Itself, which in its original form states: "Act so that you use humanity, as much in your own person as in the person of every other, always at the same time as end and never merely as means" (Kant, 1785). The scope of Kant's injunction entailed solely humans, aiming to secure their mutual respect – but in so doing it cast a long shadow over the other beings and things by suggesting that these *could* be used as 'mere means'. To repair this oversight, I suggest a supplemental formula that might be called the Formula of Nothing as Means, which states: "Act so that you use anything, whether being or thing, always with awareness of its influence on ends and never merely as means". This does not make the mountains, computers, uranium rods, cars and rainforests into Kant's ends-in-themselves, but it requires that we never forget that the means we adopt have consequences that we cannot afford to ignore.

Furthermore, I should like to offer a new formula of communal autonomy based upon Kant's Formula of the Realm of Ends variation, which in its original form states: "Act in accordance with maxims of a universally legislative member for a merely possible realm of ends" (Kant, 1785). This new formula, which I shall call (after Latour) the Formula of the Parliament of Things, states: "Act in accordance with the requirements and obligations of a hesitant member of a merely possible parliament of things." This cannot be, unlike Kant's original formulations, solely a Law Ethic, because it has to set aside claims to universal truth. But neither can it be, as with Badiou's ethic of truths, purely a Chaos Ethic, because it is institutional through-and-through. Rather, it attempts to strike, as Moorcock always advocated, a balance between Law and Chaos, between institutions and resistance, between collective representation and individual freedom (Moorcock and Bateman, 2011).

It is *this* moral fiction, Kant's realm of ends for all things or Latour's equivalent parliament of things, that might offer us a moral mythology capable of establishing duties to rainforests, to mountains, to animals, to devices, *and* to humans, and with this the possibility of a good common world for all. Both Latour and Stengers seek to reposition the relationship between politics and the sciences in order to make it possible to engage in a genuine kind of political representation. Affording to researchers a capacity to evoke final answers created an impasse since it meant a politics forever waiting for ultimate answers that the sciences could never guarantee, let alone ratify quickly enough to 'save us'. Simultaneously, giving all the authority of truth to the sciences meant silencing everyone by erecting the Vienna Wall of multiculturalism that reduced all moralities to mere opinions. This dual denial of the genuine merits of the sciences and of the necessity of morality could only lead to the bickering political carnage we seem to have accepted as unavoidable. Political ecology seeks to restart the process anew, having knocked down the Vienna Wall and thus finally admitted that researchers never had the oracular powers to pronounce truth that they were expected to possess.

However, there is a problem with the compositionist approach that has to be acknowledged. Its core proposal is that rather than letting us "wallow in multiculturalism", abstaining from making value judgments, we should instead begin talking to each other (Latour, 2004). Yet Latour's approach commences from the assumption of our giving up a perspective on the world that has emerged from the Enlightenment and that is *still the mythology of a great many people,* in particular those positivists who place their trust firmly in the sciences as a source of answers. Similarly, while many of the philosophically minded bloggers are enthusiastic about Latour's work they tend to raise concerns that it means working with conservative Christians whom they view as committed to enforcing moral and political values they deem appalling. Thus the idea that we can abstain from making value judgments and still engage in discussions seems doomed from the start – Latour cannot avoid making negative judgments about enthusiastic positivists ('the epistemology police') and those his work appeals to cannot avoid making negative judgments about enthusiastic theists ('fanatics').

One possible answer to these concerns is to recognize that since we are already at deadlock these problems reflect where we are, not where we should be going. The merit of the parliament of things, and the political ecology required to construct it, is not that it can instantly solve our problems but that it recognizes that there was *never* a way to circumvent disagreements by legislatively enforcing a Law Ethic, whatever its foundations, as Chantal Mouffe (2005) warned regarding the dangers of enforcing a 'rational consensus'. If there could eventually be something we could call the moral law, it might first have to pass through moral chaos. This was the only significant failing of Kant's realm of ends, so if a Kantian Chaos Ethic is possible we do not need to abandon the Enlightenment, we could simply repair its legacy. Oddly, Kant's mutual respect would seem to *demand* the setting aside of the moral law if it blocks the realm of ends, since it is communal autonomy that Kant saw as the ultimate goal of morality, *not* the moral law.

With the shortest route up the mountain blocked we have no choice but to stray from the trail, and if we cannot climb together we shall have to return to camp and begin our plans anew. If we do so, we may discover that precisely what has gone wrong is that we have each drawn our own maps of the mountain we are climbing, none of which have the complete picture. If there are those whose maps are so different that they cannot even talk to one another about the way forward, we will not solve this problem by leaving these rivals to shout at one another until they are hoarse. If we need to bring about a good common world, if we need to bring about Kant's realm of ends, to convene Latour's parliament of things, to compose Stengers' ecology of practices, the first step may be to stop making demands and start listening to those other voices we have tried to silence, those of other humans, other beings, and other things. If we want to climb the mountain, we might need to begin by listening to it.

9

Balance

Moral Representation

If you want to talk about your political representation, you can easily establish which politician is supposed to be representing you in government, even though you have probably never met or otherwise corresponded with them. It is even more clear who is the political representative for a nation as a whole, and indeed many people vote for their local representatives on the basis that they are voting for their national representative – the party system depends in part upon this conflation between leaders and members for its efficacy. However, it is rather less clear for most people who are their *moral* representatives – or even if they *have* a moral system to represent. It might be claimed that the Pope of the Vatican is the moral representative of Catholic Christians, but who is the moral representative of someone who has no religion, or someone like myself who has *many* religions? Who can claim to morally represent those who do not even know what morality they hold?

Democratic governments today are called representative because politicians are supposed to be selected by, and then speak for, the people in a particular geographical space. However, politicians often struggle and fail to be good spokespeople, in Bruno Latour's sense – both because the practical dimensions of contemporary politics revolve around deal-making, and because the residents of particular areas are rarely amenable to being reduced to a single attitude. Majority rule ensures political representation for the most common points of views, but guarantees the silencing of all other perspectives. This problem is not solved by merely altering the point of contact for democratic decisions: replacing politicians with polls, for instance, does not guarantee better political representation – it is just as likely to move influence into the hands of the media, and advertisers in particular.

When John Stuart Mill wrote in 1859 that it was a "commonplace" to view the balance between a party of order and a party of progress as healthy for democracy, it reflected the circumstances of Victorian life. Reform was long overdue and it was comparatively easy to orient a majority towards progressive mythologies of future emancipation. The party of order could then serve as a counterweight – reactionaries resisting the rate of change and thus preventing matters from moving forward too hastily by retaining a commitment to the past. Bruno Latour suggests that our situation has now radically changed: "everybody is reactionary today" (Kastrissianakis and Latour, 2007). The simple narrative contrast between past and future has ceased to be constitutive of politics because everyone has varying commitments to both. As the equality ideal of the Enlightenment has become part of everyone's background of understanding (admittedly operating in each case upon different exclusions), there is no future emancipation to anticipate – outside of orthodox science fiction, there is more fear than hope in our imagined futures.

So has the political distinction between left and right become meaningless? Latour implies this, but Chantal Mouffe (2005) argues precisely the opposite: "Far from having lost their relevance, the stakes to which the left and the right allude are more pertinent than ever." To see why this might be so, it is helpful to examine the significance of this question when viewed through Michael Moorcock's mythology of Law and Chaos. The ideals of future emancipation that constituted the left of Victorian politics were still very much wed to Law, for all that they advocated greater inclusiveness. The political expressions of Chaos do not manifest clearly until the twentieth century. Nestor Makhno's Black Army anarchists in Ukraine from 1918-

1921 have held a particular fascination for Moorcock, and prefigure the pacifistic Chaos explored by the counterculture of the 1960s. In both cases, the political conflicts entailed an attempt to counter Law with Chaos, whether by opposing state control through collective anarchist communism, or by rejecting social norms in favor of experimental communities.

The association of the political left and metaphorical Chaos, therefore, is a legacy of the twentieth rather than the nineteenth century, despite roots that reach back to the Enlightenment. The key issue is not so much progression towards future emancipation, as with the French origins of the division into political left and right, but resistance to the establishment (Law) in the name of greater acceptance of diversity (Chaos). The Victorians had not even begun to fathom what opening this Pandora's box might ultimately entail, and even now left-leaning politics is often seduced by the capacity for power and control inherent in Law and rejects using political Chaos as its medium. This is clear in the United States where the political 'left' is still as much a party of Law as the political 'right'. Conversely, the quintessential expression of political Chaos is not the party but the *movement*, as with the civil rights movement, women's liberation, the free software movement or the Occupy movement that set up a shanty town in Wall Street in September 2011.

This association of Chaos with movements of various kinds brings to mind some remarks of Gilles Deleuze (1985) that Stengers (2003) quotes approvingly at the end of her epic *Cosmopolitics*. Deleuze suggests that it is uncharitable to accuse the political right of being delusional since they are "no more stupid than anyone else". Rather, the method of the right, of Law, is to "oppose movement". Conversely, the method of the left, of Chaos, is not necessarily about winning arguments but about "being open about things", of setting out both situations and problems. Whereas the right refuses to accept the questions, their political opponents move to expose them, to make them an inescapable part of the discourse so that the other side must change how it talks. The purpose of the political left, Deleuze suggests, is "to uncover the problem that the right wants at all costs to hide", and this is true whether they are in or out of power.

Notice that this way of looking at the political left and right also reinforces the imagery of Law and Chaos. The forces of Law seek to maintain the current situation, while the forces of Chaos seek to uncover the problems hidden by the state of affairs – the former is necessarily a position of singularity and the latter necessarily entails multiplicity. Indeed, the further that the left moves from the assumptions that underpin the political right, the more anarchically diverse it becomes. Just as with Moorcock's mythology of Chaos as unstable and infinitely changeable, the ever growing panoply of political movements pulls not in one direction but in many. In so much as this is required to balance Law, it is desirable – but it makes it increasingly difficult to render a meaningful kind of politics as the diversity of beings and things to be included outstrips the abilities of individual movements to make sense of them. Both the power and the weakness of Chaos is inherent to its plurality.

It is this collapse into utter Chaos that Latour alludes to in his remarks about everyone being a reactionary these days. In the context of ecology, he notes that we "have odd configurations" such as being "pro-nuclear and anti-global warming", as with James Lovelock's support of nuclear power that so scandalized environmentalists who were convinced he must be on 'their' side (Lovelock, 2006). The strange new combinations of issues that confront us today make it far from clear what 'our' or 'their' side are going to mean, and Latour cautions that politics now "turns around objects of interests, 'issues', 'affairs', 'things'" such that "it is of no importance to know whether one is a reactionary or not, but to know what those objects are that one holds dear, and the types of things to which one is attached." He notes that pragmatically, politics was always about 'matters of concern', it was always "issue-oriented". The mythology of progress just obscured this for a while.

If the meanings of left and right have lost their traditional point of reference in politics, the metaphors of Law and Chaos remain relevant since they capture a commitment to the existing order on the one hand, and the cacophony of movements on the other. Latour suggests the time of succession has passed and we now need to unravel the problems entailed in co-existence – but these problems are so multifarious as to seem intractable. The only thing that comes close to uniting the diverse forces of Chaos is their commitment to opposing Law, with the ironic consequence that on some issues victory becomes impossible precisely because it is mounted as a struggle between Law and Chaos that unfolds solely on the battlefields of Law. Gay marriage is just one of many such political fault lines that could have been resolved far more easily by an approach that balanced Law and Chaos from the outset. Instead of showing the need to recognize new manifestations of the marriage ideal, the issue was immediately escalated into a legislative conflict, preemptively conceding victory to Law.

Throughout this book I have argued for a need to suspend politics in order to address ethics, on the basis of something akin to Alasdair MacIntyre's (1984) contention that politics is "civil war carried on by other means". But I have not been able to provide any evidence to support the idea that switching our focus to morality will improve our situation – you might say that I have no reliable witnesses to support this claim. Certainly, it is not my intention to suggest that we can hand over our problems to moral philosophers and they will do better than our politicians – far from it! As Stengers remarks, philosophers are no better positioned to establish a definition of 'common interest' than anyone else. The point of switching our focus to morality is to understand politics as something *other than* war, to try and imagine it in terms similar to the ancient Greeks who could see communities aiming towards some good when they acted politically (Aristotle, 384-82 BC). Our wars both within and beyond politics make imagining what is good irrelevant, and this transforms politics from the pursuit of the good to a barrier that prevents the good from being realized.

A reconstruction of politics that began at the moral would necessarily look very different from the politics of geographical representation we are used to. If such a renovation entailed the complete abandonment of our existing political apparatus it could only be a utopian dream, and quite possibly one of those nightmares that destroys itself through the revolution claimed to herald its establishment. Poor Karl Marx is far from the only thinker to have had his ideas brutalized in this way. Fortunately, there is no need to start from scratch – this is merely the fantasy of the follower of Chaos who claims that Law is so corrupting that only anarchy could be freedom. Such excesses are no better than the fantasies of the followers of Law who claim that Chaos is so diabolical that nothing is too big a sacrifice to uphold order. If there is one thing we do not need any more of it is extreme visions such as these!

At the heart of an imaginary 'moral politics' lies *moral representation*, and this is a phrase that can mean two different but related things. Its private role occurs between small groups of people, often two individuals, who confer on an ethical matter. Whenever anyone vouches to offer moral advice to someone else *while taking into account that person's perspective*, they become a (private) moral representative to the other for that purpose, or equivalently they listen to that other person's moral representations of their own behavior. Private moral representation, therefore, concerns the giving and taking of advice in ethical matters, and is epitomized both in the late night talk between two friends who wrestle with a dilemma *and* in the Catholic practice of reconciliation, what is commonly called 'confession'.

When reconciliation is effective, it is not because a Priest has conducted an arcane theological accountancy ('two affairs equals fifty three Hail Mary's'), but because they have acted as a private moral representative for their parishioner. I have never been a Catholic and have no experience of this rite, but it is clear to me that those who value it do so because they consider it an effective form of moral representation.

Although Jonathan Haidt has a tendency to deduce implausible conclusions from meager evidence, he is not so far from the truth when he says that moral reasoning is more about finding reasons why others ought to share our moral judgments than it is about reconstructing the reasons we ourselves use (Haidt, 2012). This stresses our deep desire to accord with others, *and* the ever-present risk of letting this inclination manifest by trying to force others to agree with us. While I agree with Haidt that a lot of moral judgment occurs intuitively or instinctively, I would suggest this is because a great deal of our ethical thought is embedded in the particular mythologies we are using, which most people (nerds notwithstanding) are not well-practiced in expressing verbally as reasons. Whereas Haidt tries to claim that most moral reasoning is merely post hoc justifications attempting to explain an already-made intuitive judgment, I would argue that moral reasoning is central to moral representation because *it is primarily within moral discussions that we are required to develop our reasons for action.*

Haidt and I both agree that the social dimension of moral reasoning is key to affecting how people behave ethically – the difference is, Haidt wants to dismiss rational discussion of morality as mere rationalization after-the-fact, but fails to recognize how moral intuitions are dependent upon a background of understanding that emerges from *prior* moral reasoning embedded within our moral mythologies. We have no reason to expect most people to be able to discuss their mythologies rationally – Haidt is certainly unaware of how his evolutionary mythology affects his conclusions – but this is hardly a complaint against rationality or moral reasoning. Haidt seems oddly desperate to discredit rationality in morality, but his argument can never go through while he recognizes the contribution of social relations to maintaining moral systems. As Steve Clarke (2008) remarks, even if Haidt is right that most instances of moral judgment are driven by intuition, this is probably because people have become habituated to certain moral rules or systems that were already the product of previous deliberative reasoning. Because of the social dimension entailed in moral judgment that Haidt makes central to his theory, his attack on the role of reason within morality necessarily falls short of the mark.

What this brings to light is the vital importance of private moral representation to ethical living, since it is within discussions with other people that we are most required to expose our deliberations to reasonable justification. Rather than make this a case against reason, which as Clarke argues would be highly implausible, Haidt's recognition of a social dimension to morality stresses the implausibility of the valorization of a purely individual ethics. Although it may be, as Nietzsche would want us to think, heroic to be utterly self-determining, there is no kind of practical morality that is divorced from its social circumstances – something argued passionately by MacIntyre (1999). Our forms of reason are as much a product of the traditions and mythologies that they emerge from as anything else, and even if we try to make a decisive break from their traditional forms we still can't be moral alone. At best, the ethical loner can attain something close to the minimal ethic – perhaps this is the situation for cats.

To be moral is to care about *other beings*, and to do this well as humans requires that we engage with other humans on moral subjects whenever possible. This is one way that moral philosophy is always relevant to ethics, even though most people never engage with moral philosophy: it involves private and public deliberation of moral matters that may affect not only the advice certain people give in private, but ultimately works to improve our collection of ethical systems through a gradual refinement of ideals. Not everything that does this is called moral philosophy – a great deal of literature does the same job, for instance, and for a greater range of people – but there is no basis for condemning ethical philosophy to irrelevance just because it is only one of many traditions contributing to our moral discussions.

Whereas private moral representation concerns individual ethical concerns, public moral representation is parallel to political representation – it allows someone to speak for others on an ethical matter, to try to become spokespeople in Latour's sense. Some charities exist to play this role of moral representative – Greenpeace for the environment or Amnesty International for questions of human rights, to name just two I happen to support. However, such organizations are often quite poor at moral representation because they suffer from similar problems to representative democracy in terms of synthesizing perspective. There are times, for instance, when Greenpeace campaigns against something I do not find especially problematic, and I end up accepting this as the cost of being morally represented on an issue-basis like this. There comes an inevitable trade-off between the specificity of the issue being represented and the bureaucracy's ability to morally represent its members: the narrower the topic, the more accurate the representation, with the obvious consequence that perfect moral representation for everyone might require infinite bureaucracies and thus be impossible.

In some respects, organized religion may seem to offer a more effective form of public moral representation than the alternatives, but this perspective rests on a misunderstanding concerning the moral uniformity of co-religionaries. As Charles Taylor remarks on the Vatican's relationship to the Catholic laity:

"What Vatican rule-makers and secularist ideologies unite in not being able to see, is that there are more ways of being a Catholic Christian than either have yet imagined" (Taylor, 2007). While the Pope may indeed have the formal role of being a public moral representative for the Catholic Church, his point of view *need not* be that of the laity, who in any case are not (contrary to popular perception) bound to adopt the Pope's moral perspective on any given issue. The situation here is one of *formal* moral representation in public, which is something organized religion is better positioned to conduct than most of its alternatives, including the various kinds of disorganized religion that have attracted me such as Sufi Islam, 'free range' Christianity, or Discordianism.

For those outside of religion entirely, however, there isn't the complete vacuum for public moral representation that might be expected. Those who are involved, explicitly or implicitly, with a non-religion often attain a semblance of representation through authors of both fiction and non-fiction who have become famous enough to have their voices heard in the news or other media. There are also many people who affiliate with celebrities out of admiration for their work – particularly in the cases of popular musicians, novelists, and movie stars – who may gain the kind of mono-directional public moral representation the Catholic Pope is sometimes accused of practicing. In other words, there are people whose personal ethics are swayed by the moral commitments of their heroes, and are thus morally represented by them in a very loose sense of the term, and others who are attracted to celebrity voices specifically because they seem to align with their own morality. It is quite likely we are all affected in these ways, whether we recognize it or not: there has never been a human whose moral world was woven from entirely new threads.

What this hopefully makes clear is that moral representation occurs through various different means, but suffers from similar kinds of imperfection to that affecting political representation. The problem with the latter is that any given geographical area may contain vastly different perspectives, particularly on issues that have no specific connection to the region in question. The equivalent problems for public moral representation are the fraying at the edges of consensus when a matter is issue-based, and the limiting of representation to a merely formal relationship when it is affiliative, whether this is based on religion, non-religion, or celebrity. I don't want to privilege one of these forms of moral representation over the others, and it's not clear that there is any reason to do so. However, it is a clear advantage of some religious practice that it provides both private and public moral representation, irrespective of the ethic being represented. This can be a difficult point for positivists to appreciate, but all it asks is that instead of condemning religious practice outright we aim to encourage improvement in religious practices, particularly in terms of each tradition's own moral mythologies – and this is surely a goal more likely to approach consensus.

Despite the similarities, there is a vast difference between political representation and its moral equivalent in terms of the diversity of content that can hope to be explored. In particular, when it comes to exploring new ideals of the good or imaginary visions of the future, moral representation has a capacity to engage with these possibilities that is entirely divorced from the procedures of representative democracy. Thus even with its drawbacks, moral representation offers a means to explore options that can act far more freely than politics – and in this lies its great but still largely untapped potential. An unfettered imagination is impractical in the political realm, but indispensible in thinking about moral improvement or utopian ideals, and this allows for at least the possibility of radical reform. If moral representatives can develop practical ideals that people can respect and support, this provides a path towards a politics that would be something other than war continued by other means, and these ideals can initially be developed either privately or publically.

Emmanuel Lévinas suggested that "politics must be held in check by ethics", although he never elaborated on this point (Wu, 2007). His view seems to have been that the political institutions, including the law, can relieve our responsibilities for others but still leave us responsible for the political order. However, this is a practical impossibility in a politics that is at heart warfare since we routinely disavow political consequences we did not support as having nothing to do with us. This relates to MacIntyre's concern that the nature of political obligation has become systematically unclear. It follows that if politics is to be checked by ethics, it requires public moral representatives to take responsibility for what is done in their name, and in the names of the people for whom they are only ever an inadequate spokesperson. If this is what is already happening – and the contents of the media are consistent with this claim – then it appears that our existing moral representation is ineffective. If that is so then we need new forms of moral representation that can bring our unruly national and corporate bureaucracies back in check, and this is a situation where the movements of Chaos may be the only possible source of momentum, for all that they cannot succeed in reform without also engaging with Law.

I do not want to limit the ways in which we might think about new kinds of moral representation. It could involve new perspectives being applied to existing approaches – a different kind of Church, Temple or Mosque, for instance, which saw its relationship to the beings and things around it in new ways. Or a different kind of pub, bar or drug circle, that fostered a new kind of responsibility for itself. It could involve entirely new approaches – pairs, groups, buildings or entire regions experimenting with different ways of relating, perhaps making use of the internet and social media as experimental platforms. It might involve replacing some political bureaucracies with alternatives based upon moral representation. It could involve changes to existing associations or entirely new collectives. It might entail discussing a complete ethic, or just exploring one moral issue in isolation. But without some change in how our moral representation operates we will not be in a position to significantly improve our political situation, and the capacity for people to self-organize towards this end makes this option far more desirable than revolution, and far more plausible than global consensus.

Indeed, the impossibility of attaining a truly global consensus on any issue is something that we ought to take very seriously. Although I sometimes suggest that the internet offers a valuable new medium for communication about the issues we face, I am mindful of Latour's objection that "there is a bit of an exaggeration when we hear about the web as offering the universal forums that we have lost" (Kastrissianakis and Latour, 2007). The problem is, this concept of 'universal' would require us to continue thinking in terms of the 'global', to keep pushing Kant's short cut to the realm of ends even while we know full well that it is impossible to get there by cutting corners. The more we think in global terms the more influence we cede to our efficient bureaucracies, since it is *they* that both operate on, and benefit from, global scales. Almost all the problems that we desperately need to address in and around morality must be approached bottom-up, not top-down, and we should no longer be tempted by Kant's short cuts or anyone else's for that matter. As Latour suggests, the concept of universal forums is probably something we should lose.

What all moral representation has in common is a focus on how *we ourselves* behave, what we judge as good, how we can be the people we should like to be. We can now add to this an awareness of our ideals in respect of what kind of beings and things we shall live with, and how we could relate to them. Moral representation is not about what *others* should do, although its public forms may advocate suggestions, but about what you think and feel counts as a good life, a virtuous person, a cherished right, a wise outcome, and which combinations of beings and things can contribute to these ideals. That the moral question of what we want to live with, rather than the political question of what we want to ban, is so unexpected should astound us. It is long overdue that we asked it seriously.

The small-scale collectives that might come out of experiments in moral representation also face the challenging problem of how they might form larger groupings – buildings into neighborhoods and on into towns, provinces and nations; or local associations into national and international bureaucracy. It might be best not to aggregate in these ways, but then it might not be possible to effect change without it. The problem here is political, but it *could* still be approached morally. Utopian ideals like Stengers' ecology of practices or Kant's realm of ends can help establish frameworks for thinking about how to collect an unimaginably diverse set of entities into some kind of whole. But these moral fictions must not be permitted to foreclose diplomacy by dictating any kind of ultimatum concerning *how* agreement is to be attained. As Stengers (2003) remarks, effectively against Kant, we would need to be "angels" to become "authors of a utopia that is valid for every inhabitant on Earth." Neither Kant's universal, nor anyone else's, could be a reason for excluding any and all voices from being heard.

Kant Always Gets What You Want

Throughout this exploration of moral chaos I have endeavored to be open to all approaches to morality, to erect no secure borders within the ethical triangle – and certainly not to presume that any one corner of ethics has any unassailable privilege over any others. But of course I have also repeatedly and consistently returned to Kant's ethical thought in a way that may seem to undermine my claims of moral openness. There are two reasons for these many variations on the key of Kant, the first of which I have already confessed: Kantian ethics are close to what morality has always meant for me, in part because as an imaginative Christian child I inherited many of the same ideals as Kant, and as geeks he and I both tend to systematize.

Yet you needn't have been raised Christian to have inherited this moral perspective – it can be found in anyone who supports the concepts and principles of human rights, who recognizes the tension between the laws of the state and individual freedom, or who seeks equality and respect for everyone. Most of us who live in or near English-speaking nations are participating in the same moral tradition as Kant, a tradition that is already at least three millennia old if we trace it back to Zoroastrianism, as Nietzsche (1883-85) did, and which has immeasurably changed (dare I say progressed?) over that interval. Our moral fictions may differ in many respects, sometimes in ways that lead to immense conflicts and disagreements, but enough of us share a desire to work out how we might live together that we have not, despite the twin threats of Nietzsche's abyss and the Vienna Wall, splintered into disparate moral tribes, never to participate in the same wider community ever again.

The second reason that Kant repeatedly reappears in my discussions is that, if you will excuse the pun on the *Rolling Stones* lyric, 'Kant always get what you want'. While it is debatable whether he achieved his goal of uncovering the fundamental principle of morality, Kant's system successfully traces the landscape of the ethical triangle completely. Consequently, wherever your ethics land within this space, Kant always has something to offer you. The three forms of the categorical imperative dovetail with the three corners of the triangle. Mutual respect, the cornerstone of ethical community, is as alive in contemporary virtue ethics as it is in the best Kantian ethics. Rule-focused ethics that favor proscriptive moral law align with the ethics as universal, while those that admit to a more nuanced ethical legislation settle under communal autonomy, which can be supported by both moral law and moral chaos. Even outcome-focused ethics intersects within the idea of ethics as universal, as Shelly Kagan (2002) has argued, even if doing so risks falling prey of Wood's (2002) warning about turning Kantian ethics into a 'sausage machine'.

More than this, however, communal autonomy *requires all moral perspectives to have their own voice*. This is the other way in which 'Kant always gets what you want' - even if you found nothing of value in anything that Kant wrote about, anyone who *does* honor Kant's approach *must* reflect your moral vision, or there can be no communal autonomy at all. The only moralities that can be excluded under Kantian ethics are those that make building a realm of ends (or Latour's animist variant, the parliament of things) impossible. Under moral law, this could be a serious embargo, since Kant assumed that our morality (being part of who we were as humans) would coincide sufficiently to allow for a coherent set of shared laws founded on an international basis. This part of the Kantian project has failed, but Kant could not have foreseen why it would not be possible to solve our ethical crises using a top-down solution such as this. Instead, a bottom-up solution is required – and this requires something like the slow process of composition that Stengers and Latour argue for. There is no need to presuppose what this kind of realm of ends would be like, what moral fictions it would share – or even that all collectives within its remit would indeed share the same fictions. The realm of ends can admit both moral law and moral chaos. It was not how Kant imagined it, but upon his shoulders we can see so much further.

So it is that I offer another kind of Kantian ethics – not to supplant its orthodox kinds, which I admire and hope will continue to prosper, but to complement the moral law with moral chaos. The Kantian Chaos Ethic I am defending largely rejects ethics as universal (the first formula of the categorical imperative) but it still accepts mutual respect and communal autonomy (the second and third formula). Perhaps the defenders of Kant's original vision would not welcome this anarchic neighbor – certainly my initial attempt to introduce the idea to Allen Wood horrified him, but I think mostly because my précis was an inadequate overture to such a radical reconfiguration of Kant's ideas. Wood, seeing Kantian ethics as a coherent system in which all three formulas are inseparable, was not in a position to consider if Kant's moral ideals could be rebuilt without reference to the moral law.

Perhaps I dishonor Kant in suggesting that a Kantian Chaos Ethic is a form of Kantian ethics... I hope instead that I honor him by showing just how much vaster the scope of Kant's ethical project might be, and by suggesting that *anyone* can help build the realm of ends or the parliament of things, even those for whom moral law is an impossible fiction to adopt. It is not the only kind of moral chaos – indeed, there may be no limit to the possible forms of Chaos Ethic that are conceivable – but it stands out from the near-infinity of alternatives by its thoroughly Kantian commitment to finding what might allow us all to live together. Besides, even if I am the sole representative of Kantian Chaos Ethics, I hope it will still have been worthwhile in some small way to explore this idea. Expanding the horizons of possibility sometimes requires that intrepid explorers risk getting completely lost.

Furthermore, we face an urgent crisis both as a species and as a world, one that requires a seismic shift in how we think about the relationship between ends and means. We can no longer afford to ignore cyberfetish and pretend that our tools and devices are having no effect on how we behave or on what kinds of life can survive on this planet. Allowing the voices of beings and things to speak involves human representatives, which is why Latour's parliament of things is secretly Kant's realm of ends in disguise. If a Kantian Chaos Ethic can bridge between secular animism and the older moral traditions, or indeed offer a connection between *any* moral communities that currently can only shout angrily at each other's shadows, it may yet prove its worth.

Our moral diversity has thus far proved more of a hindrance than a benefit, but this is partly because Nietzsche's abyss had a hypnotic quality that left us wallowing in the vertiginous sense of irreconcilability between us. Knocking down the Vienna Wall improves the situation immeasurably, but there is still a great deal to do and the sheer magnitude of the remaining problems can lead to lingering sense of hopelessness. MacIntyre (1984), after writing a wonderful expose on the moral confusion of the twentieth century, ended with these depressing words:

> What matters at this stage is the construction of local forms of community within which civility and the intellectual and moral life can be sustained through the new dark ages which are already upon us. And if the tradition of the virtues was able to survive the horrors of the last dark ages, we are not entirely without grounds for hope. This time however the barbarians are not waiting beyond the frontiers; they have already been governing us for quite some time. And it is our lack of consciousness of this that constitutes part of our predicament.

Compare MacIntyre's gloom and resignation to the ostensibly similar remarks Wood (1999) makes at the end of his first extended discussion of Kant's ethical thinking:

> Real solidarity between mature human beings can grow only from their shared commitment to universal principles that are given content and universal validity only by an ongoing process of free, enlightened communication. At present, we see only fragments of such a community, which we must nurture like seedlings, hoping that they will someday grow into a single social whole uniting all people, whose actions

> accord with a shared, rational plan for our common human destiny... Precisely that hope was literally Kant's own last word on the human condition.

Even if I balk at the moral law implicit in "universal principles", I still wholeheartedly support Wood's contention that we should "nurture like seedlings" those fragmentary communities that manage somehow to pursue moral living. What's more, I would far rather do this than hunker down and attempt to wait out the "new dark ages" that MacIntyre laments. There is too much at stake to sit idly by, but precisely because of this we cannot afford to let our enthusiasm trump our willingness to communicate, to co-operate, and to productively disagree about what must be done. Kantians – whether Law Ethicists or Chaos Ethicists – cannot accept inaction as a moral course of action. There is a great deal of work to be done, and we need to find ways to mobilize everyone with even a glimmer of conscience or scruple, and to include as many as possible in whatever must be done.

It is perfectly possible that moral law may yet function as a viable universal ideal at some uncertain time in the future – when the parliament of things has been carefully composed, when the realm of ends is finally convened, even I may find universal principles I can endorse. Indeed, my own Chaos Ethic never prevented me from supporting the human rights agreements we have already ratified, even if I remain disappointed by our failure to live up to their ideals – and disgusted by their constant betrayal. In suggesting that universal principles attain their validity only by an "ongoing process" of communication, Wood effectively recognizes that universality is an ideal to strive for, not a justification for tyranny. On this view, Kantian Chaos Ethics might be simply a transitional stage towards a future Kantian Law Ethic. Perhaps. But it is just as possible that moral chaos is a necessary corrective to the excesses of moral law – that we need to find ways to strike and constantly re-strike a balance between the two if we are to build any kind of moral consensus worth defending.

Exploring the Multiverse Together

About a century ago, William James asserted that "things are *with* one another in many ways, but nothing includes everything, or dominates over everything." Speaking out against the tendency to think in absolutes and universals, he objected that manyness-in-oneness was a characteristic of the world we inhabit. James suggested that this was difficult to accept when beginning at "the rationalistic block-universe, entire, unmitigated, and complete" – the 'all-form' of reality. Instead, he suggested we accept an 'each-form' of reality, and argued that an existence founded on this premise would still be "a coherent world". He remarks of anyone who accepts this diversity of existence that "our 'multiverse' still makes a 'universe'" and suggests that these two ways of viewing reality – multiverse or universe – make "pragmatically different ethical appeals" (James, 1909).

Just as Law and Chaos have penetrated deep into popular culture thanks to Moorcock's writing, so the term 'multiverse' owes a debt to him. These days, we are quite familiar with the physicist's version of the multiverse that postulates a diverse collection of parallel worlds or universes, as with the oddly metaphysical 'many worlds' interpretation of quantum mechanics (Everett, 1957). Physicist David Deutsch read Moorcock's story *The Sundered Worlds* (1962a), which first used the term in its contemporary sense, and then coined it in his own scientific work in connection with the 'many worlds' interpretation. However, what Moorcock originally deployed as a science fiction concept acquired numerous different levels of meaning and would eventually come to be deployed by the writer "as a metaphor for the mind" (Moorcock, 2008). In his fantasy novels, it has the additional, poetic name 'the Million Spheres', representing myriad alternative worlds that may be visited by the Eternal Champion, Moorcock's doomed fantasy hero. There is a sense that Moorcock's multiverse is not a physical space at all, but a *literary* one, and that while the Million Spheres represent a genuine diversity of realities for Moorcock's characters to explore, it figuratively represents the entirety of his stories – a literary superset, comprised of many different styles and settings, ancient and modern, fantastical, and down-to-earth.

The concept of the multiverse connects Moorcock's work to Latour's, since Latour makes use of William James' idea, albeit under the alternative name 'pluriverse'. Latour (2010a) suggests that "in the pluriverse there is plenty of room for other modes of existence, each with its own key." Although Moorcock never read James, this is also the ideal that animates Moorcock's multiverse, which although expressly referring to his own literary canon is also symbolic for the diversity of realities that people live within. Indeed, this is what gives Moorcock's novels their philosophical relevance – from the existentialists, he takes on the question of what it means to be a nomad, to be adrift from tradition and situation. The title of Moorcock's pioneering 'steampunk' trilogy, *Nomad of the Time Streams* (1971, 1974, 1981b) expressly plays on this concept of nomadism, which is present throughout the Eternal Champion stories. In later books, the heroes are sometimes describes as 'mukhamir' or 'players of the Game of Time' (e.g. Moorcock 1994), a theme which further develops his idea of nomads caught between worlds.

Stengers offers an insightful new take on the contrast between nomadic and settled (or sedentary) existence, one that allows the metaphorical implications of being a 'nomad' to be more carefully considered (Stengers, 2003). She suggests:

> ...when the distinction becomes metaphoric, it is the sedentary populations that become the object of scorn, people who cling to existential, professional, or cultural territories and reject the

> challenges of modernity. The sedentary belongs to popular opinion, while the nomad is willing... to detach herself from her beliefs in order to challenge them and to follow a problem wherever it may lead.

This could almost be the mission statement for Moorcock's Eternal Champion! The Million Spheres become here the diverse practices that Stengers' cosmopolitics seeks to carefully compose into an ecology, each a different world, a different reality, a different mythology. Stengers notes that those who take pride in being a nomad, in being adrift from tradition, "will feel perfectly at home" in Latour's parliament of things since it does not obligate them to pay attention to anything other than the "conflicts, rivalries, and negotiations through which others create new risks for them and constrain them to new formulations." For the cultural nomad, disagreements and tensions are entailed in every encounter with their more settled counterparts.

However, Stengers stresses that when we judge things to be 'nomadic' or 'settled', this claim is only in respect of one particular aspect of a situation. Those who "pride themselves on being nomads" deceive themselves if they believe in the illusionary freedom to invent oneself that Sartre expounded. As Moorcock repeatedly demonstrates in his novels, this freedom would be a curse – indeed, Stengers shows how it is *already* a curse: the curse of tolerance that would divide people into those who believe and those who know. In the chaos of the multiverse, there is no single sphere that contains all the others – the settled individual can only know what their tradition, their practice, means for them. They can know their own sphere, but not the million others it exists alongside with. Conversely, and despite the elevation of nomadism when opposed to opinion and tradition, the nomad can visit many spheres but can never really *know* them. Their freedom to 'travel' obscures the fact that every nomad is and always was settled somewhere – even if their valorization of the freedom to be no-one obscures this.

What's more, our current political systems *make us all nomads*. By demanding that those who participate in representational democracy be abstracted into "territorial categories", we are all reduced to no-one in politics as we know it. Such a situation, as Stengers warns, "presents a serious weakness". It "fails to take into account the danger that nomadism might become a norm." This, then, is where Stengers positions the cosmopolitical question of her ecology of practices: as a politics that does not begin by asking everyone to be no-one. She does not defend her utopia by asking that everyone submit to some universal principle, but rather entreats us to ask a universal question – the question of the values inherent to an ecology of practices, the morality that would allow the Million Spheres to form a harmonious multiverse, rather than an endless battleground. She urges us, in a manner reminiscent of the hesitation ethic of Haché and Latour (2010) to resist "the temptation to shift from 'he refuses to cooperate' to 'he has nothing to show, nothing to say...'"

The political uncertainty of Stengers' cosmopolitics that "hesitates before a problem" creates a "different kind of silence", one formed from humility in the face of what would be involved in giving up the universe as the model of truth and transforming it into the "collective adventure" of the multiverse, or the ecology of practices. She cautions:

> Who are we to evaluate what we are in the process of deciding among ourselves? Are we fully aware that we are about to connect, and thus transform through multiple and partly unpredictable acts of reciprocal capture, histories that, on Earth and until now, were distinct? ...This silence does not imply a prohibition, a limit before which everyone must bow. In itself it expresses no power, provides no response. It only has meaning in giving the question its cosmopolitical dimension, creating the space in which the voice of those who

are silent becomes present.

We need this silence, because without it we cannot hear the voices of others who had been drowned out by our certainty. Stengers gives the example of an African mother who has contracted AIDS but refuses to have the abortion that the medical bureaucracy recommends. She notes that for this person, what we call 'probability' or 'risk group' has no meaning, and this lack is not because she is ignorant. Rather, she takes on risks of her own that have no meaning to the medical bureaucracy. Her nomadic culture lives in a space where "our 'scientific' definition of disease has no meaning or, more specifically, no genuinely interesting meaning." The two spheres do not intersect, and the medical mythology has no basis for forcing its values upon her.

This is the risk inherent in the Enlightenment's elevation of reason that must be severed from the ethical traditions that it also fostered – yet another clash between Law and Chaos, the one and the many, but this time with ideals of rationality. Stengers warns that if the elimination of magical thinking, theology and superstition is viewed as a "triumph" of reason, this simultaneously results in the creation of a "belligerent reason, one that identifies with the triumph found in the destruction of the other", and thus one that cannot hope to produce peace, although it can certainly imagine the tranquility of unanimity, when all voices are silenced and thus in agreement. This is the danger that Moorcock associates with his metaphor of Law: that the multiverse will be destroyed by the forcible banishment of diversity.

The multiverse as I am presenting it here is thus a metaphor for Stengers' ecology of practices, and by extension the medium within which Latour's parliament of things and Kant's realm of ends must move. This is why Latour (2003) advocates "experimental metaphysics" as a method – we need new mythologies that are capable of dealing with the problems of communicating amidst the chaos of the Million Spheres. This is not some forced extension of Latour's approach, since it is implicit in his adoption of James' 'pluriverse' - which is only another name for James' 'multiverse', and hence also of Moorcock's.

Of course, it can still be objected that whatever the origins and history of the word 'multiverse' it has now acquired a specific meaning within physics as a marker for the 'many worlds' that some imply from quantum mechanical theory. *These* worlds, speculative physicists claim, are cut off from each other and cannot communicate in any way. There is a beautiful irony here, for the same faith in Science that would elevate this meaning of 'multiverse' above all others enforces in the multiverse-as-metaphor precisely what they say characterizes the multiverse-as-theory: a total and complete separation between each of the Million Spheres that bars communication between them. It is this that causes Latour to mark out the positivist 'epistemology police' who would enforce one world to the exclusion of all others as a problem: by insisting on one – and only one – true world, they make travel within the multiverse impossible.

However, I do not see the problems with integrating positivists into the ecology of practices quite as starkly as Latour. Indeed, I see adherents to these kinds of mythologies as no more likely to cause problems than anyone else once the concept of political ecology or an ecology of practices is grasped. The challenge is in precisely this initial grasping – and this is a problem *everyone* faces. This is why I find it potentially useful to offer many different ways of mounting the same concept, throwing Kant's realm of ends and Moorcock's multiverse into the mix as alternative ways of gesturing, however vaguely, in the direction we are blindly groping to discover. But perhaps the reason I think that some – perhaps a great many – positivists are sure to be allies is just that, from within the space I have traced via my paper time machine, the positivists and the theists are just not so far apart as their bitter arguments would make it seem.

They certainly have both been a part of me, and this gives me confidence that they can also be a part of whatever we might need to attempt to make together.

I should like to return to my whimsical friend to whom I wrote letters while he was serving in the U.S. armed forces, out in the desert. Sometime after mustering out, he had a revelatory experience in which he became acutely aware of the multiple parallel worlds of the 'many worlds' interpretation – they became as real for him in that moment as anything before or since. It would be easy to mock this, especially since crucial to the associated physical theory is the (quite hilarious!) caveat that these parallel worlds are forever cut off from ours, and thus can never be detected. But for me, the new mythology he is living is no different from that of the physicist who might give in to intolerant tolerance and mock him for his 'belief', the theist who might laugh at the irony of this revelation, or indeed any of my own strange and wondrous mythologies.

By placing his experience into a mythology, I do not reduce it to the merely subjective but elevate it to the status of world, to one of the Million Spheres that must be brought into conjunction in Stengers' cosmopolitics or Kant's realm of ends. Every mythology is a world, and none of these worlds can make a claim to absolute truth without initiating what Badiou called 'disaster'. Precisely the lesson of the Million Spheres is that, to paraphrase Shakespeare, there are more ways of being in the multiverse than are dreamt of in *any* philosophy. Our task should not be to sort these into those that are true and those that are false, which is just as well as we have absolutely no basis for doing so. Our task is to find how we might explore the multiverse together – and for this adventure, everyone is a potential champion.

Practical Chaos

Perhaps it is time to cautiously emerge from reflection upon ethics in order to consider what politics could be if we accepted our own obligations towards moral representation, rather than hiding behind the failings of political representation to assuage our guilt for the mess we have got ourselves into. It is not acceptable to blame the bureaucracies for doing what they do well, namely act efficiently towards goals specified from the outside, especially when we are the ones responsible for specifying those goals (whether tacitly or explicitly). Facing our battlegrounds of competing issues, we should remember that what we currently call 'political' is what we try to force upon others, while the ethical is how we constrain *ourselves*. If we do not manage to live within our own moralities and understand our own ideals we will make a grave error when we try to elevate our values to the political stage – and this is especially true where moral horror creates a chasm between opposing positions.

Alfred North Whitehead (1938) wrote that democracy was founded upon the common fact that everything has its own value-experience: "everything has some value for itself, for others, and for the whole." Morality for Whitehead begins in the recognition that we "have no right to deface the value-experience which is the very essence of the universe." Mariam Fraser (2006) suggests that this points towards "something like an 'ethic of ethics'", and this is also what Stengers is offering in the posing of the 'universal question' concerning which values could be used to help compose a common world. As Latour (2004) puts the matter, it is only "through a long work of collection" that we might be able to "live in common" on what could become "the same earth for all".

However, getting there may also involve opening up the question of which things and beings could be assigned rights and protections – since limiting the discussion to humans has not served us particularly well. Optimistically, Latour suggests that "a few years from now" it will seem strange that we ever thought humanity was the only thing worth representing, the only thing that could have rights. As Mary Midgley (2001) points out, we need new mythologies if we are to recognize that we might have duties to things such as rainforests. Even from the perspective of the minimal ethic, it is sobering to remember that without vast forests making oxygen, without innumerable worms maintaining the soil, without multitudinous bees to pollinate plants, humanity would be instantaneously doomed. Even if we limit our moral perspective to the human, or the individual human, it is unavoidably necessary to care for other beings and things: our survival depends upon them. This is, paradoxically, good news: it gives those who adhere solely to the minimal ethic reasons to work with us in what might melodramatically be called 'saving the planet', although it is equally 'saving ourselves'.

Getting the dialogue beyond the politics of warfare will not be easy, however, especially since we are habituated into making demands as the only intersection between the moral and the political. It is an impractical kind of Law that begins with statements such as 'everyone has a right to...' where the right in question was never discussed, much less agreed. Rephrasing this to 'everyone *should* have a right to...' is more honest, but it still represents a failure to hesitate. The challenge of moral politics, political ecology, and of composing the multiverse is precisely to avoid substituting a premature political demand for a necessary moral question. In morality as hesitation, it is precisely the relevant questions that we must seek to uncover. In a moral politics of hesitation, an answer cannot be offered before the right questions have been found. We thus need a practical kind of Chaos if we wish to create a politics worth having, a cosmopolitics that will enable the silence which might allow us to finally hear the cacophony of voices that have been excluded for so long.

There are at least three general approaches to our political problems when they are placed in a mythology of balance instead of battle. Firstly, asking better questions: Who has been silenced? Which spokespeople need to be brought into our discussions? Secondly, expanding the scope of moral concern by considering other beings and things – even if only in the limited sense of asking how human concern for those beings and things creates new moral and political questions. Lastly, avoiding the restriction of dialogue such that it occurs solely between parties that are on opposite sides of divisive moral horror – that people are horrified is a salient moral fact that cannot be ignored, but it must not be used to force a Law Ethic onto others. Diplomacy, both political and mythological, is required whenever fear and anger prevents hesitation. In short, we have three basic methods – listening, hesitating and diplomacy, and three corresponding questions to ask: Who are we not hearing? What are we ignoring? Why is an issue at an impasse?

I began with problems concerning drugs, and this is as good a place as any to commence a brief exploration of practical chaos. Having declared that 'drugs cause addicts', the required course of action seemed to be banning drugs. But this didn't work, in part because we didn't ban drugs we simply declared that some were approved by the medical bureaucracy and then denounced as immoral those that were not. The questions we must ask here are the same in both cases: 'how do we live with drugs?' Stengers (2003) recognizes that this is a question of who we are not hearing, specifically those "unrepentant drug users" who necessarily challenge the way we have chosen to represent them. To be a user of illegal drugs is not, I have argued, to be a wastrel – even if that may be a risk, but in representing drug users we have always relied upon experts to represent 'victims' and never allowed those being discussed to have a voice. Indeed, we threaten them with jail if they attempt to do so! New questions, Stengers suggests, will come about only when "both drug-using experts and drug-using diplomats" can have their voices heard.

Even in the case of the drugs with the worst reputations, we cannot expect to attain balance until we are willing to listen. I learned more about heroin from Tommy than I ever learned from an 'expert', and doing so did not encourage me to try it. But it did convince me that practicing equality by exclusion in such cases was not a solution but merely a lazy way of dealing with a genuine issue. Latour remarks that the users of some illegal drugs attach such great importance to them that "they prefer to die from them rather than do without". He suggests that the drug addicts themselves must be involved in how this situation is judged, and that – at the very least – they must "sit on the jury" that would hope to make a tentative decision. Deferring political decisions about drugs to 'experts' while ignoring the voice of those with practical experience is not a route towards anything but the extension of our existing, ineffectual, blanket prohibition.

When we consider wastrels, and set aside any connections to drugs, a vital point to understand is that the vast majority of people who fall into this state of barely-living are *miserable*. Being a wastrel is not a wise life choice – although Norton apparently set off with a strange idea that being a squatter and a beggar was glamorous, I rather suspect that this reflected the fact that at any point he could call it quits and return to his parents. Most people who dig themselves a hole to live in are despondent, and don't see any way to get out of the misery they feel trapped within. There is a circularity to this situation – once you lose your confidence, your courage, drugs can offer a way to anaesthetize the pain of worthlessness. But excessive drug use exacerbates the problem it is being used to salve, and the hole is dug ever deeper.

It may be positivist heresy to make reference to a religious concept, but Kierkegaard's (1849) understanding of sin as despair is apposite to this peculiar issue. The problem of sin for Kierkegaard wasn't defiance of a Law Ethic of rigid rules but the problem of finding out who you really are and then living the good life this discovery necessitated. Those things that Kierkegaard construes as sinful are so because they cause despair, and to be caught in sin is thus to lose yourself in despondency – this, I'm claiming, is the situation of the wastrel. Seen this way, the solution lies in sparking the individual's own courage, and reigniting their sense of self. Turning to religion works for some because this connects them to both a community and a mythology of hope, but other forms of moral representation could equally help someone who had lost their way like this – a virtuous drug circle could potentially be more effective than a Church, mosque, or temple in preventing and rescuing those who get caught in this particular hole. We will not prevent wastrels by enforcing criminal penalties for drug use, because the drugs are only a part of the problem, they are not its principal cause. Recognizing this would be a huge step forward for how we relate to drug users.

The problem of 'how to live with drugs' is even more problematic in the context of medicine, because here there is a general lack of recognition that there is a problem. The cyber-fetish of medicine deflects inquiry by assuming that doctors and medical researchers are the only people with a voice worth hearing, in part because fear of death has helped forge a mythology of eternal maintenance of human life that denies the facts of suffering and death far more effectively than any religious doctrine. Here it is a question of what we are ignoring – and pulling up the floorboards of medicine reveals numerous issues. In the case of drugs, the idea that corporate-developed pharmaceuticals are immune from scrutiny or criticism because they are qualified (as Stengers notes) as the "only rational" drugs is deeply problematic. This qualification of 'rational' is both mythological *and* dishonest: it is *not* rational to drug your children with commercial pharmaceuticals just because they are unruly, and neither is it rational to squander vast quantities of money paying for treatments that *extend* suffering and delay death, much less to pay for *research* into such counter-productive techniques.

As Ivan Illich suggested back in 1975, healthy people need

"minimal bureaucratic interference to mate, give birth, share the human condition, and die." Furthermore, 'healthy' is not an adjective that must be certified by the medical bureaucracy at all – we are healthy when we live in healthy homes, have a healthy diet, and live in a healthy environment. An effective medical community ought to be focused on minimizing its contact with patients, not upon developing an unlimited scope for the technological treatment of disease (much less an unlimited suite of definitions for disease and disability!). We need to have the discussion we have managed to avoid for so long, but it is not easy to get past the cyberfetish in this case. We ought to consider whether Illich was correct in suggesting that healthy people are "sustained by a culture that enhances the conscious acceptance of limits to population, of aging, of incomplete recovery, and ever-imminent death."

It is not just the relationship between humans and their medical institutions that are being ignored, though, since the relationship between animals and medical research is equally barred from consideration. Stengers suggests that while industrial livestock production and animal testing for cosmetics are "scandalous", the question of sacrificing "mice, rats, or even chimpanzees" in the quest for alleviating human suffering is "undecidable". She suggests we need to invent ways to bring this undecidability into focus for everyone involved. This entire topic is, alas, a minefield of moral horror, and the animal activist's strategy of publicly parading their disgust is counter-productive, inviting those who do not feel this way to exclude both the activists and the animals from further consideration. Insisting that everyone converts to veganism is not a solution to any of these problems – no political issue is ever resolved by demanding mass conversions. Similarly, the classic strategy of turning to the numbers to emphasize the scale of the problem fails because if you don't care about one animal's suffering, you don't care about a million. Superior diplomacy is desperately needed here.

The situation is parallel with abortion, and for similar reasons: the political battleground is positioned across the divide of moral horror. In discussions of both the putative rights of animals and the claimed rights of the unborn, the most vehemently opposed mythologies face off with an anger so intense that both camps believe their opponents are monsters, imbeciles or otherwise open to exclusion from consideration. This is another deadlock in desperate need of diplomacy, particularly because the moral implications of both abortion and animal exploitation are obscured when opponents rely upon their own Law Ethic to make their point for them. Something is dreadfully wrong when 'since I'm not Christian, it doesn't matter if I have an abortion' is thought to be a valid moral proposition. Something equally disturbing is embedded in the suggestion that 'since I am a Christian, I must abuse those who terminate pregnancies.' When political opponents are both driven to insanity, it is time to bring in new voices. In the United States, where this issue is especially volatile, moderate Christians might be in the best position to mediate between the extremes in the case of abortion, since they are capable of understanding both of the unique, divergent mythologies that have come into conflict over this issue – although it will certainly strain their patience to chair such discussions!

On the subject of killing humans, some of the biggest problems are also the most invisible. So it is with the murderous car, a cybernetic animal we form with the automobile that we implausibly believe allows us to get around our urban sprawls more easily, even when we are stuck for an hour in the daily gridlock that inevitably results from the topographic problem of demanding that a multitude of straight lines must pass through the same point without ever crossing. Latour remarks of the eight thousand people killed in France each year that they became "mere means for the automobile, which was raised to the rank of

Sovereign Good." This is precisely Illich's concern about what I have called cyberfetish, which in transportation manifests by the unquestioned assumption (the radical monopoly in Illich's terms) that mechanized transport is the only solution to travel. Infrastructure, and not vehicles, is the key to the problem here – the car is ineffectual without its roads, and *we do not have to build roads everywhere*. When we can't see beyond the car we not only fail to see better solutions to the problem of infrastructure (which requires much more than a merely technical solution), we exclude random victims of traffic accidents from consideration as people worth saving.

This is another case where cyberfetish blinds us so effectively we simply can't find the questions, much less discover solutions. As Illich (1973) remarks, it has become unthinkable that limiting our tools would be considered as a solution to any problem, and limiting speed by design is "an implausible idea to the rich and an irrelevant idea to the poor." He suggests that someone living in the Andes simply cannot grasp why anyone should need to travel so fast, while those who live within the tangled knots of our highways "cannot imagine a world without speed" at all. Illich offers a solution worth considering: build cars limited to the speed of a bicycle, build infrastructures that do not place the needs of the car above those of the pedestrian or cyclist, level the playing field between different forms of human transportation Even if this solution – which would save the lives of almost every person killed in a car accident anywhere in the world – is rejected, it points to another opportunity for hesitation. The cyberfetish of speed is as deadly as that of the gun, and all the more so because we fool ourselves into thinking it is inevitable and thus unavoidable.

Speaking of the cyberfetish of guns, this may seem like the easiest of issues – after all, liberals are more-or-less united in their agreement to smash this icon, and can find no reasons they might be mistaken. Here is a situation where we should be wary of what Latour (2010) calls *iconoclash,* the ambiguity involved in smashing idols. When an icon is smashed, it is never entirely clear if the person with the hammer should be viewed as a liberator (as they tend to see themselves) or as a mere scandal-monger (as they tend to be viewed), or worse as a buffoon or a terrorist. As Latour cautions: "What if we had killed the wrong people, smashed down the wrong idols? Worse, what if we had sacrificed idols for the cult of an even bloodier, bigger, and more monstrous Baal?" The lesson is simply that we should tread carefully when we seek to smash icons, idols, and cherished ideals, because no matter how sure we may be in the right-eousness of our actions we can be even more certain that there are other ways to understand what we do.

The gun is an idol to those who treasure it in much the same way as a particular drug is an idol to those who use it. Just as it would be a moral error to make political decisions about drugs without discussing it with drug-users, it would be a mistake to think that the question of guns can be raised without accepting that there are people for whom the gun is every bit as vital a part of their mythological lives as the car. It's ironic that the other examples of cyberfetish I just discussed – medicine and automo-biles – are largely invisible to all concerned. The cyberfetish of guns is far more visible, which at least makes it easier to recognize, although it is in practice no easier to solve.

In the wake of tragic shootings where guns played a role, the standard response in the United States is to call for legal restric-tions on the private purchase of firearms. But having acknowl-edged that guns play a role in such shootings it is, I suspect, rather less of a role than is sometimes credited: if there were no ostracized children to wield the gun, such horrific events would cease, and perhaps more importantly if there were no guns the ostracized children would simply turn to fire, explosives, or other devices of destruction, none of which will ever go away. The sheer volume of news coverage given to such terrible events as school shootings, enthusiastically pursued by 24-hour news presenters desperate for something worth reporting, reinforces the idea that it is easier to make a mark on the world through infamy than through honorable struggle. Norse tales certainly had their villains but the Vikings would never have viewed these shallow atrocities as worthy of song or saga, so why do we?

The cyberfetish of guns may be merely the personal reflection of the cyberfetish of war machines that is far from a new occurrence in our history. It would be misleading to suggest that previous nations didn't desire superior weaponry, nor that they never produced it. However, the asymmetry implied by contemporary weapons – including but in no way restricted to aerial drones – helps bring into focus the decline of honor as a concept of war. Some writers mock Kant for his naivety when he suggests that snipers are "underhanded means" that must be avoided in warfare (Kant, 1797). For Kant, however, assassins and snipers risked voiding "the trust requisite to establishing a lasting peace in the future". If we descendants of the Enlightenment cannot understand why war must be waged only in ways that make future peace possible, then the mythology of the 'just war' is bankrupt and our soldiers will either have to help us establish some new ideal that might replace it, or give up their profession entirely. This is a rare instance where I would endorse Kant's ethics as universal as a valuable test: if you would not permit your enemy to use a particular weapon, how can you possibly justify using it yourself? Which are the weapons you should wish to be used *against yourself*?

I doubt that we can end war, for all that I hope that we may, so we must strive to ensure that the barbarism and immorality of the battleground is kept in check by moral standards that transcend merely prudential concerns. These moral boundaries are not optional extras that military forces can try on or discard at will, for all that the state of exception may make them appear as such: they are the only defense against the dishonor of soldiers, and the best defense against future terrorist atrocities. The question I would most like to hear asked in the context of warfare is why, at a time of such sophisticated technological capabilities, do we default to killing our enemies as our basic strategy? I do not dispute that it is more convenient to be rid of enemies than to detain them, but if capture is an option – and given the tremendous asymmetry in technology it must surely be at least that – why design military equipment solely for death? Of course, given the shocking mistreatment of prisoners we have allowed in internment camps, it's hard to wish for anyone to be held captive in this way. But it is harder still to wish for an ever-escalating arsenal of deadly armaments.

Practical chaos asks that we reconsider our assumptions and find new solutions to old problems, and war need not be excluded from this project. A great many problems descend from the state of exception, the power of the head of state to both enforce and suspend the laws, which as Giorgio Agamben (2005) has suggested is intimately connected with our existing political systems. There may yet be hope that the immoral chaos of the state of exception might be transformed into moral chaos, even if it cannot become moral law, but changing this will not be easy. It is worth recognizing that a great many people feel it is perfectly acceptable for their nation to do, under the veil of secrecy when necessary, whatever is required for 'national security'. But as I have charged, the cause of 'national security' is what causes national insecurity, and this we must not accept. Bringing hesitation into espionage and intelligence will not be easy, but it must happen if we are to have national institutions that we can honor and support. If intelligence organizations will not offer open scrutiny of their actions, which of course they cannot, we must teach them to honor the maxim of those they work to protect: 'Let nothing happen in my name that I could not consent to.'

Beyond Cyberfetish

On all these questions of cyberfetish, the problems revolve around the corporation – it is the pharmaceutical corporation that drives the insanity of an unlimited medical bureaucracy, the automobile manufacturer behind the nonsense of our roads, and the 'defense' contractor behind the endless escalation of killing machines. We need not be misled here into thinking that we must submit to the tragedy of bureaucracy wherever it occurs: what is inevitable is solely that bureaucratic systems can generate only bureaucratic responses, and that commercial bureaucracies are bound to the constraints of the marketplace.

Since the concept of a 'market' has taken a quite substantial knocking in recent decades it is worth remembering the term simply labels a situation where people want things and will pay to get them. It is not so much that markets have failed in recent years as it is that our governments let banks engage in incredibly ill-conceived financial practices – and it is worth remembering that stock and currency markets are very different beasts to the markets that trade in goods and services. Unless there is a tremendous appetite for creative barter on an unprecedented scale, it is a safe bet that we will be dealing with markets for as long as we are dealing with humans: even the communists did not try to eliminate money, and with good reason. We should not mistakenly blame a medium of exchange for the problems of greed.

The ubiquity of markets creates the genuine possibility to influence those bureaucracies that depend upon them for their success. This is why a moral politics has the potential to influence corporations: if we change where the money is to be found, it will necessarily change what the corporations do to get at it. Change national defense priorities from warfighting to, say, disaster response, and military equipment will cease to be obsessed with superior devices for killing humans. Change transport and infrastructure priorities away from overpowered engines that are inappropriate for urban travel and manufacturers will rapidly respond with new vehicles. Many of these possibilities are already manifested, so all that is needed is a change in focus, not a drastic upheaval.

We cannot know what a moral politics might be able to achieve, but we can see what kind of ideas are worth considering. Illich (1973) makes the point that scientific research can be deployed in one of two different ways. We have currently used it to foster ever-growing specialization of functionality, institutionalization, and centralization of power that regrettably "turns people into the accessories of bureaucracies or machines". We could, however, use technology to increase each person's "competence, control, and initiative" in a way that was limited "only by other individual's claims to an equal range of power and freedom." This latter path, which Illich designates as that of *convivial* tools, is less well-travelled, but it is not non-existent. The bicycle in particular provides Illich with an iconic manifestation of the strengths of conviviality, since it empowers the individual without seriously limiting those around them.

Convivial society for Illich designates a space in which "technologies serve politically interrelated individuals rather than managers", and it is tools that facilitate this end that he calls convivial. Illich talks of "individual freedom realized in personal independence" as an "intrinsic ethical value", and it is clear that this concept is a perfect fit for Kant's communal autonomy. Indeed, Illich offers a technological ideal for the realm of ends that sounds irrepressibly Kantian in its flavor:

> Our imaginations have been industrially deformed to conceive only what can be molded into an engineered system of social habits that fit the logic of large-scale production. We have almost lost the ability to frame in fancy a world in which sound and shared reasoning sets limits to everybody's power to interfere with anybody's equal power to shape the world.

He stresses that what is required is not "the creation of a new man", nor even a single way of living. On the contrary, Illich's vision of tools that are limited by design would necessarily "encourage a diversity of life styles." Neither does he suggest abandoning industrial production entirely – he merely urges us to consider balancing it with tools that enable, rather than addict. The radical monopolies that corporations establish when they produce technology that fosters dependence necessarily restrict autonomy by making everyone reliant upon goods and services that *only* large institutions can provide. Moving past this requires something close to a consensus on the destructiveness of the imperialism of both nations and transnational corporations – something that has grown ever-clearer in the decades since Illich was writing, although it is still far from a unanimously held view.

It is important to appreciate the extent to which, without anyone really noticing, industrial manufacturing has created requirements for what people think they must have in order to live that are radically different from what humans actually need to live happily – namely, sustenance, shelter and community. Someone wishing to move from, say, Djibo in Burkina Faso to, say, Los Angeles in the United States goes from knowing a few people with motor vehicles they might use when they need them to being *required* to own a car in order to be part of respectable society. Only the poor and the destitute catch the bus in the City of Angels, whereas in Djibo, buses are for those nomadic souls who wish to travel to faraway lands – and even then, the option is always there to travel by camel with the Tuareg instead (even if this service mostly exists to entertain tourists). It is impossible to explain to someone who lives in Djibo why anyone in Los Angeles should think it sensible to spend hours of their day stuck inside a stationary car at 'rush hour'. I have visited both Djibo and Los Angeles: the people of Djibo have remarkably less, yet they are in my experience substantially happier than most

Los Angelenos.

The raising of the technology bar increases the costs of living but doesn't necessarily raise the quality of life, in part because our things do not in fact possess the capacity to completely satisfy us that advertisers love to promise. The established institutions of industrialized corporate production are gradually spreading radical monopolies to every corner of the world – to the detriment of everyone. Again, it is not that industrial production is a problem by itself, but when it dominates not only the exploitation of resources and tools but also "the imagination and motivational structure of people" it suddenly becomes impossible to even ponder a world in which individuals might contribute to their own space in the world via any role but consumer. The churches of the middle ages were the pride and joy of the towns that built them because they were the achievement of the entire community – no highway, office block or multi-storey car park can make the same claim, although perhaps the sports fan can feel a certain pride when their loyalty helps fund a new stadium.

What Illich warns about, and what we desperately need to become more aware of, are those situations where ludicrous goals are set on the basis that future technology will be able to fulfill them – this is the essence of the problem of cyberfetish, and the reason that techno-immortality is the exemplar of its illusions. To Illich, there is no difference between the pretence that doctors can deliver an unlimitedly superior health through technology and the equivalent fantasies that engineers can provide ever-higher speeds, or cities can provide ever-improving housing. When entirely abstract – and pragmatically impossible – goals are set, it turns the means by which these objectives are to be met into ends, while simultaneously making their fulfillment unobtainable. Just as Latour (2002) critiqued decades later, Illich warns that the neat division into means and ends falls apart in cyberfetish: we have truly reached the end of the means.

What gets "pushed into the blind spot" by cyberfetish is the possibility that – like the Africans I met in my short time on that continent – we might find "great happiness at lower affluence", as Illich puts the matter. This is heresy indeed! Our addiction to industrial growth is founded in part upon the presumption that this is the *only* way to bring wealth and contentment to everyone. But it seems apparent that this mythology is waning, even if it is not clear which new mythologies will take its place. The mothballing of the Concorde, the emblem of supersonic passenger planes, shows that when it comes to the question of speed we have finally recognized that there are far more dimensions to the question of transportation than speed alone. We need a similar breakthrough in our understanding of medical bureaucracy before the unnecessary escalation of industrial medicine bankrupts every nation that thinks of 'health' as something bestowed by doctors. It would be equally helpful to rethink the concept of transportation in a way that recognized that the only way to end gridlock in Los Angeles and everywhere else is to give people good reasons *not* to drive by entirely re-imagining urban infrastructure.

What is required for a convivial society is not a political revolution against our efficient nightmares but a new focus on the design criteria of tools rather than the industrial focus on production goals, a theme also found in secular animists such as Latour and Verbeek. At the heart of Illich's ideal is a desire to put aside the illusion that we were "born to be slaveholders", and the corresponding fantasy that the only flaw in previous attempts to do so was that we couldn't *all* own slaves. In the machine, we created the perfect slave – but Illich warns that the dream has backfired, and it is no longer clear if we are the master of the machine or its slave. Except for the more sophisticated account of agency, Illich prefigures Latour's critique of tools by some thirty years.

Computers in particular seem to be poised between both

paths at the moment – dominated by corporate institutionalization, but still capable of conviviality in the hands of interrelated individuals. It is a problem for these machines in Illich's perspective that they can *only* come out of industrial production techniques, which Illich justifiably accuses of blocking conviviality, but it is far from clear that a non-industrial computer is a plausible device. It is worth recalling here the impossibility of Google (or indeed Apple or Microsoft or any similar transnational corporation) entering into co-production with its customers – the ratio of staff to clients is too disproportionate. However, if we agree that this kind of co-operative relationship is what we want, the corporations will necessarily reconfigure to deliver it – we just have to get past the mythology that a better future will come about automatically through the gradual refinement of industrial products, and also the equally problematic idea that we can get the world we want without our involvement.

Although perhaps I should be cautious in speaking of 'better', since Illich cautions that it is precisely the dream of 'better worlds' that has hypnotized us into cyberfetish. As he puts the matter: "The commitment to the better at any cost makes the good impossible at all costs." The question we need to be asking if we want a convivial society, therefore, is the same one that the Greek philosophers asked themselves: 'what is the good life'? Or perhaps I should say 'how can we have a life that is good?' since this question leaves open the possibility – the probability – that there are many different answers. The challenge is not only to find these answers, but to work out how to make a semblance of order out of their chaos, and thus attain some hope of balance.

The Politics of Balance

It is not too much to hope that we might move beyond politics as warfare, and it is important to remember that what is needed most urgently are not political reforms (although these should also be considered) but forms of moral representation that allow an alternative politics to emerge. This is what Stengers is striving for when she talks of 'cosmopolitics' and what I mean when I talk of 'moral politics'. It is not what Kant meant by the realm of ends – although this is, I suggest, not only compatible with these other projects but also a moral fiction ideally suited to understanding the nature of the problem. Precisely because the realm of ends requires us to consider how to integrate our goals with other people's, it's very possibility excludes the premature silencing of dissent. On the contrary, every chaotic voice must be heard before any hope of convening the realm of ends or the parliament of things could be fulfilled.

In this regard, although I wholeheartedly support Mouffe's attempts to regenerate democracy by accepting that conflict and disorder are essential to political life, her arguments in respect of ending politics as war and replacing it with a more civil kind of political disagreement only go so far. Mouffe's radical recovery of democracy is necessary, but it is not sufficient to solve the crisis we face. We do need to regain political engagement, because it is only through our democratic practices that we might be able to bring our national bureaucracies back in line with our own ethics. But we cannot hope to solve all our troubles upon the stages of national and international politics. Indeed, a focus upon this aspect of political and moral life will make it hard to even *identify* all the problems that need to be addressed, and this is especially the case when politics is reduced to the domain of economics.

By being excessively focused on the distribution of money, we have empowered the political war and consequently silenced discussion of morality. I will not say that there aren't problems to be addressed when it comes to finances, but it is important to remember that not everyone's ideal of fairness entails equality – fairness as proportionality also has to be taken into account. Indeed, thinking about pay in terms of equality erroneously leads to thinking that the problems of injustice in employment are about disparity, and this isn't really the case. We should expect disparity in pay where there is a disparity in work. The problem isn't disparity but *disproportion,* and addressing disproportionate pay would hit the concerns of both fairness as equality *and* fairness as proportionality. Even if there are people who think that the CEO of a company deserves to earn seven-figure salaries, there are almost none who think that such executives work a hundred times harder than rank-and-file workers in the same organization. Diplomatically speaking, focusing on disproportionate pay would be a better agenda for change because it puts liberals and conservatives closer to talking about the same thing.

But let's not get distracted by money, because the politics of money hasn't been a great success thus far. If it rankles that there are people out in the world with astronomical sums of money at their disposal it may be helpful to remember that for a great many millionaires and billionaires their wealth has brought them nothing but isolation and misery. The few millionaires I've met have, for the most part, been incredibly lonely people, and the one that was not had changed his life specifically because he had encountered first-hand the misery of the billionaire recluse. Sometimes we are so focused on the disparity between the rich and the poor that we forget that both can be miserable with their lot. Of course, there are plenty of wealthy people who enjoy their affluence – but if we make our politics exclusively about money we can be certain to continue the war indefinitely, and whatever imaginary future you strive for it will be much easier to get there with the co-operation of the financial aristocracy than to focus change solely upon attempting to spitefully ruin them.

What forms could a new politics of balance take? We can easily consider a few possibilities. For Illich, the capacity to imagine a better world for yourself would be central:

> Alternative political arrangements would have the purpose of permitting all people to define the images of their own future. New politics would aim principally to exclude the design of artifacts and rules that are obstacles to the exercise of this personal freedom. Such politics would limit the scope of tools as demanded by the protection of three values: survival, justice, and self-defined work. I take these values to be fundamental to any convivial society, however different one such society might be from another in practice, institutions, or rationale.

This idea of 'self-defined work' is a crucial one for Illich, since he is entirely unsatisfied with the transformation of work away from something that people *do*, and towards something that people *have*. Before the industrial revolution, people worked to live – now, people 'have' jobs, and these roles are defined by bureaucracies entirely out of individual control. It is the situation of the wage-slave who hates their job but cannot quit because they need money to live that Illich is calling unacceptable here. But his goal of "survival in justice" is something that he sees as possible only through "the universal renunciation of unlimited progeny, affluence, and power on the part of both individuals and groups." His hope was that people would "relearn to depend on each other", since the transformation he saw as necessary "cannot be extorted by some despotic Leviathan, nor elicited by social engineering." Honestly, I doubt that "universal renunciation" is attainable, but of course the moral fictions of utopia that inspire us need not be possible for them to be effective. It would, however, be helpful to avoid impossibilities as a *requirement* for change, and on this front Illich's solutions come up somewhat short.

Conversely, Latour's political ecology is a far more attainable ideal precisely because it entails nothing universal. Indeed, decrying the universal is Latour's *modus operandi*! Unfortunately, the problems that Latour wrestles with are still largely invisible to most people, and this gives him a very different problem to Illich's – even if political ecology were the best course of action, it would still be necessary to present it in such a way that people could *understand* what was expected of them. Latour (2004) suggests that we need a "riskier and more ambitious slogan" than the eighteenth century cry of 'No taxation without representation', namely "No reality without representation!" But to whom does this cry make sense? Very few, alas, because to recognize the need for more co-operative representation of reality you have to already be a nomad of the Million Spheres. There is a vast gulf here between the wise proposals that Latour offers, and the ability of the majority of people to understand what he suggests, although he is never more accessible than when he proposes that "the right to ask one's own question in one's own terms could be included in the Bill of Rights."

On one point, however, Latour is vastly more lucid than most who would take on the risks associated with change: he recognizes the value of politicians. Indeed, it has become so expected that we will speak ill of our political representatives that the most shocking thing imaginable is to suggest that they might, after all, be good at what they do! I have always attempted to redirect people's ire at the nefariousness of politicians by reminding them that 'all politicians are weasels' - but to Latour, this kind of attitude entirely misses the strength of the politician's role. It is their capacity to compromise that Latour recognizes as valuable, and this is something "the most imaginative scientists cannot emulate" because to them 'compromise' is akin to 'lie'. For Latour, the much maligned deals and compromises of the political negotiation table conceal "the most indispensible of virtues" - provided one small change is accepted. Spokespeople must return from discussions with a willingness to help *change* the opinions of those they represent faithfully. In this, the meaning of 'faithfulness' acquires an additional and unexpected sense.

Distinguishing Stengers cosmopolitics from Latour's project can be difficult since the two intellectuals are in many ways of one mind. But the ecology of practices Stengers advocates is not the parliament of things, for all that it may be conducive to its convening, and it is worth appreciating how Stengers views a politics of balance developing. For her, part of the essential problem we face is how to integrate our cities, the places where politics originated, with all those other places that are nothing like either the cities or each other! To make this possible – to bring forth a common world from a patchwork of traditions – requires that we "create obstacles that prevent us from rushing towards others while requiring that they resemble what we might become". Crucially, this is a problem *for us* and not for those other practices, those other traditions that we hope to meet with. We must cultivate not our curiosity for knowledge, which ties us to one way of seeing the world, but our thirst for wonder. We have to discover how to be both settled and a nomad simultaneously, although in different ways, to be able to travel the Million Spheres without losing sight of the inescapable fact that we are all at home somewhere, mythologically if not physically.

Lisa Disch (2009) suggests that what both Latour and Stengers are putting together is an entirely new way of thinking about representation, a way that I have tried (perhaps uncomfortably) to adopt in the writing of this book. Their joint approach rests upon taking the definition of representation from the political assembly (which provides the concept of a 'spokesperson') but the practice of representation from the laboratory (which provides practices capable of establishing reliable witnesses). This has odd consequences, not least of which is the suggestion that scientists *represent*, a fortuitous concept for me since my philosophy of imagination revolves around our representations and what they mean in art, games, science, and now morality and politics. We have learned to speak to supposedly inanimate things in the laboratory far more effectively than we have ever learned to speak to one another! The problem of the politician, Latour insists, is that they dared imagine that they can speak for those they represent "without ever truly consulting them". Disch proposes that the flawed mythology (and she expressly uses this term) that surrounds the claim that we have a 'voice' through political representation is intimately connected to the failure to consult in politics, which means that whatever voice we have on the political stage it cannot be authentically *ours*!

All representations are fictions – whether we are talking about representative art and the virtual worlds of games (Bateman, 2011), the mythologies of the sciences (Bateman, 2012), the problems of political representation, or the possibilities of moral representation. In all these cases, the relevant fictions should not be treated as necessarily disjunct from facts – indeed, the fictions of the sciences are precisely of value to us not because they 'are facts' but because they *aim* at the factual. As Stengers (1993) recognizes, precisely what scientists do is "invent possibilities of representing, of constituting a statement that *nothing a priori* distinguishes from a fiction, as the legitimate representation of a phenomenon". How admirable is this capacity to apply our imagination to understanding the world! How wonderful would it be to apply the same inventiveness in morality, the same legitimacy of representation in politics? We *already* accept perspectival truth in the sciences, which attain their robustness from the community practices that refine individual claims – perhaps it is time to welcome it in morality and politics.

A politics of balance may be morally and politically desirable for a great many reasons, but it is especially important to us now because the ecological crisis that cyberfetish has inexorably drawn us into will not be resolved by politics as war. Part of the problem we suffer is an astonishing disconnect between the scope of the problem and our ability to accept it. Latour (2011) calls this 'the ecological dumbfounding':

> If we are so threatened, why is it that ecologically minded people constitute no more than a minority? I think most would agree that there is no comparison between the urgency of ecological concerns and the mobilizing energy of wars or, for that matter, religion. A threat to a temple? A blasphemy somewhere? Everyone is up in arms. Millions move like one single man. A threat to the Earth life system? A yawn, or a slow snail-like move to change our light bulbs. This is what I call the disconnect. How is it that we remain dumbfounded by the ecological crisis?

The answer that I would offer is simply that we are still caught up in those mythologies of the Enlightenment and earlier that struggle to present this problem in ways that allow it to be entirely appreciated. Cyberfetish, which was facilitated by the split into thinking subjects and inanimate objects, is so much more exciting and immediate than some future threat of extinction – which is quite amusing, really, given that it is cyberfetish that powers us rapidly towards environmental catastrophes. But really, the mythological problem is only part of the barrier – the other is that the Greens, as environmentalists are affectionately known, have the same problem as opponents of abortion and animal cruelty: they come to the table under the influence of moral horror, and it makes diplomacy far more difficult to establish. Indeed, the painting of ecological crisis as apocalyptic – while certainly dramatic – fails to motivate for the same reason that people who have some sympathy for the plight of animals harden their hearts when animal activists try to share their intensity too directly: you cannot transfer moral horror if you don't *already* have the requisite mythology that exposes the raw nerves.

It has not been possible for environmental scientists to have their case accepted thus far because, in a brutal irony, the attempt to leverage the authority of Science in the matter of humanity versus the rest of the planet has exposed the total lack of authority that is actually possessed by scientists. As long as the mythology of the sciences is that Science is Truth, it cannot be persuasive. However, once we switch to the sciences as representation – to scientists as spokespeople instead of prophets – we are in a radically new space and the ecological crises, as Latour (2004) expresses beautifully, becomes a 'revolt of means' as suddenly no entity, no matter how small or apparently insignificant, will consent "to be treated 'simply as a means' but insists on being treated 'always also as an end'". Once again, Latour's project moves hand-in-hand with Kant's, here extending the Formula of Humanity beyond humanity, as I have already traced.

So we return to Kant's realm of ends, and contemporary Kantians' continuation of his project to create a secular alternative to Christian moral ideals. Because so many humans on our planet at this time are Christian, and so many more are from related Abrahamic traditions, we absolutely require mythologies that can be accessed both by people of faith *and* by positivists and others who find religion, at best, suspicious. Christine Kosgaard (2012) offers the Kantian perspective of Latour and Stenger's 'common world' simply through her faithfulness to the tradition of Kant's moral philosophy:

> Despite its explicitly religious formulation, the idea that God gave us the world in common captures something that goes right to the heart of the moral outlook, and that can be formulated in secular terms. It is the thought that others have just as good a claim on the resources of the world as we do, and that it behooves us to limit our own claims with that in mind.

Here the theme of limitation, so explicit for Illich and Stengers, and implicit in Latour, is once again the problem around which we must devise new mythologies, or adapt existing ones. It is only by accepting our limits, and the necessary limitations of technology that cyberfetish obscures, that we can hope to discover "how to live together in liveable places", which is what 'ecology' can and perhaps should mean (Latour, 2010a). Latour is convinced of the feasibility of these new political ecologies, these ecologies of practices, precisely because the long-exaggerated influence of Europe is finally declining, and with it the *hubris* that "made its pretence at defining universality for all the others so cheap and so incoherent." If this is a dig at Kant and the Enlightenment, with its craving for universality in both the sciences and morality, it is also entirely in the spirit of Kant's moral and political projects that we should work together to establish *how* we might live together.

The politics of balance that are being advocated do not require political reform (or do not *necessarily* require it), but they *do* require moral reform, and in particular they require us to develop or adapt our moral mythologies to allow us to come face-to-face with not only the problem, but the beings and things we have managed to ignore all too easily up until now. As Midgley (2003) asks:

> Can it really be true that we bear responsibility for things that happen to people and countries so far away from us? Can we, still more oddly, have responsibilities towards the non-human realm? Our current moral tradition makes it hard for us to grasp these things. It doesn't leave room for them. Yet the changes are real. They do demand some kind of adaptation from us, adaptation of a morality that was formed for a quite different, more manageable kind of world. We can't go on acting as if we were still in that world. On that path, there is no way through.

This is the challenge of moral politics understood, as it must be, as an *ethical* dilemma, and specifically as a problem of the moral imagination. Morality, as Latour (2004) explains, has "changed direction". We are no longer in a position to define foundations, but we are perfectly positioned to "recommence the process of composition" that might allow us to understand – for the first time – the incredible diversity of beings and things that are sharing this world with us, including both those whose ancestors and ours somehow managed to survive unthinkably long eons, and those that we ourselves have created and unleashed in a few scant centuries. All these beings and things are in the world in a different way, and they are all parts of very different mythologies – sometimes mythologies that are in direct tension. We cannot make this splendid chaos into a universe any more, not unless we first accept the multiverse we were always living within.

Returning to my earlier selves, I can now ask whether religious-me and wild-me could be brought into alignment, whether their different spheres could be brought into conjunction somehow. Certainly, this would not be easy, even accepting moral chaos and the cosmopolitical demands of the multiverse. For positivists, and others of similar inclination (such as wild-me), all religions are necessarily false and hence all their practices fall under suspicion, condemnation or worse. Yet in order to reach this conclusion it is necessarily to valorize a particular mythology – that which treats the world as knowable by (and perhaps only by) the sciences, and hence restricts the very concept of 'knowledge' to that which is testable and replicable by purely physical means. This is not, despite how it may seem, a case of breaking free of the illusions of religion and escaping to the true world beyond, but rather of exchanging one mythological perspective for another. The kinds of knowledge embedded within religious traditions are so very different from those embedded within scientific traditions that it should be clear that the two standards are not the same. When instead the values of the latter come to be used to judge the former, it can only end in lunacy and error.

For those like wild-me who are suspicious of religion and

theology and either unwilling or unable to accept people of faith, there is a need to recognize and understand the moral horror behind this attitude, and to carefully consider what might need to be done going forward. We cannot afford to think the world through categories so narrow that no truth could possibly squeeze through. If you declare that every religion is without value, that it must be abandoned before anything good can come about, you will not only become indistinguishable from those bigots you detest but you will block reform by excluding the vast majority of people from consideration as allies. Yet if you merely endure what others 'believe' from the security of your own 'knowledge', then your intolerant tolerance will be your curse, and you will be forever isolated from understanding anyone whose forms of knowledge are not your own. For those like religious-me on the other side of this divide, nearly identical concerns apply, and this alone should reveal the shared ground upon which a common world might be built. Each of the Million Spheres is woven from its own mythology, and truth can be found both within and between them all.

It would be foolish for me to believe that this one insignificant book could change the world, although it perhaps would not be too much to dream. For good or ill, we have moved beyond that time in our history as a species when a few individuals could set the moral and intellectual agenda in isolation. Our technology now allows everyone the capacity to speak, out in the hinterlands of the internet and elsewhere – to the extent that there are now so many people trying to be heard that it is almost impossible to hear anything but cacophony. Fortunately, as I have tried to demonstrate through the patient composition of so many different threads in the tapestry of moral philosophy, the argument that I have tried to advance here is both well-established, and continuing to adjust itself to the circumstances at hand. We do, therefore, have cause for hope.

There is a reason I have repeatedly cited the Kantians, Allen

Wood, Christine Korsgaard, and of course Immanuel Kant himself; a reason I have endlessly referred to Bruno Latour and Isabelle Stengers; a reason to bring Alain Badiou alongside Michael Moorcock; a reason I draw upon Alasdair MacIntyre and Mary Midgley again and again to make my points – and this reason is the simplest of all. Although they are all different philosophers, with diverging perspectives that address a variety of unique problems, they all bear on the same predicament, the crisis of ethics as it faces us now. It is only by viewing this problem from every side that we can have faith that we have genuinely seen what is true, the perspectival truth of morality. This truth emerges as imperfectly in this book as it does anywhere else, but it is always there to be found when we have the willingness to be wrong so that we might eventually find what is right.

Saint I certainly am not, and I would not judge my own morality as superior to anything, except perhaps to the denial of ethics as meaningful, that most frivolous of all intellectual fantasies. Yet somehow I must hold myself in tension between the necessity of making moral judgments, and a reluctance to condemn either difference or similitude in others without first appreciating that which I am judging. I must continue in my own moral representation of myself, and strive to appreciate and encourage the moral representation of others. Just as the unity of a universal moral law is forever balanced against the infinite diversity of moral chaos, so I must maintain a tension between certainty and hesitation, to hold fast to that which is good while leaving open the ever-present possibility of finding other ways of bringing good into the world. I cannot do it alone – even the most heroic effort cannot render moral living a private concern, because even living itself is the work of the many and not the one, both human and otherwise than human. We are not alone. We were never alone. It is time we started living this eternal truth together.

References

Al-Muslimi, Farea (2013). "Drone Wars: The Constitutional and Counterterrorism Implications of Targeted Killing" [Statement], *United States Senate Judiciary Committee Subcommittee on the Constitution, Civil Rights and Human Rights,* April 23, 2013, available online: http://www.judiciary.senate.gov/pdf/04-23-13Al-MuslimiTestimony.pdf (accessed 24 April 2013).

Africa (2013a). "Sahara", BBC1, Sunday 17 March 2013, 6 pm.

Africa (2013b)."The Future", BBC1, Sunday 24 March 2013, 6 pm.

Agamben, Giorgio (2005). *State of Exception,* trans. Kevin Attell, London, UK: University of Chicago Press.

Anderson, Poul (1961). *Three Hearts and Three Lions,* New York, NY: Doubleday.

Anon (1923). "Climbing Mount Everest is Work for Supermen", *New York Times,* 18 March.

Anscombe, G. E. M (1958). "Modern Moral Philosophy", *Philosophy,* vol. 33, no. 124, pp. 1-19.

Arendt, Hannah (1958). *The Human Condition,* Chicago, IL: University of Chicago Press.

Arendt, Hannah (1961). *Between Past and Future,* New York, NY: Viking Press.

Arendt, Hannah (2005). *The Promise of Politics,* ed. Jerome Kohn, New York, NY: Schocken Books.

Aristotle (384-82 BC). *Ethics,* trans. D.P. Chase [2009], Boston, MA: MobileReference.

Asimov, Isaac (1942). "Runaround", *Astounding Science Fiction,* vol. 29, no. 1, pp. 94-103.

Attenborough, David (2008). *Life in Cold Blood,* New York, NY: Random House Group.

Badiou, Alain (2000). *Deleuze: The Clamor of Being,* trans. Louise Burchill, Minneapolis, MN: University of Minnesota Press.

Badiou, Alain (2001). *Ethics: An Essay on the Understanding of Evil*, trans. Peter Hallward, New York, NY: Verso.

Badiou, Alain (2005), "Philosophy and 'the death of communism.'" in *Infinite Thought*, ed. and trans. Oliver Feltham and Justin Clemens, New York, NY: Continuum, pp. 95-105.

Badiou, Alain (2009). *Logic of Worlds: Being and Event II*, trans. Alberto Toscano, New York, NY: Continuum.

Badiou, Alain (2011). *Being and Event*, trans. Oliver Feltham, New York, NY: Continuum.

Badiou, Alain (2013). *Plato's Republic*, trans. Susan Spitzer, New York, NY: Columbia University Press.

Baron, Jonathan (2007). *Thinking and deciding*, New York, NY: Cambridge University Press.

Barry, Roger (2008). "Revenue, Lordship, Kinship and Law", *Manaraefan Herred*, available online: http://www.manaraefan.co.uk/index_files/Page3400.htm (accessed: 19 December 2012).

Barthelmess, Eugênia (1987). "Politics and metaphysics in three novels of Philip K. Dick", Post-graduate dissertation, available online: http://dspace.c3sl.ufpr.br/dspace/bitstream/handle/1884/24340/D?sequence=1 (accessed 11 April 2013).

Bateman, Chris (2007a). "Kant's Yardstick", *Only a Game* [blog], available online: http://onlyagame.typepad.com/only_a_game/2007/06/kants_yardstick.html (accessed 14 January 2013).

Bateman, Chris (2007b). "The Trolley Problem (2)", *Only a Game* [blog], available online: http://onlyagame.typepad.com/only_a_game/2007/07/the-trolley-pro.html (accessed 7 January 2013).

Bateman, Chris (2011). *Imaginary Games*, Winchester and Washington: Zero Books.

Bateman, Chris (2012). *The Mythology of Evolution*, Winchester and Washington: Zero Books.

Baumgartner, Thomas; Heinrichs, Markus; Vonlanthen, Aline;

Fischbacher, Urs and Fehr, Ernst (2008). "Oxytocin Shapes the Neural Circuitry of Trust and Trust Adaptation in Humans", *Neuron*, vol. 58, no. 4 (May), pp. 639-650.

Beetz, Andrea; Uvnäs-Moberg, Kerstin; Julius, Henri; Kotrschal, Kurt (2012). "Psychosocial and psychophysiological effects of human-animal interactions: the possible role of oxytocin", *Front. Psychology*, vol. 3, article 234.

Bekoff, Marc and Pierce, Jessica (2009). *Wild Justice: The Moral Lives of Animals*, Chicago, IL: Chicago University Press.

Bentham, Jeremy (1776). *A Fragment on Government.*

Bentham, Jeremy (1789). *An Introduction to the Principles of Morals and Legislation.*

Berlin, Isaiah (1988). "On the Pursuit of the Ideal", *The New York Review of Books*, vol. 35, no. 4 (March 17), pp. 11-18.

Berreby, David (1994). "...That Damned Elusive Bruno Latour", *Lingua Franca*, vol. 4, no. 6, pp. 22-34.

Braver, Lee (2012)."A brief history of continental realism", *Continental Philosophy Review*, vol. 45, pp.261-289.

Brockman, John (1995). *The Third Culture: Beyond the Scientific Revolution*, Simon and Schuster.

Brożekm, Bartosz (2012). *Rule-Following. From Imitation to the Normative Mind*, Kraków, Poland: Copernicus Center Press.

Bruce, Laura, Neary, Timothy (1995). "The limbic system of tetrapods: A comparative analysis of cortical and amygdalar populations", *Brain, Behavior and Evolution*, vol. 46, no. 4-5, pp. 224-234.

Buss, Sarah (2008). "Personal Autonomy", *Stanford Encyclopedia of Philosophy*, available online: http://plato.stanford.edu /entries/personal-autonomy/ (accessed: 8 April 2013).

Butler, Joseph (1726). *Fifteen Sermons Preached at the Rolls Chapel*, London, UK: J. and J. Knapton.

Campbell, Joseph (1972). *Myths to Live By*, New York, NY, Bantam.

Campbell, Joseph (2001). *Thou Art That*, San Francisco, CA, New

World Library.

Camus, Albert (1942). *The Myth of Sisyphus*, trans. Justin O'Brien [1955], London, UK: Hamish Hamilton.

Carnap, Rudolph (1934). *The Unity of Science*, London: Kegan Paul.

Cato, Molly Scott (2009). *Green Economics: An Introduction to Theory, Policy and Practice*, London, UK: Earthscan.

Cato, Molly Scott (2013). *The Bioregional Economy: Land, liberty and the pursuit of happiness*, New York, NY: Routledge.

Clarke, Steve (2008). "SIM and the City: Rationalism in Psychology and Philosophy and Haidt's Account of Moral Judgment", *Philosophical Psychology*, vol. 21, no. 6, pp. 799-820.

Cogburn, Jon and Silcox, Mark (2012). *Dungeons and Dragons and Philosophy*, Chicago and LaSalle, IL: Open Court.

Comte, Auguste (1830). "Course of Positive Philosophy", reprinted in ed. Gertrud Lenzer, *Auguste Comte and Positivism: The Essential Writings*, New York, NY, Harper, pp. 71-86.

Comte, Auguste (1858). *The Catechism of Positive Religion*, trans. Richard Congreve [2004], Whitefish, MT: Kessinger Publishing.

Connor, Steven (2010). "I Believe That the World", in *Cultural Ways of Worldmaking: Media and Narratives*, eds. Vera Nünning, Ansgar Nünning, Birgit Neumann, Berlin and New York: Walter de Gruyter, pp. 29-46.

Costelloe, Timothy M. (2009). "The Invisibility of Evil: Moral Progress and the 'Animal Holocaust', *Philosophical Papers*, vol. 32, no. 2, pp. 109-131.

Cottle, Thomas J. (2002). "On Narratives and the Sense of Self", *Qualitative Inquiry*, no. 8, pp. 535-549.

Csányi, Vilmos (2005). *If Dogs Could Talk: Exploring the canine mind*, New York, NY: North Point Press.

Cummiskey, David (1990). "Kantian consequentialism", *Ethics*, vol. 100, no. 3, pp. 586-615.

Currie, Gregory and Ravenscroft, Ian (2002). *Recreative Minds:*

Imagination in Philosophy and Psychology, Oxford, UK: Clarendon Press.

Stretch, Euan (2011)."Beeb Faked Frozen Planet", *Daily Mirror*,12 December, p1.

Darwin, Charles (1859). *On the Origin of Species by Means of Natural Selection, or the Preservation of Favored Races in the Struggle for Life*, London: John Murray.

de Waal, Frans (1996) *Good Natured: The Origins of Right and Wrong in Humans and Other Animals.* Cambridge, MA: Harvard University Press.

Dean, Richard (2010). "Does Neuroscience Undermine Deontological Theory?", *Neuroethics*, vol. 3, no. 1 (April), pp 43-60.

Deleuze, Gilles (1985). "Mediators", trans. Martin Joughin [1995], in *Negotiations 1972-1990*, New York, NY: Columbia University Press, pp. 121-134.

Demenchonok, Edward (2009). "10. The Universal Concept of Human Rights as a Regulative Principle: Freedom Versus Paternalism", *American Journal of Economics & Sociology*, vol. 68, no. 1, pp. 273-301.

Dennett, Daniel C. (1984). *Elbow Room: The Varieties of Free Will Worth Wanting*, Cambridge, MA: The MIT Press.

Dews, Peter (2008). "Alain Badiou: Being and Event", *Philosophical Reviews*, available online: http://ndpr.nd.edu/news/23361-being-and-event/ (accessed: 21 January 2013).

Disch, Lisa J. (2009)."'Faitiche'-izing the People: What Representative Democracy Might Learn from Science Studies", *APSA 2009 Toronto Meeting Paper*, available online: http://ssrn.com/abstract=1449734Studies (accessed 8 April 2013).

Douzinas, Coastas (2007). *Human Rights and Empire: The Political Philosophy of Cosmopolitanism*, Abingdon, UK: Routledge-Cavendish.

Ecology Global Network (2013). "World Birth and Death Rates", available online: http://www.ecology.com/birth-death-rates/ (accessed 4 April 2013).

Effinger, George Alec (1988). *When Gravity Fails,* New York: Bantam.

Ekman, Paul (2003). *Emotions Revealed,* New York, NY: Times Books Henry Holt and Company.

Engels, Donald (1999). *Classical Cats: The rise and fall of the sacred cat,* New York, NY: Routledge.

Everett III, Hugh (1957) "'Relative State' Formulation of Quantum Mechanics", *Reviews of Modern Physics,* vol. 29, no. 3 pp. 454-462

Festinger, Leon (1957). *A Theory of Cognitive Dissonance,* Stanford, CA: Stanford University Press.

Feyarabend, Paul (1988). *Farewell to Reason,* New York, NY, Verso.

Fischlin, Daniel, Hollinger, Veronica, Taylor, Andrew (1991). "'The Charisma Leak': A Conversation with William Gibson and Bruce Sterling", *Science Fiction Studies,* vol. 19, no. 1 (March), available online: http://www.depauw.edu/sfs/interviews/gibsonsterling.htm (accessed 6 May 2013).

Fitzhugh, William (2005). "Who Were the Vikings?", *NOVA,* available online: http://www.pbs.org/wgbh/nova/ancient/who-were-vikings.html (accessed: 19 December 2012).

Fives, Allyn John (2008). "Human Flourishing: The Grounds of Moral Judgment", *The Journal of Value Inquiry,* no 42, pp.167-185.

Foot, Phillipa (1967). "The Problem of Abortion and the Doctrine of the Double Effect", *Oxford Review,* vol. 5, pp. 5-15.

Forbes, Mark (2004). "The most hapless tourist in the world", *The Age,* 13 March 2004, available online: http://www.theage.com.au/articles/2004/03/12/1078594562511.html?from=storyrhs (accessed 15 April 2013).

Fraser, Mariam (2006) "The ethics of reality and virtual reality: Latour, facts and values", *History of the Human Sciences,* vol. 19

no. 2, pp. 45-72

Frolich, Norman; Oppenheimer, Joe A.; Eavey, Cheryl L. (1987). "Laboratory Results on Rawls's Distributive Justice", *British Journal of Political Science*, vol. 17, no. 1, pp. 1-21.

Garry, Ann (2012). "Who Is Included? Intersectionality, Metaphors, and the Multiplicity of Gender", in *Out from the Shadows: Analytical Feminist Contributions to Traditional Philosophy*, eds. Sharon L. Crasnow and Anita M. Superson, New York: Oxford University Press, pp. 493-530.

Gauchet, Marcel (1996). "Right and Left", trans. Arthur Goldhammer, in *Realms of Memory: Rethinking the French Past, Volume I: Conflicts and Divisions*, ed. Pierre Nora, New York, NY: Columbia University Press, pp. 242-245.

Gendler, Tamar Szabó (2000). "The Puzzle of Imaginative Resistance", *The Journal of Philosophy*, vol. 97, no. 2 (February), pp. 55-81.

Gendler, Tamar Szabó (2002). "Personal Identity and Thought-Experiments", *The Philosophical Quarterly*, vol. 52, no. 206 (January), pp. 34-54.

Gendler, Tamar Szabó (2007). "Philosophical Thought Experiments, Intuitions, and Cognitive Equilibrium", *Midwest Studies in Philosophy*, vol. 31, no. 1, pp. 68-89.

Gendler, Tamar Szabó (2008a). "Alief and Belief", *Journal of Philosophy*, vol. 105, no. 10, pp. 634-663

Gendler, Tamar Szabó (2008b). "Alief and Belief in Action (and Reaction)", *Mind and Language*, vol. 23, no. 5, pp. 552-585.

Gendler, Tamar Szabó (2011). *Intuition, Imagination, and Philosophical Methodology*, Oxford, UK: Oxford University Press.

Ghezzi, Ivan and Ruggles, Clive (2007). "Chankillo: A 2300-Year-Old Solar Observatory in Coastal Peru". *Science*, vol. 315, no. 5816, pp. 1239-1243.

Gibson, William (1986). *Neuromancer*, London: Grafton.

Gibson, William and Sterling, Bruce (1991). *The Difference Engine*,

New York, NY: Bantam.

Gibson, William and Swanwick, Michael (1987). "Dogfight", in *Burning Chrome*, ed. William Gibson, New York: Ace Books, pp. 167-194

Gimpl, Gerald and Fahrenholz, Falk (2001). "The Oxytocin Receptor System: Structure, Function, and Regulation", *Physiological Reviews*, vol. 81 no. 2 (April), pp. 629-683.

Gittell, J.H., Douglass, A. (2010). "Relational Bureaucracy: At the Boundary of Relational and Bureaucratic Organizing", *Institute for Work and Employment Relations* Seminar, Cambridge, MA: MIT Sloan School of Management.

Google (2012). "Code of Conduct", available online: http://investor.google.com/corporate/code-of-conduct.html (accessed 3 April 2013).

Graham-Campbell, James (2001). *The Viking World*, 3rd edition, London, UK: Frances Lincoln Ltd..

Gregory, Derek (2006). "The Black Flag: Guantánamo Bay and the Space of Exception", *Geografiska Annaler*, vol. 88B, no. 4, pp. 405-427.

Green, Ronald M. (1992). *Kierkegaard and Kant: The Hidden Debt*, Albany, NY: SUNY Press.

Greene, Joshua D. (2008). "The secret joke of Kant's soul", in *Moral psychology, Volume 3:The Neuroscience of Morality, Emotion, Brain Disorders, and Development* , ed. Walter Sinnott-Armstrong, Cambridge: MIT Press, pp. 35-80.

Gygax, Gary and Arneson, Dave (1974). *Dungeons & Dragons* [Boxed Role-playing Game], Lake Geneva, WA: Tactical Studies Rules, Inc.

Haché, Émile and Latour, Bruno (2010)."Morality or Moralism? An Exercise in Sensitization", trans. Patrick Camiller, *Common Knowledge*, vol. 16, no 2 (Spring), pp. 311-330.

Haidt, Jonathan (2001). "The Emotional Dog and its Rational Tail: A Social Intuitionist Approach to Moral Judgment", *Psychological Review*, no 108, pp. 814-834.

Haidt, Jonathan (2012). *The Righteous Mind: Why Good People Are Divided by Politics and Religion*, London, UK: Allen Lane.

Haidt, Jonathan; Graham, Jesse (2007). "When Morality Opposes Justice: Conservatives Have Moral Intuitions that Liberals may not Recognize". *Social Justice Research*, vol. 20, no. 1, pp. 98-116.

Handlin L, Hydbring-Sandberg E, Nilsson A, Ejdebäck M, Jansson A, Uvnäs-Moberg K. (2011). "Short-term interaction between Dogs and Their owners: Effects on oxytocin, cortisol, insulin and heart rate. An Explorative Study."*Anthrozoos*, vol. 24, pp. 301-315.

Haraway, Donna (1991). "Cyborg Manifesto: Science, Technology, and Socialist-Feminism in the Late Twentieth Century" in *Simians, Cyborgs and Women: The Reinvention of Nature*, New York, NY: Routledge, pp. 149-181.

Haraway, Donna (2003). "The Companion Species Manifesto: Dogs, People, and Significant Otherness", Chicaco, IL: Prickly Paradigm Press.

Harcourt, Bernard (2011). *The Illusion of Free Markets: Punishment and the Myth of Natural Order*, Cambridge, MA: Harvard University Press.

Hardin, Gareth (1968). "The Tragedy of the Commons", *Science*, vol. 162, no. 3859, pp. 1243-1248.

Harman, Graham (2009). "On 'Latour Litanies'", *Object-Oriented Philosophy* [Blog], available online: http://doctorzamalek2.wordpress.com/2009/12/13/on-latour-litanies/ (accessed 15 April 2013).

Heger, Alexander, Stanford E. Woosley (2002). "The Nucleosynthetic Signature of Population III", *Astrophysical Journal*, vol. 567, no. 1, pp. 532-543.

Herodotus (circa 440 BC). *The Histories*, trans. George Rawlinson, New York, NY: Everyman's Library.

Hill, Greg and Thornley, Kerry Wendell (1970). *Principia Discordia*, 4th edition, Port Townsend, WA: Loompanics.

Hirsch, Walter (1958). "The Image of the Scientists in Science Fiction: A Content Analysis", *American Journal of Sociology*, vol. 63, no. 5 (March), pp. 506-512.

Hobbes, Thomas (1651). *Leviathan, or the Matter, Forme, and Power of a Commonwealth, Ecclesiasticall and Civil*, London: Andrew Crooke.

Holert, Tom (2012). "'A live monster that is fruitful and multiplies': Capitalism as Poisoned Rat?", *e-flux*, vol. 36, available online: http://www.e-flux.com/journal/%E2%80%9Ca-live-monster-that-is-fruitful-and-multiplies%E2%80%9D-capitalism-as-poisoned-rat/ (accessed 26 April 2013).

Hollifield, Ryan Brooks (2007). *Spaces of Risk, Spaces of Difference: Environmental Justice and Science in Indian Country*, Ann Arbor, MI: ProQuest.

Hu, Ying-Hsueh (2005). "The Cultural Models of the Origins of Life and Stem Cell Debate in Taiwan", *metaphorik.de*, available online: http://www.metaphorik.de/08/hu.htm (accessed 29 December 2012).

Hume, David (1739). *A Treatise of Human Nature*, Oxford: Clarendon Press.

Hume, David (1748). *An Enquiry Concerning Human Understanding*, Oxford: Clarendon Press.

Hume, David (1751). *An Enquiry Concerning the Principles of Morals*, Oxford: Clarendon Press.

Hume, David (1757). "Of the Standard of Taste".

Ignatieff, Michael (2002). "Is the Human Rights Era Ending?", *New York Times*, 5 February, Op-Ed, Late Edition, Section A, p. 25, column 2.

Illich, Ivan (1973). *Tools for Conviviality*, London and New York: Marion Boyars.

Illich, Ivan (1974). *Energy and Equity*, London, UK: Harper and Row.

Illich, Ivan (1975). *Medical Nemesis: The Expropriation of Health*, London, UK: Marion Boyers.

Jacobs, Brian and Kain, Patrick (2003). *Essays on Kant's Anthropology*, Cambridge, UK: Cambridge University Press.

Jacobson, Daniel (2012). "Moral Dumbfounding and Moral Stupefaction", *Oxford Studies in Normative Ethics*, vol. 2, pp. 289-316.

James, William (1891). "The Moral Philosopher and the Moral Life", Yale Philosophical Club Lecture.

James, William (1909). *A Pluralistic Universe: Hibbert Lectures at Manchester College on the Present Situation in Philosophy*, New York, NY: Longmans, Green and Co.

Kagan, Shelley. (2002). "Kantianism for Consequentialists", in *Groundwork for the Metaphysics of Morals*, Rethinking the Western Tradition edition, ed. Allen W. Wood, New Haven, CT: Yale University Press, pp. 111-156.

Kahane, Guy (2010). "Evolutionary Debunking Arguments", *Noûs*, vol. 45, no. 1 (March), pp. 103-125.

Kant, Immanuel (1755). *Universal Natural History and Theory of the Heavens*, trans. Ian Johnston [1998], available online: http://records.viu.ca/~johnstoi/kant/kant2e.htm (accessed 27 December 2012).

Kant, Immanuel (1785). *Groundwork for the Metaphysics of Morals*, ed. and trans. Allen W. Wood [2002], New Haven, CT: Yale University Press.

Kant, Immanuel (1790). *Critique of Judgment*, trans. J. H. Bernard [2005], Mineola, NY: Dover Publications.

Kant, Immanuel (1795). "Toward Perpetual Peace: A Philosophical Sketch", in *Toward Perpetual Peace and Other Writings on Politics, Peace, and History* [2006], ed. Pauline Kleingeld, trans. David L. Colclasure, New Haven, CT: Yale University Press.

Kant, Immanuel (1797). *The Metaphysics of Morals*, ed. and trans. Mary Gregor [1996], Cambridge, UK: Cambridge University Press.

Kant, Immanuel (1798). *Anthropology from a Pragmatic Point of*

View, ed. and trans. Robert B. Louden [2006], Cambridge, UK: Cambridge University Press.

Kastrissianakis, Konstantin and Latour, Bruno (2007). "Bruno Latour – We are all reactionaries today", *Re-Public*, available online: http://www.re-public.gr/en/?p=129 (accessed 20 February 2013).

Kaufman, Herbert (1977). *Red Tape: It's Origins, Uses, and Abuses*, Washington, DC: Brookings Institution Press.

Kennedy, Kelly (2013). "Death rates from guns, traffic accidents converging", *USA Today* available online: http://m.usatoday.com/article/news/1784595?preferredArticleViewMode=single (accessed 25 March 2013).

Kierkegaard, Søren (1843). *Fear and Trembling: A Dialectical Lyric by Johannes de Silentio*, trans. Alastair Hannay [2006], London, UK: Penguin.

Kierkegaard, Søren (1849). The *Sickness Unto Death: A Christian Psychological Exposition for Edification and Awakening*, trans. Alastair Hanney [1989], London, UK: Penguin Books.

Kierkegaard, Søren (1854-55). *Attack Upon Christendom*, trans. Walter Lowrie [1968], Princeton, NJ: Princeton University Press.

Kierkegaard, Søren (1859). *The Point of View for My Work as an Author*, trans. H.V. Hong and E.H. and Hong [1998], *Kierkegaard's Writings*, vol. 22, Princeton, NJ: Princeton University Press.

Kierkegaard, Søren (1938). *Purity of Heart is to Will One Thing; spiritual preparation for the office of confession*, trans. Douglas V. Steere [1956], New York, NY: Harper & Row.

Kierkegaard, Søren (1996). *Papers and Journals: a Selection*, trans. Alastair Hannay, London, UK: Penguin.

Klein, Colin (2011). "The Dual Track Theory of Moral Decision-Making: a Critique of the Neuroimaging Evidence", *Neuroethics*, Vol. 4, no. 2 (July), pp 143-162.

Koch, Arthur L., Silver, Simon (2005). "The First Cell". *Advances in Microbial Physiology*, vol. 50, pp. 227-59.

Korsgaard, Christine (2004). "Fellow Creatures: Kantian Ethics and Our Duties to Animals" in *The Tanner Lectures on Human Values*, ed. Grethe B. Peterson, vol. 25/26, Salt Lake City, UT: University of Utah Press, pp. 77-110.

Korsgaard, Christine (2006). "Morality and the Distinctiveness of Human Action" in *Primates and Philosophers: How Morality Evolved*, ed. Frans de Waal, Princeton, NJ, Princeton University Press, pp. 98-119.

Korsgaard, Christine M. (2012) "A Kantian Case for Animals Rights" *Animal Law: Tier und Recht*, edited by Julia Hänni, Margot Michel, Daniela Kühne, Zurich: Dike Verlag, pp. 3-27.

Kripke, Saul (1982). *Wittgenstein on Rules and Private Language*, Cambridge, MA, Harvard University Press.

Kühne, Walter G. (1949-50). "On a Triconodont tooth of a new pattern from a Fissure-filling in South Glamorgan", Proceedings of the Zoological Society of London, vol. 119, pp. 345-350.

Laird, John (1946). "Act-Ethics and Agent-Ethics", *Mind*, Vol. 55, No. 218 (April), pp. 113-132.

Lake, James A. (2009). "Evidence for an early prokaryotic endosymbiosis", *Nature*, vol. 460 (August), pp. 967-971.

Lakoff, George (1995). "Metaphor, Morality, and Politics, Or, Why Conservatives Have Left Liberals In the Dust", *Social Research*, vol. 62, no. 2, pp. 177-214.

Lakoff, George and Johnson, Mark (1980). *Metaphors We Live By*, Chicago, IL, University of Chicago Press.

Lakoff, George (2010). "The Poll Democrats Need to Know About", *The Huffington Post*, available online: http://www.huffingtonpost.com/george-lakoff/the-poll-democrats-need-t_b_537993.html (accessed 7 January 2013).

Lamarque, Peter (2010). "Wittgenstein, Literature, and the Idea of a Practice" *British Journal of Aesthetics* vol. 50, no. 4, pp. 375-388.

Latour, Bruno (1991). *We Have Never Been Modern,* trans. Catherine Porter [1993], Cambridge, MA: Harvard University Press.

Latour, Bruno (1994) "On Technical Mediation", *Common Knowledge,* vol. 3, no. 2, pp. 29-64.

Latour, Bruno (1999). *Pandora's Hope: An Essay on the Reality of Science Studies,* Cambridge, MA: Harvard University Press.

Latour, Bruno (2002). "Morality and Technology The End of the Means", trans. by Couze Venn, *Theory, Culture & Society,* vol. 19, no. 5/6, pp. 247-260.

Latour, Bruno (2004). *Politics of Nature: How to Bring the Sciences into Democracy,* trans. Catherine Porter, Cambridge, MA: Harvard University Press.

Latour, Bruno (2010a). "Coming out as a philosopher", *Social Studies of Science,* vol. 40, no. 4, pp. 599-608.

Latour, Bruno (2010b). "An Attempt at a 'Compositionist Manifesto'. *New Literary History,* vol. 41, pp. 471-90.

Latour, Bruno (2010c). *On the Modern Cult of the Factish Gods,* trans. Catherine Porter and Heather MacLean (chapter one), Durham and London: Duke University Press.

Latour, Bruno (2011). "Politics of Nature: East and West Perspectives", *Ethics and Global Politics,* vol. 4, no. 1, pp. 71-80.

Ledden, J.E. (1947). "Virtue, Obligatoriness, and Rightness", *Mind,* vol. 56, no. 224 (October), pp. 351-354.

Lévinas, Emmanuel (1963). "The Trace of the Other", trans. Alphonso Lingis, *Tijdschrift voor Philosophie* (September), pp. 605-23.

Lévinas, Emmanuel (1974). *Otherwise than Being or Beyond Essence,* trans. Alphonso Lingis [1998], Pittsburgh, PA: Duquesne University Press.

Lévinas, Emmanuel (1983). "Beyond Intentionality", in *Philosophy in France Today,* ed. Alan Montefiore, Cambridge, UK: Cambridge University Press.

Lévinas, Emmanuel (1990). "The Name of a Dog, or Natural

Rights," in *Difficult Freedom: Essays on Judaism*, trans. Seán Hand, Baltimore, MD: Johns Hopkins University Press, pp. 151-153.

Leyhausen, Paul (1978). *Cat Behavior*, New York, NY: Garland.

Linden, Eugene. *The Parrot's Lament and Other True Tales of Animal Intrigue, Intelligence, and Ingenuity*, New York, NY: Plume.

Louden, Robert B. (1986). "Kant's Virtue Ethics", *Philosophy*, vol. 61, no. 238 (October), pp. 473-489.

Lovelock, James (2006). *The Revenge of Gaia: Why the Earth is Fighting Back and How We Can Still Save Humanity*, London, UK: Penguin Books.

Lyotard, Jean-François (1979). *The Postmodern Condition*, trans. Geoff Bennington and Brian Massumi [1984], Manchester, UK: Manchester University Press.

Lyra, Wladimir; Paardekooper, Sijme-Jan; Mac Low, Mordecai-Mark (2010)."Orbital Migration of Low-mass Planets in Evolutionary Radiative Models: Avoiding Catastrophic Infall", The Astrophysical Journal Letters, vol. 715, no. 2, pp. L68-L73.

Manninen, Bertha Alvarez (2006)."Medicating the mind: a Kantian analysis of overprescribing psychoactive drugs", *Journal of Medical Ethics*, vol. 32, no. 2 (February), pp. 100-105.

Marshall, John (1999). "Critical Study: J.B. Schneewind's *The Invention of Autonomy*", *Hume Studies*, vol. 25, no. 1-2 (April/November), pp. 207-224.

McHugh, Josh (2003). "Google vs. Evil", *Wired*, vol. 11, no. 1 (January), available online: http://www.wired.com/wired/archive/11.01/google_pr.html (accessed 3 April 2013).

MacIntyre, Alasdair (1984). *After Virtue: A Study in Moral Theory*, second edition. Notre Dame, IN: University of Notre Dame Press.

MacIntyre, Alasdair (1999). *Dependent Rational Animals: Why Human Beings Need the Virtues*, London, UK: Gerald Duckworth and co.

Manjoo, Farhad (2013). "The Happiness Machine: How Google became such a great place to work", *Slate*, 21 January, available online: http://www.slate.com/articles/technology/technology/2013/01/google_people_operations_the_secrets_of_the_world_s_most_scientific_human.single.html (accessed 8 April 2013).

Marder, Michael and Francione, Gary (2012)."Michael Marder and Gary Francione Debate Plant Ethics", available online: http://www.cup.columbia.edu/static/marder-francione-debate (accessed 15 March 2013).

Margulis, Lynn (1970). *Origin of Eukaryotic Cells*, New Haven, CT: Yale University Press.

Margulis, Lynn (1994). "Symbiogenesis and symbioticism", in *Symbiosis as a Source of Evolutionary Innovation: Speciation and* Morphogenesis, eds. Lynn Margulis and René Fester, Cambridge, MA, MIT Press, pp 1-14.

Margulis, Lynn (1998). *Symbiotic Planet: A New Look at Evolution*, New York, NY, Basic Books.

Margulis, Lynn, Dolan, Michael F., and Guerrero, Ricardo (2000). "The Chimeric Eukaryote: Origin of the Nucleus from the Karyomastigont in Amitochondriate Protists", in *Variation and Evolution in Plants and Microorganisms: Towards a New Synthesis – 50 Years After Stebbins*, eds. Francisco J. Ayala, Walter M. Fitch, and Michael T. Chegg, Washington, DC: National Academies Press, pp. 21-34.

Marx, Karl (1867). *Capital, Volume One*, trans. Samuel Moore and Edward Aveling [1887], available online: http://www.marxists.org/archive/marx/works/1867-c1/index.htm (accessed 26 April 2013).

Meillassoux, Quentin (2011). "History and Event in Alain Badiou", trans. Thomas Nail, *Parrhesia*, no. 12, available online: http://parrhesiajournal.org/parrhesia12/parrhesia12_meillassoux.pdf (accessed: 21 January 2013).

Merleau-Ponty, Maurice (1945). *Phenomenology of Perception*,

trans. Colin Smith [1958], London: Routledge and Kegan Paul.
Michelangelo (1504). *David* [Sculpture], Florence, Accademia Gallery.
Midgley, Mary (1978). *Beast and Man: The Roots of Human Nature*, London and New York: Routledge.
Midgley, Mary (1983). *Animals and Why They Matter*, Athens, GA: University of Georgia Press.
Midgley, Mary (1984). *Wickedness: A Philosophical Essay*, London and New York: Routledge.
Midgley, Mary (1985). *Evolution as a Religion: Strange hopes and stranger fears*, London and New York: Methuen.
Midgley, Mary (1991). *Can't We Make Moral Judgments?*, New York, NY: St. Martin's Press.
Midgley, Mary (1992). *Science as Salvation: A Modern Myth and its Meaning*, London and New York: Routledge.
Midgley, Mary (2001). *Science and Poetry*, London and New York: Routledge.
Midgley, Mary (2003). *The Myths We Live By*, London and New York: Routledge.
Mikhail, John (2013). "Emotion, Neuroscience, and Law: A Comment on Darwin and Greene", *Emotion Review*, vol. 3, no. 3 (July), pp. 293-295.
Milgram, Stanley (1963). "Behavioral Study of Obedience", *Journal of Abnormal and Social Psychology*, vol. 67, no. 4, pp. 371-8.
Mill, John Stuart (1859). *On Liberty*, London, UK: John W. Parker and Son.
Moorcock, Michael (1962a). "The Sundered Worlds", *Science Fiction Adventures*, vol. 5, no. 29 (November), pp. 2-58.
Moorcock, Michael (1962b). "To Rescue Tanelorn", *Science Fantasy*, no. 56 (December), pp. 55-82.
Moorcock, Michael (1964). "Master of Chaos" (later re-titled "The Dream of Earl Aubec"), *Fantastic Stories of Imagination*, vol. 13, no. 5 (May), pp. 72-85.

Moorcock, Michael (1971). *The Warlord of the Air*, New York, NY: Ace Books.

Moorcock, Michael (1974). *The Land Leviathan*, London, UK: Quartet.

Moorcock, Michael (1981a). *The War Hound and the World's Pain*, New York, NY: Timescape.

Moorcock, Michael (1981b). *The Steel Tsar*, London, UK: Granada.

Moorcock, Michael (1987). *Wizardry and Wild Romance*, London, UK: Gollancz.

Moorcock, Michael (1994). *Blood: A Southern Fantasy*, New York, NY: Avon Books.

Moorcock, Michael (2001). *The Dreamthief's Daughter: A Tale of the Albino*, New York, NY: Aspect.

Moorcock, Michael (2006). *The Vengeance of Rome*, London, UK: Jonathan Cape.

Moorcock, Michael (2008). Comment on "Moorcock's Metaphysics (4): The Multiverse", *Only a Game* [Blog], available online: http://onlyagame.typepad.com/only_a_game/2008/05/moorcocks-metap.html (accessed 10 August 2013).

Moorcock, Michael and Bateman, Chris (2011). "Moorcock on Fiction", available online: http://onlyagame.typepad.com/only_a_game/2011/03/moorcock-on-fiction.html (accessed 28 January 2013).

Moorcock, Michael and Greenland, Colin (1992). *Death Is No Obstacle*, Manchester, UK: Savoy Books.

Moore, G.E. (1903). *Principia Ethica*, Cambridge, UK: Cambridge University Press.

Moraes, Ricardo (2011). "Capturing Souls", *Photographers Blog*, available online: http://blogs.reuters.com/photographers-blog/2011/05/12/capturing-souls/ (accessed 22 April 2013).

Mouffe, Chantal (2005). *The Democratic Paradox*, London: Verso.

Mulhall, Stephen (2009). "The Cat and the Camel: A Hesitant Response to 'Morality or Moralism?'", *Common Knowledge*, vol. 16, no. 2 (Spring), pp. 331-338.

Nagasawa, Miho; Kikusui, Takefumi; Onaka, Tatsushi; Ohta, Mitsuaki (2009)."Dog's gaze at its owner increases owner's urinary oxytocin during social interaction", *Hormones and Behavior*, vol. 55, pp. 434-441.

National Crime Records Bureau (2011). *Accidental Deaths & Suicides in India 2011*, available online: http://ncrb.nic.in/CD-ADSI2011/ADSI-2011%20REPORT.pdf (accessed 10 December 2012).

Nelson, Elizabeth Jean (1991). "'Nothing ever goes well enough': Mussolini and the rhetoric of perpetual struggle", *Communication Studies*, vol. 42, no. 1, pp. 22-42.

Nietzsche, Friedrich (1883-85). *Thus Spoke Zarathustra: A Book for All and None*, trans. Walter Kaufmann [1968] in *The Portable Nietzsche*, ed. Walter Kaufmann, New York, NY: Viking Press, pp. 103-439.

Nietzsche, Friedrich (1886). *Beyond Good and Evil*, trans. Helen Zimmern [2008], Rockville, MA: Serenity Publishers.

Nietzsche, Friedrich (1888). *The Antichrist*, trans. Walter Kaufmann [1968] in *The Portable Nietzsche*, ed. Walter Kaufmann, New York, NY: Viking Press, pp. 565-656.

Nietzsche, Friedrich (1968). *The Portable Nietzsche*, ed. and trans. Walter Kauffman, New York, NY: Viking Press.

Nozick, Robert (1974). *Anarchy, State, and Utopia*, New York, NY: Basic Books.

Ord, Toby (2005). "Consequentialism and Decision Procedures" [Thesis], Oxford, UK: University of Oxford.

Ostroff, Frank (1999). *The Horizontal Organization: What the organization of the future actually looks like and how it delivers value to customers*, New York, NY: Oxford University Press.

Parekh, Bhikhu (2000). *Rethinking Multiculturalism: Cultural diversity and political theory*, Cambridge, UK: Cambridge University Press.

Parfit, Derek (1984). *Reasons and Persons*, Oxford, UK: Oxford

University Press.

Parfit, Derek (2011). *On What Matters*, Volumes 1 and 2, Oxford, UK: Oxford University Press.

Parkinson, John (2002). "How Bacteria Swim to Dinner: Teams of Sensors May Change Faint Food Smells into Marching Orders." *University of Utah News and Public Relations.*

Patronek, Gary J. (2001). "Assessment of claims of short- and long-term complications associated with onychectomy in cats". *Journal of the American Veterinary Medical Association*, vol. 219, no. 7 (October): pp. 932-7.

Peterson, Martin (2009). "A Royal Road to Consequentialism?", *Ethical Theory and Moral Practice*, vol. 13, no. 2, p153-169.

Peterson, Martin and Spahn, Andreas (2011). "Can Technological Artefacts Be Moral Agents?", *Science and Engineering Ethics*, vol. 17, no. 3 (September), pp. 411-424.

Plato (380 BC). *Republic.*

Pols, Auke J. K. (2012). "How Artefacts Influence Our Actions", *Ethical Theory and Moral Practice*, available online: http://link.springer.com/content/pdf/10.1007%2Fs10677-012-9377-0 (accessed 8 April 2013).

Popper, Karl (1945). *The Open Society and its Enemies: Volume 1: The Spell of Plato*, London, UK: Routledge.

Posner, Richard A. (2002). "The Best Offense", *The New Republic*, available online: http://www.powells.com/review/2002_09_05.html (accessed 15 April 2013).

Po-wah, Julia Tao Lai (2006). "A Confucian Approach to a 'Shared Family Decision Model' in Health Care: Reflections on Moral Pluralism", in *Global Bioethics: The Collapse of Consensus*, ed. Hugo Tristram Engelhardt, Salem, MA: M & M Scrivener Press, pp. 154-179.

Powers, Thomas M. and Johnson, Deborah G. (2004). "The Moral Agency of Technology", *The Intentionality and Agency of Artifacts: Towards a Moral Account of Technology (2004 Workshop on New Directions in Understanding Ethics and Technology),* University of Virginia.

Putnam, Hilary (2002). *The Collapse of the Fact/Value Dichotomy and Other Essays,* Cambridge, MA: Harvard University Press.

Putnam, Hilary (2007) "Between Scylla and Charybdis: Does Dummett Have a Way Through?" *The Philosophy of Michael Dummett,* eds. Randall E. Auxier and Lewis Edwin Hahn, Chicago, IL: Open Court, pp. 155-167.

Rawls, John (1971). *A Theory of Justice,* Cambridge, MA: Harvard University Press.

Reuters (2012). "2011 traffic deaths a record low", available online: http://www.reuters.com/article/2012/05/08/us-autos-deaths-idUSBRE84618920120508 (accessed 10 December 2012).

Roeser, Sabine (2010). "Intuitions, emotions and gut reactions in decisions about risks: towards a different interpretation of 'neuroethics'", *Journal of Risk Research,* vol. 13, no. 2 (March), pp. 175-190.

Roosevelt, Elenaor (1948). "Statement to the United Nations' General Assembly on the Universal Declaration of Human Rights", 9 December 1948, available online: http://www.gwu.edu/~erpapers/documents/displaydoc.cfm?_t=speeches&_docid=spc057137 (accessed 22 April 2013).

Rowlands, Mark (2009). "Responding to Animals", *Common Knowledge,* vol. 16, no 2 (Spring), pp. 351-360.

Ruse, Michael (2003). *Darwin and Design: Does Evolution Have a Purpose?,* Cambridge, MA, Harvard University Press.

Russell, Bertrand (1930). *Has religion made useful contributions to civilization?,* London, UK: Watts & co.

Rynes, Sara L. (2012). "Care and Compassion in Companies and Organizations: New Trends", transcript of panel discussion for Academy of Management, available online: http://aom.org/Multi-Media/Publications/Academy-of-Management-Review/Caring-Organizations-Podcast.aspx (accessed 8 April

2013).

Sachs, Benjamin. 2010. "Consequentialism's Double-Edged Sword". *Utilitas*, vol. 22, no. 3, pp. 258-71.

Sato, Masayuki (2012). "Studies of the *Han Feizi* in China, Taiwan, and Japan" in *Dao Companion to the Philosophy of Han Fei*, ed. Paul R. Goldin, Dordrecht, Heidelberg, New York and London: Springer, pp. 257-281.

Scham, Sandra (2008). "The World's First Temple", *Archeology*, vol. 61, no. 6 (November/December), available online: http://archive.archaeology.org/0811/abstracts/turkey.html (accessed 29 April 2013).

Saul, John Ralson (2005). *The Collapse of Globalism and the Reinvention of the World*, New York, NY: Overlook.

Segal, Charles (1986). *Interpreting Greek tragedy: myth, poetry, text*, Ithaca, NY: Cornell University Press.

Sewell, Anna (1877). *Black Beauty*, Norwich, UK: Jarrold and Sons.

Shakespeare, William (1600). *Henry V*, London, UK: Thomas Millington.

Shelley, Mary (1818). *Frankenstein; or, The Modern Prometheus*, London: Lackington, Hughes, Harding, Mavor and Jones.

Short, William R. (1996). "Honor, Dueling, and Drengskapr", *Hurstwic*, available online: http://www.hurstwic.org/history/articles/society/text/drengur.htm (accessed 19 December 2012).

Sidgwick, Henry (1874). *The Methods of Ethics*, London: Macmillan and Company.

Simek, Rudolf (2004). "The Emergence of the Viking Age. Reasons and Triggers", in *Vikings on the Rhine. Recent Research on Early Medieval Relations between the Rhinelands and Scandinavia*, eds. Rudolf Simek and Ulrike Engel, Vienna, Austria: Fassbaender, pp. 9-21.

Singer, Peter (1975). *Animal Liberation*, New York, NY: Pimlico.

Singer, Peter (2005). "Ethics and Intuitions", *Journal of Ethics*, no. 9, pp. 331-52.

Smart, Ninian (1996). *Dimensions of the Sacred: An Anatomy of the World's Beliefs*, New York, NY: HarperCollins.

Solomon, Robert C. (1995). *A Passion for Justice: Emotions and the Origins of the Social Contract*, Lanham, MD: Rowman and Littlefield.

Stanford International Human Rights and Conflict Resolution Clinic (2012). "Living Under Drones: Death, Injury, and Trauma to Civilians from US Drone Practices in Pakistan", available online: http://www.livingunderdrones.org/wp-content/uploads/2012/10/Stanford-NYU-LIVING-UNDER-DRONES.pdf (accessed 15 April 2013).

Stengers, Isabelle (1993). *The Invention of Modern Science*, trans. Daniel W. Smith [2000], Minneapolis: University of Minnesota Press.

Stengers, Isabelle (1997). *Power and Invention: Situating Science*, Minneapolis: University of Minnesota Press.

Stengers, Isabelle (2003). *Cosmopolitics II*, trans. Robert Bononno [2011], Minneapolis, MN: University of Minnesota Press

Stengers, Isabelle (2012). "Reclaiming Animism", *e-Flux*, vol. 36, available online: http://www.e-flux.com/journal/reclaiming-animism/ (accessed: 24 April 2013)

Sterling, Bruce (1988). *Mirrorshades: The Cyberpunk Anthology*, London: Paladin.

Stolerman, Ian P. and Jarvis, Martin J. (1995)."The scientific case that nicotine is addictive", *Psychopharmacology*, vol. 117, no. 1 (January), pp. 2-10.

Strawser, Bradley J. (2010). "Moral Predators: The Duty to Employ Uninhabited Aerial Vehicles", *Journal of Military Ethics*, vol. 9, no. 4, pp. 343-368.

Taylor, Charles. (1992) *The Ethics of Authenticity*, Cambridge, MA: Harvard University Press.

Taylor, Charles (2007). *A Secular Age*, Cambridge, MA: Belknap of Harvard.

Temkin, Larry (1986). "Inequality," *Philosophy and Public Affairs*, vol. 15, no. 2, (Spring), pp. 99-121.

Tenenbaum, David (2002). "When Did Life on Earth Begin? Ask a Rock", *Astrobiology Magazine*, available online: http://www.astrobio.net/exclusive/293/when-did-life-on-earth-begin-ask-a-rock (accessed 27 December 2012).

Theobold, Douglas L. (2010). "A formal test of the theory of universal common ancestry", *Nature*, vol. 465, no. 7295, pp. 219-22.

Thobani, Sunera (2007) "Nationality in the Age of Global Terror", *Exalted Subjects: Studies in the Making of Race and Nation in Canada* Toronto: University of Toronto Press, 217-247.

Thomas, Morawetz (1978). *Wittgenstein and Knowledge: The Importance of 'On Certainty'*, Amherst: University of Massachusetts Press.

Thomson, Judith Jarvis (1985). "The Trolley Problem", *The Yale Law Journal*, vol. 94, no. 6 (May), pp. 1395-1415.

Thrash, J. Cameron; Boyd, Alex; Huggett, Megan J.; Grote, Jana; Carini, Paul; Yoder, Ryan J.; Robbertse, Barbara; Spatafora, Joseph W.; Rappé, Michael S.; Giovannoni, Stephen J. (2011). "Phylogenomic evidence for a common ancestor of mitochondria and the SAR11 clade". *Scientific Reports*, vol. 1, article 13.

Tolkien, J.R.R (1954-55). *The Lord of the Rings*, London, UK: George Allen and Unwin.

Tolkien, J.R.R (1981). *The Letters of J.R.R. Tolkien*, ed. Humphrey Carpenter with Christopher Tolkien, London, UK: George Allen and Unwin.

Tolkien, J.R.R. (1977). *The Silmarillion*, London, UK: George Allen and Unwin.

Tomasello, Michael (1999). *The Cultural Origins of Human Cognition*, Cambridge, MA: Harvard University Press.

Tomasello, Michael; Carpenter, Malinda; Call, Josep; Behne, Tanya; and Moll, Henrike (2005)."Understanding and sharing intentions: The origins of cultural cognition", *Behavioral and*

Brain Sciences, vol. 28, pp. 675-735.

Valevičius, Andrius (1987). "Emmanuel Lévinas: Some Basic Facts", *Lituanus*, vol. 33, no. 1, available online: http://www.lituanus.org/1987/87_1_02.htm (accessed: 21 January 2013).

van Leengoed, Eric, Kerker, E, Swanson, Heidi H. (1987)."Inhibition of post-partum maternal behavior in the rat by injecting an oxytocin antagonist into the cerebral ventricles." *Journal of Endocrinology*, vol. 112, no. 2 (February), pp. 275-82.

van Norden, Bryan W. (2003). "Virtue Ethics and Confucianism", in *Comparative Approaches to Chinese Philosophy*, ed. Bo Mou, London, UK: Ashgate Publishing, pp. 99-121.

Varela, Francisco, Thompson, Evan, and Rosch, Eleanor (1991). *The Embodied Mind: Cognitive science and human experience.* Cambridge, MA: MIT Press.

Verbeek, Peter-Paul (2006). "Materializing Morality: Design Ethics and Technological Mediation", *Science, Technology, & Human Values*, vol. 31, no. 3 (May), pp. 361-380.

Verbeek, Peter-Paul (2009a). "Cultivating Humanity: toward a non-humanist ethics of technology", in *New Waves in Philosophy of Technology*, eds. Jan Kyrre Berg Olsen, Evan Selinger, and Søren Riis, Basingstoke, UK: Palgrave Macmillan, pp. 241-263.

Verbeek, Peter-Paul (2009b). "Let's Make Things Better: A Reply to my Readers", *Human Studies*, vol. 32, no. 1, p. 251.

Vohs, Kathleen D. and Baumeister, Roy F. (2009)."Addiction and free will", *Addiction Research and Theory*, vol. 17, no. 3 (June), pp. 231-235.

Walker R.J., Brooks H.L., Holden-Dye L. (1996)."Evolution and overview of classical transmitter molecules and their receptors", *Parasitology*, vol. 113 Supplemental, pp. S3-33.

Walton, Kendall L. (1990). *Mimesis as Make-believe: On the Foundations of the Representational Arts*, Cambridge, MA, Harvard University Press.

Warman, Matt (2011). "Google reaches 1 billion users", *The Telegraph*, 22 June, available online: http://www.telegraph.co.uk/technology/google/8591032/Google-reaches-1-billion-users.html (accessed 8 April 2013).

Wells, H. G. (1934). *Experiment in Autobiography. Discoveries and Conclusions of a Very Ordinary Brain (Since 1866)*, New York, NY: The Macmillan Company.

Whitehead, Alfred North (1926). *Science and the Modern World*, Cambridge, UK: Cambridge University Press.

Whitehead, Alfred North (1938). "Civilized Universe." Lecture Six in *Modes of Thought*, New York: Macmillan, pp. 143- 171.

Wiggins, David (1987). "Truth, Invention and the Meaning of Life", in *Needs, Values and Truth*, New York, NY: Oxford University Press, pp. 87-138.

Wild, John. "Authentic Existence."*Ethics*, vol. 75, no. 4, pp. 227-39.

Wilkerson, Dale (2009). "Friedrich Nietzsche (1844-1900)", *Internet Encyclopedia of Philosophy*, available online: http://www.iep.utm.edu/nietzsch/ (accessed 17 December 2012).

Wilson, Robert Anton (1986). *The New Inquisition*, Las Vegas, NV: New Falcon Publications.

Wittgenstein, Ludwig (1962). *Philosophical Investigations*, trans. G.E.M. Anscombe, New York, NY: Macmillan.

Wittgenstein, Ludwig (1980). *Culture and Value*, Chicago, IL: University of Chicago Press.

Wonders of the Universe (2011). "Destiny", BBC2, Sunday 6 March 2011, 9 pm.

Wood, Allen (2011). "Humanity as an End in Itself" in *On What Matters*, Volume 2, Derek Parfit, Oxford, UK: Oxford University Press, pp. 58-82.

Wood, Allen W. (1999). *Kant's Ethical Thought*, Cambridge, UK: Cambridge University Press.

Wood, Allen W. (2002). "What is Kantian Ethics?" in *Groundwork for the Metaphysics of Morals*, Rethinking the Western Tradition edition, ed. Allen W. Wood, New Haven, CT: Yale University Press, pp. 157-182.

Wood, Allen W. (2006). "The supreme principle of morality." *The Cambridge Companion to Kant and Modern Philosophy*, ed. Paul Guyer. Cambridge, UK: Cambridge University Press, pp. 342-380.

Wood, Allen (2008). *Kantian Ethics*, New York: Cambridge University Press.

Wood, Allen W. and Bateman, Chris (2012a). "Allen Wood on Ethics (1): Kant and Mutual Respect", *Only a Game* [Blog], available online: http://onlyagame.typepad.com/only_a_game/2012/10/allen-wood-on-ethics-1-kant-and-mutual-respect.html (accessed 14 January 2013).

Wood, Allen W. and Bateman, Chris (2012b). "Allen Wood on Ethics (2): Political Realities", *Only a Game* [Blog], available online: http://onlyagame.typepad.com/only_a_game/2012/11/allen-wood-on-ethics-2-political-realities.html (accessed 18 December 2012).

Wu, Feng-Wei (2007). "Between Ethics and Politics – Reading Lévinas through Kant", *Taiwan Philosophical Association Annual Conference*, Tunghai University, October 21.

Yablo, Stephen (1998). "Does Ontology Rest on a Mistake?", *Proceedings of the Aristotelian Society*, Supplementary vol. 72, no. 1, pp. 229-262.

Yablo, Stephen (2002)."Abstract Objects: A Case Study", in *Individuals, essence & identity: Themes of Analytic Metaphysics*, eds. Andrew Bottani, Massimiliano Carrara and Pierdaniele Giaretta, Dordrecht, The Netherlands: Kluwer.

Zamir, Tzachi (2007). *Ethics and the Beast: A Speciesist Argument for Animal Liberation*, Princeton, NJ: Princeton University Press.

Zamir, Tzachi (2009). "How Reliable is Moral Sensitivity?", *Common Knowledge*, vol. 16, no 2 (Spring), pp. 339-345.

Žižek, Slavoj (2004). "From Purification to Subtraction: Badiou and the Real" in *Think Again: Alain Badiou and the Future of*

Philosophy, ed. Peter Hallward, New York, NY: Continuum, pp. 165-181.

Žižek, Slavoj (2008), "Tolerance as an ideological category", *Critical Inquiry*, vol. 34, no. 4 (Summer), pp. 660-682.

Žižek, Slavoj (2012). "The Apostate Children of God", New Delhi, India: *Outlook*, August 20 edition, available online: http://www.outlookindia.com/article.aspx?281931 (accessed 29December 2012).

Žižek, Slajov, and Daly, Glyn (2004). *Conversations with Žižek*. Cambridge, UK: Cambridge University Press.

Zylinska, Joanna (2009). *Bioethics in the Age of New Media*, Cambridge, MA, MIT Press.

Zylinska, Joanna and Bateman, Chris (2009). "Joanna Zylinska on Bioethics" [Blog], available online: http://onlyagame.typepad.com/only_a_game/2009/09/joanna-zylinska-on-bioethics.html (accessed 28 December 2012).

Glossary

Absolute truth: the belief that there is only one coherent account of the truth, that it is objective and knowable, and that because there can be only one such accurate account any claim that conflicts with it is by definition false. Compare *perspectival truth, relativism* (q.q.v.).

Agent: anything that can take an action, especially in the context of this book anything that can take an action of moral relevance.

Agent-focused: any form of *ethic* in which the disposition and character of the person acting is the emphasized element i.e. *virtue ethics* (q.q.v.). Compare *rule-focused* and *outcome-focused* (q.q.v.).

Alief: Gendler's term for a basic form of *imagination* that connects stimulus with mental representations and emotional states, and which is a precursor to *belief* (q.q.v.).

Animism: the endowment of things with certain properties typically reserved to beings. See also *secular animism* (q.v.).

Atheology: the examination of religious issues from a rational perspective, based on a rejection of any viable concept of God. Compare *theology* (q.v.).

Authorized story: in *pretence theory* (q.v.), any fiction that is accepted as fact can be considered an authorized story.

Autonomy: freedom of the individual to govern their own actions.

Belief: a form of *imagination* (q.v.) that models direct experience, attempting to track the world reliably. Compare *alief* and *make-believe* (q.q.v.), which are respectively the prototype and the refinement of this faculty.

Betrayal: Badiou's term for giving up on a revealed truth in order to pursue self-interest. One of three examples of what Badiou terms *Evil*, the others being *disaster* and *simulacrum* (q.q.v.).

Bureaucracy: an institution that operates according to proscribed rules.

Cambrian explosion: the appearance approximately 530 million years ago of almost all major animal forms over an interval of a few million years.

Categorical imperative: Kant's concept that morality is binding upon us because its demands are not contingent, expressed in three separate forms as *ethics as universal, mutual respect* and *communal autonomy* (q.q.v.).

Chaos Ethic: a term used in this book to describe any moral system that rejects *absolute truth* (q.v.) and thus resists any universal institutionalization of its morality. Like *Law Ethic* (q.v.), this term owes a debt to the novelist Michael Moorcock.

Christendom: Kierkegaard's term for the European culture of the nineteenth century that officially claimed to be Christian but that was only a caricature of Christian faith reduced to mere rule-following.

Cognitive dissonance: a discomforting feeling that results from trying to hold two conflicting ideas or values in mind at the same time. See also *moral horror* (q.v.).

Common world: a *moral fiction* (q.v.) of the best arrangement that can be composed out of the disparate needs of everything contained within it. Compare *realm of ends* (q.v.).

Communal autonomy: the co-operation of individuals towards both individual and mutual goals, as expressed by Kant's Formula of Autonomy account of his *categorical imperative* (q.v.). See also *realm of Ends* (q.v.).

Compositionism: see *political ecology* (q.v.).

Consequentialism: one of three major forms of moral philosophy, that which is *outcome-focused* (q.v.).

Convivial: Illich's term for societies in which technology serves politically interrelated individuals, or for tools that foster individual competence and control.

Cosmopolitanism: Kant's *moral fiction* (q.v.) of a global human community united by international laws founded upon a shared morality.

Cosmopolitics: Isabelle Stengers *moral fiction* of an ecology of practices that must be gradually assembled from vastly diverse *traditions* (q.q.v.). Compare *political ecology* (q.v.).

Creative imagination: Currie and Ravenscroft's term for the imaginative capacity for innovation, which is not constrained to humans. Compare *recreative imagination* (q.v.).

Curse of tolerance: Stengers' idea that anyone who thinks they 'know' but that others 'merely believe' fails to allow others the freedom to exist in the world upon their own terms, and are thus cursed to misunderstand both others and themselves.

Cyberfetish: the exaltation of technology, and in its more extreme manifestations, a longing to physically merge with technology. Also, technology considered as equivalent to a totem in *animism* (q.v.).

Cyborg: Haraway's term (drawn from science fiction) for hybrids of machine and organism – for example, a car is necessarily a cyborg while it is being driven.

Decision ethic: a form of *consequentialism* (q.v.) that focuses upon determining the decision procedures likely to lead to the best outcomes, rather than any attempt to calculate the best outcomes.

Deontology: a technical term for what is called *duty ethics* (q.v.) in this book.

Diplomat: Latour's term for someone who attempts to bring disparate groups into accord by carefully disentangling their disagreements and trying to establish how best to integrate their disparate needs into one *common world* (q.v.). Compare *moralist* (q.v.).

Disaster: Badiou's term for belief in the total power of a truth such that it becomes absolute and hence destructive. One of three examples of what Badiou terms *Evil*, the others being *betrayal* and *simulacrum* (q.q.v.).

Divine command: a *Law Ethic* that is *rule-focused* (q.q.v.) and which specifies that what is good is what is commanded by God.

Duty ethics: one of three major forms of moral philosophy, that which is *rule-focused* (q.v.). Also known as *deontology*. Compare *virtue ethics* and *consequentialism* (q.q.v.).

Duty: an obligation or responsibility.

Egoism: an *outcome-focused* (q.v.) ethic in which those outcomes that favor the individual's self-interest are preferred.

End: something to strive towards, a goal.

Ethic of hesitation: Haché and Latour's concept of morality as *hesitation*, and the related *virtue* of *hesitancy* (q.q.v.).

Ethic: any moral system. In this book, ethics are considered to be either *Law Ethics* or *Chaos Ethics* (q.q.v.).

Ethical triangle: a metaphor for the idea that all moral discussions entail *agent-focused, rule-focused* or *outcome-focused* elements (q.q.v.).

Ethics as universal: a restatement of Kant's Formula of Universal Law version of the *categorical imperative* (q.v.), expressing the idea that ethical behavior must be binding for everyone.

Ethic of truths: Badiou's *Chaos Ethic* (q.v.) based on viewing truth as emerging solely through a process, and advocating fidelity to these fragile truth procedures.

Event: Badiou's term for a brief glimpse of truth, an awareness of the void beyond what is known about a situation.

Evil: with a capital letter, 'Evil' is a *moral fiction* central to Badiou's condemnation of any *Law Ethic* (q.q.v.) that begins by identifying what is barbaric and is then justified in acting barbarously towards it. Also, the name Badiou gives to three forms of Evil: *simulacrum* (or terror), *betrayal* and *disaster*.

Existentialism: a philosophical approach emphasizing the freedom of the individual to determine their own life, and to take responsibility for the consequences of their actions and choices.

Exploitation ethic: the relation of the intensive factory farmer to their livestock, or the guard to a prisoner in a labor camp. One of two *ethics* that could be judged worse than the *predator ethic* (q.q.v.). See also *predator ethic, extermination ethic* (q.q.v.).

Extermination ethic: the relation of the exterminator to the vermin. One of two *ethics* that could be judged worse than the *predator ethic* (q.q.v.). See also *predator ethic, exploitation ethic* (q.q.v.).

Fact-value distinction: an attempt to distinguish between those judgments that constitute knowledge (facts) and those that constitute morality (values).

Fairness as equality: the liberal ideal that fairness is attained by striving towards maximum equality of outcomes, as typified by Rawls' concept of distributive justice.

Fairness as proportionality: the conservative ideal that fairness is attained by allocating reward in proportion to contribution, even if this guarantees unequal outcomes.

Fictional: any circumstance that is imagined can be considered fictional. The term is also a synonym for 'fictionally true' in Walton's *pretence theory* (q.v.).

Grand narrative: Lyotard's term for the stories a culture tells in order to make sense of the world. Compare Campbell's *living mythology* (q.v.).

Great chain of being: a *moral fiction* (q.v.) that was widespread prior to the Enlightenment and that arranged all life in a hierarchy from God through royalty, nobility, peasants, animals, plants and down to the rocks.

Hesitancy: the *virtue* of *hesitation* (q.q.v.).

Hesitation ethic: see *ethic of hesitation* (q.v.).

Hesitation: Haché and Latour's idea that the essence of morality is defined by our willingness to defer as opposed to our capacity to act assuredly, which they dismiss as *moralism* (q.v.). See also *sensitivity* (q.v.).

Highway code: the name of a guidebook in the UK that describes the laws and rules of conduct on the roads, and a generic name for any such 'rules of the road'.

Home community: the set of entities of primary moral concern for any given animal e.g. the home community of wolves consists of the wolves in their pack. Compare *outer community* (q.v.).

Iconoclash: Latour's term for the inescapable ambiguity involved in smashing idols, where the iconoclast cannot know if they are liberators or merely scandalmongers.

Ideal: a synonym for *moral fiction* (q.v.).

Imagination: the capacity to be aware of something, whether or not it is *fictional* (q.v.). In this book, the term is extended to include (in order of complexity) *premagination, alief, belief* and *make-believe* (q.q.v) to allow the various forms of imagination to be traced back to the beginnings of life.

Impossible to compare: a phrase used in this book to substitute for the technical term *incommensurability,* and which implies that different perspectives or traditions cannot be judged superior or inferior because there is no perspective from which to make such a judgment.

Incommensurability: the idea that there is no reliable method for determining which is superior between two particular perspectives. This book uses *impossible to compare* (q.v.) as a synonym.

Institution: a *practice,* especially a large scale *bureaucracy* (q.q.v.).

Is-ought problem: Hume's objection that there is no way to justify a moral conclusion from a factual premise, generally taken as the prototype of the *fact-value distinction* (q.v.).

Law Ethic: a term used in this book to describe any moral system that presumes *absolute truth* (q.v.) in its formulation. Like *Chaos Ethic* (q.v.), this term owes a debt to the novelist Michael Moorcock.

Living mythology: Joseph Campbell's term for a set of stories that serve an active role in a particular culture, shaping the ethics and norms of that society.

Logical positivism: the *positivist* movement of the Vienna Circle in the 1920s and 1930s that considered *metaphysics* (q.q.v) as meaningless because they could not be verified.

Make-believe: a form of *imagination* (q.v.) that entails the conceptualization of imaginary worlds of various different kinds. Compare *belief* (q.v.).

Maxim: a succinct formulation of a principle of conduct, a moral rule.

Megatext: Charles Segal's term for collections of myths or stories that imply a single fictional world.

Metaphysical: the adjective conjugated from *metaphysics* (q.v.).

Metaphysics: the philosophical exploration of that which cannot be tested or proven i.e. claims concerning reality that exceed experience or direct evidence. See also *mythology* (q.v.).

Minimal ethic: the moral system that requires the least of individuals while still making community possible, namely *egoism* (q.v.).

Moral chaos: the positive moral aspects of unpredictable, ungoverned or uncontrollable life. See also *moral law* and *Chaos Ethic* (q.v.).

Moral community: all those entities an individual has a moral relation with, including both *home community* and *outer community* (q.q.v.).

Moral fiction: an element of a *living mythology* (q.v.) with implications for morality and social norms, e.g. moral law, rights, utility.

Moral horror: intense *cognitive dissonance* (q.v.) caused by contemplating radically incompatible ethical systems or values, particularly when someone else's morality is impossible to reconcile with your own.

Moral law: the positive moral aspects of regulated, predictable or managed life, or the criteria that specifies which actions are *right* (q.v.). See also *moral chaos* and *Law Ethic* (q.q.v.).

Moral order: synonymous with *moral law* (q.v.).

Moral politics: a political circumstance guided in part by *moral representation* (q.v.). Compare *cosmopolitics, realm of ends, parliament of things* (q.q.v.).

Moral representation: the concept of a relationship that is based upon common *ideals* or *ethics* (q.q.v.). Private moral representation concerns individual ethical deliberation, while public moral representation concerns political advocacy for specific ethics.

Moral sensitivity: see *sensitivity* (q.v.).

Moral system: see *ethic* (q.v.).

Moral tradition: the *tradition* formed around any given *ethic* (q.q.v).

Moralism: Haché and Latour's term for a kind of *ethic* that acts with certainty towards those beings that are excluded from the *home community* (q.q.v.).

Moralist: Latour's term for anyone who recognizes the imperfection of any given social situation, and who will fight on behalf of those who are excluded or disadvantaged. Compare *diplomat* (q.v.).

Multiculturalism: a disastrous consequence of the *fact-value distinction,* whereby different moral perspectives are treated as entirely *impossible to compare* and so no attempt at discourse is even attempted (q.q.v.). Compare *perspectival truth* (q.v.).

Multiverse: a term coined by William James and popularized by Michael Moorcock for a diversity of realities, a 'many-in-one'. The term can either mean a plurality of parallel physical dimensions, or a plurality of parallel experiential realities. Compare *cosmopolitics* (q.v.).

Mutual respect: the agreement between individuals to respect one another's individuality, as expressed by Kant's Formula of Humanity as an End in Itself, one formulation of his *categorical imperative* (q.v.).

Mythology: a collection of imaginative patterns that use fiction or metaphor to express a particular perspective. See also *living mythology, metaphysics* (q.q.v.).

Natural rights: the *mythology* that claims *rights* (q.q.v.) are an inherent property of humanity, and thus cannot be disputed.

Nihilism: the rejection of morality as meaningful, or the belief that life is essentially meaningless.

Non-religion: a belief-system with its own *mythology* and *ethic* that is not a religious *tradition* e.g. Marxism, *positivism* (q.q.v.).

Nova effect: Charles Taylor's term for the ideological fragmentation in the modern world within which the range of possible ideals tends towards infinite diversity.

Orthodox science fiction: any fictional story that does not overtly contradict a contemporary perspective on the *science megatext* (q.v.).

Other: Lévinas' term for another being when we encounter their face (although this need not literally mean a face).

Otherness ethic: morality built on Lévinas' contention that we have infinite responsibility for the *other* (q.v.) we encounter.

Outcome-focused: any form of *ethic* in which the consequences of actions are used to judge their moral worth i.e. *consequentialism* (q.q.v.). Compare *agent-focused* and *rule-focused* (q.q.v.).

Outer community: for any animal, the set of all entities that lie outside of the *home community* (q.v.) but that are still considered to be morally relevant.

Oxytocin: a mammal hormone that underpins experiences of trust, compassion and bonding.

Parliament of things: Latour's *moral fiction* of a form of political life in which both things and beings have representation as a result of *secular animism* (q.q.v.). Compare *compositionism, realm of ends* (q.q.v.).

Person: any being possessed of a sufficient moral imagination that it can view other such beings as persons. The term is usually restricted to humans – in this book, I am agnostic about whether (say) dolphins or elephants might also be persons.

Perspectival truth: the belief that the true state of affairs can be attained only by examination from multiple different perspectives, many of which may contribute usefully to determining what is true. Compare *absolute truth, relativism* (q.q.v.).

Petty evil: an institution's willful disregard for individuals in its pursuit of some definition of utility, that is, the harm caused by the dehumanization inherent to bureaucracy.

Politics as war: a form of political life based upon defeating opposing viewpoints within the legislature and thus enforcing your own beliefs upon others. Compare *moral politics* (q.v.).

Political ecology: Latour's *moral fiction* of a *common world* (q.q.v.) that is gradually composed as an iterative process, also known as compositionism. Compare *realm of ends* (q.v.).

Positivism: a scientific *non-religion* based upon avoiding belief in untestable things, and thus an attempt to minimize *metaphysics* (q.q.v.) as much as possible.

Positivist: a person who believes in some form of *positivism* (q.v.).

Practice: a socially-grounded activity, such as language, games, currency, ethics.

Predator ethic: the relation of the predator to the prey. See also *extermination ethic, exploitation ethic* (q.q.v.).

Premagination: the most primitive form of *imagination* (q.v.), reflected in those creatures that are capable of responding to stimulus but nothing else. Thus, a single-celled organism premagines its food source when its rudimentary sensory capacities detect evidence of it.

Pretence theory: the part of Walton's philosophical make-believe theory of representation concerning the relationship between fiction and fact.

Private language: according to Ludwig Wittgenstein, a person cannot have a private language because language is constituted of rules which are socially enforced. See also *private rule* (q.v.).

Private rule: Saul Kripke, following an argument implied by Wittgenstein, denies the validity of private rules, stating that without a social context we cannot consider something to fulfill the role of a rule. See also *private language* (q.v.).

Psychological egoism: a theory about motivation claiming that we act only in our self-interest, or that our ultimate desires are self-directed. See also *egoism, psychological hedonism* (q.q.v.).

Psychological hedonism: a theory about motivation claiming that our ultimate desires are only concerned with seeking pleasure and avoiding pain. See also *psychological egoism, egoism* (q.q.v.).

Radical monopoly: Illich's term for any situation in which an industry becomes the dominant means of satisfying a need that formerly was met individually e.g. motorized transport replacing walking. The monopoly is 'radical' because once the industrial solution is adopted (e.g. once roads for cars are built everywhere) it becomes the *only* solution considered.

Realm of ends: Kant's *moral fiction* of *communal autonomy* (q.v.), whereby each person works towards the fulfillment of their own ideals and goals, while avoiding blocking other people from attaining their own objectives wherever possible. Compare *common world* (q.v.).

Recreative imagination: Currie and Ravenscroft's term for the imaginative capacity to project ourselves into the mental lives of others. Compare creative imagination (q.v.).

Relational bureaucracy: Gittell and Douglass' term for a kind of institution structured around networks of reciprocal relationship, both internally and between the inside and the outside of the organization.

Relativism: rejection of *absolute truth* (q.v.), and perhaps also of truth as a viable concept. The term is often deployed disparagingly against those who reject truth or absolute truth. Compare *perspectival truth* (q.v.).

Reliable witness: Stenger's term for a process that allows speaking on behalf of something else, e.g. when a researcher in animal behavior talks faithfully about the animals they study, the *animals* are a reliable witness, and the researcher is their *spokesperson* (q.v.).

Right: actions that concord with a particular *ethic* (q.v.) are deemed right (as opposed to wrong). Not to be confused with *rights* (q.v.).

Rights: *moral fictions* (q.v.), sustained by mutual agreement, whereby individual freedoms are protected in certain specific ways.

Rule-focused: any form of *ethic* in which the emphasized element concerns rules (or *rights*, or maxims) to be complied with e.g. *duty ethics*. (q.q.v.). Compare *agent-focused* and *outcome-focused* (q.q.v.).

Science megatext: the collection of texts (e.g. experiments, theories) that comprise the current *paradigm* for scientific research, acting as a *megatext* (q.q.v.).

Science: the mythology of the *science megatext* when it is read as a source of *absolute truth* (q.q.v.). Compare *the sciences* (q.v.).

sciences, the: collective noun for all the different scientific disciplines. This book follows Latour in distinguishing between *Science* (q.v.) with a capital 'S' and the sciences, in the plural, and lower case. The former is an artifact of a specific *mythology*, while the latter is a collection of *traditions* (q.q.v).

Scruple: a sense of doubt or reluctance concerning the moral implications of a situation, especially in the sense of a *hesitation* (q.v.).

Secular animism: those *living mythologies* (q.v.) that treat all things as having an involvement in the outcomes of actions, not just those with consciousness.

Sensitivity: Haché and Latour's concept that encounters between different kinds of beings are moral only in so much as we are sensitive to the possible inclusion of those beings in our moral world. See also *hesitation* (q.v.).

Series-person: Nagel's idea, championed by Parfit, that we can think of who we are at different times of our lives as being *different* identities (different series-persons) rather than as a single integrated identity. See also *person* (q.v.).

Simulacrum: Badiou's term for the pursuit of private interests that have been undertaken as if they were grounded in something universal (also referred to as 'terror'). One of three examples of what Badiou terms *Evil*, the others being *betrayal* and *disaster* (q.q.v.).

Spokesperson: Latour's term for those (particularly researchers) who speak on behalf of other entities (particularly non-human entities) via whatever process will allow those entities to form a *reliable witness* (q.v.) e.g. when a mathematician asserts a mathematical truth, they are a spokesperson for numbers.

State of exception: Agamben's moral limbo that represents simultaneously the sovereign's power to suspend law in an emergency and the legal vacuum this creates.

Techno-immortality: the unwise result of an imaginary technology that grants eternal life to humans.

Terror: see *simulacrum* (q.v.).

Theology: the examination of religious issues from a rational perspective, in relation to a specific concept or set of concepts of God. Compare *atheology* (q.v.).

Thought experiment: tentative research conducted solely in the imagination, intended to shed light on a particular issue by exploring conclusions that follow from its *fictional* (q.v.) scenario.

Tradition: any human activity with a specific focus, set of methods, and its own values can be considered a tradition e.g. cartography, Chess, chemistry, Christianity, cooperage, crochet. This term is broadly equivalent to Isabelle Stengers' term 'practice'.

Tragedy of the commons: Garret Hardin's term for situations in which a commonly shared resource becomes depleted because it is purportedly in the best interest of individuals to take more than their share.

Transnational corporation: a commercial *bureaucracy* (q.v.) that operates globally. In this book, this term is preferred over 'multinational corporation' as it stresses the disconnection between the institutions of a transnational corporation and the institutions of nations.

Universal ethics: see *ethics as universal* (q.v.).

Unmarriage: stable, committed, romantic relationships that have not been ratified by a marriage ceremony.

Utilitarianism: an *outcome-focused* (q.v.) ethic which aims for 'the greatest happiness for the greatest number'.

Utility: a measure of usefulness, often numerical, originating in *utilitarianism* (q.v.).

Vienna Wall: a metaphor for the *fact-value distinction* (q.v.), drawing reference to the Vienna Circle as originators of this concept.

Viking: a member of an overseas expedition from what is now Scandinavia. In this book, the adjective is used as shorthand to refer to Norse culture in general.

Virtue ethics: one of three major forms of moral philosophy, that which is *agent-focused* (q.v.). Compare *duty ethics* and *consequentialism* (q.q.v.).

Virtue: a quality of an *agent* (q.v.) that is considered desirable and meritorious.

Wastrel: someone who debilitates themselves by excessive use of intoxicants.

Wild justice: Marc Bekoff and Jessica Pierce's term for the morality of non-human animals.

Other Books by Chris Bateman

The Mythology of Evolution, Zero Books, 2012

Imaginary Games, Zero Books, 2011

Beyond Game Design: Nine Steps Towards Better Videogames (Editor), Cengage Learning, 2009

Game Writing: Narrative Skills for Videogames (Editor), Thompson Delmar Learning, 2006

21st Century Game Design (with Richard Boon), Charles River Media, 2005

Contemporary culture has eliminated both the concept of the public and the figure of the intellectual. Former public spaces – both physical and cultural – are now either derelict or colonized by advertising. A cretinous anti-intellectualism presides, cheerled by expensively educated hacks in the pay of multinational corporations who reassure their bored readers that there is no need to rouse themselves from their interpassive stupor. The informal censorship internalized and propagated by the cultural workers of late capitalism generates a banal conformity that the propaganda chiefs of Stalinism could only ever have dreamt of imposing. Zer0 Books knows that another kind of discourse – intellectual without being academic, popular without being populist – is not only possible: it is already flourishing, in the regions beyond the striplit malls of so-called mass media and the neurotically bureaucratic halls of the academy. Zer0 is committed to the idea of publishing as a making public of the intellectual. It is convinced that in the unthinking, blandly consensual culture in which we live, critical and engaged theoretical reflection is more important than ever before.